# WORLD ECONOMIC OUTLOOK

## October 1995

**A Survey by the Staff of the
International Monetary Fund**

**INTERNATIONAL MONETARY FUND
Washington, DC**

**World economic outlook (International Monetary Fund)**
World economic outlook: a survey by the staff of the International
Monetary Fund.—1980– —Washington, D.C.: The Fund, 1980–

    v.; 28 cm.—(1981–84: Occasional paper/International Monetary Fund
ISSN 0251-6365)
    Annual.
    Has occasional updates, 1984–
    ISSN 0258-7440 = World economic and financial surveys
    ISSN 0256-6877 = World economic outlook (Washington)
    1. Economic history—1971– —Periodicals.   I. International
Monetary Fund.   II. Series: Occasional paper (International Monetary
Fund)

HC10.W7979                                                      84-640155
                                       338.5'443'09048—dc19
                                                          AACR 2 MARC-S

Library of Congress                        8507

    Published biannually.
ISBN 1-55775-467-5

*The cover, charts, and interior of this publication
were designed and produced by the IMF Graphics Section*

Price: US$34.00
(US$23.00 to full-time faculty members and
students at universities and colleges)

Please send orders to:
International Monetary Fund, Publication Services
700 19th Street, N.W., Washington, D.C. 20431, U.S.A.
Tel.: (202) 623-7430      Telefax: (202) 623-7201
Internet: publications@imf.org

recycled paper

# Contents

Page

**Charts**

**Chapter**

**Boxes**

# Assumptions and Conventions

A number of assumptions have been adopted for the projections presented in the *World Economic Outlook*. It has been assumed that average real effective exchange rates will remain constant at their August 1–23, 1995 levels, except for the bilateral rates among the exchange rate mechanism (ERM) currencies, which are assumed to remain constant in nominal terms; that "established" policies of national authorities will be maintained; that the average price of oil will be $16.67 a barrel in 1995 and $15.51 a barrel in 1996, and remain unchanged in real terms over the medium term; and that the six-month U.S. dollar London interbank offered rate (LIBOR) will average 6¼ percent in 1995 and 1996. These are, of course, working hypotheses rather than forecasts, and the uncertainties surrounding them add to the margin of error that would in any event be involved in the projections. The estimates and projections are based on statistical information available on September 18, 1995.

The following conventions have been used throughout the *World Economic Outlook*:

. . .    to indicate that data are not available or not applicable;

—    to indicate that the figure is zero or less than half the final digit shown;

–    between years or months (e.g., 1994–95 or January–June) to indicate the years or months covered, including the beginning and ending years or months;

/    between years or months (e.g., 1994/95) to indicate a fiscal or financial year.

"Billion" means a thousand million; "trillion" means a thousand billion.

"Basis points" refer to hundredths of 1 percentage point (e.g., 25 basis points are equivalent to ¼ of 1 percentage point).

Minor discrepancies between constituent figures and totals are due to rounding.

\*    \*    \*

As used in this report, the term "country" does not in all cases refer to a territorial entity that is a state as understood by international law and practice. As used here, the term also covers some territorial entities that are not states but for which statistical data are maintained on a separate and independent basis.

# Preface

The projections and analysis contained in the *World Economic Outlook* are an integral element of the IMF's ongoing surveillance of economic developments and policies in its member countries and of the global economic system. The IMF has published the *World Economic Outlook* annually from 1980 through 1983 and biannually since 1984.

The survey of prospects and policies is the product of a comprehensive interdepartmental review of world economic developments, which draws primarily on information the IMF staff gathers through its consultations with member countries. These consultations are carried out in particular by the IMF's area departments together with the Policy Development and Review and Fiscal Affairs Departments.

The country projections are prepared by the IMF's area departments on the basis of internationally consistent assumptions about world activity, exchange rates, and conditions in international financial and commodity markets. For approximately 50 of the largest economies—accounting for 90 percent of world output—the projections are updated for each *World Economic Outlook* exercise. For smaller countries, the projections are based on those prepared at the time of the IMF's regular Article IV consultations with member countries or in connection with the use of IMF resources; for these countries, the projections used in the *World Economic Outlook* are incrementally adjusted to reflect changes in assumptions and global economic conditions.

The analysis in the *World Economic Outlook* draws extensively on the ongoing work of the IMF's area and specialized departments and is coordinated in the Research Department under the general direction of Michael Mussa, Economic Counsellor and Director of Research. The *World Economic Outlook* project is directed by Flemming Larsen, Senior Advisor in the Research Department, together with David T. Coe, Chief of the World Economic Studies Division.

Primary contributors to the current issue are Francesco Caramazza, Staffan Gorne, Robert F. Wescott, Vincent Koen, Mahmood Pradhan, Paula De Masi, Alexander Hoffmaister, Thomas Helbling, Hossein Samiei, and Cathy Wright. Other contributors include Sheila Bassett, Ximena Cheetham, Hema De Zoysa, Robert Feldman, Douglas Laxton, Calvin McDonald, Steven Symansky, and Anthony G. Turner. The authors of the annex are indicated in the annex. The Fiscal Analysis Division of the Fiscal Affairs Department computed the structural budget and fiscal impulse measures. Sungcha Hong Cha and Toh Kuan provided research assistance. Shamim Kassam, Allen Cobler, Nicholas Dopuch, Isabella Dymarskaia, Gretchen Gallik, Mandy Hemmati, Yasoma Liyanarachchi, and Subodh Raje processed the data and managed the computer systems. Susan Duff, Margarita Lorenz, and Margaret Dapaah were responsible for word processing. Juanita Roushdy of the External Relations Department edited the manuscript and coordinated production of the publication; Tom Walter coordinated production of the Arabic, French, and Spanish editions.

The analysis has benefited from comments and suggestions by staff from other IMF departments, as well as by Executive Directors following their discussion of the *World Economic Outlook* on September 11 and 13, 1995. However, both projections and policy considerations are those of the IMF staff and should not be attributed to Executive Directors or to their national authorities.

# Economic Prospects and Policies

Underlying trends in the world economy are encouraging in many respects (Chart 1), with economic policies contributing importantly to the favorable performance and prospects of most countries.

- In most of the industrial world, economic expansion has now been under way for some time, with inflation in many cases remaining at its lowest level since the early 1960s. Pre-emptive tightening of monetary policy in 1994 has proven successful in dampening inflationary pressures in countries most advanced in the economic cycle. Low inflation and stronger efforts and commitments to contain budget deficits have helped to reverse earlier increases in long-term interest rates, while coordinated intervention in foreign exchange markets and changes in official interest rates have helped to bring key exchange rates closer into line with fundamentals.

- Among most of the developing countries, growth has remained particularly strong, helped by successful stabilization and reform efforts in an increasing number of countries. Confidence has been quickly restored in all but a few countries following the Mexican financial crisis, and capital flows have been sustained at relatively high levels. Conditions for a pickup in growth are also improving in many of the poorest countries.

- The economies in transition from central planning are increasingly seeing the fruits of their adjustment efforts, with output now rising in many countries. Stronger stabilization policies in some of the countries less advanced in the transition suggest that conditions for a recovery of activity are improving there also.

Notwithstanding these positive developments, many challenges remain. Some of these stem from long-standing problems, including high structural unemployment and still-excessive budget deficits in most industrial countries. Many challenges also need to be addressed to further deepen the role of market forces among the developing countries and the countries in transition. Robust growth and subdued inflation in the world economy provide excellent conditions for tackling these tasks. At the same time, the integration of world financial markets underscores the urgency both for the performance of individual countries and for

**Chart 1. World Indicators[1]**
*(In percent)*

The cyclical recovery has boosted the growth of world output and trade above trend, while inflation in the industrial countries remains contained.

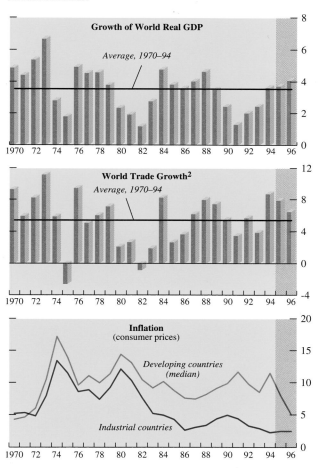

[1]Blue shaded areas indicate IMF staff projections.
[2]Goods and services, volume.

global economic and financial stability of addressing weaknesses in economic policies.

In the past eighteen months, the world economy has witnessed several episodes of turbulence in financial markets as investors have adjusted their portfolios in response to changes in risk evaluation. The timing and extent of shifts in market sentiment are often difficult to explain in terms of changes in economic fundamentals. But the large increases in bond yields seen in 1994, and the large movements in capital flows and exchange rates experienced in 1995, are at least in part traceable to concerns about the resolve or ability of governments to deal with economic problems and imbalances and to correct weaknesses in economic policies. If anything, the sensitivity of markets to such concerns seems to be increasing.

The specific focus of market concerns—be it a risk of overheating, the sustainability of fiscal or external imbalances, tensions over trade, or the credibility of an exchange rate peg—varies over time with changing economic circumstances. The shifting focus and sensitivity of investors to perceived risks contribute to market volatility. Understandably, there is concern among policymakers that shifts in market sentiment may give rise to overshooting of interest rates, misalignment of exchange rates, and destabilizing swings in international capital flows. The possibility that a government may misinterpret or ignore the first signs of a confidence crisis only aggravates the risk of more serious disruptions at a later stage. And while markets may sometimes pay insufficient attention to the longer-term consequences of an emerging and accumulating imbalance, they ultimately react forcefully if the imbalance is not corrected.

Abrupt swings in investor sentiment may contribute to fluctuations in output and employment through a variety of channels, including the effects of wealth appreciation or depreciation on the balance sheets of households, enterprises, and financial institutions. With upward trends in stocks of both real and financial assets relative to current income, and the growing use of highly leveraged instruments, the potential impact of fluctuations in asset prices is probably increasing. Asset price changes may sometimes reinforce the effects of policy actions and help to stabilize an economy. This was arguably the case in the United States in 1994 when increases in long-term interest rates helped to set the stage for a more sustainable growth path. And exchange rate changes are often helpful and desirable to promote external adjustment and balanced growth. In some instances, however, changes in financial market sentiment may make the task of policymakers more difficult, perhaps even aggravate existing problems. This was clearly the case in Japan at the exchange rate of about ¥85 per dollar prevailing in mid-1995. For Italy and Sweden, very large premiums in interest rates and persistent exchange rate weakness have also complicated the tasks of putting their public finances on a sound footing and of meeting their inflation objectives.

The critical issue, however, is not whether the liberalization of financial markets needs to be reconsidered because of the potential for market turmoil. Admittedly, markets occasionally are mistaken and often appear to react too slowly to emerging imbalances. But shifts in market sentiment are usually justified even though the resulting movements in asset prices can appear excessive. Indeed, closer attention by markets to the quality of economic policies is clearly desirable and needs to be assisted by timely provision of economic information, which would help to reduce the abruptness and costs of adjustment. In any case, closing the capital account of the balance of payments is neither feasible nor desirable. The issue facing policymakers is rather the need to address the policy problems and weak fundamentals that are often at the root of market turmoil and thereby jeopardize the great benefits from capital market liberalization and integration.

The most prominent recent episode of shifts in investor sentiment started in Mexico at the end of 1994, following a period of unsustainable current account deficits; as the economy adjusted to the abrupt reversal of capital flows, real GDP has contracted sharply this year. The impact of the crisis in Mexico was felt not only by its main trading partners but also by some other emerging market countries because of contagion effects, although these were quickly contained in most cases. Among industrial countries, Japan has suffered a serious setback to its fragile recovery as a result of the excessive strength of the yen in the first half of 1995, especially against the U.S. dollar. Several other countries have experienced an intensification of inflationary pressures due to the lagged effects of large exchange rate depreciations in recent years. And the earlier sharp rise in long-term interest rates in some countries with weak fundamentals has affected their prospects for sustained economic recovery.

Actions to lower short-term interest rates in support of concerted intervention by leading central banks have reinforced market trends and contributed to correct the misalignment of key currencies that arose in the first half of 1995. These developments, which have helped to alleviate downside risks to the expected recovery in Japan and to the prospects for continued noninflationary growth in other industrial countries, illustrate the benefits of cooperative efforts among the major industrial countries to address common concerns. Although intervention is not a reliable tool to influence exchange rates in all circumstances, the recent experience confirms that coordinated actions to affect exchange rates can be effective against serious misalignment when economic and policy developments are supportive and the timing carefully chosen.

Overall, the world economy has proven quite resilient to the recent turmoil in financial markets. While the staff has revised down the projected growth rate for the industrial countries by ½ of 1 percentage point for 1995 and somewhat less for 1996, the projections for many developing and some transition countries are now stronger than indicated in the May 1995 *World Economic Outlook* (Table 1). The projected rate of growth of world output is therefore essentially unchanged at about 4 percent in both 1995 and 1996.

Looking further ahead, the sensitivity of financial markets to economic imbalances underscores the importance of adhering to the cooperative strategy for sustained global expansion set out in the Interim Committee's Madrid Declaration and reaffirmed in its April 1995 communiqué.[1] If policy shortcomings are addressed in a timely manner, there is the potential for robust growth with low inflation over the medium to longer run. Conversely, slippages in economic policies would increase the risk of further disruptive reactions in financial markets, volatility in output and employment, and significant welfare losses for all countries. Clearly, the key challenge is to address policy weaknesses *before* markets force the required adjustments.

Prospects for world trade are critical for global economic performance. The rapid growth of trade in relation to the growth of world output—by a factor of almost two to one over the past thirty-five years—has been both a cause and a result of rising prosperity. With new multilateral agreements in place or in prospect for further liberalization of trade in goods and services, and of foreign direct investment, trade is likely to remain an engine of growth for all countries that position themselves to benefit. The new World Trade Organization provides a stronger rules-based institutional framework, but it faces formidable challenges to resist and reverse protectionist pressures. The multilateral trading system has served the world well but is threatened by frequent resort to unilateral trade measures, excessive use of antidumping actions, and the risk that regional trade agreements may lead to trade diversion.

## Industrial Countries

The pace of economic expansion in the industrial countries slowed somewhat in the first half of 1995. Among the countries where the upswing has been the strongest—the United States, Canada, the United Kingdom, and Australia—some moderation of growth was appropriate following the rapid absorption of slack during 1994. For Germany, France, and several other continental European countries still recovering from the 1992–93 recession, economic activity is expected to remain relatively strong, although growth expectations for 1995 have been marked down slightly.

---

[1]The text of the Madrid Declaration is reproduced in the October 1994 *World Economic Outlook*, p. x.

The most serious deterioration in the economic situation is in Japan, for which the staff has revised down the near-term growth projections substantially.

Japan is experiencing one of its most serious economic slowdowns in the postwar period, the result of successive financial shocks including the bursting of the asset price bubbles of the late 1980s and the continued sharp appreciation of the yen. In mid-1995, with an exchange rate of about ¥85 per dollar, the Japanese currency appeared to be significantly overvalued on most criteria that can be used to assess the consistency of exchange rates with underlying fundamentals. The subsequent depreciation of the yen has brought it back to a level that appears to be closer in line with fundamentals.

The Japanese authorities have eased fiscal and monetary policies substantially, which has helped to contain the adverse impact of the financial shocks. In recent months, the protracted nature of the downturn has prompted further action to restore confidence and to avoid an even more prolonged underutilization of resources. The further easing of monetary conditions in July and August, with the discount rate being cut to a record low of ½ of 1 percent, was warranted in light of the declining levels of most price indices and the large output gap. The decline in interest rates, supported by coordinated intervention, helped to reverse the earlier excessive appreciation of the yen. The subsequent substantial economic package announced in September has reinforced the monetary easing. While there will be a need to resume fiscal consolidation once recovery is firmly established, the latest measures appear to provide the desired support for a sustained recovery and point to the potential for somewhat higher growth in 1996 than indicated in the staff's baseline projection (Box 1).

The recent successfully managed closure of some insolvent financial institutions was a significant step toward the resolution of the bad loans problem in Japan, but many other smaller insolvent institutions may also require restructuring and there is a risk that financial sector problems will continue to slow the pace of recovery. It is therefore essential that the authorities decisively address these problems. Structural reforms also remain essential to revitalize the Japanese economy. Deregulation and other market opening reforms would increase the responsiveness of the economy to world competitive forces.

In North America and Europe, it will be important not to overreact to what is likely to be only a pause or a temporary slowdown in the expansion. In particular, the substantial reversal this year of earlier rises in long-term interest rates should provide significant support to activity during the period ahead. Against the backdrop of subdued inflationary pressures, several countries have lowered official interest rates in recent months to alleviate downside risks to economic activity. However, barring stronger efforts to reduce fiscal

## Table 1. Overview of the *World Economic Outlook* Projections

*(Annual percent change unless otherwise noted)*

| | 1993 | 1994 | Current Projections 1995 | Current Projections 1996 | Differences from May 1995 Projections 1995 | Differences from May 1995 Projections 1996 |
|---|---|---|---|---|---|---|
| **World output** | **2.5** | **3.6** | **3.7** | **4.1** | **—** | **−0.1** |
| Industrial countries | 1.1 | 3.1 | 2.5 | 2.4 | −0.5 | −0.2 |
| United States | 3.1 | 4.1 | 2.9 | 2.0 | −0.3 | 0.1 |
| Japan | −0.2 | 0.5 | 0.5 | 2.2 | −1.3 | −1.3 |
| Germany | −1.2 | 2.9 | 2.6 | 2.9 | −0.6 | −0.4 |
| France | −1.5 | 2.9 | 2.9 | 2.7 | −0.3 | −0.4 |
| Italy | −1.2 | 2.2 | 3.0 | 2.8 | — | −0.2 |
| United Kingdom | 2.2 | 3.8 | 2.7 | 2.9 | −0.5 | — |
| Canada | 2.2 | 4.6 | 2.2 | 2.7 | −2.1 | 0.1 |
| Seven countries above | 1.3 | 3.1 | 2.4 | 2.3 | −0.6 | −0.3 |
| Other industrial countries | 0.2 | 2.9 | 3.2 | 3.0 | −0.1 | −0.2 |
| *Memorandum* | | | | | | |
| European Union | −0.6 | 2.8 | 2.9 | 2.8 | −0.3 | −0.2 |
| Developing countries | 6.1 | 6.2 | 6.0 | 6.3 | 0.4 | 0.2 |
| Africa | 0.8 | 2.6 | 3.0 | 5.2 | −0.7 | −0.1 |
| Asia | 8.7 | 8.5 | 8.7 | 7.9 | 1.0 | 0.5 |
| Middle East and Europe | 3.6 | 0.3 | 2.4 | 3.2 | −0.5 | −1.5 |
| Western Hemisphere | 3.3 | 4.6 | 1.8 | 4.0 | −0.6 | 0.3 |
| Countries in transition | −9.1 | −9.5 | −2.1 | 3.4 | 1.7 | −0.1 |
| Central and eastern Europe | −6.1 | −3.8 | 0.2 | 4.3 | −0.2 | 0.8 |
| Excluding Belarus and Ukraine | −1.9 | 2.8 | 4.0 | 4.4 | 0.4 | 0.1 |
| Russia, Transcaucasus, and central Asia | −11.8 | −15.2 | −4.6 | 2.4 | 3.7 | −1.1 |
| **World trade volume (goods and services)[1]** | **3.9** | **8.7** | **7.9** | **6.5** | ... | ... |
| Imports | | | | | | |
| Industrial countries | 1.1 | 9.2 | 7.1 | 5.5 | ... | ... |
| Developing countries | 9.3 | 8.5 | 11.1 | 9.5 | ... | ... |
| Exports | | | | | | |
| Industrial countries | 2.5 | 8.1 | 6.9 | 5.0 | ... | ... |
| Developing countries | 7.3 | 11.3 | 11.0 | 9.6 | ... | ... |
| **Commodity prices in SDRs** | | | | | | |
| Oil[2] | −10.7 | −6.5 | 1.1 | −6.1 | −1.7 | −5.3 |
| Nonfuel[3] | 2.7 | 10.8 | 1.8 | −0.2 | ... | ... |
| **Consumer prices** | | | | | | |
| Industrial countries | 2.9 | 2.3 | 2.5 | 2.5 | −0.1 | −0.2 |
| Developing countries | 43.1 | 48.1 | 19.5 | 13.0 | 2.0 | 4.1 |
| Countries in transition | 675.2 | 301.3 | 147.7 | 25.4 | 20.8 | 6.5 |
| **Six-month LIBOR (in percent)[4]** | | | | | | |
| On U.S. dollar deposits | 3.4 | 5.1 | 6.2 | 6.2 | −0.6 | −0.8 |
| On Japanese yen deposits | 3.0 | 2.4 | 1.4 | 1.4 | −0.7 | −1.7 |
| On deutsche mark deposits | 6.9 | 5.3 | 4.6 | 5.2 | −0.8 | −0.8 |

Note: Real effective exchange rates are assumed to remain constant at the levels prevailing during August 1–23, 1995, except for the bilateral rates among ERM currencies, which are assumed to remain constant in nominal terms.

[1]Because services were not previously included and some methodological changes have been made to the way calculations are done, comparisons with the May 1995 projections are not presented.

[2]Simple average of spot prices of U.K. Brent, Dubai, and Alaska North Slope crude oil. The average price of oil in U.S. dollars a barrel was $15.47 in 1994; the assumed price is $16.67 in 1995 and $15.51 in 1996.

[3]Average, based on world commodity export weights. Comparisons with the May 1995 projections are not presented because the nonfuel commodity price index has been revised.

[4]London interbank offered rate.

deficits than currently envisaged, only a few countries appear to have significant scope for further monetary easing.

Almost all industrial countries are struggling to contain large budget deficits and to reduce excessive levels of public debt. It is therefore encouraging that efforts and commitments to tackle fiscal imbalances appear to be intensifying. Several countries have already made some progress and others are in the process of implementing significant medium-term deficit reduction plans. Nevertheless, underlying imbalances generally remain large and the envisaged pace of consolidation is rather slow in most cases. As a result of the still-large fiscal deficits, many countries are paying heavy costs in the form of high risk premiums in interest rates, increased inflationary pressures from currency depreciation, and diminished long-term growth potential. Under these circumstances, the best contribution fiscal policy can make to sustain the expansion is through determined action to progressively eliminate fiscal imbalances over the medium term. Postponing such action, let alone allowing slippages in needed consolidation efforts, would only increase the risk of financial instability and reduce both near-term and longer-run growth.

In the United States, a moderation of growth in 1995 was needed to prevent a buildup of excess demand pressures. The slowdown that has occurred can be attributed in part to the pre-emptive tightening of monetary policy in 1994, which was reinforced by the rise in long-term interest rates. Spillover effects from the crisis in Mexico, which necessitated a sharp correction of Mexico's external current account position, also contributed. Although growth appears to have slowed more than expected in the May 1995 *World Economic Outlook*, conditions are generally favorable for the expansion to pick up again during the second half of 1995 and in 1996.

For the U.S. expansion to be sustained, the risks of renewed upward pressure on inflation and on long-term interest rates must be averted. Since the rate of capacity utilization is still very high, there would need to be evidence of a marked slowdown to warrant a significant relaxation of monetary policy. But the key policy issue facing the U.S. authorities remains the need to eliminate the fiscal deficit and thereby strengthen national saving. Substantial progress toward fiscal consolidation was achieved in 1994, without impeding vigorous growth. In the absence of further measures, however, the underlying federal budget deficit would tend to rise again in the medium term. Budget proposals by the administration and by Congress recognize that further deficit reduction is essential to raise potential output and permit sustained increases in living standards in the future. A more front-loaded program, which postponed the introduction of significant tax cuts until substantial progress toward a balanced budget had been achieved, would allow the economy to reap the benefits of increased saving and lower interest rates more quickly and surely.

The domestic reasons for addressing the U.S. fiscal deficit are reinforced by global considerations. Although the deficit is now lower than in most other industrial countries, the fiscal shortfall is a contributing factor to the low U.S. saving rate and the persistent external current account deficits incurred since 1983. The ability to draw on other countries' saving has helped to contain the level of real interest rates in the United States but has added to pressures on global interest rates.[2] There are limits to the willingness of foreign investors to acquire dollar assets, however, which may have been a factor in the earlier weakness of the U.S. dollar against other major currencies. As discussed in the Annex, fiscal consolidation and other measures to enhance domestic saving in the United States would help to strengthen the dollar in the medium to longer run. The short-run effects of fiscal consolidation on the dollar are uncertain and would depend on the speed of consolidation, the cyclical response of the economy, and the impact on confidence and capital flows.

In the group of countries whose current business cycles are most closely synchronized with that of the United States—including the United Kingdom, Canada, and Australia—recent signs of moderation in the pace of expansion should also help to alleviate inflationary pressures. However, levels of long-term interest rates suggest that these countries have yet to fully establish the credibility of their anti-inflation policies. This makes it particularly important to consolidate the recovery through a period of more moderate growth. Safeguarding the commitment to price stability and strengthening financial market confidence will also need to be backed up by further progress on the fiscal front. In the United Kingdom and Australia, it will be important to avoid slippages in fiscal consolidation efforts. In Canada, the credibility of the government's economic policies would be strengthened by the adoption of a stronger medium-term consolidation program aimed at bringing the federal fiscal deficit well below the present target of 3 percent of GDP; further efforts to contain the deficits of provincial governments are also needed.

Among the continental European countries, where the recovery began only in the course of 1993, there have been mixed signals from recent economic indicators. The widespread moderation of growth since the beginning of 1995 may be due to the lagged effects of last year's rise in long-term interest rates, the appreciation of the deutsche mark and closely linked curren-

---

[2]The relationship between fiscal deficits, world saving, and interest rates is discussed in detail in Chapter V of the May 1995 *World Economic Outlook*.

## Box 1. September 1995 Economic Stimulus Package in Japan

The Government of Japan announced on September 20 a new economic stimulus package intended to provide additional fiscal support to activity and promote a return to a path of steady recovery. The package includes fiscal measures amounting to ¥14.2 trillion (3 percent of GDP)

and consists almost wholly of expenditure increases (*see table below*). The most important component of the package is an increase in public investment of over 1½ percent of GDP. This includes general public works; public works solely financed by local governments; education,

### Japan: Summary of Economic Stimulus Packages, 1992–95
*(In trillions of yen, unless otherwise indicated)*

| | Date Proposed | | | | |
| --- | --- | --- | --- | --- | --- |
| | August 1992 | April 1993 | September 1993 | February 1994 | September 1995 |
| Total package | 10.7 | 13.2 | 6.2 | 15.3 | 14.2 |
| (In percent of GDP) | (2.3) | (2.8) | (1.3) | (3.2) | (3.0) |
| Tax reductions | — | 0.2 | — | 5.9 | — |
| (In percent of GDP) | (—) | (—) | (—) | (1.2) | (—) |
| Public investment[1] | 5.8 | 7.6 | 2.0 | 4.0 | 8.1 |
| (In percent of GDP) | (1.2) | (1.6) | (0.4) | (0.8) | (1.7) |
| Land purchases | 1.6 | 1.2 | 0.3 | 2.8[2] | 3.2[3] |
| (In percent of GDP) | (0.5) | (0.3) | (0.1) | (0.6) | (0.7) |
| Increased lending by Housing Loan Corporation | 0.8 | 1.8 | 2.9 | 1.2 | 0.5 |
| (In percent of GDP) | (0.2) | (0.4) | (0.6) | (0.3) | (0.1) |
| Increased lending by government-affiliated financial institutions | 2.1 | 2.4 | 1.0 | 1.5 | 2.4 |
| (In percent of GDP) | (0.5) | (0.5) | (0.2) | (0.3) | (0.5) |

Sources: Japanese authorities; and IMF staff estimates.

[1]Includes disaster relief, unidentified land component of public investment, and lending by the Fiscal Investment and Loan Program to public corporations for public works.

[2]Including ¥0.5 trillion of land purchases to be conducted over a five-year period.

[3]Including ¥0.5 trillion of land purchases by a government-affiliated urban development organization.

cies, the effects on monetary conditions of tensions within the European Monetary System (EMS) in the spring of 1995, and spillovers from North America and Japan. However, with the renewed decline of long-term interest rates in most countries and the recent abatement of tensions in exchange markets, it seems likely that the European expansion will continue at a pace slightly above potential growth.

At the same time, it appears that the recovery in continental Europe may bring only relatively slow progress in reducing unemployment. There is also a danger that macroeconomic imbalances and high unemployment would pose continued risks of financial market pressures. It is critical, therefore, to address a number of key policy weaknesses, especially in the fiscal area and with respect to labor markets. Germany has set a good example with substantial progress in unwinding unification-related fiscal imbalances, although additional efforts will be required in coming years to improve further the fiscal position while also lessening the burden of taxation. In France, by contrast, the budget deficit remains sizable despite recent

efforts to raise revenues. Further efforts at fiscal consolidation are also needed in most other European countries. It is now generally recognized that Stage III of Economic and Monetary Union (EMU) is unlikely to begin before 1999, mainly because of the slow pace of fiscal consolidation. It is important that this delay does not lead to a relaxation of efforts to tackle fiscal imbalances. It is also critical to ensure continued progress toward price stability. In the current situation, countries that have established their anti-inflationary credibility and that make sufficient progress toward fiscal consolidation probably have some room to allow monetary conditions to ease further in coming months.

In Italy and Sweden, recovery is continuing, partly driven by rapid export growth. In both countries, significant measures have been taken, or are planned, to reduce the unsustainably large fiscal imbalances, but lack of confidence in financial markets has continued to cloud the outlook. This has been reflected in extremely weak currencies and substantial premiums in long-term interest rates, which have added to concerns about the fiscal outlook. There are recent signs that telecommunication networks, science, and technology projects; disaster relief; and other investments including earthquake reconstruction and agricultural support projects.[1] The package also includes measures to stimulate activity in the real estate market through land purchases. Furthermore, the Housing Loan Public Corporation is to extend additional loans, and increased public sector loans are to be provided mainly to small businesses and for investment in new business activities. Other measures include employment stabilization, import promotion, additional financial liberalization, and further acceleration of deregulation.

With the implementation of the September package, the structural deficit (excluding social security), in relation to GDP, is estimated to widen to 5½ percent in FY 1995 and to 6¼ percent in FY 1996, compared with 5 percent in FY 1994 (see table on the right). The additional stimulus provided by the package through FY 1995/96 would thus more than offset the small withdrawal of stimulus that otherwise would have occurred owing to the unwinding of the earlier packages. The projections in this issue of the World Economic Outlook, which were finalized before the September package was announced, are based on the assumption that fiscal measures would have been adopted to prevent a withdrawal of stimulus through 1996.

In addition to the direct effects on demand and activity from the further increase in public investment outlays,

---

[1]This agricultural support constitutes a part of the six-year program that was decided in the wake of the Uruguay Round agreement in 1994.

**Japan: Structural Budget Balance, Excluding Social Security**
*(In percent of GDP)*

| | Fiscal Year | | | | | |
| --- | --- | --- | --- | --- | --- | --- |
| | 1991 | 1992 | 1993 | 1994 | 1995 | 1996[1] |
| Without September 1995 package | −1.1 | −3.3 | −3.6 | −5.0 | −4.9 | −4.7 |
| With September 1995 package | −1.1 | −3.3 | −3.6 | −5.0 | −5.5 | −6.3 |

Sources: Japanese authorities; and IMF staff estimates.
[1]The estimates for FY 1996 are based on IMF staff assumptions about the FY 1996 budget as well as the phasing of the implementation of the September package.

the new measures will operate through indirect effects on consumption and investment, partly by bolstering consumer and business confidence. The measures to stimulate activity in the real estate market could help to improve the health of the financial sector, which has been weakened by the decline in land prices, thereby alleviating a potential restraint on the recovery. Moreover, structural policy measures, including further deregulation, should help to stimulate entrepreneurship and private sector vitality, and thus strengthen overall confidence in economic prospects. The effects of these measures could potentially be large. Overall, the latest measures have significantly improved the prospects for recovery during the period ahead and point to the potential for somewhat stronger growth in 1996 than indicated in the baseline forecast.

---

strengthened commitments to fiscal consolidation are beginning to break this vicious circle, but to fully restore confidence in financial markets the required reductions in fiscal deficits must be implemented as soon as possible. Concerns about the budgetary outlook have also resulted in continued high interest rate premiums in Spain and even more so in Greece. In contrast, Finland now appears to be recovering briskly, with an improving fiscal outlook, a correction of a previously sharply depreciated exchange rate, relatively low inflation, and declining interest rate premiums.

High rates of unemployment remain a central concern in most industrial countries. In Europe, where the problem is most serious, the cyclical recovery under way will help to improve labor market conditions but is unlikely to bring unemployment much below 8 to 9 percent, which is the estimated level of structural unemployment. Reducing structural unemployment will require fundamental reform of all regulations and policies that hamper incentives for creating jobs and seeking employment. The reforms should be designed to ensure that social objectives are achieved in ways that

are compatible with better functioning labor markets, including through better education and increased training to enhance productivity and real earnings potential of the labor force. In several countries, steps are being taken to reduce the levels of social security contributions, which deter the creation of low-skilled jobs in particular. Such measures, however, will need to be accompanied by other fundamental reforms and should be fully financed so as not to impede continued progress toward fiscal consolidation.

## Developing Countries

The storm that broke with the financial crisis in Mexico has been weathered well by most emerging market countries. Contagion effects have been contained, and in all but a few cases capital inflows have been sustained at relatively high levels. Growth in some developing countries has even been marked up somewhat and should average about 6 percent in both

1995 and 1996. The maintenance of market confidence and the continued solid economic performance by a large number of countries are testimony to the substantial progress throughout the developing world toward greater economic and financial stability and market-oriented structural reform.

The Mexican authorities responded to the abrupt reversal of capital flows at the end of 1994 by adopting a bold stabilization program that has received substantial international support. The program, which includes a significant improvement in the fiscal position, aims at re-establishing the basis for sustainable economic growth by strengthening domestic saving, reducing the external deficit and dependence on foreign saving, and containing inflation in the aftermath of the sharp depreciation of the peso. Despite the inevitable contraction of output early in the adjustment process, the initial results are generally encouraging and the country has been able to meet its international obligations. Moreover, investor confidence has improved as illustrated by a rising stock market, declining interest rates, and a stable currency. The rapid pace of adjustment suggests that the Mexican economy should soon begin to recover.

Argentina, which has been most affected by the Mexican crisis, has also put in place significant adjustment measures aimed at bolstering saving and reducing the external deficit. As in Mexico, the adjustment process is under way, although further efforts are required to strengthen the financial system. In Brazil, capital outflows in the wake of the Mexican crisis were less acute, and more recently there have been strong inflows. The impressive decline in inflation following the introduction of the real in mid-1994 should help to foster sustained economic recovery; consolidation of this progress requires, in particular, further efforts to strengthen the public finances and the implementation of structural reforms. Chile was virtually untouched by the Mexican crisis owing largely to its strong policy fundamentals.

For a number of developing countries, continued buoyancy of growth has increased the risk of overheating. This is a particular concern in Asia, which accounts for most of the upward revision to the output projections for developing countries. If not checked, rising inflationary pressures may eventually require more significant policy tightenings with potentially large economic costs. Despite some adverse effects on investor confidence in the immediate aftermath of the Mexican crisis, capital flows into Asia have been sustained at high levels. In many countries with inflexible exchange rates, the large capital inflows contribute to excess demand pressures, in part because of the difficulty of effectively sterilizing such inflows. A key policy requirement for many of these countries is to strengthen the public sector's financial position in order to reduce pressures on interest rates and, hence, incentives for capital inflows. Exchange rate

appreciation may also contribute to better macroeconomic balance, especially in countries where rapid productivity growth is helping to maintain external competitiveness.

In China, with efforts to tighten financial policies, demand and inflation appear to have moderated but a cautious policy stance remains appropriate. Hard budget constraints in the state-owned enterprise sector would help to reduce overall credit expansion and free up real and financial resources for the vibrant private sector. A faster pace of trade liberalization and upward flexibility of the exchange rate would also help to contain inflationary pressures. In India, recovery is now well established, with increased supply responses from structural reforms introduced since 1991, while inflation has recently abated as a result of a tightened monetary policy. To reduce the risk of a renewed rise in inflationary pressures and to increase resources available for private investment, the large fiscal deficit should be reduced further and structural reforms should be accelerated.

In the Middle East, several non-oil producing countries have achieved significant progress. However, weak oil prices and persistent macroeconomic imbalances have limited economic growth in most of the region during the recent period. Considerable strengthening of fiscal positions will be required in most countries to increase domestic saving and investment and reduce external deficits. The oil exporting countries need to expand non-oil tax revenues and improve expenditure control to ensure that improvements in fiscal positions can be sustained. To diversify their export base and strengthen growth, many countries will also need to broaden the scope and increase the pace of structural reform, including through trade liberalization and public enterprise reform. The medium-term prospects for the region should benefit from increased confidence brought about by the peace process and from greater intraregional cooperation.

Growth prospects in Africa have improved somewhat with the adoption of market-oriented policies in an increasing number of countries. Stronger adjustment efforts have fostered macroeconomic stability, and currency realignments and liberalization of exchange and trade regimes have helped to restore external competitiveness and improve the investment climate. Efforts are also under way in many countries to address distortions in resource allocation and to remove obstacles to private sector development. However, notwithstanding encouraging progress on a number of policy fronts, many African countries still suffer from declining or stagnating levels of per capita income, widespread poverty, and unsustainable external debt burdens. Significantly higher growth rates will be required to improve living standards. Domestic policies will be the key determinant of success, with policy priorities including the need to intensify efforts to strengthen government revenue mobilization, reduce fiscal imbalances, and step up structural and institutional reform. Actions in these areas are being complemented by measures to reduce debt to Paris Club creditors using Naples terms, together with comparable action by other bilateral and commercial creditors. The international community needs to ensure that all highly indebted poor countries undertaking strong adjustment programs can receive the financing and alleviation of their debt burdens needed to allow them to grow to their potential.

Strong and consistent reform and stabilization efforts have contributed importantly to the impressive growth performance of the developing world in recent years. These efforts have not only permitted greater participation by the developing countries in the world economy but also appear to have made them more resilient to cyclical downturns in the industrial countries, as seen in 1991–93. They have also given them access to financial resources to support higher levels of investment and growth. At the same time, however, the integration of the developing countries into global financial markets makes them more vulnerable to external financial disturbances. Indeed, a key issue is how these countries can best benefit from increased integration into the global economy while minimizing risks to domestic financial stability arising from external shocks.

Liberalization of capital movements helps to increase the efficiency of resource allocation. It also fosters competition in domestic financial markets and allows domestic investors to diversify their portfolios. These objectives have been the driving force behind the liberalization of capital movements by the industrial countries and more recently by many emerging market countries. Experience shows, however, that certain conditions have to be met for capital account liberalization to be successful. Because financial markets adjust more quickly than other markets, capital account liberalization requires both a reasonable degree of macroeconomic balance and structural reforms, especially of the domestic financial system.

## Transition Countries

Economic performance varies considerably across the countries in transition, largely reflecting differences in the stage of economic stabilization and restructuring. Among the countries that are still going through the process of disinflation—Russia, Belarus, Ukraine, and most Transcaucasian and central Asian countries—output continued to decline in 1994 and the first half of 1995, although official data probably exaggerate the output contraction. In contrast, those economies that are more advanced in the transition have now clearly turned the corner and are enjoying, in most cases, robust growth. These countries, which

include Poland, the Czech and Slovak Republics, Hungary, Slovenia, Albania, the Baltic countries, and Mongolia, owe their success to the achievement of relative macroeconomic stability coupled with major structural reform efforts. The results are a substantial strengthening of economic incentives, improvements in the allocation of real and financial resources, rapid increases in productive investment, and impressive growth of both exports and imports.

Even so, many challenges will need to be addressed to consolidate the initial gains and to maintain a strong growth momentum. As in the emerging market countries in the developing world, many of the transition countries are receiving significant capital inflows. Such inflows, which include repatriation of flight capital, are a sign of the confidence of both domestic and foreign investors in the strong growth prospects of the recipient countries. Inflows of foreign direct investment are particularly encouraging because of their beneficial effects on management practices and productivity. By easing financing constraints, capital inflows should help to stimulate activity and permit higher levels of investment; this is critical for future growth since much of the capital stock inherited from the command system has proven to be obsolete.

Also important to keep in mind, however, are the lessons from other parts of the world about the potential instability of such inflows and the need to guard against the risk of overheating and excessive current account imbalances. As the transition countries increasingly gain access to international capital markets and receive portfolio inflows by nonresidents, foreign saving should not become a substitute for domestic saving. A key requirement is a continued cautious stance of macroeconomic policies with further reductions in government deficits. Many of the transition countries also need to accelerate privatization, enterprise restructuring, and institution building. This will help to further deepen the role of market forces and increase the chances that both domestic and external financial resources are channeled toward productive investments.

The countries that are less advanced in the transition process suffer from a complex set of problems and policy shortcomings, although there are encouraging signs of greater determination to resolve them. Indeed, many of these countries have made good progress in reducing inflation during the first half of 1995. In Russia, there have now been significant achievements over a number of years in the area of structural reform. Tightened financial policies have brought down inflation, and there are early signs that activity may have begun to turn around. The nominal appreciation of the ruble in the second quarter of 1995 and the authorities' successful policy of maintaining it within a band during the third quarter should help to bring down inflation further. Sustained progress in reducing the large fiscal imbalances, particularly through increased revenues, will be essential to continue the process of disinflation and to free up resources needed for the restructuring of the economy. There has been substantial progress with macroeconomic stabilization since late 1994 in Ukraine, and more recently in Belarus.

A serious structural weakness in many of the transition countries, including some of the most advanced, is the fragility of their banking systems. The legacy of nonperforming assets has its roots in the old central planning regime; however, the accumulation of bad loans has continued during the early years of transition, including by many of the new banks that have been established in recent years. The slow pace of restructuring of the nonfinancial state-owned sector is an important underlying reason for these difficulties, often because of political pressures to extend bank credit to financially insolvent enterprises. In addition, banks have frequently provided financing for new ventures that turned out to be failures.

Preventing banking crises and dealing with them when they arise are major challenges in these countries as in several other countries. A key issue is the need to limit potential macroeconomic disruptions and setbacks to stabilization efforts. Problem loans to ailing enterprises need to be resolved in the context of a comprehensive enterprise and bank reform strategy, including appropriate social safety net measures. There is also a need for strengthened prudential supervision, better assessment of credit risk, more stringent capital requirements, and greater access for foreign banks, which in turn will spur the necessary strengthening of banking practices. In any case, banking reform measures will take time before they become effective, and should be preceded by clear strategies to address banking crises in a way that prevents their contagion and limits the fiscal costs, without creating an excessive risk of moral hazard.

# II

# The World Economy in 1995–96

Developments in financial markets during the past eighteen months and signs of a softening of growth in the industrial countries since the beginning of 1995 have highlighted the sensitivity of financial markets to economic imbalances and the downside risks to the outlook. However, although economic performance has been adversely affected in some countries, there are many reasons to expect that the global economic expansion will proceed at a satisfactory pace. Fears of a pickup in inflation in the industrial countries have largely abated, long-term interest rates have again fallen substantially in most countries following the sharp increases in bond yields during 1994, coordinated foreign exchange market intervention by leading central banks and supportive policy developments have helped to correct the misalignment of key currencies that had emerged earlier in the year, contagion effects from the financial crisis in Mexico have been contained, and growth in most of the emerging market countries in the developing world and among the transition countries has remained robust. While the short-term projections for the industrial countries have been marked down somewhat, the forecasts for many developing countries are now even stronger than expected in the May 1995 *World Economic Outlook* (see Table 1).

Notwithstanding the staff's relatively optimistic baseline projections, which are based on a number of positive policy developments, there are still downside risks to both the near-term and medium-term outlook. These risks derive partly from policy weaknesses in many industrial countries that may provoke renewed turbulence in financial markets. Among the developing countries, rapid growth and difficulties in managing capital inflows pose risks of overheating in many economies. And the prospects for sustained economic growth in many transition countries are tempered by possible setbacks in stabilization efforts related partly to the fragility of their financial systems. The policy requirements to address these risks are discussed in the following chapters.

## Economic Activity

A broad range of indicators seem to indicate a slowing of demand and activity in the industrial countries since the beginning of 1995. With the important exception of Japan, however, there are few signs of recession, suggesting that the slowdown represents a midcycle pause. Such a pause will help to prevent overheating in those countries that are most advanced in the economic cycle, and hence should help to prolong the expansion. But there also seems to be some softening of activity in continental Europe, where the expansion began more recently, even though the underlying growth momentum still appears to be quite strong.

The moderation of growth in the industrial countries has been reflected in a stagnant industrial output in the major industrial countries as a group during the first half of 1995. A marked decline in real commodity prices also indicates a slowdown in demand. And various leading or coincident indicators, including consumer confidence, business expectations, and real money growth (which has been slightly negative in most of the major industrial countries since the beginning of the year), suggest that the growth pause extended into the second, and possibly even into the third, quarter of 1995 (Charts 2 and 3). Quarterly GDP statistics confirm that growth was particularly weak in Japan and Canada in the first half of the year and that the other major countries also experienced a slowdown.

The reasons for the apparent slowdown include both common and country-specific factors. The run-up in long-term interest rates worldwide during 1994, which reinforced the effects of pre-emptive monetary tightenings in a number of countries that had reached high levels of capacity utilization, has probably been a key factor in affecting consumer confidence and restraining both consumption and residential investment. Generally low real wage growth and tax increases in some countries have also acted to restrain private consumption. Other factors include the spillover effects of the Mexican crisis on major trading partners, especially the United States, and the adverse effects of exchange rate appreciations on export prospects in Germany, Switzerland, and especially Japan. In Japan, the excessive strength of the yen in the first half of the year and the Kobe earthquake have compounded the difficulties that began with the collapse of the asset price bubble in the early 1990s.

Looking ahead to 1996, private consumption growth is expected to remain relatively moderate in most countries. Moreover, public consumption is likely to expand only marginally in the industrial

**Chart 2.  Selected Industrial Countries:  Output Growth and Leading Economic Indicators[1]**

*(Percent change from previous year)*

In early 1995, leading indicators were signaling declines in output growth in the United States and continental Europe.

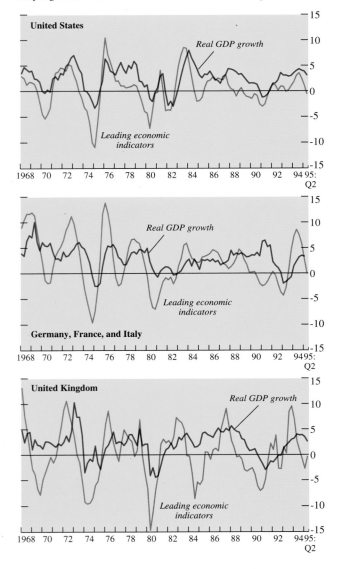

Sources: Bureau of Economic Analysis, Department of Commerce (United States); OECD *Main Economic Indicators* (Germany, France, and Italy); *Economic Trends,* Central Statistics Office (United Kingdom).

[1]The leading economic indicators are composite indices of variables that lead cyclical activity in the economy. The indices differ by country but typically include variables such as new orders, construction starts, hours worked, unfilled orders, producers' shipments, stock prices, money supply, and other variables.

countries overall, as efforts continue to control the growth of public expenditure. In contrast, the strength of investment intention surveys is extremely encouraging, suggesting that business investment should generally remain by far the most buoyant component of overall demand. High rates of capacity utilization in some countries, generally solid profits in recent years (Chart 4), continued restructuring under the pressure of global competition, and high levels of foreign direct investment should all contribute to raise overall investment levels and to stimulate rapid growth of trade in capital goods. Japan is the only country where private domestic investment is expected to be relatively weak, whereas outward foreign direct investment is likely to continue at a high level as Japanese producers adjust to the strong yen by shifting production to other countries, especially in Asia.

Turning to the outlook for individual countries, in the *United States,* following unsustainably rapid growth during 1994, the economy reached very high levels of resource use by early 1995. Although price increases remained moderate, the strains on labor markets and on capacity were threatening to boost inflation, which would ultimately have required a serious slowdown or even a recession to unwind the inflationary pressures. To prevent this, the Federal Reserve gradually tightened monetary conditions during 1994, setting the stage for a "soft landing" (Chart 5). This strategy clearly proved successful, even though activity appears to have slowed somewhat more than expected in the May 1995 *World Economic Outlook,* partly due to the decline in exports to Mexico and the rise in long-term interest rates during 1994. But the reversal of the rise in long-term interest rates since early 1995 should provide stimulus to activity during the period ahead. The risk of a rise in inflation has diminished, but it has not gone away completely and overall resource use remains close to, if not above, the level consistent with noninflationary growth. It seems unlikely that a further easing of monetary policy—beyond the small cut in the federal funds rate on July 6—will be warranted.

In the *United Kingdom, Canada,* and *Australia,* the business cycles remain closely synchronized with that of the United States (Table 2). All three countries have experienced a slowdown in key indicators since the start of the year, partly under the influence of significant increases in interest rates during 1994. Relatively weak exchange rates and buoyant export growth have helped to support activity in the United Kingdom and Canada, but rising import prices and producer prices have been threatening to spill over into broader indicators of inflation. Some moderation of growth in these countries was desirable following the rapid pace of expansion in 1994. However, should activity weaken more than expected, monetary policy would be faced with a dilemma, notably in Canada where the exchange rate has been weak and further depreciation would add to inflationary pressures. In both Canada and Australia, large external deficits underscore the need to raise domestic saving, especially through a tightening of fiscal policy. In the United Kingdom, unemployment has fallen to the lowest level since 1991, but wage increases have remained moderate and there still appears to be some margin of slack in the economy. Continued implementation of the authorities' commitments to reduce budget deficits and keep inflation low should reduce premiums on interest rates and the exchange rate and permit sustained growth over the medium term. In *New Zealand*, economic activity began to slow to a more sustainable rate in late 1994; however, the economy is still operating close to capacity. The fiscal position has strengthened markedly and the structural budget balance is now in sizable surplus, but financial policies need to remain sufficiently tight to forestall the buildup of inflationary and balance of payments pressures.

In *Germany*, the appreciation of the deutsche mark in the first half of the year has led to some downward revision of near-term growth expectations following stronger-than-expected growth in 1994. Investment intentions are still buoyant, however, in both the eastern and western Länder, and continued rapid productivity growth in manufacturing should help to offset the adverse effects of exchange rate appreciation on export growth. Although good progress toward fiscal consolidation will again dampen private consumption in 1995, planned tax reductions will contribute to raise real disposable incomes in 1996. Official interest rates were eased in March and again in August 1995 in response to the weakness of monetary indicators and the strength of the currency; low inflation and continued weak growth of M3 provide room for a further easing in support of the recovery should this prove warranted.

*France* has also felt the impact of exchange market tensions and again raised short-term money market rates substantially in the spring of 1995 to counter speculative pressures on the franc. More recently, these pressures have abated, the franc has strengthened against the deutsche mark to near its central parity, and interest rates have fallen significantly. With export demand remaining strong, the economy is not expected to be seriously affected by the earlier tensions. While some economic indicators weakened in early 1995, consumer confidence strengthened significantly in the second quarter. Unemployment is expected to decline only slowly, however, and wage increases are assumed to remain moderate. Inflation is projected to remain among the lowest in the industrial countries, which should provide scope for a further easing of monetary conditions should conditions in exchange markets allow. This will partly depend on the prospects for fiscal consolidation.

In *Italy* and *Sweden*, growth seems to have been well sustained, at least into the early part of 1995. Although domestic demand is being restrained by very

**Chart 3. Industrial Countries: Indicators of Consumer Confidence[1]**

Consumer confidence has weakened but remains relatively high.

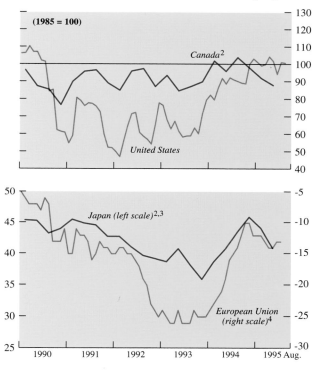

Sources: For the United States and Canada, the Conference Board; for Japan, Economic Planning Agency; and the European Commission.

[1]Indicators are not comparable across countries.

[2]Quarterly observations.

[3]Values above 50 indicate that respondents, on average, expect an improvement in their economic situation; values below 50 indicate an expected deterioration.

[4]Percent of respondents expecting an improvement in their situation minus percent expecting a deterioration.

**Chart 4. Industrial Countries: Indicators of Business Sector Profitability**

Profit shares and rates of return in the industrial countries in 1994 were the highest in twenty years.

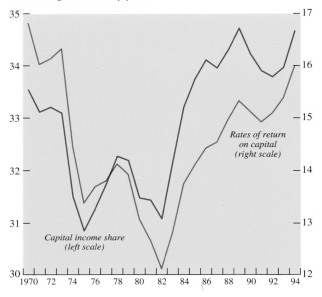

Rates of return on capital (right scale)

Capital income share (left scale)

Source: OECD, Economic Outlook data base.

Note: The data underlying these indicators are adjusted for the imputation of wage component of the self-employed.

high real interest rates, the competitive positions of both countries have improved sharply with the large depreciations of their currencies since 1992, which continued into the spring of 1995. The resulting boom in exports is providing welcome support for activity, but inflationary pressures have increased as rising import prices and producer prices are affecting consumer prices and inflation expectations. Both countries have therefore had to tighten monetary conditions quite early in the expansion. This should help to contain inflationary pressures although it puts at risk the prospects for a more balanced economic expansion. Progressive cuts in fiscal deficits, under way in both countries, are necessary to improve confidence in financial markets and to alleviate risks to their economic recoveries.

In *Austria, Belgium, Denmark*, and the *Netherlands*, growth is expected to remain relatively strong in 1995, although exports will be adversely affected by the effective appreciation of their currencies in the early part of the year. The strength of their currencies will also act as a brake on inflation, but inflationary pressures are nevertheless expected to increase somewhat in Denmark as the output gap narrows. Denmark's fiscal balance is expected to improve in 1995 and 1996 as the government reverses fiscal stimulus introduced to support the economy in 1994. In *Switzerland*, the franc appreciated against the U.S. dollar even more sharply than the deutsche mark in the first half of the year. The appreciation will restrain exports and dampen growth somewhat in 1995–96. Official and market interest rates have eased in recent months, which should help sustain activity without undermining inflation objectives. In *Spain* and *Portugal*, the economic recovery is also expected to continue at a moderate pace. Domestic demand has begun to supplement exports in supporting the upswing. Unemployment remains exceptionally high in Spain but should gradually decline this year and next as labor market reforms contribute to employment growth. The general government budget deficit declined in 1994 and is expected to decline further in 1995 to 5.9 percent of GDP. The 1996 budget will need to include substantive measures to reduce the deficit to 4.4 percent of GDP in 1996, which is the objective set in the government's Maastricht convergence plan.

Growth has been particularly buoyant in *Ireland* and, more recently, in *Finland*, and is expected to remain vigorous in both countries in 1995 and 1996. In Ireland, inflation has been well contained following the depreciation of the Irish pound in 1992, and the external position has strengthened considerably; the fiscal deficit has been kept below the Maastricht ceiling and progress has also been good in reducing the high level of public debt relative to GDP. Finland's fiscal consolidation plans have been well received by financial markets. This has allowed the markka to appreciate, relieving pressure on monetary policy and helping to contain inflation.

The *Japanese* economy has yet to show convincing signs of recovery from the deep and protracted downturn that began in late 1991. The estimated gap between potential and actual output has now widened to almost 6 percent (Chart 6). Open unemployment, although still low by the standards of other countries, is at a record high and threatens to rise further in the absence of a strong recovery. The persistent weakness of activity is due to the combined effects of sluggish domestic demand, which is affected by the balance sheet difficulties that arose after the bursting of the asset price bubble, the overhang of excess capital stocks, and the strength of the exchange rate. The sharp appreciation of the yen during the first half of 1995 threatened to set back further the prospects for recovery. However, the subsequent depreciation of the yen to levels closer to those implied by economic fundamentals and the rise in equity prices have strengthened the prospects for a pickup in growth in 1996. Both fiscal and monetary policies have been eased substantially to support activity, and the authorities have recently taken additional action that increases the chances of recovery.

Among the developing countries, the repercussions of the financial crisis in Mexico have been successfully contained in all but a few cases. In the Western Hemisphere, although growth is expected to slow in 1995 (Table 3) before picking up to 4 percent in 1996, the projections have been revised up for several countries compared with the May 1995 *World Economic Outlook*. In *Mexico*, however, output is estimated to fall by 5 percent this year as a result of necessary economic adjustments; but growth is expected to resume in 1996 as the bulk of the adjustment is completed and macroeconomic stability is achieved. In *Argentina*, which has been most affected by the Mexican crisis, growth is expected to slow in 1995–96 following a sharp decline in capital inflows and a tightening of fiscal policy that was necessary to restore confidence. In *Brazil*, by contrast, output growth so far in 1995 has been stronger than expected as a result of the positive effects on real incomes of the successful stabilization program. The authorities, however, face the challenge of avoiding overheating and containing the balance of payments deficit at a sustainable level. *Chile* and *Colombia* have been less affected by the Mexican financial crisis and are expected to experience robust output growth in 1995 and 1996. In *Venezuela*, output is expected to begin to turn around in 1995 after three consecutive years of contraction associated with a severe domestic financial crisis and inappropriate policies.

Average growth in the developing countries in Asia is expected to exceed 8 percent in 1995 for the fourth year in a row. This is providing a welcome offset to the weakness in Japan, but there are concerns that continued growth at unsustainable rates would heighten inflationary pressures. In *China*, growth in industrial

**Chart 5.  Three Major Industrial Countries:  Policy-Related Interest Rates and Ten-Year Government Bond Rates[1]**

*(In percent a year)*

Contrasting movements in policy-related interest rates reflect different cyclical positions.

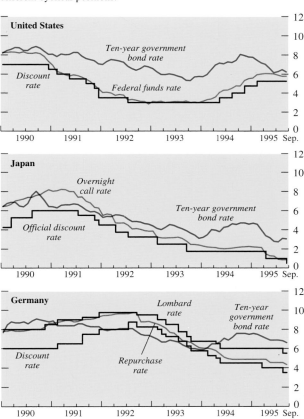

[1]The U.S. federal funds rate, Japanese overnight call rate, German repurchase rate, and all ten-year government rates are monthly averages. All other series are end of month.

**Chart 6.  Major Industrial Countries:  Output Gaps[1]**
*(Actual less potential, as a percent of potential)*

Output gaps continue to narrow in the major industrial countries
except in Japan, where the gap is expected to widen further.

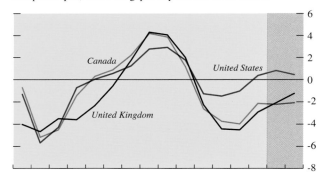

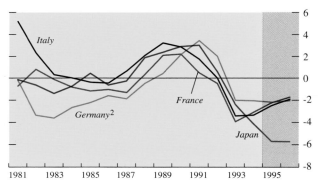

[1]Blue shaded areas indicate IMF staff projections. The gap estimates
are subject to a significant margin of uncertainty. For a discussion of the
approach to calculating potential output, see the October 1993 *World
Economic Outlook*, p. 101.
[2]Data through 1990 apply to west Germany only.

production slowed to an annual rate of around 17 percent in the first quarter of 1995 after increases in
excess of 20 percent in the second half of 1994. But
export growth and foreign direct investment remain
stronger than expected, and overheating is still a cause
for concern. Real GDP growth is expected to moderate
to single-digit levels only in 1996. The recovery in
*India* is now firmly established, partly reflecting the
supply response to structural reforms as well as the
stimulus from capital inflows. Output is expected to
increase by 5½ percent in 1995, as export volumes
continue to grow at double-digit rates and as private
investment remains robust. Further fiscal consolidation will be necessary to ensure adequate resources for
private investment and thus allow faster growth to be
sustained. Economic growth in *Korea* is expected to
pick up to 9¾ percent in 1995 driven by strong export
growth and investment, with the export sector benefit-
ing from gains in competitiveness against the yen. The
strength of activity in *Indonesia* is supported by buoyant domestic demand, whereas the contribution from
net exports is expected to remain negative. The boom
in private investment is likely to be sustained by recent
deregulation measures. In *Malaysia* and *Thailand,* the
strong expansion of domestic demand and large capital inflows have also led to widening current account
deficits despite impressive export growth; inflationary
pressures appear to be intensifying in both countries.
The *Philippine* economy performed better than expected in 1994 and appears to be on the way to recovery following the implementation of a successful
stabilization program.

Growth in the Middle East and Europe region is expected to strengthen somewhat in 1995 and 1996,
mainly because of improved prospects in several
countries that have experienced significant difficulties
recently. The recent weakening of oil prices, however,
is likely to have adverse effects on the oil exporting
countries in the region. Although demand for oil has
increased in line with world economic growth since
the beginning of the year, most of the increase in demand has been met by non-OPEC (Organization of
Petroleum Exporting Countries) producers. In *Egypt,*
despite progress in reducing the budget deficit and inflation, there has been some slippage in macroeconomic policies. The objective of maintaining a de
facto peg to the U.S. dollar has resulted in a loss of
competitiveness that is hampering growth. Real GDP
is expected to rise by only 1½ percent in 1995 but
could expand more in 1996 subject to progress with
reforms. In the *Islamic Republic of Iran,* the economic
situation remains difficult, but growth is expected to
pick up somewhat in 1995. In *Saudi Arabia,* the government is planning to cut the fiscal deficit to between
2 percent and 3 percent of GDP and little growth is expected during 1995–96. *Turkey* is gradually emerging
from a protracted crisis caused by overheating and an
abrupt loss of confidence. Output declined by 5½ per-

## Table 2. Industrial Countries: Real GDP, Consumer Prices, and Unemployment Rates

*(Annual percent change and percent of labor force)*

| | Real GDP | | | | Consumer Prices | | | | Unemployment Rates | | | |
|---|---|---|---|---|---|---|---|---|---|---|---|---|
| | 1993 | 1994 | 1995 | 1996 | 1993 | 1994 | 1995 | 1996 | 1993 | 1994 | 1995 | 1996 |
| **Industrial countries** | **1.1** | **3.1** | **2.5** | **2.4** | **2.9** | **2.3** | **2.5** | **2.5** | **8.1** | **8.1** | **7.6** | **7.5** |
| Major industrial countries | 1.3 | 3.1 | 2.4 | 2.3 | 2.8 | 2.2 | 2.4 | 2.4 | 7.3 | 7.2 | 6.8 | 6.8 |
| United States[1] | 3.1 | 4.1 | 2.9 | 2.0 | 3.0 | 2.6 | 3.0 | 3.2 | 6.8 | 6.1 | 5.7 | 5.9 |
| Japan | −0.2 | 0.5 | 0.5 | 2.2 | 1.3 | 0.7 | −0.2 | 0.1 | 2.5 | 2.9 | 3.1 | 3.2 |
| Germany[2] | −1.2 | 2.9 | 2.6 | 2.9 | 4.5 | 2.7 | 1.8 | 1.7 | 8.8 | 9.6 | 9.1 | 8.7 |
| France | −1.5 | 2.9 | 2.9 | 2.7 | 2.1 | 1.7 | 2.1 | 2.3 | 11.6 | 12.4 | 11.7 | 11.0 |
| Italy | −1.2 | 2.2 | 3.0 | 2.8 | 4.5 | 4.0 | 5.4 | 4.0 | 10.4 | 11.3 | 11.2 | 10.5 |
| United Kingdom[3] | 2.2 | 3.8 | 2.7 | 2.9 | 3.0 | 2.4 | 2.9 | 3.0 | 10.3 | 9.3 | 8.3 | 8.1 |
| Canada | 2.2 | 4.6 | 2.2 | 2.7 | 1.8 | 0.2 | 2.1 | 2.0 | 11.2 | 10.4 | 9.7 | 9.4 |
| Other industrial countries | 0.2 | 2.9 | 3.2 | 3.0 | 3.7 | 3.2 | 3.5 | 3.0 | 12.2 | 12.5 | 11.8 | 11.2 |
| Spain | −1.2 | 2.0 | 3.2 | 3.2 | 4.6 | 4.7 | 4.8 | 3.7 | 22.7 | 24.2 | 23.1 | 22.0 |
| Netherlands | 0.4 | 2.5 | 3.3 | 2.4 | 2.6 | 2.7 | 2.3 | 2.2 | 7.7 | 8.7 | 8.6 | 8.5 |
| Belgium | −1.7 | 2.4 | 2.5 | 2.5 | 2.8 | 2.4 | 1.7 | 2.0 | 9.5 | 10.3 | 9.8 | 9.4 |
| Sweden | −2.6 | 2.2 | 2.5 | 2.6 | 4.6 | 2.2 | 3.2 | 3.4 | 8.2 | 8.0 | 7.3 | 6.9 |
| Austria | −0.1 | 2.7 | 2.8 | 2.5 | 3.6 | 3.0 | 2.7 | 2.5 | 4.2 | 4.4 | 4.2 | 4.2 |
| Denmark | 1.5 | 4.4 | 3.3 | 2.5 | 1.2 | 2.0 | 2.3 | 3.0 | 12.3 | 12.1 | 10.0 | 9.7 |
| Finland | −1.6 | 3.9 | 5.2 | 4.6 | 2.2 | 1.1 | 1.4 | 2.5 | 17.9 | 18.4 | 16.8 | 14.7 |
| Greece | −0.5 | 1.5 | 1.9 | 2.3 | 14.5 | 10.9 | 9.3 | 7.4 | 9.7 | 9.6 | 9.5 | 9.3 |
| Portugal | −1.2 | 1.0 | 2.8 | 3.2 | 6.5 | 5.2 | 4.2 | 3.7 | 5.5 | 6.8 | 7.0 | 6.6 |
| Ireland | 4.0 | 5.2 | 6.2 | 4.9 | 1.4 | 2.5 | 2.5 | 2.5 | 15.7 | 14.8 | 13.8 | 13.5 |
| Luxembourg | 2.8 | 2.8 | 3.0 | 3.3 | 3.6 | 2.3 | 2.2 | 2.3 | 2.1 | 2.8 | 3.0 | 2.6 |
| Switzerland | −0.9 | 1.2 | 1.5 | 2.0 | 3.3 | 0.9 | 1.9 | 1.7 | 4.6 | 4.8 | 4.3 | 4.0 |
| Norway | 2.3 | 5.1 | 5.0 | 3.5 | 2.3 | 1.4 | 2.5 | 2.2 | 6.0 | 5.4 | 5.0 | 4.5 |
| Iceland | 1.1 | 2.8 | 3.0 | 2.6 | 4.1 | 1.6 | 2.5 | 2.5 | 4.4 | 4.8 | 4.5 | 4.3 |
| Australia | 3.9 | 5.4 | 3.8 | 3.6 | 1.8 | 1.9 | 4.5 | 3.4 | 10.9 | 9.7 | 8.4 | 7.6 |
| New Zealand[3] | 5.0 | 4.3 | 2.2 | 3.2 | 1.7 | 1.8 | 2.3 | 1.3 | 9.2 | 7.4 | 6.5 | 6.3 |
| *Memorandum* | | | | | | | | | | | | |
| European Union | −0.6 | 2.8 | 2.9 | 2.8 | 3.8 | 3.0 | 3.1 | 2.8 | 11.1 | 11.6 | 11.0 | 10.4 |

[1]The projections for unemployment have been adjusted to reflect the new survey techniques adopted by the U.S. Bureau of Labor Statistics in January 1994.

[2]Consumer prices are based on the revised consumer price index for united Germany introduced in September 1995. The revisions are estimated to have reduced measured CPI inflation by about ½ of 1 percentage point in 1994 and 1995.

[3]Consumer prices are based on the retail price index excluding mortgage interest.

cent last year, but the current account went into surplus as imports fell sharply and competitiveness improved. Growth is expected to begin to recover during 1995–96, although high inflation continues to cloud the outlook.

Africa's economic prospects have improved in recent years as a strengthening of economic policies in a number of countries has fostered greater macroeconomic stability. The projected increase in growth in 1995–96, however, remains subject to risks of policy slippages. In *South Africa*, economic activity is expected to pick up during the period ahead, reflecting increased private investment and strengthening consumer and business confidence. Nevertheless, unemployment is expected to remain very high in the foreseeable future. In *Nigeria*, political uncertainties contributed to a deterioration of the economic and financial situation in 1994. A recovery of oil production, and continued tight fiscal policy, underlies the envisaged recovery during 1995–96. In *Morocco*, a return of drought conditions is expected to adversely affect agri-

cultural production and economic activity. In *Algeria*, economic activity is expected to strengthen as the reform process continues. Growth in *Kenya* has been boosted by favorable weather and an expansion of exports and tourism receipts. In *Uganda*, economic activity has been stronger than anticipated, in part due to prudent financial policies. Growth is expected to be sustained at a relatively rapid pace, although the economy remains fragile and vulnerable to negative shocks.

In many countries of the CFA franc zone, the positive effects of the currency adjustment in early 1994 and the associated macroeconomic and structural policies are now beginning to be visible. Economic activity has picked up and growth in the CFA franc zone is expected to average 5 percent in 1995–96, supported by healthy growth of both investment and exports. In *Côte d'Ivoire*, for example, output growth is expected to reach 6½ percent in 1995. An export-led recovery in *Cameroon* is also under way. For the African countries that had arrangements at the end of 1994 under the IMF's structural adjustment facility (SAF) or en-

## Table 3. Selected Developing Countries: Real GDP and Consumer Prices

*(Annual percent change)*

| | Real GDP | | | Consumer Prices | | |
|---|---|---|---|---|---|---|
| | 1993 | 1994 | 1995 | 1993 | 1994 | 1995 |
| **Developing countries** | **6.1** | **6.2** | **6.0** | **43.1** | **48.1** | **19.5** |
| **Median** | **3.4** | **3.5** | **4.4** | **8.5** | **11.5** | **8.0** |
| **Africa** | **0.8** | **2.6** | **3.0** | **27.9** | **32.9** | **20.8** |
| Algeria | −2.2 | −0.2 | 3.0 | 29.0 | 22.5 | 6.4 |
| Cameroon | −2.2 | −3.8 | 3.3 | −3.7 | 12.7 | 26.7 |
| Côte d'Ivoire | −0.8 | 1.7 | 6.4 | 2.1 | 26.0 | 8.0 |
| Ghana | 5.0 | 3.8 | 5.0 | 25.0 | 24.9 | 28.9 |
| Kenya | −0.6 | 3.2 | 4.9 | 46.0 | 28.8 | 3.2 |
| Morocco | −1.1 | 11.5 | −5.1 | 5.2 | 5.1 | 7.0 |
| Nigeria | 2.3 | 1.3 | 3.3 | 57.2 | 57.0 | 58.3 |
| South Africa | 1.1 | 2.3 | 3.0 | 9.7 | 9.0 | 9.9 |
| Sudan | 7.6 | 5.5 | 7.2 | 111.5 | 102.0 | 58.5 |
| Tanzania | 3.7 | 3.1 | 4.5 | 26.1 | 29.0 | 22.0 |
| Tunisia | 2.3 | 3.4 | 4.2 | 4.0 | 4.7 | 5.5 |
| Uganda | 5.5 | 10.0 | 6.5 | 6.5 | 6.1 | 5.0 |
| SAF/ESAF countries[1] | 0.7 | 3.2 | 4.9 | 16.3 | 24.3 | 10.6 |
| **Asia** | **8.7** | **8.5** | **8.7** | **9.4** | **13.5** | **12.0** |
| Bangladesh | 4.9 | 4.4 | 4.9 | 1.6 | 3.2 | 4.2 |
| China | 13.7 | 11.5 | 11.4 | 13.0 | 21.7 | 18.0 |
| Hong Kong | 5.8 | 5.7 | 5.7 | 8.5 | 8.0 | 8.5 |
| India | 3.7 | 4.9 | 5.5 | 8.1 | 10.2 | 9.5 |
| Indonesia | 6.5 | 7.3 | 7.5 | 9.7 | 8.5 | 9.6 |
| Korea | 5.3 | 8.4 | 9.7 | 4.8 | 6.3 | 5.0 |
| Malaysia | 8.3 | 8.7 | 8.5 | 3.6 | 3.7 | 4.6 |
| Pakistan | 2.5 | 3.9 | 5.1 | 10.5 | 12.8 | 13.5 |
| Philippines | 2.1 | 4.3 | 5.3 | 7.6 | 9.1 | 7.1 |
| Taiwan Province of China | 6.1 | 6.5 | 6.9 | 2.9 | 4.1 | 3.9 |
| Thailand | 8.2 | 8.5 | 8.4 | 3.3 | 5.0 | 6.0 |
| Vietnam | 8.1 | 8.8 | 9.0 | 5.2 | 14.5 | 14.5 |
| **Middle East and Europe** | **3.6** | **0.3** | **2.4** | **24.5** | **32.3** | **25.3** |
| Egypt | 1.5 | 1.3 | 1.5 | 12.0 | 8.1 | 7.5 |
| Iran, Islamic Republic of | 2.3 | 1.6 | 3.0 | 22.9 | 35.2 | 30.0 |
| Israel | 3.5 | 6.5 | 5.0 | 10.9 | 12.3 | 10.2 |
| Jordan | 5.8 | 5.7 | 6.1 | 3.3 | 3.6 | 4.5 |
| Kuwait | 29.3 | 1.1 | −0.3 | −1.2 | 4.7 | 6.1 |
| Saudi Arabia | −0.5 | −0.1 | 0.5 | 0.8 | 0.6 | 2.2 |
| Turkey | 7.5 | −5.5 | 3.2 | 66.1 | 106.3 | 72.5 |
| **Western Hemisphere** | **3.3** | **4.6** | **1.8** | **212.2** | **226.7** | **38.2** |
| Argentina | 6.0 | 7.4 | 0.5 | 10.6 | 4.3 | 3.6 |
| Brazil[2] | 4.3 | 5.7 | 5.1 | 2,103.3 | 2,407.6 | ... |
| Chile | 6.3 | 4.2 | 7.0 | 12.7 | 11.4 | 8.0 |
| Colombia | 5.3 | 5.7 | 5.3 | 22.4 | 22.6 | 20.0 |
| Dominican Republic | 3.0 | 4.3 | 4.0 | 5.2 | 8.3 | 10.5 |
| Ecuador | 2.0 | 4.0 | 2.0 | 45.0 | 27.3 | 18.8 |
| Guatemala | 3.9 | 4.0 | 3.0 | 13.4 | 12.5 | 8.2 |
| Mexico | 0.6 | 3.5 | −5.0 | 9.8 | 7.0 | 31.0 |
| Peru | 6.5 | 12.9 | 6.5 | 48.6 | 23.7 | 10.8 |
| Uruguay | 2.5 | 5.1 | 1.1 | 54.1 | 44.7 | 40.2 |
| Venezuela | −0.4 | −3.3 | 0.5 | 38.1 | 60.8 | 60.0 |

[1]African countries that had arrangements, as of the end of 1994, under the IMF's structural adjustment facility (SAF) or enhanced structural adjustment facility (ESAF).

[2]From December 1993 to June 1994, consumer prices in Brazil rose 763 percent. Following the introduction of the real on July 1, 1994, monthly inflation fell to 5½ percent in July. From June 1994 to December 1994 consumer prices increased by 17 percent. From December 1994 to December 1995, consumer prices are projected to increase by about 23 percent. These figures differ from the year-on-year changes reported in the table.

hanced structural adjustment facility (ESAF), growth is expected to be sustained at a relatively robust pace of about 5 percent in 1995–96.

Among the former centrally planned economies, recorded output is now expanding in those countries that achieved financial stabilization early on in their transition. During 1995, growth in *Albania, Croatia,* the *Czech Republic, Estonia, Lithuania, Poland,* the *Slovak Republic,* and *Slovenia* is expected to reach or exceed 4 percent (Table 4). In some of these countries, strong growth has reversed the sharp increase in open unemployment characteristic of the earlier stages of the transition. Despite their slow start in achieving financial stabilization, measured output is also expected to increase during 1995 in *Armenia, Bulgaria,* the *Kyrgyz Republic, Moldova* (subject to harvest conditions), and *Romania.* In *Russia,* signs of a recovery in output are now visible with recent increases in industrial production; however, output is expected to decline overall for 1995, by about 4 percent. Continued declines in activity are expected in countries where progress toward stabilization remains fragile, including *Belarus, Ukraine,* and most countries of *central Asia* and the *Transcaucasus.* The reasons for the differences in economic performance among the transition countries are discussed in detail in Chapter V.

## Inflation and Commodity Prices

The aggregate inflation projections for the *industrial countries* have been revised down slightly, which is consistent with the revisions to demand and activity, and inflation is generally expected to remain well under control in 1995 and 1996. Nevertheless, there are some indications of an increase in inflationary pressures, especially at the producer level (Chart 7). Countries that have experienced significant exchange rate depreciations in recent years are encountering the greatest difficulties in preserving the momentum of disinflation and in meeting stated inflation objectives.[3]

Several factors, however, suggest that inflation in most industrial countries is unlikely to pick up much during the current expansion. Most important, the tightenings of monetary policy in countries where slack was being rapidly absorbed during 1994 have pre-empted potential inflationary pressures. This has demonstrated the strong commitment of monetary authorities to reasonable price stability, thereby helping to strengthen the credibility of monetary policy and reducing inflation expectations. Low inflation expectations are reflected both in the fall in long-term interest rates since early 1995 and in continued moderate wage

[3]For a discussion of explicit and implicit inflation objectives in industrial countries, see the May 1995 *World Economic Outlook,* pp. 20–22.

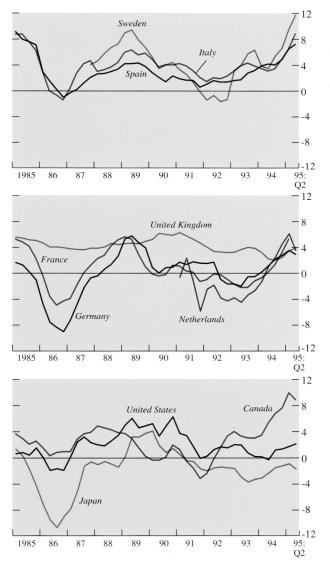

**Chart 7. Selected Industrial Countries: Producer Prices[1]**
*(Percent change from previous year)*

Producer prices indicate an increase in inflationary pressures, especially in countries with depreciating currencies.

[1]Manufacturing output price (United Kingdom); wholesale prices (Japan, Germany, and Spain); finished goods (United States).

**Table 4. Countries in Transition: Real GDP and Consumer Prices**

*(Annual percent change)*

|  | Real GDP | | | Consumer Prices | | |
| --- | --- | --- | --- | --- | --- | --- |
|  | 1993 | 1994 | 1995 | 1993 | 1994 | 1995 |
| **Countries in transition** | **−9.1** | **−9.5** | **−2.1** | **675** | **301** | **148** |
| **Median** | **−10.3** | **−1.0** | **1.7** | **686** | **207** | **53** |
| Central and eastern Europe | −6.1 | −3.8 | 0.2 | 459 | 203 | 116 |
| Excluding Belarus and Ukraine | −1.9 | 2.8 | 4.0 | 139 | 87 | 64 |
| Albania | 9.6 | 9.4 | 7.8 | 85 | 23 | 9 |
| Belarus | −10.6 | −20.2 | −13.8 | 1,188 | 2,220 | 737 |
| Bulgaria | −2.4 | 1.4 | 2.3 | 73 | 96 | 62 |
| Croatia | −3.7 | 0.8 | 5.0 | 1,516 | 97 | 2 |
| Czech Republic | −0.9 | 2.6 | 4.0 | 21 | 10 | 9 |
| Estonia | −6.6 | 6.0 | 6.0 | 89 | 48 | 26 |
| Hungary | −0.8 | 2.0 | 1.2 | 22 | 19 | 29 |
| Latvia | −14.8 | 1.9 | 0.4 | 109 | 36 | 25 |
| Lithuania | −24.2 | 1.7 | 5.3 | 410 | 72 | 36 |
| Macedonia, former Yugoslav Rep. of | −15.5 | −7.2 | 0.8 | 248 | 55 | 18 |
| Moldova | −8.7 | −22.1 | 1.5 | 837 | 111 | 30 |
| Poland | 3.8 | 6.0 | 5.5 | 35 | 32 | 29 |
| Romania | 1.3 | 3.5 | 4.5 | 256 | 137 | 34 |
| Slovak Republic | −4.1 | 4.8 | 5.0 | 23 | 13 | 10 |
| Slovenia | 1.3 | 5.0 | 4.5 | 32 | 20 | 13 |
| Ukraine | −16.8 | −23.7 | −10.3 | 4,735 | 891 | 329 |
| Russia | −12.0 | −15.0 | −4.3 | 896 | 302 | 181 |
| Transcaucasus and central Asia | −11.2 | −16.2 | −5.9 | 1,241 | 1,583 | 214 |
| Armenia | −14.1 | 5.3 | 5.1 | 3,732 | 5,273 | 185 |
| Azerbaijan | −23.1 | −22.0 | −8.7 | 1,130 | 1,664 | 464 |
| Georgia | −39.2 | −35.0 | −5.0 | 3,421 | 7,380 | 163 |
| Kazakhstan | −12.0 | −25.0 | −11.0 | 1,662 | 1,880 | 165 |
| Kyrgyz Republic | −16.0 | −26.5 | 2.0 | 1,209 | 278 | 44 |
| Mongolia | −3.0 | 2.1 | 3.5 | 268 | 88 | 28 |
| Tajikistan | −11.1 | −21.4 | −19.5 | 2,195 | 350 | 389 |
| Turkmenistan | −10.0 | −20.0 | −1.0 | 3,102 | 2,611 | 226 |
| Uzbekistan | −2.4 | −3.4 | −4.0 | 534 | 1,433 | 273 |

cost pressures in most countries. More flexible labor markets may be contributing to wage moderation in some countries. The continued rapid growth of international trade and increased global competition should also help to alleviate inflationary pressures. And relatively comfortable profit margins should provide some buffer for unforeseen cost increases. While there is no place for complacency about inflation, the maintenance of reasonable price stability in most industrial countries is particularly encouraging and bodes well for the future.

In the United States, intermediate and raw materials price inflation picked up somewhat during 1994; however, moderate wage increases and the slow growth of employee benefits have helped to contain the rise in overall inflation. While consumer prices are projected to increase by 3 percent in 1995, the continued high level of resource use is expected to raise the inflation rate slightly to 3¼ percent in 1996. In Europe, partly under the influence of exchange rate appreciations, in-

flation is likely to remain close to or below 2 percent in Germany, France, Belgium, Finland, the Netherlands, and Switzerland; and below 3 percent in the United Kingdom, Austria, Denmark, Ireland, and Norway. In Italy and Spain, the effects of significant exchange rate depreciations are complicating the task of disinflation. Inflation has also picked up under the influence of exchange rate depreciations in Canada, Australia, and Sweden, and to a lesser extent in the United Kingdom. Disinflation in Greece has been hampered by insufficient fiscal consolidation. In New Zealand, "headline" inflation has increased so far in 1995 owing to the effect of higher interest rates on the consumer price index, but underlying inflation is expected to rise only temporarily above the 2 percent upper target band. Japan is faced with the unusual challenge of preventing consumer price deflation; producer prices have been declining since 1991.

Among the *developing countries*, average inflation remained high in 1994 because of continued high inflation in a few countries, but price increases are generally expected to slow in 1995 (see Table 3). Median inflation is forecast at 8 percent in 1995, down from 11 1/2 percent in 1994. Although inflation rates are expected to remain higher in Africa than in other regions, it is for this region that the greatest progress is expected. This partly reflects projected declines in inflation in the CFA countries—contingent on tight financial policies to contain the price effects of the 1994 devaluation, and the expected successful control of hyperinflation in Zaïre. However, inflation is also expected to decline in other countries, in part owing to increased supplies of agricultural products associated with favorable weather. In Kenya, for example, inflation is expected to fall into single digits for the first time since 1989.

Inflationary pressures are a matter of concern in many Asian countries. High levels of capacity utilization exerted considerable pressure on prices in 1994. The impact of large capital inflows on liquidity and demand has aggravated the problem. Despite measures of restraint in several countries, inflation is expected to moderate only slightly in 1995 and may well rise again in 1996 given the continued rapid pace of growth in the region. Price increases in China fell below 20 percent in the first half of 1995 as a result of strengthened stabilization efforts, and there are recent signs that the growth of demand and activity is moderating, but resource pressures remain strong. In India, monetary policy became progressively tighter in the early months of 1995, and the inflation rate has come down to single-digit levels. Many of the successful emerging market countries in southeast Asia will also need to tighten financial policies to contain inflationary pressures.

Inflation in the Middle East and Europe region is projected to fall from over 30 percent in 1994 to about 25 percent in 1995. Inflation was over 100 percent in Turkey during 1994, boosted by a sharp exchange rate depreciation and lax financial policies, but is expected to fall to 50 percent during 1995–96 as stabilization policies take hold. In the Islamic Republic of Iran, inflation was over 30 percent in the first half of 1995, in part a result of strongly negative real interest rates, exchange rate depreciation, and supply bottlenecks, but is expected to decline in 1996. Elsewhere in the region, inflation is expected to moderate during 1995–96 in Egypt and in Israel, and remain subdued in Saudi Arabia.

Among the developing countries of the Western Hemisphere, inflation is also projected to decline in 1995. In Brazil, where progress has been most significant, monthly inflation rates have fallen from about 40 percent before the real was introduced in July 1994 to an average monthly rate of about 1 1/2 percent during the first half of 1995. For the second half of the year, monthly inflation is expected to increase somewhat as a result of adjustments in certain administered and market prices that were kept constant for a year after

the introduction of the real, a more flexible exchange rate policy, and continued strong demand. Other countries in the region—such as Chile and Ecuador—have also experienced substantial reductions in inflation. And in Mexico, following large price increases in the first half of the year in the wake of the depreciation of the peso, inflation is expected to abate as a result of the country's stabilization efforts. Inflation in Venezuela is expected to remain high owing to lax financial policies in recent years.

Many *economies in transition* have achieved considerable progress in bringing down inflation from the high rates prevailing in the initial years of the transition. Inflation in Albania, Croatia, the Czech Republic, and the Slovak Republic has approached rates typically observed in western economies but remain higher than in major trading partner countries. Strict monetary and credit policies recently brought monthly inflation down to low single-digit levels in Belarus, Bulgaria, Kazakhstan, the Kyrgyz Republic, Moldova, Romania, and Ukraine. Despite these accomplishments, inflation still remains relatively high in most of these countries, reflecting persistent fiscal imbalances that are typically financed through money creation, the widespread use of indexation mechanisms, and continued relative price adjustments. Further progress in reducing inflation hinges on steadfast adherence to tight money and credit policies. Inflation has recently picked up in Poland and Hungary, as large increases in net international reserves resulted in rapid monetary expansion that fueled inflation in Poland, while large increases in energy prices in January 1995 and a devaluation in March contributed to higher inflation in Hungary. Struggles to gain control over inflation continue in a number of other countries. In Russia, a decline in effective reserve requirements and high growth in base money have contributed to the disappointing inflation performance.

Oil prices strengthened in the early months of 1995 as market conditions firmed. However, prices began to decline in May, owing to a marginal increase in OPEC production and easing political tensions, and fell further in late June and in July as it became apparent that OPEC quotas would not be reduced. Prices firmed somewhat in August, mainly on a seasonal upturn in demand. For 1995 as a whole, oil prices are assumed to average $16.67 a barrel, an increase of 7 3/4 percent over the previous year; in SDR terms, oil prices are expected to increase by only 1 percent in 1995 and to decline by 6 percent in 1996.

The prices of many nonfuel primary commodities measured in terms of SDRs fell steeply in the first half of 1995, after rising sharply in 1994 (Chart 8). Much of the upward pressure on commodity prices in 1994 stemmed from increased demand in the industrial countries and buoyant demand in the fast-growing Asian economies. Demand factors, in particular the slowdown in economic activity in the industrial coun-

## Chart 8. Commodity Prices
*(1990 = 100)*

Primary commodity prices began to decline in early 1995 as economic activity in industrial countries slackened.

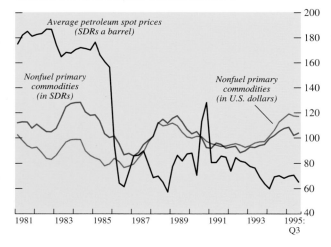

Note: The values for the third quarter of 1995 are averages for July and August.

tries, also appear to have contributed to the weakening of commodity prices in the first half of 1995.

Some special factors have also played an important role, however. Coffee prices in 1994 rose to their highest levels since 1986 in the wake of midyear frosts and subsequent drought in Brazil's coffee growing regions and prospects of tight supply in 1995. Large price changes have also been recorded by metals and a number of agricultural raw materials. For metals, improved market fundamentals and speculative purchases by commodity investment funds raised prices throughout 1994. The boom in metal prices ended in the first quarter of 1995, when investor sentiment changed amid signs that the U.S. economy was slowing. Uncertainty regarding prospects for exports of metals from some transition countries also contributed to the volatility of metal prices. Strong demand, and production problems in major producing countries, led to steep increases in the prices of agricultural raw materials, especially for natural rubber, wool, and cotton. Speculative activity drove the price of natural rubber at the end of 1994 to its highest level since 1980. Subsequently, rubber prices declined but remained above average prices in 1994. The downward trend in the prices of most commodities that began in the second quarter of 1995 is expected to continue in subsequent quarters as new supplies come on the market and the growth in demand slows somewhat. In 1996, commodity prices are expected to weaken somewhat further in a context of moderate demand and favorable supply conditions. The IMF's indices of prices of non-oil primary commodities have recently been revised using 1987–89 export weights (Box 2).

## Foreign Exchange and Financial Markets

The pressures that developed in foreign exchange markets in the spring of 1995 have abated, and exchange rate developments since midyear generally have been in the direction implied by economic fundamentals. After falling sharply to record lows against the Japanese and German currencies in April, the U.S. dollar mostly traded in a narrow range of DM1.38–1.41 and ¥84–85 in June. It continued in this range in July and early August against the deutsche mark; against the yen, it moved up to around ¥91 per dollar in early August. The dollar subsequently appreciated sharply against the yen, reaching ¥104 in mid-September, a level last seen in May 1994. Against the deutsche mark, the dollar had appreciated to DM1.48 by mid-September, a level only slightly lower than at the beginning of 1995.[4]

---

[4]The exchange rate assumptions underlying the staff's projections are based on the average levels during August 1–23, 1995.

## Box 2. Nonfuel Primary Commodity Prices

The IMF's index of nonfuel primary commodity prices has been revised to reflect more recent information on the composition of world trade in commodities and to incorporate more representative price series for some items. The weights used to calculate the commodity price index are now based on average world exports of commodities during 1987–89. Compared with the previous weights based on 1979–81 exports, the weight of food has been reduced to 33 percent from 43 percent and the weight of tropical beverages to 6¾ percent from 11¾ percent, while the weight of agricultural raw materials has increased to 32¼ percent from 23¼ percent and the weight of metals has increased to 26¾ percent from 22 percent. Other changes include a more comprehensive price index for timber, a separate index for fertilizers, and new price series for rice and tobacco.[1]

Until the early 1990s, movements in the revised world index of nonfuel commodity prices were similar to those in the old index (*see chart*). The most important differences are that the most recent trough in commodity prices

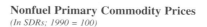

**Nonfuel Primary Commodity Prices**
*(In SDRs; 1990 = 100)*

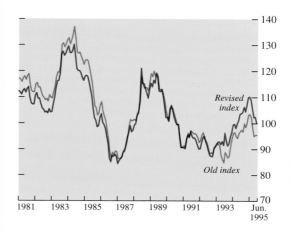

[1]The commodity price indices are calculated by the Research Department and published monthly in *International Financial Statistics*, which contains additional information on the specifications and weights for the commodities included in the revised indices. See also Table A26 in the Statistical Appendix for more detail and projections. Because of data limitations, the weights do not incorporate information on commodity exports of the Baltic countries, Russia, and the other countries of the former Soviet Union.

occurred earlier and was less deep in the revised index, and the recovery in prices since late 1992 is significantly stronger in the revised index than in the old index. These differences mainly reflect the larger weight assigned to timber and some metals, such as copper, whose prices have risen sharply since 1992.

Several factors may have contributed at various times to the weakness of the dollar in the first half of the year, including the effects of the Mexican crisis, diminished expectations of further U.S. interest rate increases—which were related to signs of a slowdown in U.S. economic growth—the persistence of the U.S. current account deficit, and a shift in currency preferences of Japanese investors away from U.S. dollar-denominated assets in the context of the general strength of the Japanese yen.[5]

Whatever the precise reasons for the earlier weakness of the dollar, especially against the yen, it appears that policy actions played an important role in the significant correction of key exchange rates that subsequently occurred. In mid-July and early August, the dollar began to strengthen against the yen as the Bank of Japan eased monetary conditions—following the 25 basis point cut in the federal funds rate by the Federal Reserve—and the monetary authorities of both Japan and the United States intervened jointly, surprising the

market by purchasing dollars even as the currency was rising. In addition, on August 2, Japan announced measures to promote increased outflows of capital. The more recent strengthening of the U.S. dollar occurred in the wake of coordinated intervention in the foreign exchange market by leading central banks in mid-August and in the context of a further easing of monetary conditions in Japan and Germany. The effect of the intervention was to reinforce the modest appreciation of the dollar that was under way and to persuade market participants that a further strengthening of the U.S. dollar was warranted. Two factors contributed to the success of the official intervention. First, it was increasingly evident that markets had taken the value of the dollar below levels that were justified by economic fundamentals, especially against the Japanese yen. Second, incoming data and evidence about policies were supportive of official efforts to promote a stronger dollar.

In assessing recent movements in the three major currencies, it is also important to consider the exchange rates of other currencies, including those of developing countries. This is especially the case when considering movements in the U.S. and Japanese

[5]The consequences of exchange market volatility and currency misalignment are discussed in detail in Chapter III.

**Chart 9.  Three Major Industrial Countries: Real Effective Exchange Rates[1]**

*(Based on CPI; January 1990 = 100)*

Recent fluctuations in the value of the yen have been far greater than movements in the dollar or the deutsche mark.

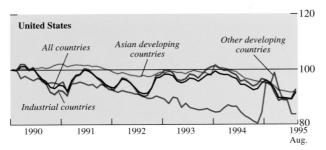

United States

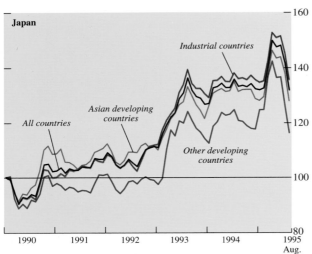

Japan

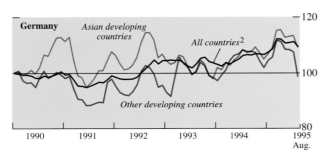

Germany

[1]Price data for July and August are partly estimated.
[2]The index for "industrial countries" is indistinguishable from that for "all countries."

currencies, but less so for the German currency. Chart 9 shows the real effective exchange rates of the U.S. dollar, Japanese yen, and deutsche mark that take account of the developing countries and use competitiveness weights.[6]

For Germany, developing countries have a comparatively small weight, and it is the European industrial countries that are really key. Although there has been considerable variation in the movement of the deutsche mark in real terms against the various European currencies, the German currency overall has moved within a fairly narrow range, appreciating in the 1990s by roughly 10 percent. From a nearer-term perspective, exchange rate tensions within Europe have subsided compared with the earlier pressures in the spring of 1995: several currencies, including the French franc and the Spanish peseta, have reversed most of their earlier declines against the deutsche mark this year, while the Italian lira and the Swedish krona have reversed some, but not all, of their earlier depreciations. By mid-September, the lira, the krona, and the peseta had appreciated by around 14 percent, 11 percent, and 7½ percent, respectively, against the deutsche mark from their lows in early-to-mid April. Still, the most recent exchange rate changes have offset the earlier appreciation of the deutsche mark to only a small extent.

For the U.S. dollar, the real effective exchange rate across the widest array of trading partners has declined by about 8 percent since 1990. While the U.S. dollar moved substantially downward against some currencies in the first half of 1995, notably the German and Japanese currencies, the movement was offset to a degree by the weakness of the Canadian dollar and the Mexican peso against the U.S. currency. For the United States, Mexico has a particularly large weight and this is reflected in the steep slope of the line labeled "other developing countries" beginning near the end of 1994. Chart 9 shows that the dollar overall reached new lows in spring 1995, especially when the developing countries are excluded, but has since retraced some of the earlier losses. Even abstracting from Mexico, in August the dollar was only about 4 percent below the average for the decade.

Changes in the Japanese yen have been considerably larger than those for the other two major currencies. Taking the period from the autumn of 1991 through 1992 as a base, the yen has appreciated by about 25 percent in overall effective terms and has shown a broadly similar real appreciation against all the country groupings in Chart 9, including other Asian currencies. The weakening of the Asian currencies against the Japanese yen during the first half of 1995 mirrored the fact that a number of these countries

---

[6]The weights are derived from 1989–91 trade flows and encompass both direct trade and so-called third-market effects.

are closely-linked to the dollar. The most recent exchange rate developments have brought the effective value of the yen back to levels broadly corresponding to those prevailing at the end of 1994.

Among other industrial countries, Canada, Italy, the United Kingdom, Australia, and Sweden have experienced significant real effective exchange rate depreciations in recent years (Chart 10). Since the early 1990s, the Canadian dollar and the Italian lira have depreciated by some 25 percent to 30 percent, while the United Kingdom, Australia, and Sweden have seen their currencies fall by between 10 and 20 percent. In contrast, the Swiss franc has appreciated by around 15 percent, while the French franc has been broadly stable. The appreciation of the Swiss franc reflects its strength not only against the U.S. dollar, but also against other European currencies, including the deutsche mark. Like other currencies, however, the Swiss franc has depreciated significantly against the yen in recent years, albeit less steeply. These exchange rate trends were generally being accentuated during the early months of 1995, with the lira, the krona, and the pound sterling all depreciating significantly, the Australian dollar reversing the appreciation during 1994, and the Swiss franc appreciating quite sharply. Since April, however, the Canadian dollar, the lira, and the krona have all appreciated significantly, while the Swiss franc has retraced some of the earlier gains. The French franc and the pound sterling have remained broadly stable, while the Australian dollar has appreciated since June.

In government bond markets, despite upticks in June and July, long-term interest rates in mid-September had dropped from their peaks last autumn by about 2 percentage points in the United States and Japan and by about 1 percentage point in France, Germany, and the United Kingdom. (For trends in long-term interest rates, see Table A18 in the Statistical Appendix.) These declines, which have substantially reversed the rise in interest rates in 1994, have occurred under circumstances of more moderate growth expectations, reduced fears of an upsurge in inflationary pressures, and increased commitments to fiscal consolidation in some countries. In Italy, Spain, and Sweden, long-term interest rates in mid-September were between 1 and 1¼ percentage points below their end-1994 levels; however, sizable premiums relative to German interest rates remained, reflecting the weak fiscal fundamentals and other policy concerns of these countries. Some of the possible reasons for the large movements in bond yields in recent years are discussed in Chapter III.

In equity markets, prices in many European countries fell in the second half of 1994 and remained at comparatively low levels into early 1995, with the strength of the deutsche mark adversely affecting share prices. As exchange market tensions subsided, and as inflation fears and interest rates eased, equity

**Chart 10. Selected Industrial Countries: Real Effective Exchange Rates**
*(Based on CPI; January 1990 = 100)*

A number of currencies have depreciated sharply in recent years.

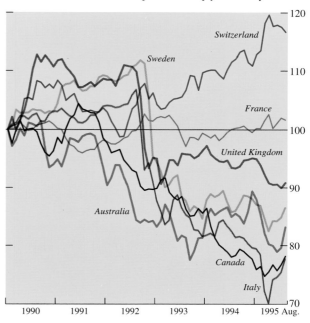

Note: Price data for July and August are partly estimated.

prices rebounded strongly. Between early April and mid-September, they rose by 16 percent in Germany, 12 percent in the United Kingdom, and 8 percent in Italy. Equity prices in France were essentially unchanged. Meanwhile, equity prices in the United States and Canada have tested new highs. By comparison, equity prices in Japan are still down by over 5 percent this year, notwithstanding gains of some 20 percent since early July.

The movements in the foreign exchange values of the major currencies, in particular the earlier appreciation of the yen, had significant potential repercussions for a number of developing countries. For many southeast Asian economies, the rise in the value of the yen, coupled with the relative stability of their currencies against the dollar, although strengthening their international competitiveness in the short term, threatened to heighten inflationary pressures. Moreover, for countries that have substantial liabilities denominated in Japanese yen and export earnings that are tied mainly to the dollar—for instance, Indonesia—the strength of the yen was cause for concern. These concerns have subsequently abated with the depreciation of the yen. Elsewhere in Asia, the Chinese yuan has appreciated by about 5 percent against the U.S. dollar since the unification of yuan exchange markets in January 1994. In the Western Hemisphere region, the Mexican new peso, which depreciated sharply during the financial crisis early in 1995, fell to almost MexN$8 to the U.S. dollar in April. By June, however, it had recovered to around MexN$6 to the dollar, on evident progress under the adjustment program and increased confidence in the economy, and it has remained around that level. In Brazil, following its introduction in July 1994, the real appreciated substantially until the early part of this year. Subsequently it has depreciated somewhat and in June the band around the real was changed from R$0.88–0.93 to the U.S. dollar to R$0.91–0.99. In contrast, the Argentinean peso depreciated somewhat in real terms during 1994 and in early 1995, in part owing to the decline in the inflation rate, thus offsetting some of the peso's real appreciation since it was pegged to the dollar in 1991.

In the Middle East and Europe region, the pressure on the Turkish currency has eased somewhat in recent months, owing in part to the introduction of a ceiling on the rate of depreciation. In Egypt, the objective of preserving a de facto peg against the U.S. dollar was supported by a high interest rate policy. In Africa, the South African rand was unified in March by abolishing the financial rand system that applied to nonresident capital transactions. In Nigeria, the large spread between the official exchange rate and the market-determined rate persisted as high inflation and macroeconomic imbalances continued. In Uganda, the authorities imposed a coffee stabilization tax to prevent the boom in coffee prices leading to an appreciation of

the currency and a loss of competitiveness. The real effective exchange rates of the CFA franc countries have appreciated modestly over the past year, but a large part of the gains in competitiveness stemming from the January 1994 devaluation have been preserved.

For most of the transition countries that have brought inflation under relative control, nominal exchange rates have stabilized. However, since domestic inflation rates are still quite high, real exchange rates have tended to appreciate. In the Czech Republic, appreciation of the currency has begun to threaten external competitiveness. In Hungary, similar concerns prompted the government to devalue the forint by $8\frac{1}{4}$ percent in March 1995. In contrast, in Russia—where inflation remains very high—the nominal exchange rate was allowed to appreciate substantially in recent months albeit from very low levels. As a result, the real exchange of the ruble against the U.S. dollar rose by about 33 percent during the second quarter of 1995. To stabilize the ruble, the Russian authorities in July announced their intention to maintain the nominal exchange rate against the U.S. dollar within a band of Rub 4,300 to Rub 4,900 during the third quarter of 1995. Many countries in transition have made further efforts to remove foreign exchange restrictions, underscoring their commitment to an open and transparent exchange system for current transactions.

Net capital flows to developing countries declined substantially in the immediate aftermath of the Mexican financial crisis, but have subsequently returned to a relatively high level. The aggregate picture, however, masks considerable variations both in the composition of capital flows and across different countries and regions. Foreign direct investment flows, which remained stable through 1994, have declined only marginally this year. By contrast, portfolio flows, which had already slowed significantly in the second half of 1994 as interest rates in the industrial countries rose, fell sharply further in the first half of 1995. In the recent episode of declining capital flows, financial markets appear to have become considerably more selective, depending on countries' saving performance and degree of macroeconomic stability. Latin American countries, with the exception of Chile, have experienced the largest declines in capital inflows. Among the large recipient countries in Asia, the decline in portfolio capital inflows has been less pronounced. Indeed, capital flows to many of these countries have rebounded in recent months, increasing the risk of overheating.

On the assumption that policies in the emerging market economies continue to strengthen, capital inflows are expected to increase gradually over the medium term, but aggregate flows are assumed to remain below the high levels experienced during the early 1990s (Chart 11). Developing countries in Asia and the Western Hemisphere will continue to account for the major share of private capital flows. Economic prospects of some African countries such as Côte d'Ivoire and Uganda have significantly improved and have to some extent been reflected in moderate increases of private capital flows. Most African countries, however, are still primarily dependent on official flows, especially development assistance from bilateral donors. With recent trends in aggregate official development assistance indicating a continuing slowdown, external financing constraints for many of these countries are likely to tighten further; thus, improvements in macroeconomic policies and reform efforts will be crucial to sustain growth.

Among the countries in transition, Poland and Romania recently joined the Czech Republic, Hungary, and the Slovak Republic in regaining access to private international capital markets, marking a shift from exceptional to normal financing. Following Poland's first Eurobond issue in late June, Russia is considering doing the same later in 1995. Large capital inflows have occurred in many transition countries including the Czech Republic, Russia, and the Slovak Republic and reflect in varying degrees external borrowing by enterprises, the return of flight capital, and foreign portfolio and direct investment.

The initial effects of the Mexican financial crisis were felt strongly in emerging equity markets, with sharp declines in equity prices in January and February of this year. Most Latin American and Asian markets proved to be remarkably resilient, however, and rebounded during the second quarter of 1995 (Chart 12). In Latin America, growing confidence among investors that economic adjustment programs were broadly on track, and declining bond yields in the industrial countries, contributed to a recovery of stock markets, especially in Argentina, Brazil, and Mexico. However, except in Chile, where the repercussions were smallest, and in Peru, prices remain below their mid-December 1994 levels. Equity prices staged even stronger recoveries in Asian countries, in part boosted by gains in competitiveness against the Japanese yen. More recently, some of the gains were reversed, but by mid-September stock prices in Indonesia, Malaysia, the Philippines, and Thailand were above their pre-Mexico crisis levels. In contrast, in India, equity prices were about 25 percent lower in mid-September compared with mid-December 1994, reflecting the significant tightening of monetary policy and rise in interest rates over this period, and as uncertainties regarding the pace of reforms contributed to a rather lackluster performance of the equity market.

Notwithstanding the rebound in equity prices, price-earnings ratios in the major developing country equity markets have been declining since mid-1994 and are now close to their 1992 levels. Rising interest rates in the industrial countries during 1994, and more recently a more cautious attitude toward emerging markets among international investors, are likely to be important contributory factors, but the growth and

**Chart 11. Developing Countries: Net Capital Flows[1]**
*(In billions of U.S. dollars)*

Net capital flows to developing countries are expected to remain only slightly lower than in 1991–93.

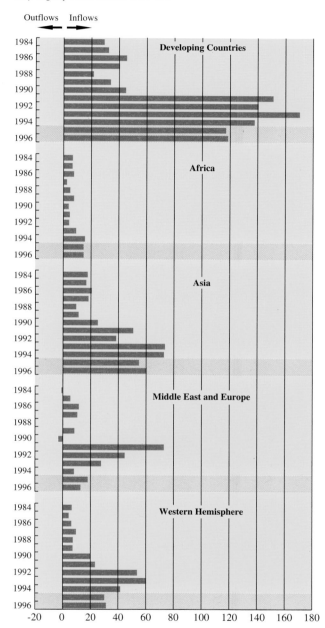

[1]Net capital flows comprise net direct investment, net portfolio investment, and other long- and short-term net investment flows, including official and private borrowing. Blue shaded areas indicate IMF staff projections.

27

deepening of these markets may also have led to greater convergence in the valuation of developing and industrial country equity markets.

## Trade, External Payments, and Debt

Following the sharp cyclical rebound in 1994, when the volume of world trade in goods and services rose by 8¾ percent, the expansion of trade is expected to continue at a rapid pace of 8 percent in 1995 and about 6½ percent in 1996. Outsourcing from industrial countries with strong exchange rates, increased trade among the developing countries, and the continued recovery of trade in the transition countries are among the factors that will contribute to rapid trade growth. Prices of internationally traded goods (measured in SDRs) are expected to change only marginally over the short term, as productivity increases, trade is further liberalized, and competitive forces (including in commodity markets) contribute to keep global inflationary pressures at bay. Despite the significant correction of the exchange rate changes that occurred in the first half of the year, trade flows will be heavily influenced by past changes in exchange rates. In particular, Japan is expected to continue to lose export market shares (between 1991 and 1996, the projections suggest that Japanese merchandise export volumes will have risen by only 6 percent compared with a rise in world trade by 34 percent over the same period); at the same time, import penetration is rising rapidly, albeit from relatively low levels. Many of the Asian emerging market countries are expected to continue to gain market shares (Table 5).

The large shifts in external competitiveness in recent years, together with changes in relative rates of capacity utilization, will have a significant bearing on the global pattern of current account positions (Table 6). However, while some payments imbalances are diminishing, others are widening, in many cases increasing the urgency of policy actions to contain domestic demand or improve external competitiveness. In several cases, already significant external surpluses are expected to grow further, possibly indicating the scope for currency appreciation.

For the two largest economies, the degree of improvement in external positions associated with the cumulative effects of past exchange rate changes is being masked to some extent by the effects of a significant further widening of the output gap differential in favor of the United States. In addition, the persistent widening of net international investment positions will continue to affect net investment income and the balance of payments in the two countries (Chart 13). Thus, for the United States, the forces affecting the external position, including the substantial correction of Mexico's external deficit, are expected to raise the current ac-

## Chart 12. Emerging Markets: Equity Prices
*(In U.S. dollars; 1993 = 100)*

Equity markets have recovered in the wake of the Mexican crisis.

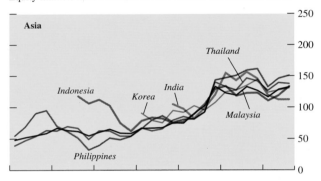

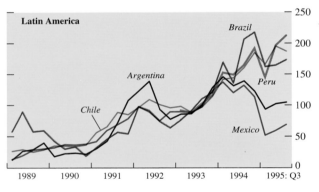

Note: The values for the third quarter of 1995 are averages for July and August.

**Table 5. Selected Countries: World Export Market Shares**
*(In percent of world exports of goods and services)*

| | 1970–79 | 1980–89 | 1991 | 1992 | 1993 | 1994 | Projections 1995 | 1996 |
|---|---|---|---|---|---|---|---|---|
| United States | 12.1 | 12.1 | 13.0 | 12.9 | 13.5 | 13.3 | 12.8 | 13.0 |
| Japan | 6.3 | 7.8 | 8.0 | 8.0 | 8.5 | 8.4 | 8.3 | 7.8 |
| Germany | 10.2 | 9.4 | 10.5 | 10.4 | 9.3 | 9.2 | 9.4 | 9.1 |
| France | 7.0 | 6.7 | 7.0 | 7.3 | 6.6 | 6.5 | 6.7 | 6.6 |
| Italy | 4.5 | 4.6 | 5.4 | 5.6 | 5.4 | 5.3 | 5.1 | 5.1 |
| United Kingdom | 6.0 | 5.6 | 5.3 | 5.2 | 5.0 | 5.0 | 5.1 | 5.2 |
| Canada | 4.0 | 3.7 | 3.2 | 3.1 | 3.4 | 3.5 | 3.3 | 3.3 |
| Belgium | 2.9 | 2.9 | 3.2 | 3.3 | 3.0 | 3.0 | 3.1 | 3.1 |
| Netherlands | 3.9 | 3.7 | 4.0 | 3.9 | 3.8 | 3.6 | 3.7 | 3.7 |
| Sweden | 1.9 | 1.6 | 1.5 | 1.4 | 1.3 | 1.4 | 1.4 | 1.4 |
| Switzerland | 2.2 | 2.2 | 2.5 | 2.4 | 2.3 | 2.3 | 2.1 | 2.1 |
| China | 0.8 | 1.2 | 1.6 | 1.8 | 1.9 | 2.4 | 2.5 | 2.7 |
| Hong Kong | 1.0 | 1.6 | 2.7 | 3.0 | 3.4 | 3.5 | 3.4 | 3.6 |
| Korea | 0.7 | 1.5 | 1.9 | 1.9 | 2.0 | 2.2 | 2.4 | 2.6 |
| Malaysia | 0.5 | 0.7 | 0.9 | 0.9 | 1.1 | 1.2 | 1.3 | 1.4 |
| Singapore | 0.7 | 1.2 | 1.7 | 1.7 | 1.9 | 1.9 | 1.8 | 1.9 |
| Taiwan Province of China | 0.7 | 1.4 | 1.9 | 1.9 | 2.0 | 2.0 | 2.0 | 2.0 |
| Thailand | 0.3 | 0.4 | 0.8 | 0.9 | 1.0 | 1.1 | 1.1 | 1.2 |
| Argentina | 0.5 | 0.4 | 0.3 | 0.3 | 0.3 | 0.4 | 0.4 | 0.4 |
| Brazil | 0.9 | 1.0 | 0.8 | 0.8 | 0.9 | 0.9 | 0.8 | 0.8 |
| Mexico | 0.6 | 1.0 | 1.0 | 0.9 | 1.0 | 1.0 | 1.1 | 1.1 |

count deficit to 2½ percent of GDP in 1995, with a relatively modest improvement expected in 1996. For Japan, although the weakness of the economy plays a major role in masking the underlying degree of adjustment, the net result is a decline in the external surplus to about 2 percent of GDP by 1996. In both cases, adjustments in relative cyclical positions and the lagged effects of current exchange rates point in the direction of a larger reduction of underlying imbalances. For these potential changes in current account positions to materialize, however, domestic absorption will need to be reduced relative to potential output in the United States to allow the economy to take full advantage of conditions in export markets and external competitiveness. This would be facilitated by stepped-up fiscal consolidation in the United States. In Japan, increased absorption would be encouraged by greater openness, deregulation, and structural reform.

Among the other industrial countries, Canada's external deficit is expected to be more than halved from its level of only a few years ago as a result of improvements in competitiveness and the recovery in the United States; at less than 2 percent of GDP in 1995–96, Canada's deficit is projected to be at its lowest since 1985. Germany's relatively small deficit is expected to increase somewhat in 1996 owing to the strength of the deutsche mark. In contrast, strong competitive positions are likely to raise the external surpluses further in Italy and Sweden. A relatively large current account deficit is expected to persist in Australia. Switzerland's large surplus is expected to decline to a range of from 5 to 6 percent of GDP, while Belgium's is projected to rise to about 6 percent.

In the emerging market countries, the most dramatic change in external position is for Mexico, where the deficit on current account is projected to decline by about 7 percent of GDP in 1995 owing to the sharp reversal of capital inflows and the resulting adjustment policies. Argentina's external position is also expected to improve significantly as a result of strengthened stabilization efforts. In Côte d'Ivoire, the depreciation of the CFA franc and accompanying adjustment measures are also expected to continue to contain the external deficit. Likewise, external deficits are projected to diminish in 1995 in Hungary, the Philippines, Saudi Arabia, and Ukraine, in all cases in the context of strengthened stabilization efforts.

Several emerging market countries are expected to register a worsening of their external positions. Such worsening may reflect a combination of factors, but excess demand pressures—often fueled by cyclical inflows—are typically the driving force. For some of these countries, which include Brazil, Colombia, Indonesia, Malaysia, South Africa, and Thailand, there may be a need to reappraise the overall stance and mix of policies to address the underlying causes of the worsening trend in external positions. In Algeria, where the external deficit is projected to widen sharply in 1995, an IMF-supported adjustment program is expected to permit a reduction of the deficit in 1996.

## Chart 13. Major Industrial Countries: Net Investment Income
*(In billions of U.S. dollars)*

U.S. net investment income turned negative in 1994.

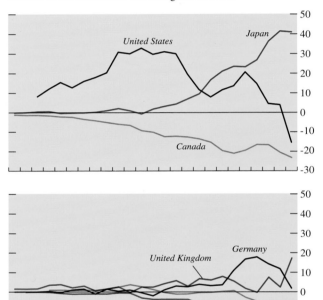

## Table 6. Selected Countries: Current Account Positions
*(In percent GDP)*

| | 1992 | 1993 | 1994 | Projections 1995 | 1996 |
|---|---|---|---|---|---|
| United States | −1.0 | −1.6 | −2.2 | −2.5 | −2.3 |
| Japan | 3.2 | 3.1 | 2.8 | 2.3 | 2.0 |
| Germany | −1.1 | −0.8 | −1.0 | −0.7 | −1.1 |
| France | 0.3 | 0.8 | 0.7 | 1.0 | 1.0 |
| Italy | −2.3 | 1.1 | 1.5 | 2.1 | 2.3 |
| United Kingdom | −1.6 | −1.8 | −0.3 | −0.7 | −0.4 |
| Canada | −3.8 | −4.0 | −3.0 | −2.3 | −1.5 |
| Australia | −3.5 | −3.7 | −4.8 | −5.7 | −5.3 |
| Belgium-Luxembourg | 3.0 | 5.4 | 5.6 | 6.1 | 6.1 |
| Denmark | 3.0 | 3.5 | 2.4 | 2.1 | 2.0 |
| Finland | −4.6 | −1.0 | 1.1 | 2.1 | 1.0 |
| Netherlands | 2.4 | 3.3 | 3.1 | 3.3 | 2.8 |
| Norway | 2.6 | 2.3 | 2.9 | 4.4 | 8.1 |
| Spain | −3.2 | −0.8 | −0.8 | −0.4 | −0.2 |
| Sweden | −3.2 | −2.2 | 0.4 | 2.2 | 3.2 |
| Switzerland | 6.3 | 7.9 | 7.2 | 5.9 | 5.4 |
| Algeria | 2.7 | 1.6 | −4.3 | −7.1 | −3.9 |
| Argentina | −2.8 | −2.9 | −3.5 | −1.3 | −1.3 |
| Brazil | 1.6 | −0.2 | −0.3 | −2.4 | −1.6 |
| Cameroon | −3.9 | −5.6 | −3.1 | −3.0 | −0.6 |
| Chile | −1.6 | −4.6 | −1.4 | 0.8 | −1.5 |
| China | 1.3 | −2.0 | 1.5 | 1.7 | 0.3 |
| Côte d' Ivoire | −12.6 | −10.0 | −2.4 | −2.2 | −3.0 |
| Egypt | 8.4 | 3.3 | 0.2 | 0.9 | 2.1 |
| India | −1.4 | −0.6 | −0.4 | −0.9 | −1.2 |
| Indonesia | −2.4 | −1.9 | −2.0 | −2.7 | −2.7 |
| Israel | 0.3 | −2.1 | −3.8 | −5.6 | −6.1 |
| Korea | −1.5 | 0.1 | −1.3 | −2.0 | −1.6 |
| Mexico | −7.4 | −6.5 | −7.8 | −0.2 | −1.2 |
| Nigeria | −1.9 | −2.9 | −2.4 | −0.9 | −2.2 |
| Pakistan | −3.7 | −4.9 | −3.8 | −3.8 | −3.1 |
| Philippines | −1.9 | −5.3 | −4.3 | −3.5 | −1.8 |
| Saudi Arabia | −14.4 | −14.6 | −7.5 | −3.9 | −4.7 |
| South Africa | 1.2 | 1.5 | −0.5 | −2.0 | −1.7 |
| Taiwan Province of China | 3.9 | 3.1 | 2.5 | 1.9 | 1.8 |
| Thailand | −5.5 | −5.4 | −5.7 | −6.6 | −6.8 |
| Turkey | −0.6 | −3.7 | 2.0 | 0.8 | 0.5 |
| Czech Republic | −1.6 | 2.2 | −0.0 | −3.4 | −4.0 |
| Hungary | 0.9 | −9.0 | −9.5 | −7.7 | −5.7 |
| Poland | 1.1 | −0.6 | 2.3 | 1.9 | −0.1 |
| Russia | −1.5 | 3.4 | 1.2 | −0.2 | −1.2 |

With the important exception of Africa, the debt burden of both the developing and the transition countries is expected to continue to ease. With a large share of non-debt-creating flows in total capital inflows, overall indebtedness is growing only modestly.[7] Relative to output and export earnings, the external debt burden of the developing countries has declined steadily during the past decade and is expected to reach 29 percent of GDP and 108 percent of export earnings in 1996, the lowest levels since 1982. For the Western Hemisphere,

---

[7]Because of exchange rate changes, the dollar-based debt indicators in Tables A38–40 are somewhat misleading.

the debt-service ratio in 1994 was 40 percent of export earnings as opposed to a peak debt-servicing burden of 57 percent in 1982. The improving debt situation has been reflected in a considerable strengthening of secondary market prices of developing country debt instruments during the past decade. This trend was temporarily disrupted by the uncertainties that arose in the wake of the Mexican financial crisis, but in most cases secondary market prices have turned around again in recent months (Chart 14).

In Africa, only a few countries, including Ghana and Uganda, have managed to reduce substantially their debt burdens in the context of strengthened adjustment efforts, supported in some cases by debt restructuring and debt forgiveness. For most of the region, however, the debt burden remains extremely high and the accumulation of arrears continues to raise overall debt burdens, which in much of sub-Saharan Africa have reached levels that exceed 400 percent of export earnings. Few countries appear to have any realistic scope for servicing debt burdens of such a magnitude. In most countries, however, actual debt service is less than one half of the amount of new inflows from donors. There is a risk that excessive debt burdens may deter foreign direct investment and other private flows to some of these countries.

Paris Club creditors agreed in December 1994 to "Naples terms" for low-income rescheduling countries.[8] These offer a 67 percent net present value reduction of eligible debt for most eligible countries and the prospect of an exit from the rescheduling process through stock-of-debt operations. Eleven reschedulings have taken place so far under these terms, including one stock-of-debt operation (for Uganda). Paris Club reschedulings on Naples terms have been complemented for certain countries by bilateral debt forgiveness as well as by debt reduction from commercial banks. The Group of Seven industrial countries at their Halifax summit in June 1995, encouraged the Bretton Woods institutions to develop a comprehensive approach to assist the small number of countries with multilateral debt problems, both through the flexible implementation of existing instruments and, where necessary, through new mechanisms.

**Chart 14. Selected Developing Countries: Secondary Market Prices for Bank Loans**
*(In percent of face value)*

Secondary market prices for bank loans have begun to recover from their 1994 decline.

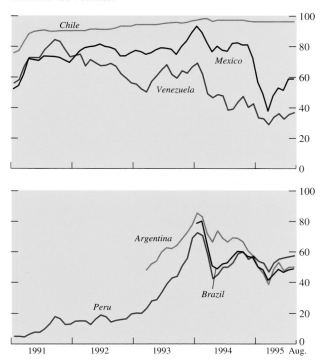

Source: Solomon Brothers.

___
[8]The 1994 Group of Seven summit in Naples encouraged the Paris Club to favor reductions in the stock of debt and increased concessionality for those countries facing special difficulties.

# III

# Financial Market Turmoil and Economic Policies in Industrial Countries

**B**ond yields and exchange rates have posted relatively large movements over the past year and a half. During 1994, long-term interest rates rose between 175 and 500 basis points across the industrial countries. They then tumbled in 1995, largely reversing the 1994 run-up in many cases. Although such swings are not unusual by the standards of the 1970s and 1980s, they were nevertheless surprisingly large in view of the high degree of price stability that has been reestablished in most countries (Chart 15). There have also been wide shifts in exchange rates. By mid-1995, for example, the effective exchange rate of the yen had appreciated by almost 25 percent from its already high level at the end of 1993. Then between mid-1995 and early fall, the yen depreciated sharply, roughly reverting to its late 1993 value. Movements in other currencies have been less dramatic but have nevertheless contributed to widespread concerns that exchange rate movements may have been restraining growth in countries with strong currencies, while adding to inflationary pressures in countries with depreciated currencies.

It is difficult to find complete explanations based on economic fundamentals for these movements in asset prices that are applicable to all countries. The sharp appreciation of the yen and then its subsequent decline is particularly difficult to explain in terms of fundamental economic factors. On the other hand, recent adverse swings in market sentiment have affected financial market prices in a number of countries with relatively weak policy fundamentals. Throughout 1994, countries with large budget deficits tended to experience the biggest increases in long-term interest rates.[9] Sweden and Italy, for instance, had among the highest ratios of budget deficits to GDP over the 1990–94 period and suffered some of the largest interest rate hikes. Despite partial reversals in 1995, these countries continue to experience exceptionally wide interest rate differentials relative to Germany. And over the first half of 1995, countries with persistently large external deficits saw their currencies depreciate relative to countries with stronger external positions, perhaps reflecting increased market concerns about the sustainability of external imbalances in the wake of the Mexican crisis.

---

[9]For a discussion of the relationship between deficits and long-term interest rates, see Thomas Helbling and Robert Wescott, "The Global Real Interest Rate," in *Staff Studies for the World Economic Outlook* (IMF, September 1995), pp. 28–51.

**Chart 15. Major Industrial Countries: Long-Term Interest Rates and Consumer Price Inflation**

Recent swings in long-term interest rates contrast with generally subdued inflation

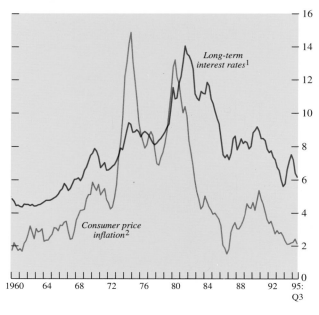

[1]GDP-weighted average of ten-year (or nearest maturity) government bond rates for the United States, Japan, Germany, France, Italy, United Kingdom, and Canada. Excluding Japan prior to 1967.
[2]Percent change from four quarters earlier.

Countries with depreciating currencies in the first half of 1995 also generally had a less successful track record in controlling inflation (Chart 16). It seems clear that fundamentals do influence market sentiment, and that international investors recognize actual or potential policy weaknesses and adjust their portfolios accordingly, albeit sometimes with a lag. It is also clear that financial markets can serve to discipline and reinforce policy decisions in a helpful way.

At the same time, there are valid concerns that shifts in market sentiment may exacerbate problems in countries with weak fundamentals, create new problems in other countries, and generally complicate policymaking. In Sweden and Italy, for example, high interest rates have led to mounting interest payments on their public debt, making attempts at fiscal consolidation even more difficult, while sharply depreciated exchange rates have increased inflationary pressures. In addition, the appreciation of some European currencies that had been the counterpart to the weakness of the lira, the krona, and the peseta dampened business confidence in some countries and led to downward revisions of growth expectations. The sharp appreciation of the yen until mid-1995 clearly worked in the opposite direction from what was needed to foster economic recovery. The strong yen meant lower net exports and hence reduced aggregate demand in an economy that is still struggling to break out of a protracted downturn. The yen's appreciation also contributed to declining price levels in Japan and heavy losses in the yen value of Japan's foreign assets denominated in foreign currency.

## Market Volatility Versus Fundamental Misalignment

A certain amount of financial sector volatility is natural and reflects the healthy flow of information among market participants. Normal week-to-week or month-to-month fluctuations in financial prices do not necessarily hurt overall economic performance.[10] Occasionally, fundamental misalignments do occur, however, when markets push prices decidedly away from their long-run equilibrium values for long periods. In this case, the costs can be much more significant. It is admittedly difficult to judge when a misalignment has occurred, because a temporary overshooting of financial market prices may simply re-

**Chart 16. Selected Industrial Countries: Inflation and Changes in Effective Exchange Rates[1]**

Countries with historically higher inflation saw their currencies depreciate the most in the first half of 1995.

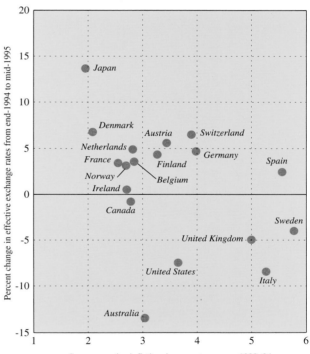

Consumer price inflation, in percent, average 1990–94

[1]The effective exchange rates take account of relative importance of a country's trading partners, of competitive relations with "third countries," of differences in the importance of the foreign sector, of the commodity composition of trade, and of estimated trade elasticities.

---

[10]There is an extensive literature suggesting that the negative effects of short-run exchange rate volatility on trade and investment are small. See the discussion in Michael Mussa and others, *Improving the International Monetary System: Constraints and Possibilities*, IMF Occasional Paper No. 116 (December 1994), pp. 20–22. More noticeable negative effects are reported in Linda S. Goldberg, "Exchange Rates and Investment in United States Industry," *Review of Economics and Statistics*, Vol. 75 (November 1993), pp. 575–88.

flect different speeds of adjustment in financial and goods markets in response to changes in economic policies or other shocks.[11] The possibility of misalignments was acknowledged in the Interim Committee's communiqué of April 1995, which said that recent exchange rate movements for some major currencies had gone farther than warranted by fundamentals. Subsequent currency reversals strengthen the argument that the early 1995 movements did represent a misalignment. The sharp drops in world long-term interest rates in 1993, the spiking of rates in 1994, and the subsequent decline again in 1995, also suggest the possibility of overshooting in bond markets in some countries.

Misalignments of exchange rates may be due to inappropriate policies, incorrect views about future policies, or anomalies in market behavior unrelated to fundamentals. While a policy-related imbalance may justify a large movement in an exchange rate based on short-term fundamentals, the currency may still be misaligned from a longer-term perspective. One clear case in recent history of significant misalignment of a major currency was the surge of the U.S. dollar during the early 1980s, which at least partly reflected the combination of a highly stimulative fiscal policy and a restrictive monetary policy in the United States. During the later stages of that episode, especially by late 1984 and early 1985, bandwagon or speculative bubble effects also appear to have played a role.

Currency misalignments have undesirable welfare consequences for both the country with the misaligned currency and its trading partners. First, misalignments give the wrong price signals to investors, labor market participants, producers, and consumers, so resources are not allocated efficiently. Resources are shifted into or out of tradable goods sectors to a greater extent than may be desirable or sustainable on a long-term basis. If there were no barriers to the migration of labor, if capital were perfectly fungible, and if there were no startup or shutdown costs, then such disruptions might not matter much. But there are many rigidities in the world's investment and labor markets, and disruptions occur both when the misalignment builds up and when it is eventually unwound, leading to cumulative economic welfare losses that could be very large.

Misalignments can also worsen macroeconomic problems and complicate stabilization policy. A sharp depreciation of a currency below its fundamental equilibrium value, for example, would tend to boost inflation, and thereby contribute to escalating wage demands. While there would be a beneficial effect on inflation in the country with the overvalued currency, there could be negative welfare effects if the overvaluation leads to a decline in prices. Misalignments could also spill over to third parties whose currencies

are linked to an overshooting currency, and such linkages will tend to amplify welfare losses across the world economy. Overvaluation can also lead to protectionist pressures and exacerbate trade frictions. Obviously economies need to adjust if an exchange rate movement is in line with fundamentals, and the sooner the better. But if the movement will eventually be reversed because markets have overshot, then the costs may be significant.

Since there are welfare losses from currency misalignments, what should governments do to avoid them? First and foremost, governments should correct macroeconomic imbalances as soon as they appear to reduce the risk of future market turmoil. As is generally the case when imbalances are allowed to persist and credibility suffers, stronger action may eventually become necessary, at potentially great cost, to focus market attention on a government's resolve. There may also be a role for currency intervention, not as a substitute for correcting fundamental policy imbalances, but as a temporary prod to help guide markets to a better reading of the underlying fundamentals and the balance of risks. In some cases, publicly announced multilateral actions such as the Plaza Agreement of 1985 may be useful in correcting large and persistent currency misalignments. Even in this case, however, governments will need to adjust economic policies including through coordinated policy actions. Without such policy changes, it may be difficult to convince the currency markets that exchange rates are out of line with longer-term fundamentals.

## Did Currencies Overshoot?

Before discussing whether exchange rates, as they stood in mid-1995, may have been misaligned, it is useful to recall that the exchange rate is a price that will inevitably change over time. The need for such changes arises from disturbances and policy changes that affect countries asymmetrically, from differences in cyclical developments across countries, from differences in productivity growth and inflation performance, and from changes in investment opportunities that affect the international flow of capital. Such changes in exchange rates may not always be welcomed by the countries concerned but are nonetheless necessary and desirable. With pegged exchange rates, this implies that occasional realignments may be necessary to avoid the buildup of unsustainable external imbalances and to alleviate the costs of having to compensate for the lack of exchange rate flexibility exclusively through demand management policies. An assessment of the appropriateness of movements in exchange rates needs to distinguish between economically justified and desirable exchange rate changes and fluctuations that appear to go beyond what seems to be warranted by fundamentals.

---

[11]See Rudiger Dornbusch, "Expectations and Exchange Rate Dynamics," *Journal of Political Economy*, Vol. 84 (December 1976), pp. 1161–76.

The lira and the Swedish krona depreciated sharply after the two currencies were floated during the 1992 crisis in the European Monetary System. These depreciations largely reflected the need to adjust for earlier losses of competitiveness as well as cyclical factors, particularly in Sweden where the recent recession was unusually severe, but there may have been an element of overshooting. The continued steep depreciation of these currencies in early 1995 may have been related to political uncertainties (in the case of Italy), and to continued doubts in financial markets about the prospects for reducing the large fiscal imbalances in the two countries. However, in view of strong export performance and the sizable swing into external surplus of both countries since 1992, as well as strengthened commitments to fiscal consolidation, the lira and the krona do appear to have been somewhat undervalued by the spring of 1995. The weakness of these currencies until recently also began to exert pressure on inflation, complicating macroeconomic stabilization efforts for both countries. As their budget consolidation efforts translate into lower actual budget deficits—which markets now may have begun to expect with greater confidence—there should be scope for some further exchange rate appreciation as well as for a significant reduction of the large premiums in their long-term interest rates. In Canada, where the weakness of the currency may have been exacerbated by political uncertainties, the dollar also appeared to be somewhat undervalued relative to the fundamentals. While the desirability of reducing Canada's long-standing external deficit is an important consideration, the recent level of the exchange rate appears to be consistent with a substantial improvement in the external position.

The sharp appreciation of the yen against the dollar between early 1993 and mid-1995 is particularly difficult to reconcile with the changes in the fundamental determinants of exchange rates that occurred. Admittedly, during this period the inflation differential and the U.S. bilateral trade deficit with Japan would have suggested some yen appreciation. Over the nine quarters from the first quarter of 1993 to the second quarter of 1995, for example, the consumer price inflation differential would have indicated about a $4\frac{1}{2}$ percent cumulative yen appreciation for the exchange rate to be kept unchanged in real terms. But other factors should have worked in the direction of a weaker yen relative to the dollar. Cyclical movements over this period more than explain the increase in the U.S. trade deficit with Japan and the underlying or cyclically adjusted external imbalances of both countries tended to decline as a result of earlier exchange rate changes. In addition, interest rates swung significantly in favor of the dollar over this period. The weakness of activity and low returns on many financial investments in Japan would normally also have been expected to increase

the incentive for Japanese investors to invest in markets with stronger performance.[12]

Of course, it cannot be excluded that the appreciation of the yen over this period served to correct a previously undervalued exchange rate. However, a macroeconomic balance approach for assessing long-run equilibrium values for exchange rates supports the view that the yen was overvalued in mid-1995. Such an approach, although based upon important assumptions and therefore not very precise, calculates exchange rates that are consistent with internal and external balance, where internal balance means full employment with reasonable price stability and external balance means that the current account position is consistent with desired and sustainable levels of private saving and investment at full employment.[13] As the private sector in Japan has a very high saving rate, and because population aging indicates a need for the Japanese fiscal balance to shift to surplus over the medium term, it is plausible that total national saving would continue to exceed total domestic investment at full employment. This excess of national saving over domestic investment would be reflected in a current account surplus and associated net capital outflows to the rest of the world. The staff's analysis suggests that a moderate external surplus would be consistent with Japan's saving-investment needs over the medium term. The very high value of the yen in the summer of 1995, however, would not have been consistent with the maintenance of such a moderate surplus. In this sense the yen can be said to have been overvalued.

What then accounted for the strength of the yen? Many factors were at work, but reduced recycling by Japanese investors of large current account surpluses may have been particularly important. Because of the secular rise in the value of the yen, the value of Japanese foreign assets measured in yen has been reduced by as much as $400 billion since 1980, implying a large-scale depreciation of Japanese overseas wealth. Many of these losses occurred between early 1993 and mid-1995, and may well have increased the aversion of Japanese investors to currency exposure. This may have led to a vicious circle, whereby reduced Japanese capital outflows led to yen appreciation, which increased yen-based losses on foreign assets, which then caused more sales of foreign assets or fewer foreign purchases. Political or confidence fac-

---

[12]Some analysts would also point to purchasing power parity assessments as indicating that the dollar should have appreciated against the yen.

[13]For an overview of the internal-external balance approach for assessing exchange rates in terms of their long-run equilibrium values, see Peter Clark and others, *Exchange Rates and Economic Fundamentals: A Framework for Analysis,* IMF Occasional Paper No. 115 (December 1994). See also John Williamson, "Estimates of FEERs," in *Estimating Equilibrium Exchange Rates,* ed. by John Williamson (Washington: Institute for International Economics, September 1994).

tors may also have been important during this period. Policy considerations related to Japan's difficult economic situation are discussed below.

While a reasonable case can be made that movements in the yen, the lira, the krona, and possibly the Canadian dollar through the middle of 1995 had overshot relative to the fundamentals, it is less clear that the U.S. dollar overshot significantly. The dollar's weakness against other major currencies was partly compensated by its strength against the Canadian dollar, the Mexican peso, and several other currencies. As a result, the U.S. currency did not appear to be significantly undervalued relative to medium-term fundamentals on a real effective basis, although it certainly did depreciate to the lower end of its trading range of recent years. Of course, assessment of the appropriate value of the dollar also needs to take into account the desirability of reducing the external deficit. At the current level of the dollar, U.S. tradable goods industries still enjoy a high degree of international cost competitiveness; and a substantial improvement in the U.S. current account, which is desirable for both domestic and external reasons, would appear to be potentially achievable. Whether this desirable adjustment will materialize will depend on the degree to which macroeconomic policy, especially fiscal policy, will restrain the growth of domestic absorption, thereby allowing resources to be shifted toward net exports.

The third major currency, the deutsche mark, appreciated significantly in early 1995 against the U.S. dollar and against several European currencies, including the lira and the krona, as already discussed, as well as against the pound sterling and the peseta. The appreciation came on top of earlier rises in the effective value of the deutsche mark, particularly in 1992, which had to a large extent been consistent with the deterioration in Germany's external position necessary to finance the high level of investment in the eastern Länder. The early 1995 rise was, however, less easy to justify on fundamental grounds, and it has since fallen by a few percentage points. Fiscal consolidation in several European countries with highly depreciated exchange rates could help to reverse some of the deutsche mark's appreciation in recent years.

## Fiscal Consolidation and Currency Values

The Fund has often emphasized the need for fiscal consolidation for both domestic reasons and to help correct external imbalances. As part of the process of adjustment to a smaller current account deficit, for example, it has been widely recognized that a currency would generally need to depreciate to make a country's exports more competitive, and domestic saving would have to increase relative to investment demand. That is, the exchange rate and fiscal consolidation would work together to correct a large external imbalance.

How would these factors help to reduce persistent $150 billion a year U.S. current account deficits? The sharp decline in the value of the dollar since 1985 has greatly improved the U.S. competitive position in world markets, which has helped to reduce the external deficit from a peak of $3\frac{3}{4}$ percent of GDP in 1987 to a projected deficit of $2\frac{1}{2}$ percent of GDP in 1995. However, the dollar's depreciation might have produced a larger reduction of the external deficit if the adjustment process had not been tempered by high levels of domestic demand. In an economy close to full employment with a large external deficit such as the United States, reducing the external imbalance will require a decline in domestic demand relative to output, for example through fiscal tightening, if increased net exports are not to overheat the economy and erode the competitive position through higher inflation.

In the long run, a stronger equilibrium net foreign investment position should imply a stronger currency. As discussed in the Annex, lower budget deficits should lead to a higher level of national saving, an improved current account position, and less need to borrow from foreigners. Lower external deficits and lower net foreign liabilities would mean lower interest payments to foreigners, and this would reduce the trade surplus necessary to service the foreign liabilities. To induce a smaller trade surplus with the rest of the world, the real exchange rate must eventually appreciate. This result is intuitively plausible in that a country that saves more than its trading partners will accumulate more foreign assets and ultimately its currency will strengthen relative to other currencies.

In the short run, the effects of fiscal tightening on the exchange rate are more ambiguous. Fiscal consolidation would normally cause a country's aggregate demand to decline and its real interest rate to fall, and this would tend to cause the real exchange rate to depreciate, according to the standard Mundell-Fleming model of an open economy. In this model, changes in the real interest rate and the real exchange rate are the mechanisms that equilibrate aggregate demand and aggregate supply in the various regions of the world. But risk premium factors might work in the opposite direction of the interest rate effects. From a portfolio balance perspective, international investors allocate their portfolios on the basis of total expected returns available from assets denominated in different currencies. If the supply of a country's securities is relatively large, then risk-averse investors may require a larger total return to induce them to hold a higher share of those securities in their investment portfolios. The total expected return in domestic currency on a security denominated in foreign currency is equal to the interest rate plus the expected change in the value of the currency in which the security is denominated. The higher total return required by investors could be provided either through a higher interest rate or through a temporary decline in the value of the currency that would imply an expected appreciation (or a smaller expected further deprecia-tion). Thus, following a fiscal tightening, a lower sup-ply of securities would tend to reduce the total risk-ad-justed return that financial markets would demand. As a result the exchange rate might appreciate and risk premiums in interest rates might decline.[14]

For Sweden and Italy, and perhaps also Canada, the size of the premiums in long-term interest rates and the persistent weakness of exchange rates suggest that confidence effects may well dominate, and that these currencies could appreciate as credible progress is made with fiscal consolidation, even in the short run. For the United States, where confidence effects seem much smaller and only appear to affect the exchange rate, the initial effects of fiscal consolidation, espe-cially a heavily front-loaded package in the face of a weak economy, would probably be a depreciation, in accordance with the standard Mundell-Fleming result. However, with a more gradual fiscal consolidation package and a sustained expansion of economic activ-ity, confidence effects should provide a substantial off-set to the Mundell-Fleming interest rate effect. On bal-ance, taking into account the recent depreciation of the dollar against the other major currencies, the dollar might well tend to strengthen relatively quickly, at least relative to what otherwise might transpire, if the fiscal deficit were progressively eliminated over the medium term.

## Priorities for Policy Action

The Madrid Declaration and the April 1995 com-muniqué by the Interim Committee spelled out a set of policy commitments to promote sustained global eco-nomic expansion and to reduce foreign exchange and financial market tensions. These commitments in-cluded continued trade and capital account liberaliza-tion, strengthened fiscal consolidation efforts, and a readiness to use monetary policy to fight incipient in-flationary pressures. The Declaration specifically ad-vocated fiscal tightening in 1995 and over the medium term, and noted that countries with serious fiscal prob-lems should not delay corrective actions, because fi-nancial markets would be unsympathetic and would demand ever larger real interest premiums.

How have the industrial countries done by these cri-teria? Although there have been few new measures since the adoption of the Madrid Declaration, there does appear to have been some progress in recent years in reducing underlying or structural budget deficits over and above the normal improvements that

have come with the recent economic recoveries (Table 7). These underlying improvements, including ex-pected progress this year under current legislation, have been quite significant in Germany, the United States, Italy, the United Kingdom, and Canada. Among the smaller industrial countries, there has been significant progress in reducing structural deficits in Spain, the Netherlands, and, more recently, Sweden. There also appears to be strong, and in some cases in-creased, commitments to step up efforts at fiscal con-solidation over the medium term. Many countries have established strengthened medium-term targets for deficit reduction, including in countries such as Italy and Sweden, that have been struggling with particu-larly large fiscal imbalances.

Despite the generally positive trends in fiscal posi-tions, it is apparent from the still-large fiscal deficits that much remains to be done to restore an adequate degree of fiscal balance and to put ratios of public debt to GDP on a clearly declining trend in all countries, thereby alleviating pressures on global real interest rates. In many cases, the planned medium-term objec-tives may not take fully into account the need to build up assets in public pension systems in view of aging populations. In most countries, hoped-for deficit re-ductions are yet to be spelled out in legislation. And many countries are only making slow progress, miss-ing the opportunity posed by the generally favorable global economic situation to achieve more significant deficit cuts.

In Japan, the fiscal position has weakened consider-ably in recent years as the authorities have appropri-ately supported activity through a series of expansion-ary fiscal measures. As the recovery eventually picks up, the fiscal position should improve. Under current policies, however, the underlying position would worsen substantially in the future as the aging popula-tion increases public spending and as a result of the high levels of public investment envisaged in the au-thorities' ten-year investment plan. While there is a need for continuing fiscal support in the near term, sig-nificant new measures will be needed over the medium term to contain the fiscal deficit at a sustainable level.

Achieving the needed additional reduction in fiscal deficits will not be an easy task, suggesting consider-able risks of policy slippages. In some countries, tax revenues may need to be increased, which could be done by eliminating economically or socially unjusti-fied tax breaks. In most cases, however, the emphasis needs to be on expenditure cuts. As the scope for achieving minor cuts in existing expenditure programs is exhausted, governments will increasingly need to reform major programs. Among the issues that need to be addressed are unsustainable pension plans, the sharply rising costs of health care, distortionary and costly subsidies, and the modification of overly gener-ous and unsustainable indexing schemes and formulas. In this context, the recent declarations of intent by

---

[14]If fiscal consolidation leads to a substantial decline in risk pre-miums, significant capital inflows, and an appreciation of the ex-change rate, the current external account would tend to deteriorate, unless the fiscal consolidation is combined with monetary tighten-ing and a significant fall in output.

**Table 7. Industrial Countries: General Government Fiscal Balances and Debt[1]**

*(In percent of GDP)*

| | | | | | | Projections | | |
|---|---|---|---|---|---|---|---|---|
| | 1981–90 | 1991 | 1992 | 1993 | 1994 | 1995 | 1996 | 2000 |
| **Major industrial countries** | | | | | | | | |
| Actual balance | −2.9 | −2.6 | −3.7 | −4.1 | −3.5 | −3.3 | −3.0 | −1.9 |
| Output gap | −0.1 | 0.2 | −0.8 | −2.2 | −1.6 | −1.5 | −1.5 | — |
| Structural balance | −2.8 | −2.9 | −3.3 | −3.0 | −2.6 | −2.5 | −2.2 | −1.9 |
| **United States** | | | | | | | | |
| Actual balance | −2.5 | −3.2 | −4.3 | −3.4 | −2.0 | −1.9 | −2.0 | −1.4 |
| Output gap | −0.4 | −1.3 | −1.5 | −1.1 | 0.3 | 0.8 | 0.4 | — |
| Structural balance | −2.4 | −2.8 | −3.6 | −2.9 | −2.0 | −2.1 | −2.1 | −1.4 |
| Net debt | 36.7 | 49.8 | 53.8 | 56.2 | 57.6 | 57.6 | 57.7 | 55.3 |
| Gross debt | 50.5 | 63.7 | 66.8 | 68.8 | 68.9 | 68.9 | 69.0 | 66.2 |
| **Japan** | | | | | | | | |
| Actual balance | −1.1 | 3.0 | 1.5 | −1.4 | −3.0 | −3.7 | −3.9 | −3.5 |
| Output gap | 0.3 | 3.0 | 0.6 | −2.4 | −4.1 | −5.7 | −5.8 | — |
| Structural balance | −1.2 | 1.9 | 1.2 | −0.5 | −1.4 | −1.5 | −1.6 | −3.5 |
| Net debt | 20.9 | 5.3 | 4.4 | 4.8 | 7.8 | 11.6 | 15.2 | 24.1 |
| Gross debt | 66.7 | 67.7 | 71.2 | 76.6 | 83.2 | 90.6 | 95.9 | 103.6 |
| *Memorandum* | | | | | | | | |
| Actual balance excluding social security | −4.0 | −0.7 | −2.0 | −4.9 | −6.5 | −7.0 | −7.0 | −5.6 |
| Structural balance excluding social security | −4.1 | −1.7 | −2.2 | −4.0 | −5.0 | −5.0 | −5.0 | −5.6 |
| **Germany[2]** | | | | | | | | |
| Actual balance | −2.1 | −3.3 | −2.9 | −3.3 | −2.5 | −2.5 | −2.1 | −1.2 |
| Output gap | −1.2 | 3.4 | 2.0 | −2.0 | −2.0 | −2.2 | −2.0 | — |
| Structural balance | −1.5 | −5.2 | −3.9 | −2.2 | −1.2 | −1.2 | −1.0 | −1.2 |
| Net debt | 20.6 | 21.4 | 27.7 | 35.0 | 40.1 | 48.0 | 48.7 | 47.6 |
| Gross debt | 39.8 | 41.1 | 43.7 | 47.8 | 49.8 | 57.8 | 58.5 | 57.4 |
| **France** | | | | | | | | |
| Actual balance | −2.0 | −2.2 | −4.0 | −6.1 | −6.0 | −5.2 | −4.5 | −2.7 |
| Output gap | 0.1 | 0.5 | −0.5 | −3.9 | −3.1 | −2.2 | −1.7 | 0.1 |
| Structural balance | −2.1 | −2.4 | −3.6 | −3.6 | −3.8 | −3.6 | −3.2 | −2.8 |
| Net debt[3] | 22.0 | 27.1 | 30.2 | 34.4 | 40.3 | 43.2 | 44.9 | 47.1 |
| Gross debt | 29.6 | 35.8 | 39.6 | 45.3 | 48.4 | 51.1 | 53.1 | 55.5 |

both the U.S. Congress and the administration to balance the budget over the next seven or ten years are constructive because they have shown that policymakers are willing to consider reforming a range of social programs. But the intended pace of implementation seems very slow. In Sweden, sustained implementation of the recently announced medium-term consolidation program is essential to the restoration of credibility. Italy also is reducing its large deficit and debt problems, but further measures to achieve the targets of the three-year fiscal plan remain to be specified and financial markets still appear to have doubts about the ability of Italy's political system to deliver these measures. In Greece, uncertainties about the fiscal outlook continue to be reflected in large premiums on long-term interest rates. And in Spain, where interest-rate premiums are also substantial, it is critical that measures be adopted to achieve the objectives in the government's convergence plan.

In contrast to the significant further progress that is still needed in the fiscal area, the maintenance of inflation levels closer to price stability than seen in close to thirty years in many industrial countries is a major policy achievement. Monetary authorities in the United Kingdom, the United States, New Zealand, and Australia have demonstrated their readiness to tighten policy to prevent inflation from increasing. Because of this, inflation remains low in many countries that are relatively far along the expansion path. In those countries where inflation has picked up lately, it is mainly because of currency depreciations. Higher import prices have contributed to inflationary pressures in Italy and Australia, and to a smaller extent in Sweden, Canada, and the United Kingdom. Nevertheless, the domestic inflation effects of the large depreciations experienced in recent years appear to have been smaller than past experience would have suggested. Import price inflation is also higher than domestic inflation in the United States for the first time in half a decade, but the relatively small weight of imports in GDP tends to mute the impact on inflation. Most of the rest of the industrial countries are not yet close to full employment, and it is too early to tell how quickly and vigorously their policymakers will respond when inflation signals do appear. But commitments to safeguard progress toward price stability appear strong

Table 7 *(concluded)*

| | 1981–90 | 1991 | 1992 | 1993 | 1994 | Projections | | |
| | | | | | | 1995 | 1996 | 2000 |
|---|---|---|---|---|---|---|---|---|
| **Italy**[4] | | | | | | | | |
| Actual balance | −10.9 | −10.2 | −9.5 | −9.6 | −9.0 | −7.7 | −6.5 | −2.8 |
| Output gap | 2.1 | 1.8 | — | −3.4 | −3.3 | −2.5 | −1.9 | −0.1 |
| Structural balance | −11.8 | −11.2 | −9.6 | −7.9 | −7.3 | −6.5 | −5.6 | −2.7 |
| Net debt | 73.3 | 96.2 | 103.0 | 112.0 | 117.2 | 114.9 | 113.0 | 101.9 |
| Gross debt | 80.7 | 105.9 | 113.4 | 123.2 | 129.0 | 126.5 | 124.3 | 112.1 |
| **United Kingdom** | | | | | | | | |
| Actual balance | −2.0 | −2.6 | −6.1 | −7.8 | −6.8 | −4.9 | −3.2 | −0.7 |
| Output gap | −0.6 | −2.3 | −4.4 | −4.5 | −2.9 | −2.1 | −1.2 | — |
| Structural balance | −1.3 | −2.7 | −3.7 | −4.4 | −4.1 | −3.1 | −2.0 | −0.6 |
| Net debt | 40.3 | 26.7 | 28.1 | 32.5 | 37.7 | 42.4 | 43.1 | 38.9 |
| Gross debt | 48.0 | 33.6 | 34.9 | 40.4 | 45.9 | 49.0 | 49.6 | 45.4 |
| **Canada** | | | | | | | | |
| Actual balance | −4.5 | −6.6 | −7.4 | −7.3 | −5.3 | −4.6 | −3.4 | −1.3 |
| Output gap | 0.1 | −2.6 | −3.7 | −4.0 | −2.1 | −2.2 | −2.1 | −0.2 |
| Structural balance | −4.4 | −4.9 | −4.8 | −4.6 | −3.8 | −3.3 | −2.3 | −1.2 |
| Net debt | 30.1 | 49.7 | 56.9 | 61.9 | 64.4 | 67.2 | 68.4 | 65.0 |
| Gross debt | 60.9 | 79.9 | 87.3 | 92.1 | 95.4 | 98.0 | 98.7 | 92.7 |
| **Other industrial countries**[5] | | | | | | | | |
| Actual balance | −2.3 | −3.5 | −4.5 | −5.9 | −4.9 | −3.9 | −3.1 | −2.1 |
| Output gap | 0.1 | −0.2 | −1.5 | −3.4 | −2.6 | −1.8 | −1.3 | −0.1 |
| Structural balance | −2.9 | −3.7 | −3.7 | −3.4 | −2.8 | −2.6 | −2.2 | −2.1 |

[1]The output gap is actual less potential output, as a percent of potential output. Structural balances are expressed as a percent of potential output. The structural budget balance is the budgetary position that would be observed if the level of actual output coincided with potential output. Changes in the structural budget balance consequently include effects of temporary fiscal measures, the impact of fluctuations in interest rates and debt-service costs, and other noncyclical fluctuations in the budget balance. The computations of structural budget balances are based on IMF staff estimates of potential GDP and revenue and expenditure elasticities (see the October 1993 *World Economic Outlook*, Annex I). Net debt is defined as gross debt less financial assets, which include assets held by the social security insurance system. Estimates of the output gap and of the structural budget balance are subject to significant margins of uncertainty.

[2]Data before 1990 refer to west Germany. For net debt, the first column refers to 1986–90. Beginning in 1995 the debt and debt-service obligations of the Treuhandanstalt (and of various other agencies) are to be taken over by the general government. This debt is equivalent to 8 percent of GDP, and the associated debt service to $1/2$ of 1 percent of GDP.

[3]Figure for 1981–90 is average of 1983–90.

[4]Net debt includes tax refund liabilities. Net debt figure for 1981–90 is for 1984–90.

[5]Includes Spain, the Netherlands, Belgium, Denmark, Ireland, Sweden, Austria, Finland, Norway, Australia, and New Zealand.

everywhere. Meanwhile in Japan, the strength of the yen and persistently weak demand have combined to produce a special problem, declining price levels.

## Rebalancing Policies for More Sustainable Growth

Further progress in fiscal consolidation would help to foster sustainable economic expansions by reducing the risk of financial market turbulence and through generally lower long-term interest rates. Countries that take determined steps toward fiscal consolidation may also be candidates for some monetary easing. Such rebalancing of policies would have the effect of switching expenditure away from government spending and toward interest-sensitive components of demand, especially private investment, which in turn should raise productivity and real incomes.

With inflation generally under control in most of the major industrial countries, a gradual easing of money market conditions in the context of fiscal consolidation and potential declines in long-term interest rates

need not compromise hard-earned anti-inflationary credentials. The behavior of exchange rates is an important consideration in many countries, especially European countries working toward monetary union by the end of the decade. For these countries, the risks of precipitating an unwanted depreciation must be weighed against the benefits of stronger macroeconomic performance and a consequently improved fiscal situation. However, stronger efforts at fiscal consolidation and stronger growth prospects should help to alleviate some of the principal causes of tension in European currency markets.

The medium-term baseline projections foresee a soft landing with moderate growth on the basis of policies currently in place.[15] Even better results would be expected with the implementation of bolder policies to eliminate budget deficits and make labor markets more flexible. This is illustrated in a scenario that assumes that all of the industrial countries tighten fiscal

---

[15]The medium-term projections for industrial countries are shown in Table A45 in the Statistical Appendix.

**Table 8. Industrial Countries: Balanced Government Deficits in Five Years and Reduced Structural Unemployment Rates Scenario**
*(Percentage deviation from baseline unless otherwise noted)*

|  | 1996–97 | 1998–99 | 2000–01 | Long Run |
|---|---|---|---|---|
| **Industrial countries** | | | | |
| Real GDP | –0.4 | 1.5 | 1.2 | 2.3 |
| Capital stock | 0.2 | 0.9 | 2.1 | 5.5 |
| Inflation (GDP deflator)[1] | 0.5 | –0.5 | –1.0 | — |
| Unemployment rate | 0.2 | –0.6 | –0.9 | –1.0 |
| Short-term interest rate[1] | –0.3 | –1.2 | –2.2 | –0.4 |
| Long-term interest rate[1] | –0.1 | –1.9 | –1.9 | –0.4 |
| Real long-term interest rate[1] | –0.1 | –1.5 | –2.0 | –0.4 |
| General government balance/GDP[1] | 0.8 | 1.9 | 3.4 | 0.9 |
| Government debt/GDP[1] | –1.7 | –4.5 | –9.3 | –17.9 |
| **Contribution to real GDP** | | | | |
| Real government spending[1] | –0.6 | –1.4 | –2.2 | — |
| Real consumption[1] | — | 1.5 | 1.4 | 1.3 |
| Real investment[1] | 0.2 | 1.3 | 1.9 | 1.0 |
| Real net exports[1] | — | –* | 0.1 | 0.1 |

Note: The simulation assumes that a gradual reduction in public debt stocks is achieved through cuts in real spending and nondistortionary transfers. The fiscal consolidation is enough to achieve fiscal balance by 2000 but is not credibly viewed as permanent until 1998. In addition, it is assumed that revenue-neutral cuts in unemployment compensation and labor taxes reduce the natural rate of unemployment by approximately 1½ percent in Europe, over 2 percent in Canada, and 1 percent in the United States.

[1]In percentage points.

policy to reduce demands on world saving and implement labor market reforms to reduce structural unemployment rates (Table 8).[16] Budgets are assumed to be balanced by 2000, and it is assumed that budgets remain in balance until about half of the 30 percentage point increase in the industrial country aggregate debt-to-GDP ratio—built up between 1980 and 1995—is unwound. Spending cuts comprise the bulk of the deficit reductions. It is assumed that payroll taxes and unemployment compensation benefits are cut and that other labor market rigidities are reduced so that structural unemployment rates fall by about 1 percentage point on average.

Assuming that it takes bond markets a few years to view the deficit reduction actions as fully credible, the simulation suggests that long-term interest rates would thereafter be between 100 and 200 basis points lower than otherwise. Short-term interest rates would also decline as monetary policies reflected the improved fiscal environment. Investment would respond to the lower interest rates, resulting in a faster growing capital stock. This would boost productivity and tend to reduce inflation. This tendency toward lower inflation, even with higher output, would be reinforced by more flexible labor markets, and the unemployment rate

---

[16]Simulation exercises were performed with the Fund's international econometric model, MULTIMOD.

would be lower, which would improve fiscal positions. Real GDP would be permanently higher. If financial markets view the policy change as credible from the start, long-term interest rates would fall faster and growth would be even higher.

The simulation exercise underscores several key lessons. First, falling interest rates should come to the aid of governments that undertake fiscal consolidation. Second, labor market reform is critical for achieving long-run fiscal consolidation and for raising real incomes in the long run—of the 2½ percent increase in real output in the long run, 1 percent is due to the assumed reduction in structural unemployment. Finally, there may well be some moderate up-front costs during the early phase of the consolidation process, implying that the best time to start would be when inflation fundamentals are favorable and growth is strong. With industrial countries currently enjoying some of the best inflation fundamentals in decades, and with generally solid growth prospects, the next few years offer an excellent window of opportunity to put fiscal houses in order. The short-term costs of the necessary fiscal belt-tightening would be small and the long-term gains would be substantial and durable.

## Costs of Policy Slippage

The favorable scenario can be put in perspective by comparing it with a less attractive outcome. The future may not unfold so smoothly as in the soft-landing baseline projection. In particular, it cannot be excluded that policymakers will overreact to the current softening of growth and inappropriately relax both monetary and fiscal policies. Signs of sluggish growth have already led to some monetary easing in several countries. With tax reductions publicly debated or in the pipeline in the United States, the United Kingdom, and Germany, and possibly insufficient expenditure restraint in many other countries, there is also a risk of fiscal backsliding.

As noted in Chapter II, the risks of an undesirable and persistent economic slowdown in countries such as the United States, the United Kingdom, Canada, France, and Germany seem to be rather low, and there are few signs of the inflationary pressures that traditionally appear near business cycle peaks. Wage demands for the most part remain moderate, there is no heavy overhang of inventories or new construction, bank lending is adequate, stock markets are reasonably strong, and the bond market rally of 1995 has reduced long-term interest rates so that housing activity and investment should rebound with a normal three or four quarter lag. Clearly, policymakers must carefully monitor inflation signals and make sure that they do not overstimulate economies today, only to suffer a much harder landing in 1997 or 1998 and possibly earlier financial market reactions.

**Table 9. Industrial Countries:
Hard-Landing Scenario**
*(Percentage deviation from baseline unless otherwise noted)*

| | 1996–97 | 1998–99 | 2000–01 | Long Run |
|---|---|---|---|---|
| **Industrial countries** | | | | |
| Real GDP | 0.8 | −0.5 | −1.0 | −1.7 |
| Capital stock | −0.2 | −0.8 | −1.5 | −5.3 |
| Inflation (GDP deflator)[1] | 1.9 | 0.9 | −0.1 | — |
| Unemployment rate | −0.6 | −0.2 | 0.4 | — |
| Short-term interest rate[1] | — | 1.2 | 1.4 | 0.3 |
| Long-term interest rate[1] | 0.9 | 1.0 | 0.6 | 0.3 |
| Real long-term interest rate[1] | 0.5 | 1.2 | 0.7 | 0.3 |
| General government balance/GDP[1] | 1.4 | −2.5 | −2.1 | −0.5 |
| Government debt/GDP[1] | 0.5 | 4.5 | 8.8 | 9.9 |
| **Contribution to real GDP** | | | | |
| Real government spending[1] | 0.6 | 1.0 | 1.0 | 1.0 |
| Real consumption[1] | 0.4 | −0.5 | −0.9 | −1.6 |
| Real investment[1] | −0.3 | −1.0 | −1.1 | −1.0 |
| Real net exports[1] | — | — | −0.1 | — |

Note: The simulation assumes that the growth rate of money increases by approximately 2 percent a year in 1996 and 1997 before returning to its baseline rate of growth. It is also assumed that fiscal policy is eased so as to increase debt stocks by around 10 percent of GDP, phased in gradually over five years. It is assumed that these policy changes are known in 1996 and consequently are reflected in expectations. The estimates for the long run represent the permanent effects of the shocks.

[1]In percentage points.

A "hard-landing" scenario illustrates the dangers of such mistakenly procyclical policies, and shows that the benefits would be fleeting and the costs high (Table 9). The simulation assumes that governments increase spending and cut tax rates, while at the same time the monetary authorities reduce short-term interest rates. Although real GDP might be boosted over the first year, inflation would soon spike upward, requiring a severe monetary clamp down. Budget deficits and debt-to-GDP ratios would be higher than the baseline, boosting long-term real interest rates. This would dampen investment spending, cause the capital-income ratio to decline, and reduce long-term productivity growth and potential output. In addition to a possible recession in 1997 or 1998, real GDP in the industrial countries would be permanently reduced relative to the baseline projections.

## Labor Market Policies

Labor markets are a key priority policy area for the industrial countries. The lack of progress is most apparent in Europe, where structural unemployment has risen dramatically during the past twenty-five years. The level of structural unemployment in Europe may now be on the order of 8–9 percent. This compares with broadly stable levels of structural unemployment of about 6 percent in the United States and 2½ percent

in Japan. Structural unemployment has also increased substantially in Canada and Australia, over the past two decades, although not to the levels now prevailing in Europe.[17]

In economic terms, the largest cost of unemployment is the forgone output that could have been produced by the unemployed. The temporary output losses from the typical postwar recession are trivial compared with, for example, the yearly loss of about 3 percent of GDP that would result from a structural unemployment rate of 9 percent rather than 6 percent.[18] Other costs of sustained levels of high unemployment are also important. These include the social exclusion and loss of social cohesion that come with long-duration unemployment, a distinguishing feature of European labor markets; the budgetary costs to governments of labor market programs, which averaged more than 3 percent of GDP in Europe in 1993–94, two thirds of which were on passive income support to the unemployed;[19] and the leaching of economic dynamism from the economic system that, together with the labor market rigidities that contribute to high unemployment, makes economies less able to respond to adverse shocks or to take advantage of new opportunities in an increasingly competitive global market.[20]

Given the high levels of unemployment, it is not surprising that this issue has been near the top of the political agenda recently. Many countries have in fact taken steps to reduce distortions that contribute to high unemployment. The policy actions that have been taken include measures to reduce employers' social insurance contributions for the young, low-skilled, or unemployed; to exempt, or to lessen the impact of, minimum wages for young workers; to increase wage flexibility by reducing or eliminating indexation provisions and by increasing the importance of local conditions in the wage formation process; to increase the flexibility of working time; to improve education and training; to encourage job search by reforming unemployment benefits and related welfare payments; and to improve the effectiveness of active labor market policies.[21] While these policies should help to lower unemployment, other recent policies, such as increases in minimum wages and restrictions on fixed-term contracts, are likely to raise unemployment.

[17]See the discussion in the May 1994 *World Economic Outlook*, pp. 34–41.

[18]This assumes that the capital-labor ratio and average labor productivity would be broadly unchanged.

[19]See OECD, *Employment Outlook* (Paris, July 1994), p. 53.

[20]See Assaer Lindbeck, "Hazardous Welfare-State Dynamics," *American Economic Review, Papers and Proceedings*, Vol. 85 (May 1995), pp. 9–15; and Lars Ljungqvist and Thomas J. Sargent, "The Swedish Unemployment Experience," *European Economic Review*, Vol. 39 (May 1995), pp. 1043–70.

[21]For a discussion of policies adopted, and remaining priorities, in specific countries, see *The OECD Jobs Study: Implementing the Strategy* (Paris, 1995) and previous issues of the *World Economic Outlook*.

It is too early to tell if, on balance, the policies that have been recently adopted will be sufficient to lower structural unemployment significantly. Thus far, unemployment remains at or near its cyclical peaks in most continental European countries, and projections by most private and official analysts suggest little further decline as expansions mature. This points to the need for more fundamental, broad-based reforms to address the root causes of high unemployment. There is evidence that efforts to make labor markets more flexible in countries such as the United Kingdom and New Zealand may have lowered the level of structural unemployment. In New Zealand, for example, the unemployment rate has fallen by a remarkable 4 percentage points during the current expansion with little evidence of higher wage pressures, suggesting a fall in the equilibrium level of unemployment.[22] In the absence of more fundamental labor market reforms in continental Europe, current cyclical unemployment may be transformed into another step increase in structural unemployment.

Progress in this area will require that governments address sensitive issues of equity and fairness. Structural reforms to reduce unemployment may sometimes have unfavorable distributional consequences in the short run. To address these concerns, labor market reforms should be accompanied by appropriately designed, well-targeted transfer programs. Labor market reforms may adversely affect some insiders already employed, implying that reforms will be politically difficult to implement. Policies that mainly protect the interests of the employed are often justified by the need to foster social cohesion and to prevent social exclusion, which is paradoxical because these same policies often contribute to high levels of structural unemployment. In the long run, the only durable solution to social exclusion and low wages of the low skilled is improved training and education to raise labor productivity and incomes.

## Special Policy Challenges in Japan

After four years of protracted weakness, and with no immediate signs of recovery, Japan faces a unique policy challenge. Labor market slack is high by Japanese standards, there is a threat of spreading price declines, and the continued weakness of asset prices hurts business and consumer confidence.[23] The de-

clines in land prices, stock prices, and in the yen value of foreign assets, all down by roughly one half, have had widespread negative wealth effects. Additional obstacles have included the pressure that the strong yen placed on the economy until very recently, and the financial sector disruptions caused by some high-profile insolvencies. The result is that even with the recent sharp depreciation of the yen, the recently upgraded Fund forecast for economic growth in 1996 implies no narrowing of the wide output gap.

Policy responses have gone a long way to mitigate the effects of repeated shocks to the Japanese economy. On the monetary policy side, the recent series of reductions of market interest rates and the official discount rate have been useful. With consumer prices stable or falling, and with significant price declines at the producer level, real short-term interest rates had not been particularly low, and the decline in short-term interest rates in late summer have provided a welcome measure of monetary easing (Chart 17). Given the overall tepid economic environment, however, it is important for the authorities to keep the supply of liquidity ample, especially since the risks of inflation remain low. Lower interest rates tend to ameliorate problems in the financial sector, and with land prices and asset prices still falling, there should be plenty of time for monetary authorities to remove monetary stimulus to prevent any risk of a future speculative bubble when economic conditions begin to show improvement. In the area of fiscal policy, the recent ¥14 trillion stimulus package should help to place the economy firmly on a path of sustained economic recovery. Some observers have raised concerns that the stimulatory effects of the package may be partly offset by adverse reactions in financial markets. Although the fiscal deficit has widened sharply during the economic slowdown, it is important to view the deficit as providing necessary support during an exceptionally difficult period. Of course, once the recovery is firmly established, Japan will need to undertake fiscal consolidation.

Actions by the authorities also have been helpful in correcting the previous overvaluation of the yen. These actions included measures to promote Japanese overseas investments and loans, the reductions in short-term interest rates, and persistent intervention to drive down the value of the yen. The large losses on foreign assets that Japanese investors suffered in yen terms may have contributed to a relative shift of portfolio preferences in favor of yen-based assets—a vicious circle that further strengthened the yen. Guided in part by government actions, this pattern appeared to have run its course by mid-1995, and renewed willingness of Japanese investors to acquire foreign currency-denominated assets has probably been an important factor behind the recent depreciation of the yen.

Other problems need to be addressed to reinvigorate the Japanese economy. Regulation of the Japanese economy imposes deadweight costs because resources are not used as efficiently as they could be. It also

---

[22]New Zealand's comprehensive structural reform efforts are reviewed in Box 3 of the May 1995 *World Economic Outlook.*

[23]Unanticipated price deflation may hurt economic welfare because real interest rates may become very high given that nominal interest rates cannot be negative. In this context, falling prices may induce delays in expenditures, which could result in a downward economic spiral; increase the real burden of debt, with potentially undesirable distributional consequences; and reduce profits and increase bankruptcies if product price deflation is combined with rigid wages.

slowed the economy's pace of macroeconomic adjustment to the yen's appreciation over 1994 and the first half of 1995. Even though currency appreciation is painful, it partially sows the seeds for adjustment if an economy responds strongly to price signals. A strong currency, for example, would tend to cause import prices to decline, which would boost real disposable incomes and spur real consumption. But some analysts have found that the Japanese economy suffers from rigidities in market practices that have slowed the corrective macroeconomic adjustment. Although declines in import prices are generally found to feed through to retail prices, studies have concluded that only part of the rise of the yen appears to have been passed on to import prices.[24] Overregulation also reduces the number of sectors of the economy that undertake the adjustment to a sharp currency appreciation. This means that the adjustment is concentrated on sectors that face international competition, and this can lead to painful industry and regional effects.

Finally, financial sector problems remain significant, contribute to the lack of confidence in the financial system, and might continue to slow the pace of recovery. The recent successfully managed closure of some insolvent financial institutions was an important step toward the resolution of the bad loan problem, and illustrated that prompt and comprehensive action by the authorities can contain the spillover effects to other institutions. Still, other financial institutions might need restructuring. The government needs to facilitate loan write-offs, encourage the use of loan securitization, make more flexible the use of deposit insurance funds, and decisively address the problems of housing loan companies. When confidence is questioned, small or incremental steps to deal with a problem often have the opposite effect from what policymakers desire. In such circumstances, a broad-based policy response may be necessary to convince markets that policymakers appreciate the full extent of the problem and are ready to deal with it.

**Chart 17. Japan: Real Prime Interest Rate[1]**

Recent moves by the Japanese monetary authorities have lowered real short-term interest rates to their lowest levels since the late 1980s.

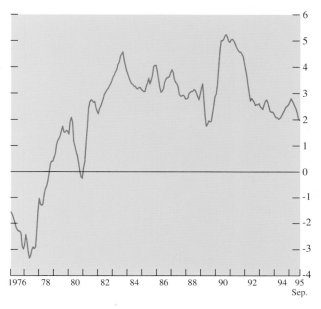

[1]Three-month centered moving average of the nominal interest rate deflated by the percent change of the consumer price index from 12 months earlier.

[24]The apparent preference of foreign firms to sell at higher prices to Japanese importers rather than seeking to expand market shares may be attributable to a variety of factors, including the importance of relatively price-inelastic consumer goods exports to Japan, and the reluctance of foreign exporters to incur the costs necessary to gain a larger foothold in a market that many foreign exporters perceive as difficult to penetrate. See Michael M. Knetter, "Why Are Retail Prices in Japan So High? Evidence from German Export Prices," National Bureau of Economic Research Working Paper, No. 4894 (October 1994). There is also evidence that the passthrough of exchange rate changes into Japanese export prices has been partial, as Japanese exporters have reduced their profit margins in response to yen appreciation in an attempt to maintain market share. See Kenichi Ohno, "Exchange Rate Fluctuations, Pass-Through and Market Shares," *Staff Papers,* International Monetary Fund, No. 37 (1990), pp. 294–310; and Giorgia Giovanneti and Hossein Samiei, "Hysteresis in Exports," IMF Working Paper 95/52 (May 1995).

# IV

# Increasing Openness of Developing Countries—Opportunities and Risks

**R**obust growth in developing countries in recent years has been associated with increasing openness and greater integration into the global economy (Chart 18). Traditional trade linkages have been deepened and new linkages developed by more open trade and exchange regimes, increased diversification of developing country exports, and closer financial linkages. Increasing financial integration has both contributed to and reflected the successful performance of the developing countries. The industrial countries have clearly benefited from this process, especially during the recent slowdown when rapid growth in developing countries helped to sustain world trade and industrial country growth.

Closer integration in both goods and financial markets promises unprecedented opportunities, but it also poses new risks. With increased openness to both trade and financial flows, the external environment for all countries will be more competitive and more demanding. Many countries continue to be challenged by large capital inflows, and the Mexican financial crisis has highlighted the risk of economic disruptions from sudden reversals of capital flows, especially in countries where macroeconomic fundamentals are not sufficiently strong. For some countries, it will be essential to strengthen domestic financial markets and address macroeconomic policy imbalances both to fully benefit from the opportunities that present themselves in a closely integrated world economy and to reduce their vulnerability to shifts in financial market sentiment and in economic conditions in industrial countries.

## Changing Relationships Between Developing and Industrial Countries

The close correlation that used to exist between growth in industrial countries and growth in developing countries appears to have broken down in the late 1980s (Chart 19). For most of the postwar period, growth in industrial and developing countries was relatively synchronized, with business cycles in industrial countries typically leading those in developing countries. During 1990–93, however, growth in the developing countries increased sharply in spite of the marked slowdown in the industrial countries, and it

**Chart 18. Developing and Industrial Countries: Openness[1]**
*(In percent of GDP)*

Openness in developing countries has increased sharply.

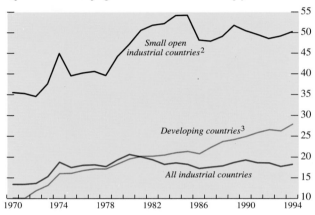

[1]Average of exports and imports of goods and services as a percent of GDP.
[2]Belgium, Denmark, the Netherlands, and Sweden.
[3]Excludes oil exporting countries.

**Chart 19. Developing and Industrial Countries: Output Growth[1]**
*(In percent)*

Developing countries have become more resilient to output fluctuations in industrial countries.

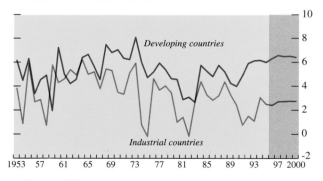

[1]Prior to 1970, growth in industrial and developing countries is based on a subset of countries for which data are available from *International Financial Statistics*. Blue shaded area indicates IMF staff projections.

has remained robust as industrial country growth has subsequently recovered.[25]

This apparent increased resilience to cyclical downturns in the industrial countries masks considerable regional disparities in the developing world. It primarily reflects a strengthening of growth in Asia and the Western Hemisphere since the late 1980s. Economic conditions in Africa and the Middle East have continued to be closely influenced by developments in the industrial countries. Many countries in these regions have made less progress with reforms and adjustment efforts and continue to be heavily dependent on exports of primary commodities. The lack of diversification is also reflected in relatively low growth of intraregional trade in Africa and the Middle East compared with Asia and Latin America.

Economic growth in the developing countries has exceeded industrial country growth throughout the past twenty-five years, and the importance of developing countries in the global economy can be expected to continue to increase in the years ahead. Developing countries as a group continue to grow at about 6½ percent a year in the staff's medium-term baseline projections. These projections assume that policy reform efforts are sustained, that industrial country interest rates remain close to current levels, and that there are no major disturbances that might provoke a sharp reversal of capital flows.[26] If industrial countries continue to grow at around 2½ percent a year, broadly in line with past trends and current estimates of potential output growth, and countries in transition expand at a rate of 6 percent a year, the share of global output produced by the developing countries could surpass that produced by the industrial countries by the middle of the next decade (Chart 20).[27] Their share of world trade may exceed 33 percent in 2004, compared with about 27 percent in 1994.

The increased openness of developing countries and their greater integration into the world economy do not necessarily mean greater vulnerability to external conditions. Paradoxically, increased openness and greater integration may reduce vulnerability because of stronger growth momentum in individual developing countries and in the developing countries as a group, and because of increasing export diversification. In addition, the impact on developing countries of changes in the demand for their exports may be partially offset by countercyclical changes in capital flows, as has

---

[25]For recent analysis of the cyclical relationship between growth in industrial and developing countries, see Alexander W. Hoffmaister, Mahmood Pradhan, and S. Hossein Samiei, "North-South Growth Linkages," IMF Working Paper (forthcoming).

[26]The implications of policy slippages for the medium-term projections are discussed below. The medium-term projections for developing countries are shown in Tables A45 and A46 in the Statistical Appendix.

[27]Convergence in terms of per capita incomes will, of course, take much longer.

**Chart 20. Shares of World Output[1]**
*(In percent)*

By the year 2004, output in developing countries is expected to exceed that of industrial countries.

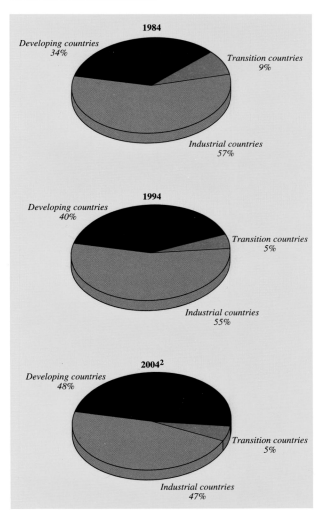

1984
Developing countries 34%
Transition countries 9%
Industrial countries 57%

1994
Developing countries 40%
Transition countries 5%
Industrial countries 55%

2004[2]
Developing countries 48%
Transition countries 5%
Industrial countries 47%

[1]Based on real PPP weights in 1987 dollars.
[2]Assuming annual growth rates of 2.5 percent in the industrial countries, 6.5 percent in the developing countries, and 6 percent in the transition countries.

## Chart 21.  Developing Countries:  Export Shares

*(In percent of total world exports)*

The share of world exports going to developing countries has been rising rapidly in recent years.

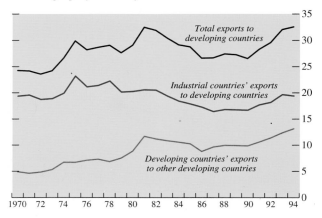

## Chart 22.  Developing and Industrial Countries: Current Account Convertibility[1]

*(In percent)*

The pace of liberalization of exchange regimes in developing countries has quickened in recent years.

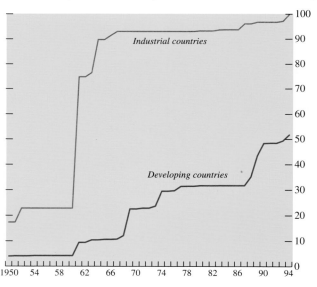

[1]Percent of developing and industrial countries that have accepted Article VIII of the IMF's Articles of Agreement; countries are weighted by their share of aggregate exports of either all developing or all industrial countries.

been the case recently, implying a dampening of overall cyclical impulses from the industrial countries. The ability of developing countries to benefit from stronger trade and financial linkages, however, will depend critically on their own domestic policies.

## Growth and Diversification of Trade

The adoption of more liberal exchange and trade regimes and the abandonment of the protectionist, import-substitution policies of the 1960s and 1970s have enabled many developing countries to substantially expand both intraregional trade and, more recently, trade with industrial countries (Chart 21). The remarkable performance of many east Asian countries and some Latin American countries that have pursued outward-oriented policies over the past two decades clearly illustrates the benefits of more open trade policies. In most Latin American countries, both tariff levels and the incidence of nontariff barriers have been lowered significantly. For example, average tariff levels in Colombia and Peru have fallen from over 60 percent in the early 1980s to under 20 percent, and the dispersion of import tariffs has been drastically reduced. And Chile now has one of the most liberal trading systems in the world. A few Latin American countries, however, have imposed trade restrictions in the wake of the Mexican crisis, partially reversing previous liberalizations. Trade liberalization in Africa and in the Middle East and Europe region has been more gradual and limited, although several countries, notably Ghana, Mauritius, and Turkey, have significantly reduced restrictions on trade recently. The increasing trend toward more open trade regimes has been accompanied by liberalization of exchange arrangements, as suggested by the number of countries that have liberalized payments for current international transactions (Chart 22).

Diversification of the export base, especially an expanded manufacturing sector, has reduced vulnerability to external shocks for many developing countries. Compared with manufactures, the demand for primary commodities is more cyclical and has risen less rapidly. This is reflected in marked differences in the evolution of prices of manufactures and primary commodities: primary commodities have been subject to particularly large price swings and a secular decline in real prices, with resulting terms of trade losses for exporters of commodities (Chart 23). Exporters of manufactures and countries with diversified export bases have experienced higher export growth and smaller terms of trade losses, which have contributed to increased resilience, higher investment, and more rapid growth during the recent period (Table 10). In Asia, the share of manufacturing exports relative to primary commodities has increased substantially since 1970 and was 74 percent of total exports of goods in 1990

**Table 10. Developing Countries: Trade and Economic Performance, 1988–94**

(Annual percent change, unless otherwise indicated)

|  | Real GDP | Terms of Trade | Terms of Trade Volatility[1] | Export Volumes | Investment[2] |
|---|---|---|---|---|---|
| Exporters of nonfuel primary products | 2.8 | −1.5 | 9.1 | 5.8 | 18.3 |
| Exporters of fuels (mainly oil) | 2.5 | −3.1 | 9.1 | 6.5 | 22.7 |
| Exporters of services | 2.4 | — | 6.5 | 8.9 | 20.4 |
| Exporters of manufactures | 8.7 | 0.3 | 0.6 | 8.6 | 35.6 |
| Diversified exporters | 4.3 | 0.7 | 3.0 | 8.4 | 24.5 |

[1]The standard deviation as a percent of the mean.
[2]In percent of GDP.

(Table 11). Although the share of manufactures has also increased markedly in the Western Hemisphere and the Middle East, it remains relatively low at 34 percent and 21 percent, respectively. In Africa, by contrast, the export share of manufactured goods has declined from 27 percent in 1980 to 22 percent in 1990.

The changing composition of developing country exports has been aided by the removal of distortions in domestic markets and reductions in trade barriers, but it also reflects an underlying shift in the comparative advantage of many developing countries toward manufacturing. Relatively low wage costs coupled with rising investment have made some developing countries highly competitive in the production of many manufactured goods. This is particularly so in some of the Asian countries where high-domestic saving has been reflected in sharp increases in the stock of capital. The composition of manufactured exports in a number of Asian countries now includes a significant proportion of advanced, high-technology manufactured goods. At the same time, the comparative advantage of many industrial countries has shifted toward services, many of which are now tradable owing to changes in technology, especially improvements in communications and information technology.

Diversification of export markets and a marked rise in intraregional trade have also contributed to the increased resilience. This is particularly true in Asia where almost 40 percent of the region's exports are now destined for other Asian countries (Table 12). The expansion of markets in Asia has benefited other regions—all industrial and developing country regions have increased the share of their exports going to Asia. Intraregional trade has also risen markedly among Latin American countries, although export diversification has been limited with almost 50 percent of the region's exports being shipped to North America. Export markets have also remained relatively undiversified among African countries, with almost 50 percent of the region's exports destined for Europe, and the level of intraregional trade, while increasing, remains modest. The level of intraregional trade among the countries of the Middle East and Europe region is also relatively small, and in contrast to the other developing country regions, the importance of intraregional trade actually diminished from 1984 to 1994.

For many developing countries, the growth of the manufacturing sector has been associated with greater efficiency in agricultural production, which has released resources for industrialization. With the benefits of the green revolution, increased productivity of both labor and land in agriculture has allowed the developing countries of Asia and the Western Hemisphere to devote a declining share of the labor force to agriculture (Table 13). Sub-Saharan African countries have been less successful in diversifying

**Table 11. Developing Countries: Diversification of Exports[1]**

(Percent of merchandise exports)

|  | Africa | | | Asia | | | Middle East and Europe | | | Western Hemisphere | | |
|---|---|---|---|---|---|---|---|---|---|---|---|---|
|  | 1970 | 1980 | 1990 | 1970 | 1980 | 1990 | 1970 | 1980 | 1990 | 1970 | 1980 | 1990 |
| Nonfuel primary products | 62.8 | 17.0 | 31.2 | 49.4 | 30.7 | 16.0 | 10.7 | 1.8 | 5.7 | 64.5 | 42.1 | 39.9 |
| Fuel | 22.8 | 56.0 | 47.2 | 8.8 | 21.4 | 10.2 | 80.1 | 93.0 | 73.6 | 23.7 | 39.9 | 26.6 |
| Manufactures | 14.5 | 27.0 | 21.6 | 41.8 | 47.9 | 73.8 | 9.2 | 5.1 | 20.7 | 11.8 | 18.1 | 33.5 |

Source: United Nations Conference on Trade and Development data base.
[1]Based on 65 developing countries for which data are available.

**Chart 23. Trends and Cycles in Prices of Commodities and Manufactured Goods**
*(1970 = 100)*

Commodity prices have declined relative to manufactures prices and are more volatile.

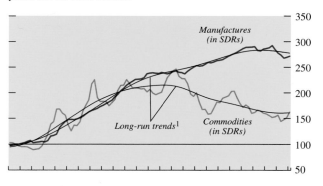

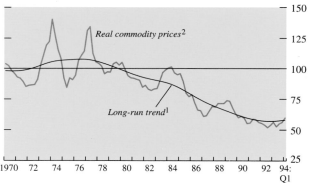

[1]Derived from the Hodrick-Prescott filter.
[2]Commodity prices deflated by the price of manufactures.

their economies, and labor productivity in agriculture has been virtually unchanged over the past two decades. This is partly due to excessive government regulation of agriculture and inadequate price incentives to producers, although a number of countries have also been adversely affected by frequent and severe droughts. The slow pace with which new technologies have been adopted in Africa, and some countries in other regions, is symptomatic in many cases of such fundamental problems as systems of land tenure that reduce the incentives for long-term investments.[28] Increases in agricultural productivity will require sustained efforts to reduce regulations and distortionary taxes on agriculture in many countries.

Increased openness has allowed many countries to narrow the technological gap with industrial countries. International trade enables developing countries to employ a larger variety of intermediate products and capital equipment that embodies foreign know-how, production methods, and product design. The potential benefits from such technological spillovers will be larger the more a country trades with technologically advanced countries.[29] Many countries have also benefited from technological spillovers through foreign direct investment, which is closely related to trade.[30] With foreign direct investment comes direct access to state of the art technology, production techniques, and management practices.

## Changing Nature of Financial Linkages

Following almost a decade of limited access to international capital markets in the wake of the debt crisis, the recent surge in capital flows to developing countries has helped to alleviate the relative scarcity of capital in these countries. The 1990s have also been characterized by radical changes in the composition of capital flows to many developing countries. In contrast to earlier episodes that were dominated by official flows and commercial bank lending to public sector borrowers, recent capital flows have been largely private direct investment and portfolio flows to private sector borrowers, often motivated by higher returns on developing country investments and their low correlation with the returns on investments in the industrial countries. Moreover, the substantial rise in both gross and net flows indicates that investments have become

---

[28]See Mahmood H. Khan and Mohsin S. Khan, "Agricultural Growth in Sub-Saharan African Countries and China," IMF Paper on Policy Analysis and Assessment 95/7 (April 1995).

[29]See Box 6 in the May 1995 *World Economic Outlook*.

[30]The strong relationship between foreign direct investment and trade is discussed by Edward M. Graham, "Foreign Direct Investment in the World Economy," in *Staff Studies for the World Economic Outlook* (IMF, September 1995).

**Table 12. Developing and Industrial Countries: Diversification of Export Markets**

*(Percent of total exports)*

| | Exports to Developing Countries | | | | | | | | | |
|---|---|---|---|---|---|---|---|---|---|---|
| | Africa | | Asia | | Middle East and Europe | | Western Hemisphere | | Total[1] | |
| | 1984 | 1994 | 1984 | 1994 | 1984 | 1994 | 1984 | 1994 | 1984 | 1994 |
| **Exports from** | | | | | | | | | | |
| **Developing countries** | | | | | | | | | | |
| Africa | 5.0 | 9.7 | 3.0 | 6.8 | 1.9 | 2.4 | 2.6 | 2.6 | 12.5 | 21.5 |
| Asia | 1.8 | 1.3 | 26.2 | 38.6 | 5.8 | 2.9 | 2.0 | 2.4 | 35.8 | 45.1 |
| Middle East and Europe | 1.9 | 2.0 | 13.8 | 19.9 | 10.9 | 8.9 | 3.9 | 2.1 | 30.4 | 32.9 |
| Western Hemisphere | 2.2 | 1.0 | 3.2 | 5.6 | 2.8 | 1.5 | 13.7 | 19.8 | 21.9 | 27.9 |
| **Industrial countries** | | | | | | | | | | |
| North America | 2.2 | 1.0 | 10.8 | 14.6 | 5.4 | 3.4 | 10.3 | 14.2 | 28.7 | 33.2 |
| Pacific[2] | 2.2 | 1.4 | 25.9 | 39.6 | 8.4 | 3.0 | 4.0 | 4.1 | 40.5 | 48.1 |
| Europe | 4.4 | 2.5 | 3.9 | 6.8 | 7.5 | 4.2 | 2.3 | 2.6 | 18.0 | 16.2 |

| | Exports to Industrial Countries | | | | | | | |
|---|---|---|---|---|---|---|---|---|
| | North America | | Pacific[2] | | Europe | | Total[1] | |
| | 1984 | 1994 | 1984 | 1994 | 1984 | 1994 | 1984 | 1994 |
| **Exports from** | | | | | | | | |
| **Developing countries** | | | | | | | | |
| Africa | 15.9 | 15.8 | 3.6 | 3.5 | 52.4 | 46.7 | 71.8 | 66.0 |
| Asia | 27.9 | 22.6 | 19.8 | 14.4 | 13.0 | 15.4 | 60.7 | 52.4 |
| Middle East and Europe | 7.9 | 11.2 | 20.8 | 16.6 | 30.6 | 28.0 | 59.3 | 55.8 |
| Western Hemisphere | 43.1 | 46.1 | 5.4 | 4.8 | 22.5 | 19.3 | 71.0 | 70.2 |
| **Industrial countries** | | | | | | | | |
| North America | 36.6 | 36.7 | 11.1 | 10.7 | 20.3 | 18.4 | 68.0 | 65.9 |
| Pacific[2] | 34.4 | 28.6 | 7.8 | 6.5 | 14.2 | 15.8 | 56.4 | 51.0 |
| Europe | 10.3 | 8.5 | 2.2 | 3.0 | 64.2 | 66.4 | 76.7 | 77.9 |

Source: IMF, *Direction of Trade Statistics*.

[1]Export shares of each region to all developing and industrial countries do not add to 100 percent because trade with the countries in transition is excluded and because of some underreporting of trade.

[2]Australia, Japan, and New Zealand.

more diversified in both the capital-exporting and the recipient countries.

Most of the recipient countries appear to have employed foreign capital more efficiently than in the 1970s, when the recycling of oil revenues sometimes led to large capital inflows into countries with serious policy weaknesses. The recent flows, by contrast, have been attracted by improvements in economic policies and performance in many of the recipient countries. In addition, a significant proportion of the capital flows in 1990–94 occurred during recessions and periods of declining interest rates in the industrial countries. Such cyclically driven flows started to moderate as industrial country activity strengthened and interest rates rose, suggesting an inverse relation between economic conditions in the industrial countries and capital flows to developing countries.

The substantial increase in gross capital flows in recent years and the narrowing of interest differentials between industrial countries and some of the emerging market economies are indicative of increasing finan-cial integration. At the same time, domestic investment in most countries has continued to be financed largely by domestic saving.[31] Indeed, with integrated financial markets there may be even tighter limits on how much countries can rely on foreign saving on a sustained basis. As suggested by Mexico's experience, the risks of sudden reversals of capital inflows are particularly important in countries where increased use of foreign saving is accompanied by lower domestic saving rather than by higher domestic investment.

Net capital flows to developing countries averaged over $130 billion a year during 1990–94, almost a fourfold increase over the 1983–89 period. In contrast

---

[31]The correlation between investment and saving rates has, however, been declining since the mid-1980s, see for example, Maurice Obstfeld, "International Capital Mobility in the 1990s," in *Understanding Interdependence: The Macroeconomics of the Open Economy*, ed. by Peter B. Kenen (Princeton: University of Princeton Press, 1995).

## Chart 24. Developing Countries: Capital Flows

*(In billions of U.S. dollars)*

Recent capital flows have been dominated by direct investment and portfolio flows.

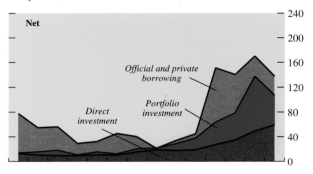

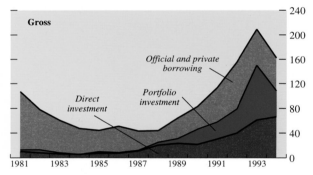

## Table 13. Developing Countries: Trends in Agriculture

*(In percent unless otherwise indicated)*

|  | 1970 | 1980 | 1990 |
|---|---|---|---|
| **Sub-Saharan Africa** | | | |
| Share of agriculture in GDP[1] | 35 | 33 | 31 |
| Share of labor force in agriculture | 78 | 73 | 68 |
| Share of irrigated land[2] | 3 | 4 | 4 |
| Fertilizer usage (kilograms per hectare) | 7 | 14 | 14 |
| Average productivity[3] | | | |
| Labor (output per employee) | 434 | 407 | 432 |
| Land (output per hectare) | 232 | 233 | 283 |
| **Asia** | | | |
| Share of agriculture in GDP[1] | 33 | 28 | 24 |
| Share of labor force in agriculture | 71 | 67 | 61 |
| Share of irrigated land[2] | 26 | 31 | 35 |
| Fertilizer usage (kilograms per hectare) | | | |
| Average productivity[3] | | | |
| Labor (output per employee) | 1,971 | 2,514 | 3,167 |
| Land (output per hectare) | 477 | 589 | 827 |
| **Middle East and Europe[4]** | | | |
| Share of agriculture in GDP[1] | 14 | 13 | 16 |
| Share of labor force in agriculture | 55 | 44 | 35 |
| Share of irrigated land[2] | 21 | 21 | 25 |
| Fertilizer usage (kilograms per hectare) | 18 | 52 | 85 |
| Average productivity[3] | | | |
| Labor (output per employee) | 1,020 | 1,371 | 1,754 |
| Land (output per hectare) | 278 | 396 | 534 |
| **Western Hemisphere** | | | |
| Share of agriculture in GDP[1] | 10 | 9 | 9 |
| Share of labor force in agriculture | 41 | 32 | 26 |
| Share of irrigated land[2] | 9 | 10 | 10 |
| Fertilizer usage (kilograms per hectare) | 25 | 54 | 52 |
| Average productivity[3] | | | |
| Labor (output per employee) | 2,160 | 2,666 | 3,203 |
| Land (output per hectare) | 433 | 477 | 549 |

Sources: World Bank; and Food and Agricultural Organization, *Production Yearbook*.

[1]Data for 1970 correspond to 1975.

[2]Percent of arable and permanant cropland that is provided with water.

[3]Measured in constant 1979–81 U.S. dollars.

[4]Excludes Malta, Qatar, and Yemen for which data are not available.

to the experience of the 1970s and early 1980s, when the bulk of private capital inflows to developing countries was bank lending, often to public entities, recent flows have been dominated by portfolio investment in bond and equity markets and by foreign direct investment (Chart 24). In part, this reflects the ongoing process of securitization and the international diversification of investment portfolios of institutional investors. It also reflects a number of structural changes in developing countries. In particular, the deregulation of financial sectors, including the liberalization of domestic interest rates and the removal of restrictions on the activities of nonbank financial institutions, paved the way for an expansion of domestic bond and equity markets.

In some of the most successful countries, the depth of equity markets now matches that of many industrial countries, at least by some measures. In Chile, Korea, Malaysia, Mexico, and Singapore, for example, stock market capitalization as a proportion of GDP exceeds that of industrial countries such as Germany, France, and Italy. The development of domestic equity and bond markets has helped to strengthen financial systems by enabling underlying investment risks to be spread across a broader investor base, and by allowing a more efficient pricing of financial assets in active secondary markets.

The surge in foreign direct investment flows to developing countries since the late 1980s stands out as a particularly promising trend. As noted above, the liberalization of trade and investment regimes in many developing countries has been a key factor, but foreign direct investment has also been spurred by the growth of intraregional trade and by the attraction of some countries as low-cost locations for production by multinational enterprises. In a number of developing countries, privatization programs have also attracted foreign direct investment. In some of the larger developing countries, especially in Asia, rising per capita incomes and more hospitable environments for foreign investors in recent years have been instrumental. The importance of such medium-term considerations is underscored by the fact that direct investment flows, although marginally lower, have remained at relatively high levels following the Mexican crisis.

Among the developing country regions, there are marked differences in the composition of recent capital flows (Chart 25). In the Asian countries, over 40 percent of net capital flows during 1989–94 has been in the form of foreign direct investment, while portfolio flows account for the bulk of capital flows to Latin America. The greater export orientation of the Asian countries compared with most Latin American countries and the recent appreciation of the Japanese yen have been key factors attracting foreign direct investment. Although Latin America and Asia account for most of the recent surge in capital flows, some countries in the Middle East and Europe, such as Egypt and Turkey, have also received relatively large inflows since the late 1980s.

In Africa, aggregate net capital inflows are still largely official flows, which remained substantial throughout the 1980s and early 1990s. However, some African countries—the CFA franc zone countries, Kenya, and Uganda, for example—have recently attracted private capital flows, as policy reform efforts have strengthened and structural adjustment measures have helped to maintain gains in competitiveness resulting from more appropriate exchange rate policies. For many other countries in Africa, debt burdens incurred during the first half of the 1980s continue to hamper adjustment efforts and the high debt burdens can deter foreign investors, although debt indicators

**Chart 25. Developing Countries: Net Capital Flows by Region, 1989–94**
*(Annual average; in billions of U.S. dollars)*

Most capital flows to Asia have been direct investment flows, while portfolio flows have accounted for the bulk of capital flows to the Western Hemisphere.

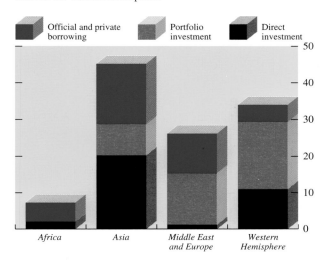

51

**Table 14. Developing Countries: Macroeconomic Stability and Trade**

*(Annual percent change unless otherwise noted)*

|  | 1978–82 | 1983–88 | 1989–94 |
|---|---|---|---|
| **Africa** | | | |
| GDP | 2.0 | 2.4 | 1.9 |
| Consumer prices | 15.9 | 15.5 | 25.6 |
| Fiscal balance (in percent of GDP) | −3.9 | −4.9 | −5.5 |
| Investment (in percent of GDP) | 29.3 | 21.3 | 19.6 |
| Saving (in percent of GDP) | 25.3 | 19.1 | 17.7 |
| Export volume | −0.3 | 2.4 | 2.1 |
| Current account balance (in percent of GDP) | −4.0 | −2.2 | −1.9 |
| Openness (average of exports and imports as percent of GDP) | 25.3 | 22.9 | 25.5 |
| **Asia** | | | |
| GDP | 5.9 | 7.8 | 7.2 |
| Consumer prices | 8.6 | 7.4 | 9.2 |
| Fiscal balance (in percent of GDP) | −3.8 | −3.7 | −2.6 |
| Investment (in percent of GDP) | 26.5 | 27.3 | 30.4 |
| Saving (in percent of GDP) | 24.8 | 27.3 | 30.5 |
| Export volume | 7.8 | 13.5 | 10.9 |
| Current account balance (in percent of GDP) | −1.7 | — | 0.1 |
| Openness (average of exports and imports as percent of GDP) | 22.0 | 25.5 | 33.9 |
| **Middle East and Europe** | | | |
| GDP | 1.7 | 2.4 | 3.4 |
| Consumer prices | 20.3 | 22.4 | 25.4 |
| Fiscal balance (in percent of GDP) | −4.8 | −12.6 | −8.1 |
| Investment (in percent of GDP) | 24.6 | 22.4 | 22.0 |
| Saving (in percent of GDP) | 32.7 | 19.7 | 18.8 |
| Export volume | −8.8 | 1.2 | 4.3 |
| Current account balance (in percent of GDP) | 8.0 | −2.7 | −3.2 |
| Openness (average of exports and imports as percent of GDP) | 39.4 | 30.1 | 29.2 |
| **Western Hemisphere** | | | |
| GDP | 4.0 | 2.1 | 2.7 |
| Consumer prices | 49.6 | 130.7 | 249.9 |
| Fiscal balance (in percent of GDP) | −2.5 | −4.4 | −0.9 |
| Investment (in percent of GDP) | 24.1 | 19.3 | 20.6 |
| Saving (in percent of GDP) | 20.3 | 18.3 | 18.7 |
| Export volume | 5.9 | 4.5 | 6.0 |
| Current account balance (in percent of GDP) | −3.8 | −1.0 | −1.9 |
| Openness (average of exports and imports as percent of GDP) | 13.7 | 13.9 | 13.9 |

have improved somewhat since the late 1980s (see Chapter II). The high debt burdens of many low-income countries point to the continuing importance of concessional financial assistance, both from multilateral institutions like the IMF and from bilateral donors.

## Reaping the Opportunities of Increased Integration

A key requirement for maximizing the benefits from greater integration is to maintain a stable macroeco-

nomic environment that promotes high rates of saving and investment. By reducing uncertainty, macroeconomic stability creates an environment where future profitability is more predictable and resources are allocated more efficiently. Macroeconomic stability also tends to be associated with strong external performance and large inflows of foreign direct investment. Among the developing country regions, the benefits of macroeconomic stability in terms of rising investment and growth are most evident in Asia, where most countries have maintained low and stable inflation rates and moderate fiscal deficits. Inflation has been higher in other regions, and investment and output growth have been lower (Table 14). In many African countries, unfavorable external conditions and high indebtedness, as well as domestic political instability, have hampered the attainment of macroeconomic stability. However, the experience of countries such as Uganda illustrates that such difficulties can be overcome through sustained adjustment and stabilization policies (Box 3).

In some developing countries, the combination of fixed exchange rates and high inflation has reduced competitiveness and limited the expansion of trade. In such cases, nominal exchange rate depreciations are necessary to restore competitiveness, especially in the face of terms of trade shocks. However, as the experience of the CFA countries illustrates, the success of devaluations depends critically on the implementation of macroeconomic policies strong enough to prevent increases in domestic inflation that would quickly erode the gains in competitiveness. In some countries, fixed exchange rates have helped to restrain inflation pressures and, in the context of low inflation, have led to improved competitiveness.

In many instances, persistent fiscal imbalances are the underlying cause of low saving and investment rates. Although countries may be able to resort to foreign saving in the short term, the correction of fiscal deficits is often a critical requirement for increasing overall saving.[32] Fiscal policies can also affect private saving through microeconomic channels, such as taxes and subsidies, that raise the rate of return to saving and through public pension schemes. A mandatory fully funded pension system may lead to higher saving by making people more aware of the need to save for the future and by increasing forced saving.[33]

---

[32]Part of the resulting increase in public saving may be offset by lower private saving, and recent estimates suggest that a 1 percentage point decline in the fiscal deficit as a percent of GDP typically lowers private saving relative to GDP by about ½ of 1 percentage point. See Paul Masson, Tamim Bayoumi, and Hossein Samiei, "Saving Behavior in Industrial and Developing Countries," in *Staff Studies for the World Economic Outlook* (IMF, September 1995), pp. 1–27.

[33]The fully funded pension systems in Malaysia and Singapore, and privatized compulsory pension system in Chile, appear to have

Structural reform and trade liberalization are also essential for a country to benefit fully from greater integration. The removal of distortions created by price controls, subsidies, and licensing requirements enables domestic industries to benefit from increased access to industrial country markets and greater opportunities for diversification. Previous issues of the *World Economic Outlook* have extensively addressed many of these policy requirements. In the context of stronger trade linkages, the critical requirement is to remove distortions that can mask the comparative advantage of domestic producers. The removal of quantitative restrictions on imports is a key aspect of trade liberalization as such restrictions prevent the price system from operating effectively: if domestic industries are not able to compete successfully with imports in their home market, it is unlikely that they will be able to compete in international markets.

Despite widespread consensus on the benefits of open trade regimes, significant barriers to trade are prevalent in a number of developing countries. In some African countries, such as Malawi, Mozambique, and Tanzania, concerns about the availability of foreign exchange have limited progress in the areas of payments and trade liberalization. In addition, exports are frequently discouraged by controls that hold prices significantly below international levels, further exacerbating foreign exchange constraints.[34] Governments are also often concerned with the fiscal implications of reductions in tariffs, and this has hindered trade liberalization in some countries. It is clear that shortfalls in government revenues from lower tariffs can be a very serious problem in the short term. Over the longer term, however, these losses will tend to be offset through higher volumes of trade, reduced incentives for illegal trade, and higher allocational efficiency.[35]

A number of developing countries have attempted to liberalize trade within the framework of regional trading arrangements such as the North American Free Trade Agreement and MERCOSUR in Latin America, the ASEAN Free Trade Area in Asia, and the Gulf Cooperation Council in the Middle East. In Africa, where regional arrangements have in the past had limited success, there have been renewed efforts to strengthen regional integration, including the Cross-Border Initiative in east and southern Africa. Regional trading arrangements can, in principle, promote trade, industrialization, and growth, especially in developing countries where domestic markets are small and fragmented. However, they are unlikely to boost trade where they involve relatively undiversified economies with limited scope for intraregional trade. Moreover, regional trading arrangements may result in trade diversion, creating potential friction for the multilateral trading system.

Developing countries will potentially benefit more from multilateral trade liberalization under the Uruguay Round than from regional trading arrangements. The realization of benefits, however, depends critically on the extent of unilateral liberalization measures and the implementation of appropriate domestic policies to make economies more responsive to the new trading opportunities. Although a number of developing countries have made commitments to reduce tariffs within the context of the Uruguay Round, many will need to increase the pace of liberalization by binding specific tariff reduction measures to the international framework offered by the Round. Countries that have as yet made no commitment to reduce tariffs will need to liberalize their trade regimes unilaterally.

With the exception of the members of the Southern African Union, most sub-Saharan African countries have made few significant liberalization commitments on border protection in agriculture, manufacturing, or services.[36] This reflects concerns that the immediate effects of the Round on low-income net importers of food, many of which are in Africa, might be a decline of the terms of trade because of higher world agricultural prices resulting from lower agricultural subsidies, principally in the industrial countries.[37] The resulting declines in income will occur gradually as Uruguay Round commitments are phased in. Provided these countries successfully diversify exports, declines in income will tend to be reversed over time through gains in efficiency and increases in trade and global activity.

For exporters of primary commodities, the volatility of commodity prices has posed considerable difficulties for macroeconomic management as fiscal revenues and external positions fluctuate with export earnings. These difficulties have been exacerbated by poorly designed stabilization funds and, in some cases,

---

contributed to marked increases in private saving and to financial sector deepening. See Giancarlo Corsetti and Klaus Schmidt-Hebbel, "Pension Reform and Growth," paper presented at the Conference on Pensions: Funding, Privatization and Macroeconomic Policy, Catholic University of Chile, January 1994.

[34]See Eduardo Borensztein, "Structural Policies in Developing Countries," IMF Paper on Policy Analysis and Assessment 94/19 (September 1994).

[35]Among African countries, for example, estimates for Burundi, Kenya, Tanzania, and Uganda show that with appropriate reforms of the tax system, the fiscal implications of trade liberalization with neighboring countries are likely to be modest after a few years. See Ferdinand Bakoup, Abdelrahmi Bessaha, and Luca Errico, "Regional Integration in Eastern and Southern Africa: The Cross-Border Initiative and Its Fiscal Implications," IMF Working Paper 95/23 (February 1995).

[36]As a result, the benefits of the Uruguay Round agreement may also be relatively small for these countries, see Piritta Sorsa, "The Burden of Sub-Saharan African Own Commitments in the Uruguay Round—Myth or Reality?" IMF Working Paper 95/48 (May 1995).

[37]For a review of the implications of the Uruguay Round agreement for developing countries, see Annex I of the May 1994 *World Economic Outlook*.

## Box 3.  Uganda: Successful Adjustment Under Difficult Circumstances

Since the end of the civil war in 1986, Uganda has made significant and impressive strides to improve economic performance under the government's Economic Recovery Program. The adjustment policies aimed at economic stabilization, the restoration of balanced growth, and the normalization of relations with external creditors. In pursuit of these policy objectives, important structural reforms were required in price and trade arrangements, the financial sector, public and quasi-public enterprises, the civil service, and the size of the military.[1]

Uganda faced a difficult situation in the mid-1980s and throughout much of the adjustment period. The civil war had devastated transportation, power, and water facilities. In 1986, per capita GDP was 60 percent below its level of 1970, inflation had risen to 240 percent, and external debt service was more than 50 percent of exports.[2] A fixed exchange rate had eroded the country's competitiveness leading to an acute shortage of foreign exchange, the development of parallel exchange markets, and increasing external payment arrears. By 1987, exports other than coffee had virtually ceased. Coffee prices declined steadily from 1985 to 1993 and Uganda suffered annual declines in its terms of trade every year from 1986 through 1992. Largely as a result of these declines in the terms of trade, Uganda's ratio of scheduled debt service to exports increased sharply, peaking at almost 130 percent of exports in 1992.

Despite the difficult preconditions, Uganda has staged a remarkable economic recovery (*see chart*). Economic growth has averaged about 6 percent a year since 1987, and is estimated to have been at least 7 percent in 1994. Inflation has fallen consistently, to an average of 6 percent in 1994, and the overall fiscal deficit has been contained. As a result, bank credit to the government is now negative and is no longer contributing to inflationary pressures. Total government revenues, which had shrunk to less than 5 percent of GDP recovered to 8 percent by 1993 and are estimated to have been over 10 percent of GDP in 1994. Despite unfavorable terms of trade movements, the external current account deficit (excluding grants) declined markedly, from a peak of 17 percent of GDP in 1988 to an estimated 5 percent of GDP in 1994.

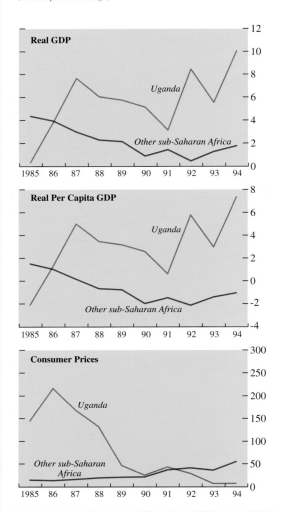

**Uganda and Other Sub-Saharan Africa: Growth and Inflation**
*(Annual percent change)*

[1]For a detailed discussion of Uganda's adjustment efforts, see Robert L. Sharer, Hema R. De Zoysa, and Calvin A. McDonald, *Uganda: Adjustment with Growth, 1987–94*, IMF Occasional Paper 121 (March 1995).

[2]Most figures refer to fiscal years starting in July of the year noted and ending in June of the following year.

Exports have become more diversified, with noncoffee exports now representing about 26 percent of total exports—despite the surge in coffee prices in 1994. The domestic economy has also become more market oriented, by state-owned agricultural boards. Windfall gains associated with temporary price rises are often transferred to the government, which may find it difficult to resist political pressures to raise expenditures on a permanent basis. In Nigeria, for example, the temporary boom in oil prices in 1990 was used to finance higher government expenditures, which led to a serious fiscal crisis when oil prices declined in 1991.[38]

[38]See David Bevan, Paul Collier, and Jan Willem Gunning, "Trade Shocks in Developing Countries: Consequences and Policy Responses," *European Economic Review,* Vol. 37 (April 1993), pp. 557–65.

with the liberalized pricing and interest rate environment providing positive incentives for saving and investment. Uganda's saving rate has risen from negative 12½ percent in 1986 to an estimated 13 percent in 1994, while over the same period investment has risen from 9¼ percent of GDP to 17¾ percent of GDP. Although still below the average for sub-Saharan Africa, saving and investment have responded positively to the adjustment policies.

The consistent implementation of strong fiscal policies was the cornerstone of these adjustments. Although the achievement of financial stabilization called for the pursuit of restrictive fiscal policies, the need to strengthen economic performance required increased outlays to restore and rehabilitate devastated infrastructure. The authorities reconciled these objectives by implementing tax reforms, including discretionary measures and the strengthening of tax administration to augment revenues, and by raising donor disbursements. To complement this, monetary and credit policies were kept tight while increasingly shifting the composition of domestic credit in favor of the productive private sector. A number of financial sector reforms, including the development of an active government securities market, a strengthening of central bank operations, and restructuring of weak banks, increased monetary control. Many of these reforms are ongoing and require deepening to improve further the efficiency of the financial sector.

In recognition of Uganda's heavy debt burden, Paris Club creditors reached agreement in June 1992 on concessional rescheduling (London terms) of Uganda's debt. In February 1995, Uganda became the first country to receive a stock-of-debt operation under the new Naples terms—the rescheduling agreement provided for a 67 percent net present value reduction of eligible debt. That eligible debt, however, represented less than 4 percent of Uganda's total outstanding debt. This reduction, together with comparable action by non-Paris Club creditors and a significant improvement in the terms of trade, helped reduce the debt-service ratio to an estimated 25 percent of exports in 1994; this ratio is expected to stabilize at about 20 percent in the next decade. Nevertheless, Uganda's debt burden remains high, with a sizable level of multilateral debt, and its debt-servicing capacity is sensitive to external developments and other circumstances that can change quickly over time.

The liberalization of the foreign exchange market coupled with supporting foreign and domestic trade reforms improved incentives and enhanced growth prospects. To improve competitiveness, the official exchange rate was devalued in several discrete steps between 1987 and 1989. In 1990, foreign exchange bureaus were established and in November 1993 the exchange market was unified with the introduction of an interbank market. Important trade and payments reforms complemented the reforms in the foreign exchange market. As foreign exchange bureaus began operations, increasingly more transactions were shifted to this market. On the supply side, foreign exchange surrender requirements for noncoffee exports and private transfers were abolished, and all restrictions on current international transactions were eliminated with the introduction of the interbank market.

Price liberalization began in 1987 with a 182 percent increase in producer prices paid to coffee farmers. By 1992, virtually all domestic price controls had been abolished, removing significant distortions and providing needed incentives for domestic producers and exporters. The liberalization of agricultural prices was accompanied by the abolition of various marketing boards, thus raising revenues to farmers and lowering marketing costs. As a result, agricultural production expanded substantially and smuggling was eliminated.

Significant progress has also been made in other structural areas. The size of the civil service has been reduced from over 300,000 to about 150,000, and ministries continue to be restructured and rationalized. The size of the military has also been reduced by about 33,000 in two phases of army demobilization. With the expected completion of the third and final stage during the coming year, the size of the army will have been reduced to about 45,000, half its former size. To speed up privatization of public enterprises, the organizational structure of the government's Privatization Unit has been revised to overcome operational and jurisdictional problems. Enterprises to be retained in the public sector are being put on a commercial footing.

The successful implementation of reforms was made possible by the political stability of recent years. The credibility of the adjustment programs was enhanced by the commitment of policymakers, the consistency of policy implementation, the appropriate sequencing of reforms, and improved governance through the institutionalization of administrative procedures and practices. Nevertheless, several challenges remain. These include accelerating many of the structural reforms, particularly in the financial system and the privatization of public enterprises, to raise productivity, saving, and investment and thereby improve prospects for long-term sustainable growth.

Many developing countries also have found it difficult to hedge commodity price risks beyond the short term owing to relatively high transactions costs and the absence of futures and forward markets beyond a year or two. While financial markets may offer limited insurance against large declines in export prices, there is some evidence that private agents have been better able to increase precautionary savings when faced with temporary price movements. Rice farmers in Thailand, for example, have been able to smooth consumption patterns quite successfully, both within and between harvest

---

### Box 4. Financial Liberalization in Africa and Asia

In many developing countries, macroeconomic stabilization and structural reform policies, especially the liberalization of financial markets, have been implemented simultaneously. The experiences of a number of developing countries, including many of the early liberalizers in Asia and Latin America, suggest that financial liberalization has been more successful in countries with a stable macroeconomic environment. For developing countries in Africa that are only now beginning to deregulate their financial sectors, the experience of the Asian countries, where deregulation has been most widespread, is particularly instructive.

A number of Asian countries liberalized their domestic financial systems during the 1980s through a combination of deregulation of interest rates and abolition of administrative controls on credit expansion and allocation. Further liberalizations in some Asian countries permitted the establishment and expansion of securities and equity markets and other nonbank sources of credit. In many African countries, the liberalization of domestic financial systems only began in earnest in the late 1980s and early 1990s. Despite the abolition of formal controls, however, continued government intervention in the allocation of credit and ongoing problems of insolvent banks, often stemming from subsidized credit extended to public sector entities, have limited the development of financial sectors in Africa. In large part reflecting the lack of progress in these areas, financial sector liberalization in Africa has generally been associated with only modest increases in the amount of financial intermediation.[1]

Following the liberalization of domestic interest rates, real interest rates rose to positive levels in Indonesia, Malaysia, and Thailand, and financial intermediation increased substantially. In Indonesia, the ratio of broad money to GDP rose dramatically from about 9 percent in

1983 to over 40 percent in 1991, while the ratio of private sector bank borrowing to GDP increased markedly from under 15 percent in 1983 to well over 45 percent in 1991. Interest rates were liberalized earlier in Malaysia, and financial deepening was over 60 percent by 1982 compared with about 40 percent in the mid-1970s. In Korea and Thailand, real interest rates were maintained at positive levels even before nominal rates were liberalized, resulting in substantial financial deepening prior to the reforms. In the Philippines, by contrast, real interest rates were both less stable and, during brief periods of high inflation, substantially negative; financial deepening was, accordingly, considerably lower, at about 20 percent, in the early 1980s, although it did increase to over 30 percent in the early 1990s following the implementation of reforms.

The Gambia and Ghana were among the first countries in Africa to liberalize financial markets in the mid-1980s. Interest rate deregulation resulted in a dramatic move to positive real rates in The Gambia, whereas in Ghana the liberalization process has been considerably slower, although real interest rates have been modestly positive recently. In both countries, the ratio of private credit to GDP has remained virtually unchanged since interest rate deregulation; the ratio of broad money to GDP has increased, however, mainly reflecting government borrowing from the banking system to finance continuing fiscal imbalances. In Kenya, Madagascar, and Malawi, liberalization prompted a fall in real interest rates on deposits as banks widened margins, and there has been little financial deepening. As in The Gambia and Ghana, progress since financial liberalization in these countries has been concentrated on the deposit rather than the lending side of bank balance sheets. Recent reforms undertaken in Uganda have led to a rise in real interest rates to modestly positive levels, although the liberalization process is too recent to assess the extent of any concurrent or subsequent financial deepening.

On the basis of conventional measures of financial deepening, such as the ratio of broad money (M2) to GDP, financial liberalization has clearly been less suc-

---

[1]See Huw Pill and Mahmood Pradhan, "Financial Indicators and Financial Change in Africa and Asia," IMF Working Paper (forthcoming).

---

years.[39] And coffee producers in Kenya saved about 70 percent of the windfall profits from the coffee price boom associated with the frost in Brazil during 1976–79.

## External Financial Liberalization

As part of the integration process, many developing countries need to address the issue of domestic and ex-

ternal financial liberalization to improve the allocation of saving. The benefits from external financial liberalization include improved access to foreign capital, which can supplement domestic saving; greater scope for domestic investors to diversify internationally; strengthening of the financial system; and greater discipline on governments that can promote sustainable macroeconomic policies. There are, however, valid concerns about the necessary prerequisites to ensure that liberalization of the external capital account is viable, and in particular that it does not result in destabilizing capital flows.

In most of the countries that have witnessed large capital inflows in recent years, the positive sentiment of foreign investors has reflected improvements in un-

---

[39]See Christina H. Paxson, "Consumption and Income Seasonality in Thailand," *Journal of Political Economy*, Vol. 101 (February 1993), pp. 39–72.

cessful in Africa than in Asia. Although financial deepening in Asia has been supported by the higher levels of income and saving than in Africa, financial liberalization and market-oriented economic policies in Asia have also boosted growth of the financial sector. Among African countries, much of the increase in the ratio of broad money to GDP that has occurred since financial liberalization reflects lending to the public sector, with the ratio of private sector credit to GDP rising only marginally, which is in sharp contrast to the experience of the Asian countries (*see chart*). Key factors that appear to have retarded the development of financial systems in Africa include unstable macroeconomic environments, widespread public ownership of financial institutions and their principal clients, and the lack of viable institutions to mobilize saving, particularly in rural areas. In the absence of well-developed domestic capital markets, fiscal deficits have been financed largely by the banking system, much of which is publicly owned and often compelled to finance government deficits at below-market interest rates. This has effectively crowded out credit to the private sector. A number of African countries implemented financial liberalization in an environment of large fiscal deficits and relatively high inflation. Inflation was more than 20 percent in Ghana when interest rates were deregulated. With the exception of the Philippines and Sri Lanka, the Asian countries were characterized by moderate macroeconomic imbalances and inflation rates well below those in the African countries.

While a stable macroeconomic environment is essential for successful financial liberalization, a sound banking system is also important. In many African countries, and also in some Asian countries such as Indonesia, public ownership of banks has resulted in financial institutions that face "soft budget constraints," and rely on the provision of subsidized credit by the central bank to remain solvent. The activities of such banks more closely resemble the provision of government subsidies financed by borrowing from the central bank, rather than commercial lending. In these cases, the deregulation of interest

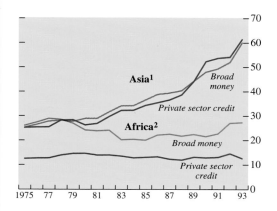

**Selected African and Asian Countries: Indicators of Financial Deepening**
(*In percent of GDP*)

[1]Indonesia, Korea, Malaysia, Philippines, Sri Lanka, and Thailand. Data for 1993 exclude Indonesia.
[2]The Gambia, Ghana, Kenya, Madagascar, and Malawi.

rates and the removal of controls on credit allocation may be insufficient to spur financial deepening or to improve the allocation of saving. Where nonperforming assets are inherited from the prereform era, interest rate liberalization should be accompanied by a number of structural measures, including restructuring of bank balance sheets, privatization of publicly owned banks, and improvements in prudential supervision of financial sector institutions. Strengthening the management and risk assessment capabilities of bank managers should also be an integral part of the restructuring process.

derlying economic fundamentals and market-oriented policies that have increased efficiency and raised the rate of return on investments. The capital inflows attracted in response to these developments have helped to ease balance of payments constraints, allowed domestic enterprises to reduce the cost of capital by borrowing from international capital markets, and enhanced longer-term growth prospects.

In some countries, however, capital inflows have also been attracted by relatively high short-term interest rates resulting from macroeconomic imbalances, including excessive fiscal deficits and inadequate levels of national saving. In such circumstances, capital inflows may exacerbate problems of overheating. Moreover, financial markets in most developing coun-

tries lack sufficient depth to intermediate large inflows. Together with ineffective prudential supervision, this may increase the vulnerability of financial systems to reversals of foreign capital inflows. The Mexican financial crisis underscores the risks of such reversals and the potential costs from the abruptness of the required adjustment process. While the prerequisites for capital account liberalization are desirable in their own right, countries that have made little progress toward macroeconomic stability and strengthening domestic financial markets need to be cautious about removing barriers to capital flows. Caution is particularly warranted with regard to short-term capital flows intermediated through the domestic banking system.

**Chart 26.  Developing Countries:  Medium-Term Effects of a Reversal of Capital Inflows[1]**

Smaller capital inflows, reduced trade, and policy slippages in developing countries would dampen medium-term growth.

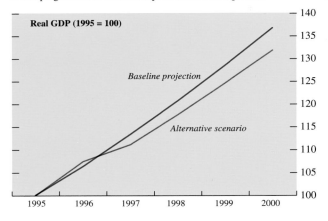

[1]Based on simulations using the IMF's developing country model.

Sustainable macroeconomic policies are clearly an important prerequisite for successful capital account liberalization. Weak fiscal positions place an excessive burden on monetary policy to contain increases in aggregate demand and to prevent rises in inflation, which is often reflected in high interest rates. Removing restrictions on short-term capital flows under these circumstances attracts portfolio flows that add to inflation pressures—especially under fixed exchange rates—and pose further difficulties for monetary control. The experience of countries such as Argentina, Chile, and Uruguay that liberalized their capital accounts during the late 1970s and early 1980s illustrates the risks of capital account liberalization before macroeconomic stability has been established.

In many developing countries, administrative controls on interest rates have been liberalized relatively recently. The experience of some countries in Africa and Asia suggests that successful liberalization requires a well-capitalized and profitable domestic banking system (Box 4, on previous page). When direct controls on credit allocation are removed, a common feature in most countries is a rapid expansion of bank credit, often fueling booms in consumption expenditure. Under these circumstances, the liberalization of the capital account may expose domestic banks to new types of risks. Prudential and supervisory regulations are often inadequate to guard against these new risks. Rising domestic interest rates may induce banks to finance local currency lending with foreign currency deposits without adequate cover for foreign exchange risk. In the event of capital outflows, banks may face large deposit withdrawals that would force balance sheet contractions, with potentially strong repercussions for their domestic borrowers. Moreover, with poor internal monitoring systems, banks may not identify problem assets, making it difficult for regulators to assess the quality of their portfolios.

Liberalization of the capital account also has strong implications for the conduct of macroeconomic policy. A number of countries have found it difficult to reconcile monetary policy and exchange rate objectives in a regime of free capital mobility. In countries such as Chile and Colombia, large capital inflows have necessitated greater exchange rate flexibility. In some emerging market countries, attempts to sterilize capital inflows while limiting upward flexibility of the exchange rate have only led to even larger inflows, and the eventual reimposition of controls. Malaysia, for example, imposed extensive administrative controls in early 1994 to deter further inflows, while Venezuela imposed relatively stringent controls on inflows in mid-1994. A number of emerging market countries continue to maintain some restrictions on portfolio inflows, and in some cases these appear to have been a deterrent to excessively volatile short-term inflows that are driven more by changes in financial market sentiment than by the underlying fundamentals.

For developing countries that are less advanced in their reform programs, it is important to strengthen financial market regulation and supervision and address policy imbalances. Although freedom of capital movements will promote growth and improve the allocation of resources over the longer term, liberalization of capital movements can be undertaken gradually. The transition to a regime of full convertibility for capital account transactions can start with the liberalization of trade-related investment flows and foreign direct investment that allows countries to reap many of the benefits of foreign capital flows while avoiding some of the pitfalls. The risk of capital flow reversals, especially when capital flows are intermediated largely through the domestic banking system, does appear to be higher in countries that institute a liberal regime for capital movements before all of the complementary policies are in place. However, restrictions on capital movements should not be viewed as a substitute for stronger adjustment efforts. It is also important to recognize that although they may help to dampen capital inflows, restrictions on capital flows have limited effectiveness in preventing capital outflows in the face of unsustainable macroeconomic and exchange rate policies.

## Implications of a Reversal of Capital Inflows

The new environment of greater openness and integration may well penalize countries with macroeconomic imbalances and inadequate structural reforms to a greater extent than in earlier periods. Recent crises in some emerging market countries have highlighted the potential for large and sudden reversals of capital

flows and the consequent sharp contractions in domestic demand. An alternative scenario has been constructed using the IMF's developing country model to illustrate the potential consequences of a partial reversal of capital flows as a result of an external financial shock.[40] The scenario builds on the policy slippage scenario for the industrial countries discussed in Chapter III and assumes a sharp reversal of capital inflows in 1996 in response to higher long-term interest rates in the industrial countries. This negative external shock leads to policy slippages in the developing countries.[41] The lower capital inflows reduce investment and imports relative to the baseline, including imports of capital goods. This, in turn, is assumed to reduce the beneficial effects of trade on productivity growth. The net effect would be to lower the level of output in the developing countries in the year 2000 by almost 4 percent relative to the baseline projection (Chart 26). Economies with low domestic saving rates and large external deficits would be hardest hit by the decline in capital flows while higher world interest rates would have the largest impact on growth in the heavily indebted countries.

---

[40]For a description of the IMF's developing country model, see Manmohan S. Kumar, S. Hossein Samiei, and Sheila Bassett, "An Extended Scenario and Forecast Adjustment Model for Developing Countries," in *Staff Studies for the World Economic Outlook* (IMF, December 1993), pp. 47–75.

[41]Capital flows are assumed to be reduced to about one half of their value in the baseline for the period 1996 through 2000. Policy slippages in developing countries are assumed to take the form of higher fiscal deficits on the order of about 2 percent of GDP a year during 1996–2000.

# V

# Policy Challenges Facing Transition Countries

For the first time since the late 1980s, recorded output is growing in most countries in transition. In some, such as Albania, Poland, and Slovenia, real GDP has already surged far above its trough. In others, including Armenia, the Baltic countries, Bulgaria, Croatia, the former Yugoslav Republic of Macedonia, Moldova, Mongolia, and Romania, economic recovery materialized later but is becoming more broadly based. At the same time, inflation is under better control in most transition countries, including Ukraine, Belarus, and most countries of central Asia and the Transcaucasus. Output performance continues to be bleaker in Russia, Ukraine, Belarus, and most of the countries of central Asia and the Transcaucasus, with further large declines in real GDP expected in 1995.

Correspondingly, the policy challenges now faced by the countries more advanced in the transition differ from the challenges confronting countries that started later or moved more slowly. The priority for the former group is to sustain growth and disinflation and to make further progress with structural reforms, particularly with respect to the deepening of market-oriented principles. For the latter group of countries, consolidating or even achieving macroeconomic stabilization remains paramount, and much is still to be done to set up the institutions of a market economy.

A central feature of successful market economies is a well-functioning financial system. In almost all countries in transition, however, financial systems suffer from deep-seated weaknesses. In several countries, banking crises have erupted into the open. In others, crises have been contained, but contingent fiscal liabilities have been building up at a disquieting pace. Bank failures endanger stabilization gains, and slow progress with financial sector reform is impeding improvements in corporate efficiency in the enterprise sector. At the same time, insufficient restructuring and financial discipline in the enterprise sector continue to burden banks with nonperforming loans, undermining the stability of the financial sector.

## Sustaining Disinflation and Growth in Countries More Advanced in the Transition

The countries that started earliest and moved most decisively with stabilization and structural reforms have made considerable progress. Disinflation has

**Chart 27. Countries More Advanced in the Transition: Inflation**
*(Twelve-month percent change in the consumer price index)*

Inflation has come down but generally remains high.

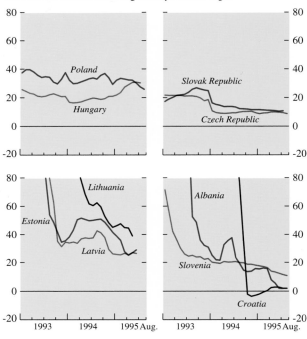

generally been fairly swift after the initial price jumps associated with decontrol. Output is expanding at a median rate of 4–5 percent. The main policy challenge now facing these countries is to ensure the sustainability of disinflation and growth.

Annual inflation rates have been brought down significantly from the triple-digit levels prevailing in the early phase of the transition. In Albania, Croatia, the Czech Republic, and the Slovak Republic, annual rates of inflation have approached or reached single-digit levels (Chart 27). Nevertheless, inflation remains stubbornly high in most countries, typically fluctuating in the 20–40 percent range. In Hungary, inflation has even picked up anew. The persistence of high inflation is mainly due to the spread of indexation mechanisms and enduring fiscal imbalances (Table 15).[42] But it is also related to continuing relative price adjustments, with prices of nontradables rising faster than prices of tradables (Box 5).[43]

Unexpectedly large capital inflows have been one of the challenges associated with relatively successful stabilization. These inflows are a welcome sign of the confidence of foreign and domestic investors in the economic prospects of the recipient countries.[44] However, the inflows have also added to inflationary pressures, most notably in the Czech Republic and Poland but also in Albania, the Slovak Republic, and Slovenia. In the Czech Republic, where the exchange rate is fixed, external borrowing by enterprises, foreign portfolio and direct investment, and short-term borrowing by banks have all contributed to a surge in official reserves, which were equivalent to nearly six months of imports by the end of August 1995. Similarly, in Poland, in the context of a crawling peg, a rapid accumulation of official reserves took place as a result of buoyant exports and, as in the Czech Republic, of expectations that the exchange rate would be revalued. In both cases, restricted exchange rate flexibility coupled with limited scope for sterilization led to rapid money supply growth.[45]

The ensuing inflationary pressures cannot be durably contained by administrative measures. Price controls, for example, such as the caps on energy prices introduced in Poland, risk delaying structural adjustment. A reintroduction of restrictions on capital

### Table 15. Countries More Advanced in the Transition: General Government Budget Balance[1]
*(In percent of GDP)*

|  | 1993 | 1994 | Projections 1995 | Projections 1996 |
|---|---|---|---|---|
| Albania[2,3] | −16.0 | −13.0 | −13.2 | −12.0 |
| Croatia | −0.8 | 1.7 | −0.5 | −0.5 |
| Czech Republic | 0.6 | −1.3 | −2.4 | −1.0 |
| Estonia | −0.7 | 0.0 | −2.3 | −3.5 |
| Hungary[2] | −7.5 | −7.9 | −7.0 | −6.1 |
| Latvia[2] | 0.2 | −4.1 | −2.2 | −1.0 |
| Lithuania[2] | −0.1 | −1.0 | −1.3 | −1.7 |
| Poland | −2.9 | −2.5 | −2.9 | −2.7 |
| Slovak Republic | −7.6 | −1.5 | −3.0 | −2.4 |
| Slovenia | 0.3 | −0.2 | −0.1 | −0.5 |

Sources: National authorities; and IMF staff estimates.

[1]Defined as total expenditure (including extrabudgetary funds) plus net lending minus total revenue and grants.

[2]Central government balance.

[3]Excludes concessional external financing of development projects on the order of 6–8 percent of GDP.

flows would also represent a setback to the liberalization and opening up of the economy and deter foreign direct investment. Rather than imposing new restrictions, measures should be implemented to remove distortions in domestic financial markets that might encourage external borrowing or discourage capital outflows. The Czech Republic has announced tighter regulation of short-term borrowing by banks, effective August 1, 1995, in view of the threat that capital inflows have posed to monetary control, while at the same time a draft foreign exchange law would further liberalize outflows of foreign direct investment. Macroeconomic policies, however, have a key role to play in reducing inflationary pressures stemming from large capital inflows. In particular, it may be appropriate to tighten fiscal policy more than planned to reduce the pressures on inflation and interest rates. In some cases, it may even be appropriate to achieve a fiscal surplus. With due regard for competitiveness considerations, it may also be desirable to allow some exchange rate appreciation or to slow down the predetermined rate of depreciation, as has been done in Poland.[46]

Most of the countries that achieved a fair measure of financial stability early on in the transition have subsequently enjoyed vigorous growth. In 1995, real GDP is projected to exceed its trough by 29 percent in

---

[42]Fiscal deficits for the countries more advanced in the transition better reflect the underlying stance of financial policies than in other transition countries where quasi-fiscal deficits remain larger (see the discussion below).

[43]See also Box 7 in the May 1995 *World Economic Outlook*.

[44]Transition countries, such as Belarus, Bulgaria, Kazakhstan, Russia, and Ukraine, that have made less progress in stabilization have also recently been the recipients of large capital inflows, stemming, in part, from high real interest rates. For a discussion of capital inflows in developing countries, see Chapter IV; and Chapter III of the May 1995 *World Economic Outlook*.

[45]The scope for sterilization is limited by its short-run fiscal cost and by the lack of financial instruments.

---

[46]The Czech authorities are concerned about the experience of the 1920s, when revaluation of the currency in response to heavy capital inflows induced by successful stabilization was followed by an export slump and a banking crisis; see Marcello de Cecco, "Central Banking in Central and Eastern Europe: Lessons from the Interwar Years' Experience," IMF Working Paper 94/127 (October 1994).

**Box 5. Price Liberalization and Inflation Dynamics in Transition Economies**

Price liberalization allows the structure of relative prices in transition economies to adjust and move toward that characterizing market-oriented economies with similar levels of per capita income.[1] Accordingly, the variability of relative prices is large in the early phase of the transition but declines as prices are realigned closer to market levels.

In Russia, for example, a relatively comprehensive price liberalization took place at the beginning of 1992, causing major shifts in relative prices. After a few months, however, relative price variability had declined substantially (*see chart*). Price liberalization was more gradual in the transition countries of central Asia. In Kazakhstan, for example, many prices remained administered until late 1994. Before they were decontrolled, these prices were adjusted infrequently and by large amounts, resulting in many spikes in relative price variability.[2] The pace of liberalization varied across types of items: in most transition countries, prices for tradables were freed first, and more or less across the board, although the prices of some staples often remained controlled; prices for services were freed last and more gradually. Relative price variability for services thus remained much higher than for tradable goods. As the relative price structure starts to resemble that in comparable market economies and as agents seek to adjust to chronic open inflation, price setting will tend to become increasingly synchronized.

In addition to the ongoing adjustment of relative prices, high and stubborn inflation in most transition countries also reflects the reliance on the inflation tax whereby money creation is used to finance persistently large fiscal and quasi-fiscal deficits.[3] In 1993–94, the ratio of the change in base money to GDP—a measure of seigniorage—averaged 1 percent in Poland and the Slovak Republic, 3½ percent in Hungary, 7 percent in Romania, and 9 percent in Russia. The scope for extracting seigniorage diminishes, however, as the demand for money drops in response to higher inflation. Moreover, the efficiency losses caused by high inflation and the inflationary erosion of tax receipts associated with tax collection lags offset seigniorage as a source of off-budget fiscal revenue. If, for example, tax payments are collected with a one-month lag and tax revenues represent 30 percent of GDP, a monthly inflation rate of 10 percent

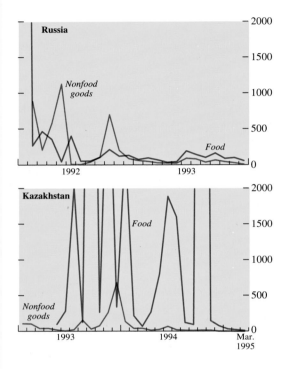

**Russia and Kazakhstan: Relative Price Variability[1]**
*(In percent)*

[1]Measured as a weighted average of the variance of monthly inflation rates for specific items.

would imply a loss in real fiscal revenue amounting to 3 percent of GDP (assuming no penalties for late payment). Persistent inflation may also reflect the more widespread use of indexation mechanisms, affecting the formation of wages and pensions, and the design of financial contracts. Indexation may help to reduce some of the costs of high inflation, but it causes inflation to become more entrenched. Disinflation under such circumstances requires decisive fiscal adjustment. The reduction of inflation may be facilitated by measures to reduce the inertia in the inflation process stemming from indexation. Institutional reforms enhancing the credibility of financial policies, such as conferring more independence to the central bank, can also reduce inflationary inertia and speed up disinflation.

[1]See Paula De Masi and Vincent Koen, "Price Convergence in Transition Economies," IMF Working Paper (forthcoming).

[2]See Mark De Broeck, Paula De Masi, and Vincent Koen, "Inflation Dynamics in Kazakhstan," IMF Working Paper (forthcoming).

[3]See Rudiger Dornbusch and Stanley Fischer, "Moderate Inflation," *World Bank Economic Review*, Vol. 7 (January 1993), pp. 1–44.

Albania, 19 percent in Poland, and 11 percent in Slovenia. Strong recoveries have helped arrest and in some cases reverse the sharp increases in open

unemployment rates that characterized the early stages of the transition (Chart 28). In accordance with the experience of other countries, the contribution of growth to job creation will depend on the degree of flexibility of new and emerging labor market institutions, particularly with respect to wage setting (Box 6).[47] Even under favorable conditions, however, high unemployment will remain a major problem in the years ahead in most of the transition countries.

To a large extent, robust output growth has thus far been driven on the demand side by a rapid expansion of exports, especially to western Europe but increasingly also to other transition economies (Chart 29). However, even if the revival of east-east trade continues (Box 7), it may be difficult for these economies to sustain rapid export growth without substantial investment to rebuild largely obsolete capital stocks inherited from the command system. Investment is generally beginning to recover and in many cases is rising rapidly from relatively depressed levels. High rates of domestic saving are essential to sustain the pickup in investment. This is an important reason why steady reductions of fiscal deficits will be needed to prevent the crowding out of needed private investments. Provided their macroeconomic consequences are taken into account in the overall policy stance, as discussed earlier, capital inflows, including the return of flight capital, can also help to finance investment. As suggested by the experience of developing countries, foreign direct investment may be particularly helpful to raise overall investment levels, strengthen productivity, improve management practices, and foster export-oriented activities.

The continued process of transformation also requires further progress with enterprise restructuring, financial sector reform, and institution building. Although much of the formal framework of a market economy is now in place in the countries that are relatively advanced in the transition,[48] corporate efficiency, management practices, and business ethics still have a long way to go to meet international standards, especially among state-owned enterprises. Moreover, in several countries, including Hungary, Poland, and the Slovak Republic, the pace of privatization has remained too slow. Lastly, some of the institutions of a market economy remain to be established, such as well-functioning housing markets, reliable systems of commercial courts, and efficient financial systems. In the longer run, increases in productivity, output, and living standards will be commensurate with improvements in those areas.

**Chart 28. Selected Countries in Transition: Open Unemployment Rates**
*(In percent of the labor force)*

Unemployment rates may have peaked in several countries.

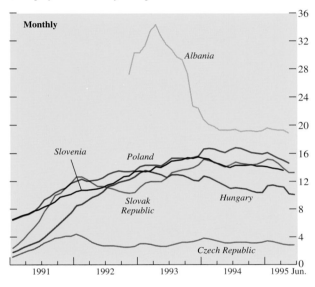

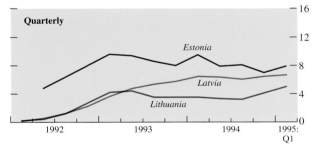

---

[47]See Robert J. Flanagan, "Institutional Structure and Labor Market Outcomes: Western Lessons for European Countries in Transition," in *Staff Studies for the World Economic Outlook* (IMF, September 1995), pp. 92–105.

[48]See Commission of the European Communities, *Preparation of the Associated Countries of Central and Eastern Europe for Integration into the Internal Market of the Union* (Luxembourg, 1995).

## Chart 29.  Selected Countries in Transition: Growth in GDP and Exports of Goods and Services
*(In percent, average for 1994–95)*

Exports have contributed substantially to output growth.

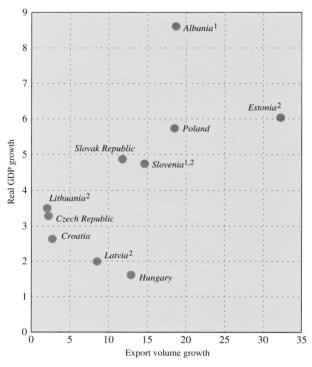

[1]Based on value in U.S. dollars.
[2]Merchandise trade.

**Box 6.  Changing Wage Structures in the Czech Republic**

Recent evidence suggests that wage structures in the Czech Republic are moving toward those observed in market economies.[1] Under central planning, the goal was to encourage the expansion of the goods-producing sector, and in particular heavy industry, and discourage activities in the service sector and most intellectual activities outside of the hard sciences. In designing national wage structures in the early postwar period, central planners took account of education, experience, the attractiveness of jobs, and other factors. However, relative wages were mainly set to allocate labor in accordance with the production goals of the central plans. Accordingly, vocational education was emphasized over advanced academic training. Average economic returns to schooling in central European countries therefore tended to be lower than in most market economies. Thus, the labor force of central European economies began the transition with overinvestments in vocational training and underinvestments in university education.

With the end of central planning, wages in a large number of occupations were free to adjust to market forces. Data from employment and labor force surveys conducted between June 1988 and November 1993 in the Czech Republic suggest that wage structures appear to be moving toward those typically associated with a market economy. Since 1988, for example, it is estimated that average returns to schooling and wage inequality have increased, suggesting a reversal of some of the wage distortions created under central planning. New private firms seem to be playing a leading role in changing the wage structures. For example, returns to university education have increased, and these gains have been particularly noteworthy in the private sector. The survey data also indicate that workers with a vocational degree are no longer guaranteed higher wages than workers with a primary school degree. Although state enterprises and recently privatized state enterprises have mostly retained the old relative wage structures, there may have been some changes—such as increases in the returns to high school and university education—because of labor market competition from the new private sector.

Adjustments in relative wages and the central role of the private sector in bringing about these changes are not unique to the Czech Republic. Estimates of the returns to schooling and wage inequality have increased in Poland and in Hungary, for example. In Romania, by contrast, which has yet to develop a significant private sector, returns to education appear to have changed very little. In a number of transition countries, workers with vocational training have experienced falling relative wages and disproportionately higher unemployment.

[1]Robert J. Flanagan, "Wage Structures in the Transition of the Czech Economy," *Staff Papers* (IMF, forthcoming).

# Countries Less Advanced in the Process of Stabilization and Restructuring

The key lesson from the countries more advanced in the transition process is that stabilization of prices and resumption of output growth require sound macroeconomic policies coupled with comprehensive structural reforms. In light of this experience, almost all the countries that initially put off fundamental adjustment policies or moved less boldly have more recently been making headway with reforms. Natural disasters and armed conflicts have hindered or undermined the implementation of stabilization and reform policies in a number of countries. Armenia has suffered from the aftermath of the 1988 earthquake, while Moldova endured a severe drought followed by storms with hurricane-force winds. Other countries were set back by the economic disruption and destruction of war, as in Armenia, Azerbaijan, Bosnia-Herzegovina, Georgia, and Tajikistan. Alongside the deleterious effects of such developments, the relatively poor starting point of some countries has tended to exacerbate the adjustment costs associated with the transition. Longer histories of central planning in many of these countries, and lack of basic understanding of market economy principles, have also inhibited the political support for the reform process. Many of these obstacles have gradually been overcome and reforms are under way. There are now visible signs of genuine progress in all but a few countries.

Despite a slow start, the stabilizing effects of tight financial policies are clearly apparent in Moldova and the Kyrgyz Republic. In Moldova, these policies, initiated in late 1993 and steadfastly adhered to since, reduced monthly inflation to less than 1 percent by March 1995 (Chart 30). Real output is expected to bottom out in 1995, harvests permitting (Chart 31). These achievements are particularly impressive in light of the adverse shocks the Moldovan economy has endured since independence, including the armed conflict following the unilateral secession of the Trans-Dniester region and a series of natural disasters. The Kyrgyz Republic, which initiated similar policy measures in late 1993, has reduced monthly inflation to low single-digits and arrested the depreciation in the nominal exchange rate. Real output is expected to begin to turn around during 1995.

Following a relatively early start with reforms, progress with stabilization has lagged in Romania and Bulgaria. Since 1994, Romania has tightened financial policies and significantly slowed inflation, while the recovery of output has continued to strengthen. During the first half of 1995, however, the current account deficit widened considerably, partly due to a surge in imports related to devaluation expectations. In Bulgaria, inflation also slowed considerably during the first half of 1995, but, as in Romania, an ailing banking sector and the failure to enforce hard budget

**Chart 30. Selected Countries in Transition: Inflation**

*(Monthly percent change in consumer price index)*

Inflation has slowed considerably during the first half of 1995.

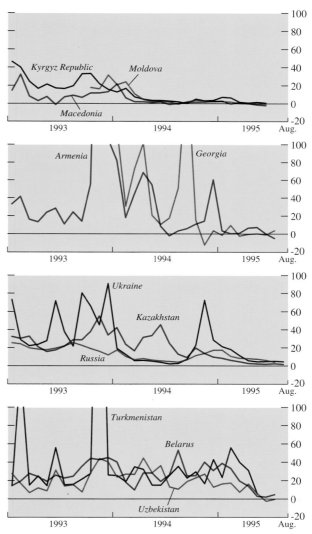

65

## Chart 31.  Selected Countries in Transition: Real GDP[1]

*(1991 = 100)*

The decline of output appears to have bottomed out in a number of countries.

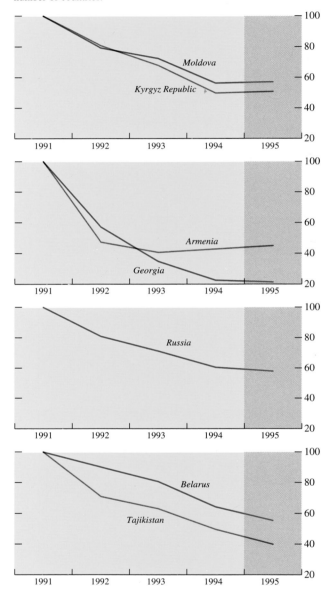

[1]Official national accounts data through 1994 and IMF staff projections (blue shaded areas) for 1995.

constraints on state-owned firms threaten to reverse disinflation.

Clear signs of stabilization have recently become visible in a number of other countries, although progress is still fragile. Following the implementation of tight financial policies, monthly inflation has reached low single-digit levels in Armenia, Azerbaijan, Belarus, Georgia, Kazakhstan, the former Yugoslav Republic of Macedonia, and Uzbekistan. Emerging or existing problems in each of these countries, however, jeopardize the success achieved thus far: in Armenia and Belarus, large capital inflows have complicated monetary policy; in Azerbaijan, output has continued to decline, partly reflecting ongoing disruptions of transportation routes and the conflict in Chechnya; in Georgia, external financing needs remain very high and public finances are particularly weak; in Kazakhstan, where large capital inflows have also made monetary policy more difficult, insufficient financial discipline in the enterprise sector could still derail progress in stabilization; in Uzbekistan, stabilization needs to be solidified and recent efforts to speed up structural reform will need to gain momentum to improve growth prospects; and in the former Yugoslav Republic of Macedonia and in Uzbekistan, the limited scope and slow pace of structural reform continue to dampen growth prospects.

Efforts to bring inflation under control continue in Russia. Notwithstanding the tightening of monetary and fiscal policies since early 1995, inflation barely declined during the second quarter, continuing at a pace exceeding $1\frac{1}{2}$ percent a week, corresponding to annual rates of over 100 percent. Russia's somewhat disappointing inflation performance through mid-1995 is in part due to a decline in the effective reserve requirement ratio, and to the surge in base money resulting from intervention on the foreign exchange market aimed at containing the nominal appreciation of the ruble. Inertia in the inflation process may also reflect lingering doubts about the stance of financial policies, and the memory of earlier failures to stabilize. Meanwhile, there are some signs that output has begun to recover, although measured real GDP is still expected to show a significant further decline in 1995.[49]

Tight financial policies implemented in Ukraine since October 1994 and in Belarus since early 1995 brought inflation down below Russian levels by the second quarter of 1995. In both countries, the nominal exchange rate stopped depreciating while inflation was falling. Inflation nevertheless remained high and the real exchange rate appreciated substantially

---

[49]Official estimates of real GDP probably exaggerate the magnitude of the decline in activity; see Evgeny Gavrilenkov and Vincent Koen, "How Large was the Output Collapse in Russia? Alternative Estimates and Welfare Implications," in *Staff Studies for the World Economic Outlook* (IMF, September 1995), pp. 106–19.

### Box 7. Trade Among Transition Countries

With the collapse of central planning, foreign trade among the transition countries declined sharply during 1989–93. Previous trade patterns determined by central plans became less relevant in an environment of trade based increasingly on comparative advantage. Some of the more rapidly reforming transition economies found new markets for their goods in the west, but many struggled to establish trade links based on market principles with their former partners. Recent evidence suggests that intraregional trade flows have recovered somewhat among a number of transition countries.

Trade with the east picked up in 1994 for some of the central European countries, including the Czech Republic, the Slovak Republic, Hungary, and Poland, albeit from very low levels. The strongest gains were in Poland: in 1994, Polish exports to other transition countries rose by 34 percent, with food and manufactured items accounting for more than half of the total, while Polish imports from transition countries increased 21 percent, mainly in fuels, chemicals, and intermediate manufactured products such as iron and steel (*see table*). Economic recovery in central Europe and multilateral trade arrangements have contributed to the revival of east-east trade. The Central Europe Free Trade Agreement (CEFTA), enacted in 1994 by the Visegrád countries—the Czech and Slovak Republics, Hungary, and Poland—mandates that all trade barriers on industrial products be removed by the year 2001. Slovenia became a full member of CEFTA in 1995. Recently, Poland became the last of the Visegrád countries to sign a separate agreement with Slovenia abolishing all import duties over the next two years.

For the Baltic countries, Russia, and the other countries of the former Soviet Union, the collapse of central planning has meant a gradual disappearance of bilateral interstate barter clearing and settlements through correspondent accounts in central banks. In many countries, these outmoded practices have been replaced by settlements in national currencies through correspondent accounts in commercial banks, forming the basis for expanded international trade.

**Poland: Foreign Trade by Direction**

| | Value (*In millions of dollars*) | Percentage Change from Previous Year | |
| --- | --- | --- | --- |
| | 1994 | 1993 | 1994 |
| Total Exports | 17,240 | 7 | 22 |
| Industrial countries | 12,991 | 12 | 22 |
| Transition countries | 2,499 | –8 | 34 |
| Developing countries | 1,750 | –2 | 6 |
| Total Imports | 21,569 | 18 | 15 |
| Industrial countries | 16,212 | 25 | 13 |
| Transition countries | 3,063 | –2 | 21 |
| Developing countries | 2,294 | 7 | 19 |

Sources: National authorities; and IMF staff estimates.

The Baltic countries have successfully established trade links with other transition countries, especially with one another. In 1994, intra-Baltic trade rose about 30 percent, reflecting the impact of the Baltic Free Trade Agreement, which eliminated all trade barriers, and the geographic proximity of these countries. More recently, in an effort to expand trade relations further, Estonia and Ukraine have been negotiating a bilateral free trade agreement that covers all products.

Trade among the Baltic countries, Russia, and the other countries of the former Soviet Union has also started to pick up. After a number of years of sharp declines, Russian exports to the Baltic countries increased strongly in 1994, as did exports of gas and diesel fuel to Ukraine and Belarus in 1995. In the past two years, Russia has signed free trade agreements with many of the countries of the former Soviet Union waiving import duties and, in some countries, export taxes. In particular, Russia and Belarus have agreed to create a customs union with a common system of external tariffs. Trade among most of the central Asian and Transcaucasian countries has yet to recover owing to ongoing payments difficulties (resulting in mounting arrears) and continued declines in domestic demand and production.

against the U.S. dollar and other western currencies. The exchange rate appears to have remained competitive, however: in May 1995, for example, monthly wages stood at less than $50 in Ukraine and at about $65 in Belarus, compared with $70 in Russia and more than $150 on average in the Baltic countries.

Tajikistan—until recently the last country other than Russia still using the ruble as legal tender—introduced its own currency, the Tajik ruble, in May 1995. A temporary freeze on bank credit and other emergency measures initially helped support the new currency, but the scope for exchange rate stabilization is limited by the paucity of foreign exchange reserves and foreign financial assistance. In recent months, inflation in Turkmenistan has been much higher than in the other

central Asian countries, fueled by an expansionary monetary policy and general hesitation to pursue decisive adjustment and reform policies.

Although success with economic stabilization has varied substantially across the countries less advanced in the transition process, fiscal performance, despite some improvements, remains a serious source of concern in all of these countries (Chart 32).[50] As budget deficits are financed in large part through money

---

[50]Deficits shown in Chart 32 in many cases understate the magnitude of fiscal problems. The cash estimates of government expenditures are typically smaller than the expenditure commitments because of sequestration or the buildup of arrears.

**Chart 32. Selected Countries in Transition: General Government Expenditure, Revenue, and Deficit[1]**
*(In percent of GDP)*

Deficits are generally narrowing but remain large.

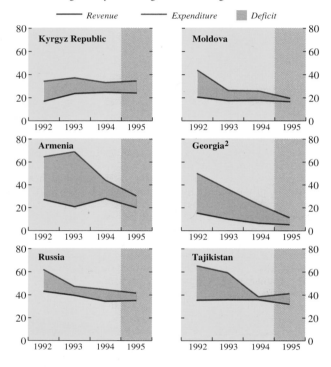

[1]Expenditure equals total expenditure (including extrabudgetary funds) plus net lending; revenue equals total revenue plus grants. Blue shaded areas indicate IMF staff projections.

[2]Central government.

creation, failure to achieve fiscal consolidation threatens to undermine progress in reducing inflation. The persistence of deficits stems from chronic problems impeding revenue collection and expenditure restraint. To some extent, revenue collection can be bolstered by strengthening tax administration, expanding tax coverage to include the emerging private sector, eliminating tax exemptions, and broadening tax bases. In a number of countries, however, the inability to collect sufficient revenues is due more to political than to economic considerations. In Russia, for example, there has been substantial political resistance to increases in taxing oil production, and tax revenues from the natural gas sector have remained low by international standards. Another source of revenue loss in Russia and in many other countries is tax arrears of unprofitable enterprises. These arrears are unlikely to be repaid in full and, in effect, represent financial transfers from the budget to enterprises (Box 8).

Gaining better control over expenditures requires considerable changes in the budget process and in the financial management of government operations. Establishing a treasury system centralizing payment and cash management can markedly improve the allocation of government resources.[51] Although such a system is being introduced in some countries, including Belarus, Kazakhstan, the Kyrgyz Republic, Russia, and Turkmenistan, it will take time before new procedures yield more effective control over spending. Other pressing expenditure issues merit immediate attention. For example, many countries still rely on cash rationing as an expedient to contain expenditures. Running up arrears, however, is an unsustainable way to achieve budget balance. Off-budget expenditure categories, and especially subsidies, are also difficult to control and therefore should be more carefully monitored. Downsizing and restructuring of the civil service, and more effective targeting of social benefits, are areas where budget savings could be realized.

Implementation and perseverance with sound macroeconomic policies are necessary, but not sufficient, to bring about sustained growth. Structural reforms and in particular price liberalization and privatization are also critical for a durable recovery of output. The different experiences of transition countries indicate that delaying these reforms, as with delaying macroeconomic stabilization, at best postpones output declines and is likely to make them larger. The process of structural reform is relatively advanced in Armenia, Georgia, the Kyrgyz Republic, Kazakhstan, and Russia, but severely lagging in the former Yugoslav Republic of Macedonia, Turkmenistan, and Tajikistan.

---

[51]See Teresa Ter-Minassian, Pedro P. Parente, and Pedro Martínez-Mendez, "Setting up a Treasury in Economies in Transition," IMF Working Paper 95/16 (February 1995).

---

**Box 8. Subsidies and Tax Arrears**

The scale of direct budgetary subsidies to enterprises in the transition economies was sharply reduced when prices were liberalized. In the Visegrád countries—the Czech and Slovak Republics, Hungary, and Poland—for example, subsidies dropped from 15–25 percent of GDP before liberalization to 3–5 percent of GDP after liberalization. Large declines in direct subsidies also occurred in most other transition countries.

The curtailment of subsidies paid out of the government budget to firms is one of the ways in which hard budget constraints are established. Progress, however, has been slower than what the contraction of budgetary subsidies may suggest. Other forms of explicit or implicit transfers to enterprises—such as arrears, guarantees for bank credit, interest rate subsidies, licenses, quotas, multiple exchange rate arrangements, and tax exemptions—have not declined to the same extent, or have even increased. In particular, arrears on tax payments (including VAT, excises, profit, and excess wage taxes) and social security payments have risen to levels comparable with those of direct budgetary subsidies.

Because eventual payment of most tax arrears may not be enforced, and because inflation erodes the real value of taxes that are paid late, tax arrears often represent a financial transfer from the budget to the enterprise sector.[1] Around 1993, the stock of tax arrears was about 5–10 percent of annual GDP in the Visegrád countries, while the flow of tax arrears typically hovered in the neighborhood of 2 percent of GDP.[2] The flow of tax arrears also averaged 2 percent of GDP in Russia in 1994.[3] These es-

timates far exceed write-offs of uncollectible taxes in most industrial countries: in the United Kingdom, for example, write-offs are typically about $1/2$ of 1 percent of GDP.

Survey evidence for Hungary and Poland suggests, not surprisingly, that the bulk of the tax arrears are owed by the least profitable firms. Balance sheet data for Polish firms show that the losses of financially distressed enterprises were covered mainly by increases in tax liabilities, and much less by increases in trade or bank credit. Paying suppliers and workers thus appears to be given priority. Because bank credit is scarce, the government ends up absorbing a large portion of the losses. As long as no bankruptcy procedures are initiated by the government or other creditors, enterprises can avoid immediate closure by running up arrears.

The tax authorities may have several reasons not to pursue these firms into bankruptcy. First, their net value may be so low that a lengthy and costly bankruptcy procedure would not yield much revenue for the budget in the short run. Second, local tax authorities may face political pressures to resist layoffs and maintain the status quo; moreover, they may hope or expect that the firms will be rescued by the government, that a debt workout scheme will be implemented by bank creditors, or simply that the firms may become viable in the context of a general economic recovery. Partly reflecting such concerns, a scheme has been introduced in Russia allowing the settlement of tax liabilities by oil companies through deliveries of fuel to the agricultural sector.

A full accounting of government aids to enterprises should thus incorporate tax arrears alongside budgetary subsidies and other quasi-fiscal transfers. Hard budget constraints are increasingly ruling most of the financial relations among banks, enterprises, and households in the transition economies. However, effective budget constraints have proven to be harder to impose on obligations between governments and enterprises. Transfers that have disappeared as subsidies have resurfaced as tax arrears.

[1] Penalties for late payment, insofar as they are paid, mitigate the inflationary erosion of tax receipts.

[2] See Mark E. Schaffer, "Government Subsidies to Enterprises in Central and Eastern Europe: Budgetary Subsidies and Tax Arrears," in *Tax and Benefit Reform in Central and Eastern Europe*, ed. by David M. Newbery (London: Centre for Economic Policy Research, 1995).

[3] See Gilles Alfandari and Mark Schaffer, "On 'Arrears' in Russia," paper presented at a Joint Conference of the World Bank and the Ministry of Economy of the Russian Federation, St. Petersburg, Russia, June 12–13, 1995.

---

Price liberalization is necessary to improve the efficiency of resource allocation. All countries have implemented significant price reforms in the markets for domestic goods and services, even though much remains to be done in a few countries such as Turkmenistan. The prices that remain controlled, typically for selected staples, rents, and other services, are periodically adjusted with the objective of full cost recovery in the longer term. Concomitantly, budgetary subsidies in most countries have declined sharply as a share of total expenditure since 1991.[52] Nevertheless,

numerous off-budget and indirect subsidies persist. In Russia, for example, these subsidies include foreign trade regulations keeping domestic energy prices excessively low, credits carrying below-market interest rates, and tax exemptions. These hidden subsidies are sources of distortion and will need to be cut further as part of the effort to reduce broadly defined fiscal deficits.

The decontrol of domestic prices and quantities must be accompanied by similar measures on the external side. These measures include exchange rate unification and liberalization, abolition of open and hidden import subsidies, harmonization of import tariffs, and elimination or at least streamlining of quotas, licensing requirements, and export tariffs.

[52] See Francesca Recanatini and Adrienne Cheasty, "Subsidies in the Countries of the Former Soviet Union," IMF Working Paper (forthcoming).

Progress in some of these areas has been slow, but reforms are proceeding. The Kyrgyz Republic and Moldova have accepted the obligations of Article VIII of the IMF Articles of Agreement, thus marking their transition to convertibility for current account transactions. Postponing reforms in this area only fosters rent seeking and corruption, generates capital flight, and provides a fertile ground for growth of vested interests strongly opposed to further structural reforms.

Privatizing the bulk of state-owned enterprises and improving enterprise management and corporate efficiency are also essential for these economies to realize their growth potential. In addition, legal structures safeguarding market-based incentives must be established and activated, including legislation governing property rights, contracts, bankruptcy, banking, competition policy, and foreign investment. Russia has made the most headway with privatization. In 1992, the Russian government launched a mass privatization program that in eighteen months shifted ownership of a large proportion of state enterprises to the private sector.[53] Restructuring, however, has typically lagged the transfer of title. While many Russian privatized enterprises are still overstaffed, handicapped by obsolete technologies, and poorly managed, survey evidence points to improvements in product lines, marketing capabilities, employment levels, and wage structures.[54] However, the leasing of land, dwellings, and industrial premises is still often carried out on an administrative basis, giving local authorities scope for discretion and discrimination.[55]

In Kazakhstan, privatization has advanced more slowly, but the ongoing mass coupon privatization scheme is expected to transfer the ownership of at least 150 large- and medium-scale enterprises each month in 1995. Although initially off to a slow start, efforts are now under way to accelerate the privatization process in Armenia, Georgia, the Kyrgyz Republic, the former Yugoslav Republic of Macedonia, and Moldova. Other countries are moving very slowly in this area: in Bulgaria, high unemployment, resistance from state-owned enterprise workers and managers, and a myriad of bureaucratic obstacles have severely hindered progress; similar difficulties exist in Belarus, Croatia, Romania, Turkmenistan, and Ukraine.

Agricultural reforms are equally necessary in all transition countries. The share of agriculture in employment and output is typically much larger than in industrial countries, approaching one third in Moldova and one half in Albania. Overall growth performance will be significantly affected by the speed with which this sector is revitalized and modernized. In many cases, however, the pace of structural change has tended to be slower in agriculture than in industry and services.

## Financial Fragility and Macroeconomic Stability

A sound banking system is indispensable for resources to be efficiently allocated as well as for the protection and encouragement of domestic saving. A healthy financial sector can also contribute to the improvement of corporate governance in the enterprise sector. Through these various channels, financial sector deepening will contribute to higher growth of output and living standards.

Banking systems in most economies in transition, however, are very fragile, as illustrated most recently by crises in Latvia and Russia. Saddled with a legacy of poor assets, but also with more recently committed nonperforming loans, many banks throughout the transition countries either have been closed or are vulnerable to adverse shocks. The fragility of the financial system poses a major risk for the recovery of activity and may exacerbate fiscal imbalances, and thereby increase inflation pressures.

The main functions of financial institutions under central planning involved payments and accounting rather than risk evaluation, allocation of financial resources, and monitoring of borrowers. In the 1980s, the monobank system still prevailing in many countries was split up and some commercial incentives were introduced. In the early 1990s, when the transition to a market economy started in earnest, small banks proliferated and other financial institutions emerged, including private insurance companies, pension funds, mutual funds, security firms, and equity and bond markets.[56] In Poland, for instance, 60 new commercial banks were started in 1990–91. In Latvia, the number of banks soared from 6 in 1990 to 63 by 1993. Russia had over 2,500 banks by the end of 1994.

The pre-existing establishments inherited several handicaps, including a lack of experience in credit operations and an excessive dependence on a small number of state-owned enterprise borrowers. Bad loans carried over from the old regime were less of a

---

[53]See Maxim Boycko, Andrei Shleifer, and Robert Vishny, *Privatizing Russia* (Cambridge: MIT Press, 1995).

[54]Based on a mid-1994 survey of 439 firms; see Qimiao Fan and Bingsong Fang, "Are Russian Enterprises Restructuring?" paper presented at the Joint Conference of the World Bank and the Ministry of Economy of the Russian Federation, Russian Economic Policy and Enterprise Restructuring, St. Petersburg, Russia, June 12–13, 1995.

[55]See Lev Freinkman, "Financial-Industrial Groups in Russia: Emergence of Large Diversified Private Companies," *Communist Economies and Economic Transformation*, Vol. 7 (March 1995), pp. 51–66.

[56]Pyramid investment schemes, such as Caritas in Romania and MMM in Russia, were also among the new institutions.

problem in countries like Poland, where high inflation wiped out their real value, than in countries like the Czech Republic and the Slovak Republic, where inflation was better controlled. The new banks were often set up with a minimal capital base.[57] A number of them—the so-called pocket banks—were little more than the financial subsidiaries of state-owned enterprises, serving as a conduit for directed credits (and sometimes as a channel for tax evasion and capital flight). Prudential regulations and supervision were almost everywhere insufficient to deal with the rapid development of the financial system.

Many banks accumulated new bad loans during the early years of the transition, sometimes at the behest of the government. State-owned enterprises faced with abrupt cuts in demand turned to banks to obtain credit, allowing them to defer adjustment. In the face of a rapidly increasing portfolio of nonperforming loans, banks often preferred to acquiesce, including through the capitalization of interest or the extension of fresh loans to debtors in arrears, rather than to record a loss. In many countries, the agricultural sector managed to continue to obtain soft loans and debt forgiveness from state banks. Often, banks tried to preserve revenue by augmenting spreads, thus exacerbating moral hazard and adverse selection problems, and crowding out some economically viable projects in the new private sector. Outright fraudulent behavior was also rife: bank shareholders, for example, often took out loans worth substantially more than the value of their shares, sometimes with the collusion of bank managers, with little intention of repaying.

As a result, numerous banks became virtually or openly insolvent. In Poland, 15 out of the 73 private banks were near bankrupt in early 1994, and close to 700 of the 1,660 cooperative banks were in crisis or subject to recovery programs. In Russia, the stock of overdue loans increased from 12 percent of bank credit at the end of 1993 to over a third in early 1995, and the central bank has already revoked the licenses of 160 banks since 1993. In Kazakhstan, a recent asset quality survey showed that 40 percent of all loans were effectively lost and should be fully provisioned. In the Kyrgyz Republic, half of the commercial banks had negative net worth in early 1995. In Turkmenistan, 7 out of the 18 commercial banks closed between February and May 1995. In Georgia, 65 of the 229 banks have had their licenses suspended, and all of the state banks have negative net worth. There have been similar developments in Armenia, Bulgaria, Ukraine, and most other countries in transition.

A large-scale banking crisis erupted in Estonia in late 1992 when three of the major commercial banks, holding deposits accounting for almost 40 percent of broad money, suddenly turned out to be insolvent. The three banks were promptly closed down. Two of them were recapitalized with public funds and merged, and the third was liquidated. Although there was not a run on the healthy banks, the public's confidence in the banking system was shaken, causing some disintermediation. In the wake of the banking crisis, and as capital requirements were increased, the number of commercial banks in Estonia halved. A second banking crisis occurred in 1994, when a large bank became insolvent. Despite some equivocation on the part of the authorities, the systemic repercussions of this bank failure were contained as well.

A major banking crisis also surfaced in Latvia. The largest commercial bank collapsed, after a few other banks had gone bankrupt or lost their licenses. This bank in particular had been offering extremely high interest rates to attract money to finance ventures with questionable prospects. The bank failed to complete its 1994 audit, and customers started to withdraw deposits. The government stepped in and took over the management of the bank. The economic court has appointed an administrator to determine the fate of the bank, including possible liquidation. The confidence crisis also affected the foreign exchange market, where there were large capital outflows and calls for a devaluation of the lat before monetary policy was tightened and the situation calmed down.

More recently, signs of the underlying weaknesses in Russia's banking system have become visible. During the last week of August 1995, the inability of a few banks to honor interbank obligations led to a sharp rise in overnight interest rates to as high as 1,000 percent a year and to a virtual standstill in interbank trading. In response, the government stepped in to provide liquidity, but emphasized that this action was a temporary measure and that the government would not directly intervene to support any ailing bank. In the aftermath of the crisis, interbank market activity has gradually resumed, starting with trading among a group of large banks, and interest rates have generally returned to previously prevailing levels. By early September, the payments problem appeared to be confined to a small number of banks. Nevertheless, these events have highlighted the need to improve banking supervision and accelerate the structural reform of the banking system.

Preventing such crises and the associated macroeconomic disruptions requires a number of precautionary measures. Supervision—both on-site examination and off-site monitoring—needs to be considerably strengthened in virtually all transition countries. Accounting standards have to be adapted so that enterprise performance can be assessed on the basis of market criteria. Banks should be allowed to deduct provisions for bad loans for tax purposes. Minimum capital requirements should be raised, which would help to consolidate an often overly fragmented bank-

---

[57]In Georgia, the legal minimum paid-in capital amounted to only $1,300 in March 1994.

ing sector.[58] Deposit insurance is desirable to protect savers but should not be unconditional and unlimited, so as to encourage caution on the part of depositors. Insolvent banks ought to be liquidated rather than kept alive through implicit or explicit . subsidization schemes. State guarantees on loans should be avoided because of the potential cost to the budget and to ensure that loans finance economically viable projects. Limits on insider lending need to be tightened, and malfeasance investigated more thoroughly and punished. Finally, the entry of foreign banks should be facilitated to spur the modernization of banking practices in domestic institutions.

Banking crises once they emerge should be dealt with promptly and vigorously, and in a way that will prevent their recurrence. As the experience of Estonia has shown, taking a tough line and proceeding with liquidations need not lead to a broader systemic crisis. Recapitalization in particular should be conducted as a one-time rescue operation and not as a prelude to future bailouts, as turned out to be the case in Hungary where several rounds of capital injections took place at considerable budgetary cost. To the extent possible, recapitalization should be combined with privatization. When government rescue operations involve state banks, recapitalization should be accompanied by commercialization. To safeguard financial stability, the fiscal costs of capital replenishment should lead to added restraint in other public expenditures, as was done in the former Czechoslovakia.[59]

Successful crisis management also requires that the central bank, or, more generally, the supervisory authorities, be given the legal powers to act decisively. Close coordination between the central bank and the government is also needed. Crisis management will be more effective the better is the authorities' prior knowledge of the dimension and distribution of the bad loans problem, including the quality of collateral, the extent of state guarantees, and the magnitude of the provisioning associated with nonperforming loans.

The soundness of the financial system also has implications for corporate efficiency in the nonfinancial sector. Weak banks are not in a position to act as agents of restructuring and of strengthened management principles in nonfinancial enterprises. Shaky investment funds are also unlikely to impose much discipline on enterprise managers. Conversely, for financial institutions to monitor enterprises effectively, the incentives facing enterprises need to be changed. For example, large state enterprises should

no longer be led to expect that they can induce the state to force banks to roll over loans that are not serviced. Indeed, reforms in the banking sector alone are insufficient to ensure financial discipline in the nonfinancial sector. Structural reform efforts must also include improvements in corporate efficiency through comprehensive enterprise reforms and social safety net restructuring. Reforms in these areas will, in turn, help to strengthen banks by increasing the number of economically viable borrowers.

* * *

Half a decade into the transition, the main challenge facing the countries more advanced on the path to a market economy is to safeguard macroeconomic stability while maintaining or, where possible, increasing the momentum of structural reform. While substantial stabilization has been broadly achieved, numerous rigidities remain that could undermine disinflation and growth performance. Particularly worrisome in this regard are signs of backtracking, as observed in the Slovak Republic with respect to privatization. It is also important to streamline social safety nets further, for fiscal as well as for efficiency reasons. The prospect of closer relations with the European Union, and perhaps eventual membership, provides added encouragement for many of these countries to persevere with their reform efforts.

While much progress with stabilization has been accomplished recently by most of the other countries, the risk of setbacks is higher than in the more advanced countries. The main challenge, therefore, is to make stabilization stick, particularly by persevering with fiscal adjustment efforts. The recent quickening of structural change noticeable in a number of these countries is encouraging. Sufficient and timely external financial assistance is also crucial, particularly in countries such as Armenia and Georgia that have undertaken courageous adjustment policies, but where the success of these policies is contingent on external assistance.

In most of the transition countries, structural change in financial systems has been substantial, helped by assistance from international institutions. Nonetheless, financial sector reforms still have a long way to go. Financial fragility poses a major risk in many countries. The way bad debt problems are handled is key; covering up bad debts by rolling over hopeless loans will increase the ultimate costs of addressing this problem. A large-scale banking crisis would spoil the fruits of past adjustment efforts and intensify pressures to soften budget constraints. It is essential to recognize and cope with the issue of nonperforming assets early on, to tackle the distortions contributing to the weakness of bank balance sheets, and possibly to spread out the implied financial burden over time, rather than to let the problems grow into a full-fledged crisis.

---

[58]Higher capital requirements may reveal fragilities in the banking system, as in the Czech Republic in 1994, but do not cause them.

[59]For a survey of the measures taken in 23 transition countries, see Michael S. Borish, Millard F. Long, and Michel Noël, *Restructuring Banks and Enterprises: Recent Lessons from Transition Countries*, World Bank Discussion Papers No. 279 (January 1995).

# Annex

# Exchange Rate Effects of Fiscal Consolidation

The connection between fiscal policy and exchange rates is not obvious from the experience of a number of industrial countries. In the United States, the increase in the fiscal deficit in the early 1980s was associated with a strong appreciation of the dollar. Similarly, the shift in Germany from a balanced fiscal position in 1989 to a large deficit in the early 1990s in the wake of unification was accompanied by a real appreciation of the deutsche mark. In Japan, the shift from a substantial structural surplus to a deficit in the general government budget between 1990 and 1994 coincided with a large appreciation of the yen. However, in other industrial countries such as Finland, Italy, and Sweden, fiscal deficits in the early 1990s have tended to be associated with depreciating real exchange rates. Fiscal expansions in France in the early 1980s and in Canada in the mid-1980s were also accompanied by exchange rate depreciations. And the significant fiscal consolidation undertaken by the German authorities during the past three years has not been associated with a weakening of the deutsche mark.

These different experiences suggest that the impact of changes in fiscal policy on nominal and real exchange rates is ambiguous. With a large number of industrial countries undertaking or planning substantial fiscal consolidation, it is useful to explore the factors that may account for this ambiguity. As discussed in the first section of this Annex, the uncertainty regarding the theoretical direction of the effect of fiscal policy on exchange rates relates mainly to the short-run impact. By contrast, the theoretical direction of the longer-run effects of a sustained change in the fiscal position, which are described in the second section, appears to be more clear cut. The third section summarizes some of the empirical evidence.

The relationship between fiscal policy and exchange rates is mainly addressed from the perspective of industrial countries. Although the framework used in the analysis is applicable to developing and transition countries, they are not discussed because in many cases they share characteristics that are quite different from industrial countries. For example, many developing and transition economies peg their exchange rates to other currencies, enjoy only limited access to international capital markets, and tend to monetize

fiscal deficits to a much greater extent than industrial countries.[1]

## Short-Run Effects of Changes in Government Budgets

The experiences of the United States, Japan, and Germany noted above are consistent with the predictions of the standard Mundell-Fleming model: a fiscal expansion combined with an unchanged stance of monetary policy leads to a real appreciation of the domestic currency in a world with high capital mobility. In this model, domestic prices are assumed to be fixed, interest rates are determined in domestic money markets, and expectations are static in the sense that current economic conditions and policies are not expected to change. This last assumption implies that net capital flows are simply a function of the interest rate differential because exchange rates are not expected to change in the future. Finally, the exchange rate floats freely and reserves are unchanged, so the current account is equal to net capital flows.

A fiscal expansion—either through an increased level of government expenditures or a reduction in taxes—raises domestic demand and, with unchanged money growth, leads to a rise in domestic interest rates. The higher level of demand increases imports, implying a deterioration in the current account, and the higher interest rates generate a capital inflow that finances the change in the current account. The net effect on the exchange rate depends on the degree of capital mobility. In the extreme case of perfect capital mobility, the domestic interest rate cannot differ from that abroad and consequently the fiscal expansion would have no impact on the domestic interest rate. The real exchange rate must therefore appreciate so that the deterioration in net exports matches the demand stimulus from the expansionary fiscal policy. Conversely, with zero capital mobility the exchange rate must depreciate so as to keep net exports unchanged. As capital is highly mobile among the industrial countries and comparable financial instruments

---

This annex was prepared by Peter Clark and Douglas Laxton.

[1]See Rebelo and Végh (forthcoming) for a discussion of the exchange rate effects of fiscal consolidation in the context of stabilization programs in developing countries.

(in terms of maturity, tax status, default risk, and so forth) issued in the currencies of these countries appear to be very close substitutes, it is reasonable to assume that the interest rate effect dominates. Consequently the fiscal expansion will tend to produce an appreciation of the nominal exchange rate.[2] The real exchange rate will also tend to appreciate if prices respond with a lag to the increase in domestic demand.

This result is based on a number of assumptions. First, monetary and fiscal policies are independent and the possibility of future monetization of government debt is ignored. If this assumption is not valid and the monetary authorities fully accommodate the fiscal expansion, then the standard result may no longer hold. Second, as noted above, expectations are static: the current level of the exchange rate does not depend on expectations of the future spot exchange rate, or, more precisely, the expected evolution of future policies does not affect the future spot rate. Violation of any of these two assumptions could account for the episodes described above in which fiscal expansions were associated with exchange rate depreciations. Third, the standard Mundell-Fleming model does not allow for a government intertemporal budget constraint, which implies that government bonds are perceived as net wealth by the private sector, and takes no account of the implications of a growing stock of liabilities to foreigners. For this reason, and because the model is static, there is no difference between the short- and long-run effects on the exchange rate of a change in fiscal policy. As described below, these effects are likely to be in different directions.

Relaxing the last two assumptions does not necessarily overturn the standard result. This can be seen in the simulation reported in Table 16, which shows the effects of an illustrative fiscal contraction in the United States using the Fund's multicountry macro-econometric model (MULTIMOD), which incorporates intertemporal budget constraints and forward-looking expectations. In this framework, the nominal exchange rate is approximately determined by the uncovered interest parity condition, whereby the interest rate differential is equal to the expected change in the exchange rate. In the scenario reported in Table 16, the public is assumed to know the future path of fiscal policy. Because the government announcement that there will be a permanent reduction in the ratio of government debt to GDP is assumed to be fully credible, the public immediately adjusts its economic actions and plans to take account of the change in policy. Finally, the effects of changes in saving and investment on the capital stock and domestic and foreign wealth are taken into account in a consistent fashion.

In the illustrative scenario reported in Table 16, fiscal policy is tightened to reduce government debt in the United States by 10 percent of baseline GDP.[3] This is accomplished by increasing the tax rate on household income by 1 percent for a period of ten years beginning in 1996. Thereafter, the tax rate is reduced to stabilize the debt-to-GDP ratio at a level 10 percent below the baseline. This fiscal action, which results in an improvement in the general government balance of about 1 percent, has a short-term contractionary effect on consumption and total demand.[4] As the monetary authorities are assumed to keep the monetary aggregates close to their baseline values, the decline in aggregate demand results in a fall in interest rates. The standard Mundell-Fleming result—a short-run nominal and real depreciation—reflects the uncovered interest parity assumption: as interest rates in the United States fall relative to those in the rest of the world, there must be an initial fall in the dollar so that the expected future appreciation of the currency offsets the lower nominal interest rate. The lower real interest rate "crowds in" real domestic investment. Furthermore, the fiscal-induced reduction in domestic demand, combined with the real exchange rate depreciation, improves the current account balance. These two channels more than offset the decline in consumption (relative to baseline) by 1998, and real output and the stock of capital are permanently higher.

This stylized scenario describes a ceteris paribus result that does not necessarily take account of the initial conditions prevailing at the time of the assumed change in fiscal policy. The depreciation of the U.S. dollar since late 1994, for example, may already reflect the anticipation of fiscal actions in the latter half of 1995 and beyond. In this case, the exchange rate may not depreciate further once these fiscal actions are actually announced or implemented. An alternative

---

[2]This result is qualitatively the same irrespective of whether the fiscal expansion results from a cut in taxes or a rise in government expenditures. The magnitude of the effect will be larger, however, if the same change in the budget position is achieved with an increase in expenditures rather than a cut in taxes. The quantitative effect also depends on whether the taxes are distortionary or nondistortionary. Finally, in models that distinguish between traded and non-traded goods, changes in public spending on nontradables rather than tradables have different effects on the relative price of these two goods, as discussed in Reinhart (1991).

[3]The magnitude of the fiscal consolidation measures in this scenario is only illustrative, as the reduction in government deficits and debt that are needed in many industrial countries are significantly larger than assumed here. If fiscal consolidation were undertaken simultaneously in a number of countries, the impacts on exchange rates would be considerably smaller.

[4]The scenario in Table 16 does not include any positive confidence effects on investment or consumption. These could arise from perceptions of an improved investment climate and lower future taxes. In principle, such positive domestic expenditure effects could outweigh the initial negative fiscal impulse, resulting in a positive impact on domestic demand. In this case, the domestic demand effect, as opposed to expectation effects related to interest premiums discussed below, might lead to an exchange rate appreciation in the short run. For a discussion of possible short-run aggregate demand effects of fiscal policy, see Box 2 in the May 1995 *World Economic Outlook*, pp. 24–25.

**Table 16. United States: Effects of Fiscal Consolidation on the Exchange Rate**
*(Percentage deviation from baseline unless otherwise noted)*

| | 1996 | 1997 | 1998 | 1999 | 2000 | 2001 | 2002 | Long Run[1] |
|---|---|---|---|---|---|---|---|---|
| Nominal effective exchange rate[2] | −2.7 | −2.8 | −2.8 | −2.6 | −2.4 | −2.2 | −1.9 | 0.4 |
| Real effective exchange rate[2] | −2.2 | −2.5 | −2.6 | −2.6 | −2.4 | −2.2 | −2.1 | 0.3 |
| Real GDP | −0.7 | −0.2 | 0.1 | 0.3 | 0.3 | 0.3 | 0.2 | 0.2 |
| Capital Stock | 0.1 | 0.2 | 0.3 | 0.4 | 0.6 | 0.7 | 0.7 | 0.8 |
| Inflation (GDP deflator)[3] | −0.3 | −0.4 | −0.2 | 0.0 | 0.0 | 0.0 | 0.0 | 0.0 |
| Long-term interest rate[3] | −0.3 | −0.4 | −0.4 | −0.4 | −0.4 | −0.4 | −0.4 | −0.1 |
| Real long-term interest rate[3] | −0.2 | −0.3 | −0.4 | −0.3 | −0.3 | −0.4 | −0.4 | −0.1 |
| General government balance/GDP[3] | 0.9 | 1.1 | 1.2 | 1.2 | 1.2 | 1.3 | 1.3 | 0.5 |
| Government debt/GDP[3] | −0.5 | −1.6 | −2.8 | −4.0 | −5.0 | −6.0 | −7.0 | −10.0 |
| Current account balance/GDP[3] | 0.2 | 0.3 | 0.3 | 0.4 | 0.4 | 0.4 | 0.4 | 0.4 |
| Net foreign liabilities/GDP[3] | −0.0 | −0.3 | −0.6 | −1.0 | −1.4 | −1.8 | −2.1 | −7.0 |
| Contribution to real GDP | | | | | | | | |
| Real consumption[3] | −1.2 | −1.0 | −0.9 | −0.7 | −0.7 | −0.7 | −0.7 | 0.2 |
| Real investment[3] | 0.1 | 0.2 | 0.3 | 0.3 | 0.3 | 0.3 | 0.3 | 0.1 |
| Real trade balance[3] | 0.5 | 0.6 | 0.7 | 0.7 | 0.7 | 0.6 | 0.6 | −0.1 |

[1]The estimates for the long run reflect the permanent effects of the shock measured as the difference between the steady-state solution of the model with and without the shock.
[2]A negative figure denotes a depreciation of the domestic currency.
[3]In percentage points.

way to look at this issue is to note that the recent dollar depreciation is expected to improve the U.S. current account balance substantially from its currently prevailing level. To accommodate this improvement in the current account, there must be a corresponding improvement in the national savings and investment balance. If there were no improvement in public saving (through fiscal consolidation), then either private saving would need to rise (for reasons that are not clear) or investment would need to be curtailed (presumably through a rise in interest rates). Alternatively, excess demand pressures in the U.S. economy, resulting from the combination of continued growth of domestic demand and a highly competitive dollar, might push up U.S. inflation and reverse the recent real depreciation of the U.S. dollar. In other words, the anticipation of further fiscal consolidation (and an improvement in public saving) may already be embodied in the current real exchange rate of the dollar. Thus, despite the theoretical prediction that an anticipated fiscal consolidation will result in an exchange rate depreciation, the ex post link between these two variables may not be apparent.

Moreover, in applying economic theory to the foreign exchange value of the U.S. dollar (or other national currencies), it is important to remember that the world has more than two important currencies. During the past year and a half, the U.S. dollar has depreciated considerably against the Japanese yen and the deutsche mark and European currencies closely linked to the deutsche mark; it has held steady or appreciated against the currencies of most of the United States' other leading trading partners.

## Interest Premiums

The illustrative scenario discussed above also does not allow for the possibility of changes in the perceived riskiness of assets in the country implementing the fiscal consolidation measures. Indeed, countries with large budget deficits and public debts have often experienced an increase in interest rates, downward pressure on exchange rates, and an improvement in the current account. By requiring higher yields on government debt in countries with large deficits and by shifting to investments in other countries, investors have frequently signaled their lack of trust in both fiscal and monetary policies.[5] Given that deteriorating actual and prospective fiscal positions and widening interest differentials have at times been associated with depreciating exchange rates, it is possible that the adoption of strong, front-loaded, credible fiscal consolidation measures could narrow interest differentials, appreciate the currency, and—possibly—worsen the current account position.

Standard intertemporal models such as MULTIMOD do not incorporate links between fiscal policy and exchange rates stemming from changes in risk premiums. The ways in which fiscal stabilization may raise investors' demand for domestic assets, and hence appreciate the domestic currency, can be summarized

---

[5]In Finland, Italy, Spain, and Sweden, for example, high fiscal deficit ratios were associated with particularly large interest rate increases in 1994. For a discussion of these developments, see Box 1 in the October 1994 *World Economic Outlook*, pp. 16–18.

with reference to a log-linear version of the standard covered interest parity condition. This condition states that the interest differential between assets denominated in different currencies and issued on the same terms in a common offshore center is approximately equal to the difference between the (log) spot exchange rate ($X$) and the (log) forward exchange rate ($F$) for delivery on the date corresponding to the interest rate.

$$i_E - i_E^* = X - F, \qquad (1)$$

where the subscript $E$ denotes Euro- (i.e., offshore) rates, the asterisk denotes foreign variables, and exchange rates are expressed as units of foreign currency per unit of domestic currency.

The interest parity condition can be rewritten in a form that is useful to discuss a variety of possible determinants of the interest differential, defined as the spread required by international investors to hold domestic assets rather than offshore assets denominated in foreign currency:

$$i_D - i_E^* = \left[X^e - F\right] + \left[i_D - i_E\right] + \left[X - X^e\right], \quad (2)$$

where $i_D$ is the interest rate paid *domestically* on assets with the same maturity as those earning $i_E$ offshore, and $X^e$ is the spot exchange rate expected by investors over the same term.

This expression decomposes the interest differential between domestic assets (issued in domestic currency in the domestic market) and foreign assets (issued in foreign currency in the Euromarket) into three components. It thereby provides a way of accounting for the large gap between domestic interest rates in currencies such as the Italian lira and interest rates on comparable instruments denominated in deutsche mark. The first component, $(X^e - F)$, is the difference between the expected future spot exchange rate and the forward rate at the same maturity. This is the properly defined measure of the foreign exchange risk premiums: the compensation required by risk-averse investors to hold an asset whose only risk depends on it being issued in a particular currency. Although empirically satisfactory structural models of exchange risk premiums have proven elusive, ad hoc empirical models and insights gained from theoretical models suggest that risk premiums on the currencies of industrial countries are unlikely to exceed 1 percent in absolute terms.[6]

The second component of the interest differential, $(i_D - i_E)$, which has come to be known in the literature as "political risk," encompasses a variety of factors linked to domestic policies that may drive a wedge between yields on domestic and offshore assets issued in the *same currency* and with the same maturity and other characteristics. Political risk has traditionally been associated with the possibility of capital controls but may be extended to include "default risk" associated with outright default, debt consolidation, or the possibility of taxation of interest income and financial wealth.

Empirically, this source of risk is likely to be small, at least in the case of industrial countries. A recent study by Lane and Symansky (1993), for example, estimated political risk in Italy at the height of the ERM crisis in 1992 to be less than 80 basis points (on an annualized basis), with noncrisis values ranging from 5 to 30 basis points. These estimates were obtained by comparing bonds issued by the Italian government in foreign currency with those issued by (presumed) default-free agents, such as the World Bank, for assets with maturities of twenty to thirty years. Political risk on shorter maturities is likely to be even smaller. Similar results were found by Alesina and others (1992), who found a strong correlation between the size of public indebtedness and the spread between public and private rates of return, but very small default premiums of less than 40 basis points in most cases.

The last component of the interest differential examined here, $(X - X^e)$, is the expectation of currency depreciation. This can reflect a variety of anticipated sources of nominal and real shocks, including changes in equilibrium real exchange rates resulting from demand and productivity shifts or expected changes in economic policies. Based on the general finding that the first two components of the interest differential appear to be fairly small, this third component of the interest differential would therefore appear to be the largest. Direct survey data for exchange rate expectations, such as reported by Consensus Economics, Inc., for example, often indicate significant expected depreciations. Much of the expected depreciation may, of course, simply reflect anticipation of higher inflation than in other countries.

Based on this taxonomy, one can envisage several channels through which changes in fiscal policy can lead to exchange rate changes, all of them implying that fiscal consolidation may result in a short-run appreciation of the home currency. First, debt reduction may cause a fall in the foreign exchange risk premium by reducing the relative stock of domestically issued liabilities held in the portfolio of both domestic and foreign investors. With assets imperfect substitutes and investors risk averse, the required rate of return on these liabilities declines with a reduction in the relative size of the liabilities issued by the government.

---

[6]For estimates of the magnitude of foreign exchange risk premiums, see Frankel (1982, 1988) and Svensson (1992).

**Table 17. Italy: Effects of Fiscal Consolidation and a Reduced Interest Premium on the Exchange Rate**

*(Percentage deviation from baseline unless otherwise noted)*

|  | 1996 | 1997 | 1998 | 1999 | 2000 | 2001 | 2002 |
|---|---|---|---|---|---|---|---|
| Nominal effective exchange rate[1] | 9.3 | 7.5 | 6.6 | 6.3 | 6.6 | 6.9 | 7.0 |
| Real effective exchange rate[1] | 4.5 | 3.1 | 2.1 | 1.6 | 1.4 | 1.4 | 1.3 |
| Real GDP | −0.4 | 0.2 | 0.3 | 1.0 | 1.6 | 1.9 | 2.0 |
| Capital stock | 0.4 | 1.3 | 2.2 | 3.1 | 4.0 | 4.9 | 5.7 |
| Inflation (GDP deflator)[2] | −1.1 | −1.1 | −1.1 | −0.9 | −0.5 | −0.3 | −0.3 |
| Long-term interest rate[2] | −2.1 | −2.4 | −2.6 | −2.6 | −2.4 | −2.4 | −2.4 |
| Real long-term interest rate[2] | −1.3 | −1.8 | −2.0 | −2.1 | −1.9 | −1.8 | −1.9 |
| General government balance/GDP[2] | 0.8 | 1.9 | 3.5 | 3.7 | 3.5 | 3.3 | 3.3 |
| Government debt/GDP[2] | 1.0 | −0.4 | −2.7 | −6.2 | −9.5 | −12.4 | −14.9 |
| Current account balance/GDP[2] | −0.2 | −0.9 | −0.8 | −1.2 | −1.4 | −1.4 | −1.3 |
| Net foreign liabilities/GDP[2] | −0.2 | 0.7 | 1.5 | 2.7 | 4.0 | 5.2 | 6.3 |
| Contribution to real GDP |  |  |  |  |  |  |  |
| Real consumption[2] | −0.4 | −0.3 | −0.7 | 0.1 | 0.7 | 0.9 | 0.8 |
| Real investment[2] | 1.0 | 1.9 | 2.2 | 2.4 | 2.5 | 2.5 | 2.5 |
| Real trade balance[2] | −1.0 | −1.5 | −1.2 | −1.5 | −1.6 | −1.5 | −1.3 |

[1]A positive figure denotes an appreciation of the domestic currency.
[2]In percentage points.

Debt reduction may also reduce the volatility of future exchange rates around their expected values. A lower debt stock may reduce uncertainty about taxation and other policies undertaken to service debt, reduce the likelihood of a financial crisis, and—most fundamentally—reduce the exposure of the domestic economy to world shocks (e.g., interest rate shocks). If a reduction in macroeconomic uncertainty causes a reduction in the systemic component of exchange rate risks, investors' demand for the home currency may increase, thus allowing *both* a fall in domestic interest rates *and* an appreciation of the currency. These effects are only likely to occur if the fiscal measures are implemented on a durable basis and are viewed as such by investors.

The second channel is that a lower outstanding stock of debt may lead investors to reduce the perceived likelihood of default, including the imposition of restrictions on capital mobility to prevent capital outflows, or of taxes on interest income and financial wealth. As "default" and "political" risk premiums fall, the domestic currency may appreciate in response to the increase in demand for domestic instruments.

A lower actual and prospective stock of government debt may also lead investors to lower their expectation of the likelihood of an eventual monetization of debt, thereby mitigating inflation expectations and exchange rate devaluation expectations. In this case, the decline in the interest differential reflects a fall in $(X - X^e)$, that is, a reduction in the expected future spot rate that exceeds the appreciation of the current spot rate. Note that the forward-looking nature of exchange rates does not require monetization to take place over the maturity of the forward contract: an anticipated future change in monetary policy and inflation will af-

fect the whole stream of exchange rates, even spot rates prior to the actual policy change (though with a decreasing intensity that reflects discounting). For there to be a decline in the interest differential and an exchange rate appreciation, the fiscal improvement must be implemented on a sustained basis.

One way to gauge the potential size of these various types of interest premiums is to look at the current configuration of long-term interest rate differentials of various assets. The low level of U.S. long-term interest rates relative to Germany suggests that there is currently little, if any, interest premium for the U.S. dollar vis-à-vis the deutsche mark. A stronger case could be made for an interest premium on the lira, given the current spread of about 500 basis points between Italian long-term interest rates and comparable German rates and the recent experience whereby exchange rates and, to a lesser extent, interest rates have shown a positive response to renewed commitments to greater fiscal discipline. Long-term interest rates in Sweden and Canada also appear to embody interest premiums.

As noted above, changes in interest premiums of this kind are not an integral part of most standard open economy macroeconomic models such as MULTI-MOD. Such changes can, however, be introduced into the model as an exogenous shock to gain a sense of the likely effects. Table 17 presents an illustrative MULTIMOD scenario of a fiscal contraction combined with a decline in the interest rate differential. This stylized scenario is discussed with reference to Italy, although the size of the fiscal and interest rate shocks are arbitrary, and the actual change in interest differentials associated with fiscal adjustment could be substantially different from that assumed in the simulation. Nevertheless, this scenario demonstrates how the effects of fiscal policy could be substantially different from the standard dynamic Mundell-Fleming result if there are substantial changes in interest premiums, while maintaining the basic underlying theoretical framework.

It is assumed in the scenario that the Italian authorities implement fiscal consolidation measures that gradually reduce the debt stock by 30 percent of GDP.[7] This is assumed to reduce the premium on Italian lira assets by 250 basis points. In this case, long-term interest rates in Italy fall by about 240 basis points and the nominal effective exchange rate appreciates by an average of about 7 percent. Although there is a negative fiscal impact on domestic demand, the decline in interest rates tends to increase investment and consumption. Combined with the appreciation of the real exchange rate, the external position worsens. Thus, a fiscal contraction combined with a decline in the interest premium can result in an increase in output, an appreciation of the currency, and, in the short run, a deterioration in the current account.

Thus, in countries where large interest differentials suggest the presence of substantial interest premiums, reductions in the fiscal deficit may, in principle, bring about an immediate appreciation of the domestic currency. This is an exception to the standard theoretical case whereby fiscal consolidation leads, ceteris paribus, to a short-run depreciation of the currency. Comparing the two cases, it is noteworthy that in the standard case, fiscal consolidation and exchange rate depreciation are associated with a short-run improvement in the current account; whereas in the reduced interest premium case, fiscal consolidation and exchange rate appreciation are associated with a short-run deterioration in the current account. Thus, economic theory suggests that, in the short run, it is unlikely that fiscal consolidation would lead, ceteris paribus, to exchange rate appreciation and to improvement in the current account, unless the fiscal consolidation is combined with monetary tightening and with a significant fall in output.

## Long-Term Implications of Fiscal Consolidation

The standard Mundell-Fleming model does not provide an adequate framework for examining the long-term implications of fiscal consolidation because this model does not account for the dynamic effects of reductions in the stock of government debt. Indeed, as

shown below, models that incorporate the dynamic effects of fiscal policy generally indicate that the real exchange rate will appreciate in the long run in response to fiscal consolidation, which brings a permanent reduction in the stock of government debt and a permanent improvement in a country's net foreign asset position.

In a long-run steady-state equilibrium, when the ratio of a country's net foreign assets (or liabilities) to GDP is stable, the country will receive (or pay) net income on its international asset (or liability) position that is a constant fraction of its GDP. The payments received by a net creditor country will finance a steady-state trade deficit with imports exceeding exports. Conversely, payments by net a debtor country to its creditors will require a steady-state trade surplus. This steady-state equilibrium condition can be represented by the following equation.[8]

$$\frac{CA}{Y} = \left(\frac{g}{1+g}\right)\left(\frac{NFA}{Y}\right), \qquad (3)$$

where $CA$ is the current account balance, $Y$ is nominal GDP, $NFA$ is the country's net foreign asset position, and $g$ is the growth rate (divided by 100) of all nominal variables. For example, if all nominal variables in the economy are growing at 5 percent and net foreign assets are equal to 100 percent of GDP, the current account surplus must be equal to about 5 percent of GDP. Conversely, if the country is a debtor country, it would be running a current account deficit in long-run equilibrium. A country can only remain a debtor or a creditor in the long run if its deficit or surplus grows at the same rate as nominal income.

The current account can be expressed as the sum of two main components: the net interest payments received from foreigners, $r\,NFA_{t-1}$, and the nominal trade balance, $TB$. Then the current account equation becomes

$$\frac{CA}{Y} = \frac{r}{1+g}\,\frac{NFA}{Y} + \frac{TB}{Y}, \qquad (4)$$

because $NFA_{-1}$ is equal to $NFA/(1+g)$. Substituting equation (3) into equation (4) gives

$$\frac{TB}{Y} = \left(\frac{g-r}{1+g}\right)\frac{NFA}{Y}. \qquad (5)$$

---

[7]Although the debt stock falls in the first year of the simulation, the larger percentage decline in nominal income results in a rise in the debt-to-GDP ratio.

[8]Equation (1) follows from the balance of payments condition that the current account balance ($CA$) has to be equal to the change in net foreign assets ($CA = \Delta NFA = NFA - NFA_{-1}$). If $g$ is the steady-state growth rate of all nominal variables, then ($NFA/NFA_{-1} - 1) = g$ or $NFA_{-1} = NFA/(1+g)$. Substituting this last expression into the $CA$ equation and dividing by nominal GDP gives equation (3).

Under the condition that the real interest rate is greater than the real growth rate of the economy, the term in parentheses in equation 5 will be negative, which implies that countries that have positive net claims on the rest of the world ($NFA > 0$) will be running a trade deficit, while countries that are debtor countries ($NFA < 0$) will have trade surpluses.[9] In other words, net creditor countries will receive a permanent flow of interest payments from the rest of the world and thus will be able to maintain a level of imports that is consistently higher than exports.

The discussion above is helpful in shedding light on the long-run results reported in Table 16. The last column shows that a fiscal contraction that reduces the long-run level of government debt to GDP will increase the country's net foreign asset-to-GDP ratio, or, equivalently, reduce the ratio of its net foreign liabilities to GDP. The increase in net interest receipts means that a higher trade deficit can be sustained in the long run. In the long run, an appreciation of the real exchange rate is required to generate the adjustment in trade flows. As the United States is a net debtor internationally, the rise in total national saving results in a reduction in the ratio of its net foreign liability to income. As can be seen from equation 5 above, this eventually would imply lower net interest payments to foreigners and a smaller trade surplus with the rest of the world. To induce a smaller trade surplus (higher imports or lower exports, or both) with the rest of the world, the real exchange rate must eventually appreciate.

In the simulation reported in Table 16, the real exchange rate depreciates in the short run, but starts to appreciate by the fifth year. In the long run, the real value of the exchange rate is higher relative to its baseline value by 0.3 percent. As discussed above, this appreciation is necessary to sustain a higher level of net imports; as interest obligations to foreigners are reduced, there will be a larger sustainable net flow of goods to U.S. consumers. And under normal assumptions about demand and supply curves, this can only come about if the relative price of these goods falls.

The different short- and long-run exchange rate effects of fiscal consolidation reflect the same macroeconomic adjustment mechanism at work. The short-run real depreciation arises from the fact that aggregate demand for domestic output is initially below capacity output as a result of the fiscal action, and consequently the relative price of domestic output (the real exchange rate) falls. Over time, however, the

increased national saving that results from fiscal consolidation in the absence of full Ricardian equivalence leads to a higher stock of domestic and foreign assets held by domestic residents. This increase in domestic wealth results in higher consumption (relative to baseline) and a rise in overall total demand (in real terms) for domestic output that exceeds capacity output. This excess demand is equilibrated by a rise in the relative price, that is, by a real appreciation.

## Empirical Evidence on the Exchange Rate Effects of Fiscal Policy

Given the theoretical possibility that changes in fiscal policy could either weaken or strengthen the currency, it is not surprising that empirical studies of the linkages are not uniform in their findings. The empirical results discussed below relate to two major episodes of recent exchange rate changes: the appreciation and subsequent depreciation of the U.S. dollar during the 1980s, and expected changes in the parities of selected ERM currencies. There is also a brief discussion of the experience of developing countries.

Several studies have found a positive link between fiscal expansion and the exchange value of the U.S. dollar. Throop (1989), for example, used a model in which the short-run real value of the U.S. dollar over the period 1973–88 is explained by real long-term interest rate differentials, and the long-run expected real value is determined by domestic and foreign structural fiscal balances relative to full-employment GNP. He finds that the dollar appreciated in response to a fiscal expansion in the United States or a fiscal contraction abroad. Melvin, Schlagenhauf, and Talu (1989) take an explicitly forward-looking approach in which today's real exchange rate is a function of the future discounted value of a number of exogenous variables (relative outputs, money stocks, and budget deficits). Using expected fiscal positions obtained from opinion surveys, they found that over the period 1974–87 higher expected budget deficits caused on average a significant real appreciation of the U.S. dollar against the pound, the deutsche mark, and the yen. Beck (1993) examined the effects of both deficit and government spending announcements on spot and forward U.S. dollar exchange rates. Using daily observations in the proximity of official federal budget announcements during the period from 1980 through July 1990, she found that the dollar appreciated in response to larger-than-expected federal deficits but did not respond to unexpected increases in government spending.

Other studies, however, have not found statistically significant evidence of a positive link between fiscal expansions and the exchange value of the U.S. dollar. Kramer (1995), for example, uses cointegration techniques to estimate the long-run effect on the U.S. real effective exchange rate of the U.S. fiscal balance rela-

---

[9]The assumption that the rate of interest exceeds the rate of growth is a standard efficiency condition in many macroeconomic models; see Blanchard and Fischer (1989), Chapter 2. Historically, however, output growth rates have exceeded real interest rates in most industrial countries during much of the twentieth century, although the opposite was true for the nineteenth century and for the 1980s; see, for example, Mishkin (1984).

tive to partner countries. Using annual data over the period 1955-90, and taking account of the effects of other variables (net foreign assets, the terms of trade, and the relative price of traded to nontraded goods), he finds that a reduction in the U.S. fiscal deficit tends to appreciate the real exchange rate in the long run. Evans (1986) uses an ad hoc reduced form model explaining bilateral dollar exchange rates from 1973 to 1984 in terms of unanticipated real federal government deficits and other macroeconomic variables. He found no evidence of a U.S. dollar appreciation in response to higher federal budget deficits, but rather some evidence of a depreciation. McMillin and Koray (1990) used a reduced form approach to assess the impact of unanticipated changes in government debt in the United States relative to Canada on the bilateral real U.S.-Canadian dollar exchange rate. They found that over the period 1963–84 an unanticipated fiscal expansion in the United States that raised U.S. debt relative to that in Canada produced a temporary depreciation on the U.S. dollar. Given the symmetry of their model, this result can be interpreted as implying that a decrease in Canadian government debt (relative to that in the United States) caused a real appreciation of the Canadian dollar because it reduced the importance of the Canadian interest premium.[10] Finally, Koray and Chan (1991) looked at the deutsche mark-U.S. dollar exchange rate over the period 1975–89. They found that although the real and nominal bilateral rate appreciated in response to anticipated and unanticipated increases in German government spending, the effect was not statistically significant.

The literature on the link between fiscal policy and exchange rates in the context of the ERM also does not reach unambiguous conclusions. Caramazza (1993) looks at the impact of fiscal variables on realignment expectations and finds fairly strong effects. For example, lower government deficits in France relative to Germany in the post-1987 period are found to reduce the expected devaluation of the French franc against the deutsche mark. By contrast, focusing on the whole EMS history (from 1979 to 1992), Chen and Giovannini (1993) find that fiscal deficits in Italy and in France relative to Germany do not have explanatory power for realignment expectations in the case of the Italian lira and French franc. Thomas (1994) obtains similar results for the same currencies and time period using government debt instead of deficits. Froot and Rogoff (1991) use pooled data for eight EMS countries to test the prediction of a simple intertemporal neoclassical model, according to which higher domes-

tic or lower foreign government spending as a percentage of GDP causes a real appreciation of the domestic currency. Estimation results for the period 1979 to 1989 indicate that higher domestic (or lower foreign) government expenditure is directly and significantly associated with real appreciations of EMS currencies, while government budget deficits are not found to be significantly related to real exchange rates.

In the developing countries, the many episodes of high inflation and consequent nominal depreciations are generally attributed to a mix of expansionary fiscal and accommodating monetary policies. Rebelo and Végh (1995) document that exchange-rate-based stabilization programs introduced in several developing countries—Chile, Israel, and Mexico in the late 1970s and the 1980s, and Argentina in the 1990s—are characterized by real appreciations and fiscal adjustments. This empirical regularity, however, does not seem to reflect any causal connection since the real appreciation could be the result of inflation inertia in the presence of pegging the nominal exchange rate. Further insights on the causal link between fiscal contractions and movements in real exchange rates can be gauged from the simulation results of the intertemporal general equilibrium model specified and calibrated for the Argentine economy by Rebelo and Végh. The authors show that, in general, a fiscal contraction does not bring about a real appreciation but rather a depreciation. In fact, only in one special case does a contractionary fiscal policy (a reduction of government spending for tradable goods that increases the relative price of tradables) cause an appreciation of the domestic currency. The magnitude of this effect, however, is very small and is not capable of replicating the observed appreciations. These are captured in the simulation experiments only by pegging the nominal exchange rate to anchor the nominal variables.

* * *

The existing theoretical literature suggests that under conditions of high international capital mobility, the short-run effect of fiscal consolidation, ceteris paribus, is to depreciate the exchange rate and improve the current account. This result is found across a fairly wide range of models. If, however, fiscal consolidation has substantial effects on confidence and reduces interest premiums, it is possible that it could lead to an appreciation of the exchange rate in the short run and to a deterioration in the current account. There appear to be some countries, with large existing interest premiums apparent in bond yields, for which this latter outcome seems to be a realistic possibility. For the long run, there is a more general presumption that a sustained reduction in the government budget deficit that raises national saving and reduces the ratio of government debt to GDP will eventually lead to a real exchange rate appreciation. This result is intu-

---

[10] This interpretation is consistent with the steady-state simulation results of the Bank of Canada quarterly model presented in Macklem, Rose, and Tetlow (1995). According to this model, a decrease in the debt-to-GDP ratio from a baseline value of 60 percent produces a long-run appreciation of the Canadian real exchange rate.

itively plausible in that a country that saves more than its trading partners will accumulate more foreign assets and ultimately its currency will strengthen relative to other currencies.

# References

Alesina, Alberto, and others, "Default Risk on Government Debt in OECD Countries," *Economic Policy: A European Forum*, No. 15 (October 1992), pp. 428–63.

Beck, Stacie E., "The Ricardian Equivalence Proposition: Evidence from Foreign Exchange Markets," *Journal of International Money and Finance*, Vol. 12 (April 1993), pp. 154–69.

Blanchard, Olivier Jean, and Stanley Fischer, *Lectures on Macroeconomics* (Cambridge, Massachusetts: MIT Press, 1989).

Caramazza, Francesco, "French-German Interest Rate Differentials and Time-Varying Realignment Risk," *Staff Papers*, International Monetary Fund, Vol. 40 (September 1993), pp. 567–83.

Chen, Zhaohui, and Alberto Giovannini, "The Determinants of Realignment Expectations Under the EMS: Some Empirical Regularities," CEPR Discussion Paper No. 790 (London: Centre for Economic Policy Research, June 1993).

Evans, Paul, "Is the Dollar High Because of Large Budget Deficits?" *Journal of Monetary Economics*, No. 18 (November 1986), pp. 227–49.

Fleming, J. Marcus, "Domestic Financial Policies Under Fixed and Under Floating Exchange Rates," *Staff Papers*, International Monetary Fund, Vol. 9 (November 1962), pp. 369–80.

Frankel, Jeffrey A., "In Search of the Exchange Risk Premium: A Six-Currency Test Assuming Mean-Variance Optimization," *Journal of International Money and Finance*, Vol. 1 (December 1982), pp. 255–74.

_____, "Recent Estimates of Time-Variation in the Conditional Variance and in the Exchange Risk Premium," *Journal of International Money and Finance*, Vol. 7 (March 1988), pp. 115–25.

Froot, Kenneth, and Kenneth Rogoff, "The EMS, EMU, and the Transition to a Common Currency," *NBER Macroeconomics Annual*, ed. by Olivier Jean Blanchard and Stanley Fischer (Cambridge, Massachusetts: MIT Press, 1991).

Koray, Faik, and Pingfai Chan, "Government Spending and the Exchange Rate," *Applied Economics*, Vol. 23 (September 1991), pp. 1551–58.

Kramer, Charles, "The Real Effective Value of the U.S. Dollar, the Fiscal Deficit, and Long-Run Balance of Payments Equilibrium," in *United States—Background Papers*, IMF Staff Country Report No. 95/94 (Washington, 1995).

Lane, Timothy, and Steve Symansky, "Italy: The Impact of the Crisis on Financial Markets in 1992" (unpublished; Washington: International Monetary Fund, 1993).

Macklem, R. Tiff, David Rose, and Robert Tetlow, "Government Debt and Deficits in Canada: A Macro Simulation Analysis," Bank of Canada Working Paper No. 95-4 (Ottawa: Bank of Canada, May 1995).

McMillin, Douglas, and Faik Koray, "Does Government Debt Affect the Exchange Rate? An Empirical Analysis of the U.S.-Canadian Exchange Rate," *Journal of Economics and Business*, Vol. 42 (November 1990), pp. 279–88.

Melvin, Michael, Don Schlagenhauf, and Ayhan Talu, "The U.S. Budget Deficit and the Foreign Exchange Value of the Dollar," *Review of Economics and Statistics*, Vol. 71 (August 1989), pp. 500–05.

Mishkin, Frederick S., "The Real Interest Rate: A Multi-Country Empirical Study," *Canadian Journal of Economics*, Vol. 17 (1984), pp. 282–311.

Mundell, Robert A., "Capital Mobility and Stabilization Policy under Fixed and Flexible Exchange Rates," *Canadian Journal of Economics and Political Science*, Vol. 29 (November 1963), pp. 413–31.

Rebelo, Sergio, and Carlos Végh, "Real Effects of Exchange-Rate Based Stabilization: An Analysis of Competing Theories," *NBER Macroeconomics Annual* (forthcoming).

Reinhart, Carmen, "Fiscal Policy, the Real Exchange Rate, and Commodity Prices," *Staff Papers*, International Monetary Fund, Vol. 38 (September 1991), pp. 506–24.

Svensson, Lars E.O., "The Foreign Exchange Risk Premium in a Target Zone with Devaluation Risk," *Journal of International Economics*, Vol. 33 (August 1992), pp. 21–40.

Thomas, Alun, "Expected Devaluation and Economic Fundamentals," *Staff Papers*, International Monetary Fund, Vol. 41 (June 1994), pp. 262–85.

Throop, Adrian W., "Fiscal Policy, the Dollar and International Trade: A Synthesis of Two Views," *Federal Reserve Bank of San Francisco Economic Review* (Summer 1989), pp. 27–44.

# Statistical Appendix

## Assumptions

The statistical tables in this appendix have been compiled on the basis of information available on September 18, 1995. The estimates and projections for 1995 and 1996, as well as the 1997–2000 medium-term scenarios, are based on the following assumptions.

- For the industrial countries, real effective exchange rates are assumed to remain constant at their average level during August 1–23, 1995, except for the bilateral exchange rates among the ERM currencies, which are assumed to remain constant in nominal terms. For 1995 and 1996, these assumptions imply average U.S. dollar/SDR conversion rates of 1.526 and 1.513, respectively.
- Established policies of national authorities will be maintained.
- The price of oil will average $16.67 a barrel in 1995 and $15.51 a barrel in 1996. In the medium term, the oil price is assumed to remain unchanged in real terms.
- Interest rates, as represented by the London interbank offered rate (LIBOR) on six-month U.S. dollar deposits, will average $6\frac{1}{4}$ percent in 1995 and 1996; the three-month certificate of deposit rate in Japan will average 1 percent in 1995 and 1996; and the three-month interbank deposit rate in Germany will average $4\frac{1}{2}$ percent in 1995 and slightly less than 5 percent in 1996.

## Data and Conventions

Data and projections for more than 180 countries form the statistical basis for the *World Economic Outlook* (the World Economic Outlook data base). The data are maintained jointly by the IMF's Research Department and area departments, with the latter regularly updating country projections based on consistent global assumptions.

Although national statistical agencies are the ultimate providers of historical data and definitions, international organizations are also involved in statistical issues, with the objectives of harmonizing differences among national statistical systems, of setting international standards with respect to definitions, and of providing conceptual frameworks for measurement and presentation of economic statistics. The World Economic Outlook data base reflects information from both national source agencies and international organizations.

The completion of the comprehensive revision of the United Nations' standardized *System of National Accounts* (*SNA*) and the IMF's *Balance of Payments Manual* is an important improvement in the standards of economic statistics and analysis.[1] The IMF was actively involved in both projects, particularly the new *Balance of Payments Manual*, which is central to the IMF's interest in countries' external positions. Key changes introduced with the new *Manual* were summarized in Box 13 of the May 1994 *World Economic Outlook*. The process of adapting country balance of payments data to the definitions of the new *Balance of Payments Manual* began with the May 1995 *World Economic Outlook*. However, full concordance with the *BPM* is ultimately dependent on national statistical compilers providing revised country data, and hence the *World Economic Outlook* estimates are still only partly adapted to the *BPM*.

The focus on world trade in this *World Economic Outlook* has been broadened to include estimates for international trade in goods and services in addition to the traditional focus on trade in goods. This is in recognition of the fact that trade in services presently accounts for a substantial share of the total value of world trade and is likely to become increasingly important. Estimates of foreign trade volumes for both goods and services are drawn as far as possible from national accounts data. For the relatively few countries lacking national accounts estimates in constant prices, balance of payments data for goods are deflated by trade unit values, and for services by GDP deflators, to generate constant price estimates.

Composite data for country groups in the *World Economic Outlook* are either sums or weighted averages of data for individual countries. Arithmetic weighted averages are used for all data except inflation and money growth for nonindustrial country groups, for which geometric averages are used. The following conventions are used.

---

[1]Commission of the European Communities, IMF, OECD, UN, and World Bank, *System of National Accounts 1993* (Brussels/Luxembourg, New York, Paris, and Washington, 1993); and IMF, *Balance of Payments Manual* (5th ed., 1993).

- Country group composites for interest rates, exchange rates, and the growth of monetary aggregates are weighted by GDP converted to U.S. dollars at market exchange rates (averaged over the preceding three years) as a share of world or group GDP.
- Composites for other data relating to the domestic economy, whether growth rates or ratios, are weighted by GDP valued at purchasing power parities (PPPs) as a share of total world or group GDP.[2]
- Composite unemployment rates and employment growth are weighted by labor force as a share of group labor force.
- Composites for data relating to the external economy are sums of individual country data after conversion to U.S. dollars at the average exchange rates in the years indicated for balance of payments, and at end-of-period exchange rates for debt denominated in currencies other than U.S. dollars. Composites of foreign trade volumes and prices, however, are arithmetic averages of percentage changes for individual countries weighted by the U.S. dollar value of exports or imports as a share of total world or group exports or imports (in the preceding year).

For central and eastern European countries in existence before 1991, external transactions in nonconvertible currencies (through 1990) are converted to U.S. dollars at the implicit U.S. dollar/ruble conversion rates obtained from each country's national currency exchange rate for the U.S. dollar and for the ruble.

Unless otherwise indicated, multiyear averages of growth rates are expressed as compound annual rates of change.

## Classification of Countries

### Summary of the Country Classification

The country classification in the *World Economic Outlook* divides the world into three major groups: industrial countries, developing countries, and countries in transition.[3] Rather than being based on strict criteria, economic or otherwise, this classification has evolved over time with the objective of facilitating the analysis by providing a reasonably meaningful organization of data. Each of the three main country groups is further divided into a number of subgroups. Tables A and B provide an overview of these standard groups in the *World Economic Outlook*, showing the number of countries in each group and the average 1994 shares of groups in aggregate PPP-valued GDP, total exports of goods and services, and total debt outstanding.

The general features and the compositions of groups in the *World Economic Outlook* classification are as follows.[4]

The group of *industrial countries* (23 countries) comprises

| | | |
|---|---|---|
| Australia | Greece | Norway |
| Austria | Iceland | Portugal |
| Belgium | Ireland | Spain |
| Canada | Italy | Sweden |
| Denmark | Japan | Switzerland |
| Finland | Luxembourg | United Kingdom |
| France | Netherlands | United States |
| Germany | New Zealand | |

The seven largest countries in this group in terms of GDP—the United States, Japan, Germany, France, Italy, the United Kingdom, and Canada—are collectively referred to as the *major industrial countries.*

The current members of the *European Union* (15 countries) are also distinguished as a subgroup. They are

| | | |
|---|---|---|
| Austria | Germany | Netherlands |
| Belgium | Greece | Portugal |
| Denmark | Ireland | Spain |
| Finland | Italy | Sweden |
| France | Luxembourg | United Kingdom |

Composite data shown in the tables under the heading "European Union" cover the current 15 members of the European Union for all years, even though the membership has changed over time.

In 1991 and subsequent years, data for *Germany* refer to west Germany *and* the new eastern Länder (i.e., the former German Democratic Republic). Before 1991, economic data are not available on a unified basis or in a consistent manner. In general, data on national accounts and domestic economic and financial activity through 1990 cover west Germany only,

---

[2]See Annex IV of the May 1993 *World Economic Outlook* and Anne-Marie Gulde and Marianne Schulze-Ghattas, "Purchasing Power Parity Based Weights for the *World Economic Outlook*," in *Staff Studies for the World Economic Outlook* (Washington: IMF, December 1993), pp. 106–23.

[3]As used here, the term "country" does not in all cases refer to a territorial entity that is a state as understood by international law and practice. It also covers some territorial entities that are not states, but for which economic policies are formulated, and statistical data are maintained, on a separate and independent basis.

[4]A few countries are presently not included in the industrial and developing country groups featured below, either because they are not IMF members, and their economies are not monitored by the IMF, or because data bases have not yet been compiled. Cuba and the Democratic People's Republic of Korea are examples of countries that are not IMF members, whereas San Marino, among the industrial countries, and Eritrea, among the developing countries, are examples of economies for which data bases have not been completed. It should also be noted that, owing to lack of data, only three of the former republics of the dissolved Socialist Federal Republic of Yugoslavia (Croatia, the former Yugoslav Republic of Macedonia, and Slovenia) are included in the group composites for countries in transition.

**Table A. Industrial Countries: Classification by Standard *World Economic Outlook* Groups, and Their Shares in Aggregate GDP and Exports of Goods and Services, 1994[1]**

| | Number of Countries Included in Group | Total GDP of | | Total exports of goods and services of | |
|---|---|---|---|---|---|
| | | Industrial countries | World | Industrial countries | World |
| **Industrial countries** | **23** | **100.0** | **54.6** | **100.0** | **70.2** |
| United States | | 38.8 | 21.2 | 18.8 | 13.2 |
| Japan | | 15.4 | 8.4 | 12.0 | 8.4 |
| Germany | | 9.2 | 5.0 | 13.1 | 9.2 |
| France | | 6.6 | 3.6 | 9.2 | 6.5 |
| Italy | | 6.2 | 3.4 | 7.5 | 5.2 |
| United Kingdom | | 6.1 | 3.3 | 7.2 | 5.0 |
| Canada | | 3.4 | 1.9 | 4.9 | 3.4 |
| Other industrial countries | 16 | 14.3 | 7.8 | 27.4 | 19.2 |
| **Industrial country groups** | | | | | |
| Seven major industrial countries | 7 | 85.7 | 46.8 | 72.6 | 50.9 |
| European Union | 15 | 38.6 | 21.1 | 57.6 | 40.4 |
| Industrial countries except the United States, Japan, and Germany | 20 | 36.6 | 20.0 | 56.1 | 39.4 |
| Industrial countries except the United States, the European Union, and Japan | 6 | 9.5 | 5.2 | 16.7 | 11.7 |
| Major European industrial countries | 4 | 28.0 | 15.3 | 36.9 | 25.9 |

Column header over GDP/exports: Percentage of

[1]The GDP shares are based on the purchasing power parity (PPP) valuation of country GDPs.

whereas data for the central government, foreign trade, and balance of payments apply to west Germany through June 1990 and to unified Germany thereafter.

The group of *developing countries* (132 countries) includes all countries that are not classified as industrial countries or as countries in transition, together with a few dependent territories for which adequate statistics are available.

The *regional breakdowns* of developing countries in the *World Economic Outlook* conform to the IMF's *International Financial Statistics (IFS)* classification, with one important exception. Because all of the developing countries in Europe except Cyprus, Malta, and Turkey are included in the group of countries in transition, the *World Economic Outlook* classification places these three countries in a combined Middle East and Europe region. It should also be noted that in both classifications, Egypt and the Libyan Arab Jamahiriya are included in this region, not in Africa. Two additional regional groupings are included in the *World Economic Outlook* because of their analytical significance. These are sub-Saharan Africa[5] and four newly industrializing Asian economies.[6]

The developing countries are also grouped according to *analytical criteria*: predominant export, financial, and other groups. The first analytical criterion, by *predominant export*, distinguishes among five groups: fuel (Standard International Trade Classification—SITC 3); manufactures (SITC 5 to 9, less 68); nonfuel primary products (SITC 0, 1, 2, 4, and 68); services, income, and private transfers (factor and nonfactor service receipts plus workers' remittances); and diversified export base. A further distinction is made among the exporters of nonfuel primary products on the basis of whether countries' exports of primary commodities consist primarily of agricultural commodities (SITC 0, 1, 2 except 27, 28, and 4) or minerals (SITC 27, 28, and 68). The export criteria, which have been updated to correspond more closely to the current World Bank classification, are now based on countries' export composition in 1988–92.

The *financial* criterion first distinguishes between net creditor and net debtor countries. Countries in the latter, much larger group are then differentiated on the basis of two additional financial criteria: by predominant type of creditor and by experience with debt servicing. The financial criteria reflect net creditor and debtor positions as of 1987, sources of borrowing as of the end of 1989, and experience with debt servicing during 1986–90.

[5]Excluding Nigeria and South Africa.
[6]Hong Kong, Korea, Singapore, and Taiwan Province of China.

**Table B. Developing Countries and Countries in Transition: Classification by Standard *World Economic Outlook* Groups and Their Shares in Aggregate GDP, Exports of Goods and Services, and Total Debt Outstanding, 1994[1]**

| | | Percentage of | | | | |
| | | Total GDP of | | Total exports of goods and services of | | Total debt of developing countries |
| | Number of Countries Included in Group | Developing countries | World | Developing countries | World | |
|---|---|---|---|---|---|---|
| **Developing countries** | **132** | **100.0** | **40.1** | **100.0** | **26.1** | **100.0** |
| By region | | | | | | |
| Africa | 50 | 8.2 | 3.3 | 6.7 | 1.7 | 15.2 |
| Asia | 30 | 57.6 | 23.1 | 63.4 | 16.6 | 34.6 |
| Middle East and Europe | 18 | 12.0 | 4.8 | 15.0 | 3.9 | 17.4 |
| Western Hemisphere | 34 | 22.2 | 8.9 | 14.9 | 3.9 | 32.8 |
| Sub-Saharan Africa | 45 | 3.3 | 1.3 | 2.3 | 0.6 | 8.8 |
| Four newly industrializing Asian economies | 4 | 7.7 | 3.1 | 36.5 | 9.5 | 5.8 |
| **By predominant export** | | | | | | |
| Fuel | 15 | 9.4 | 3.8 | 11.2 | 2.9 | 11.5 |
| Nonfuel exports | 117 | 90.6 | 36.3 | 88.8 | 23.2 | 88.5 |
| Manufactures | 7 | 32.6 | 13.1 | 47.5 | 12.4 | 14.4 |
| Primary products | 43 | 7.0 | 2.8 | 5.3 | 1.4 | 16.6 |
| Agricultural products | 29 | 4.8 | 1.9 | 3.3 | 0.9 | 10.9 |
| Minerals | 14 | 2.2 | 0.9 | 1.9 | 0.5 | 5.7 |
| Services, income, and private transfers | 37 | 3.7 | 1.5 | 3.9 | 1.0 | 6.1 |
| Diversified export base | 30 | 47.3 | 19.0 | 32.2 | 8.4 | 51.5 |
| **By financial criteria** | | | | | | |
| Net creditor countries | 7 | 5.2 | 2.1 | 14.9 | 3.9 | 2.7 |
| Net debtor countries | 125 | 94.8 | 38.0 | 85.1 | 22.2 | 97.3 |
| Market borrowers | 23 | 57.4 | 23.0 | 63.0 | 16.5 | 48.5 |
| Diversified borrowers | 33 | 25.6 | 10.3 | 15.5 | 4.0 | 30.5 |
| Official borrowers | 69 | 11.9 | 4.8 | 6.6 | 1.7 | 18.3 |
| Countries with recent debt-servicing difficulties | 72 | 31.0 | 12.4 | 21.6 | 5.6 | 55.1 |
| Countries without debt-servicing difficulties | 53 | 63.9 | 25.6 | 63.5 | 16.6 | 42.2 |
| **Other groups** | | | | | | |
| Small low-income economies | 50 | 10.8 | 4.3 | 5.0 | 1.3 | 17.1 |
| Least developed countries | 46 | 4.1 | 1.7 | 1.6 | 0.4 | 8.2 |
| **Countries in transition** | **28** | ... | **5.3** | ... | **3.7** | ... |
| Central and eastern Europe | 18 | ... | 2.7 | ... | 2.1 | ... |
| Excluding Belarus and Ukraine | 16 | ... | 2.0 | ... | 1.7 | ... |
| Russia | | ... | 2.1 | ... | 1.4 | ... |
| Transcaucasus and central Asia | 9 | ... | 0.5 | ... | 0.2 | ... |

[1]The GDP shares are based on the purchasing power parity (PPP) valuation of country GDPs.

The country groups shown under *other groups* constitute the small low-income economies and the least developed countries.

The group of *countries in transition* (28 countries) comprises central and eastern European countries, Russia, non-European states of the former Soviet Union, and Mongolia. A common characteristic of these countries is the transitional state of their economies from a centrally administered system to one based on market principles. The group of countries in transition comprises

| | | |
|---|---|---|
| Albania | Hungary | Russia |
| Armenia | Kazakhstan | Slovak Republic |
| Azerbaijan | Kyrgyz Republic | Slovenia |
| Belarus | Latvia | Tajikistan |
| Bosnia and Herzegovina[7] | Lithuania | Turkmenistan |
| Bulgaria | Macedonia, former Yugoslav Rep. of | Ukraine |
| Croatia | Moldova | Uzbekistan |
| Czech Republic | Mongolia | Yugoslavia, Fed. Rep. of (Serbia/Montenegro)[7] |
| Estonia | Poland | |
| Georgia | Romania | |

[7]Not included in the World Economic Outlook data base.

The countries in transition are classified in three subgroups: *central and eastern Europe*, *Russia*, and *Transcaucasus and central Asia*. The Transcaucasian and central Asian countries include Kazakhstan for purposes of the *World Economic Outlook*. The countries in central and eastern Europe (18 countries) are

| | | |
|---|---|---|
| Albania | Estonia | Poland |
| Belarus | Hungary | Romania |
| Bosnia and | Latvia | Slovak Republic |
| Herzegovina[8] | Lithuania | Slovenia |
| Bulgaria | Macedonia, former | Ukraine |
| Croatia | Yugoslav Rep. of | Yugoslavia, Fed. Rep. of |
| Czech Republic | Moldova | (Serbia/Montenegro)[8] |

The countries in the Transcaucasian and central Asian group (9 countries) are

| | | |
|---|---|---|
| Armenia | Kazakhstan | Tajikistan |
| Azerbaijan | Kyrgyz Republic | Turkmenistan |
| Georgia | Mongolia | Uzbekistan |

## Detailed Description of the Developing Country Classification by Analytical Group

### Countries Classified by Predominant Export

*Fuel exporters* (15 countries) are countries whose average ratio of fuel exports to total exports in 1988–92 exceeded 50 percent. The group comprises

| | | |
|---|---|---|
| Angola | Iran, Islamic Rep. of | Qatar |
| Algeria | Iraq | Saudi Arabia |
| Bahrain | Libya | Trinidad and Tobago |
| Congo | Nigeria | United Arab Emirates |
| Gabon | Oman | Venezuela |

*Nonfuel exporters* (117 countries) are countries with total exports of goods and services including a substantial share of (a) manufactures, (b) primary products, or (c) services, factor income, and private transfers. However, those countries whose export structure is so diversified that they do not fall clearly into any one of these three groups are assigned to a fourth group, (d) diversified export base.

(a) Economies whose exports of manufactures accounted for 50 percent or more of their total exports on average in 1988–92 are included in the group of *exporters of manufactures* (7 countries). This group includes

| | | |
|---|---|---|
| China | Korea | Singapore |
| Hong Kong | Lebanon | Taiwan Province of China |
| Israel | | |

(b) The group of *exporters of primary products* (43 countries) consists of those countries whose exports of agricultural and mineral primary products (SITC 0, 1, 2, 4, and 68) accounted for at least half of their total exports on average in 1988–92. These countries are

| | | |
|---|---|---|
| Afghanistan, | Guyana | São Tomé and Principe |
| Islamic State of | Honduras | Solomon Islands |
| Argentina | Liberia | Somalia |
| Bolivia | Madagascar | St. Vincent and |
| Botswana | Malawi | the Grenadines |
| Burundi | Mali | Sudan |
| Chad | Mauritania | Suriname |
| Chile | Myanmar | Swaziland |
| Côte d'Ivoire | Namibia | Tanzania |
| Equatorial Guinea | Nicaragua | Togo |
| Ethiopia | Niger | Uganda |
| Ghana | Papua New Guinea | Vietnam |
| Guatemala | Paraguay | Zaïre |
| Guinea | Peru | Zambia |
| Guinea-Bissau | Rwanda | Zimbabwe |

Among exporters of primary products, a further distinction is made between exporters of agricultural products and minerals. The group of *mineral exporters* (14 countries) comprises

| | | |
|---|---|---|
| Bolivia | Liberia | Suriname |
| Botswana | Mauritania | Togo |
| Chile | Namibia | Zaïre |
| Guinea | Niger | Zambia |
| Guyana | Peru | |

All other exporters of primary products are classified as *agricultural exporters* (29 countries).

(c) The *exporters of services and recipients of factor income and private transfers* (37 countries) are defined as those countries whose average income from services, factor income, and workers' remittances accounted for half or more of total average export earnings in 1988–92. This group comprises

| | | |
|---|---|---|
| Antigua and Barbuda | Egypt | Marshall Islands |
| Aruba | El Salvador | Micronesia, The |
| Bahamas, The | Fiji | Federated States of |
| Barbados | Gambia, The | Nepal |
| Belize | Grenada | Panama |
| Benin | Haiti | Seychelles |
| Bhutan | Jamaica | St. Kitts and Nevis |
| Burkina Faso | Jordan | St. Lucia |
| Cambodia | Kiribati | Tonga |
| Cape Verde | Kuwait | Vanuatu |
| Cyprus | Lesotho | Western Samoa |
| Djibouti | Maldives | Yemen, Rep. of |
| Dominican Rep. | Malta | |

(d) *Countries with a diversified export base* (30 countries) are those whose export earnings in 1988–92 were not dominated by any one of the categories mentioned under (a) through (c) above. This group comprises

| | | |
|---|---|---|
| Bangladesh | Indonesia | Philippines |
| Brazil | Kenya | Senegal |
| Cameroon | Lao People's Dem. Rep. | Sierra Leone |
| Central African Rep. | Malaysia | South Africa |
| Colombia | Mauritius | Sri Lanka |
| Comoros | Mexico | Syrian Arab Rep. |
| Costa Rica | Morocco | Thailand |
| Dominica | Mozambique, Rep. of | Tunisia |
| Ecuador | Netherlands Antilles | Turkey |
| India | Pakistan | Uruguay |

---

[8]Not included in the World Economic Outlook data base.

## Countries Classified by Financial Criteria

*Net creditor countries* (7 countries) are defined as developing countries that were net external creditors in 1987 or that experienced substantial cumulated current account surpluses (excluding official transfers) between 1967 (the beginning of most balance of payments series in the World Economic Outlook data base) and 1987. The net creditor group consists of the following economies:

| | | |
|---|---|---|
| Kuwait | Qatar | Taiwan Province of China |
| Libya | Saudi Arabia | United Arab Emirates |
| Oman | | |

*Net debtor countries* (125 countries) are disaggregated according to two criteria: (a) predominant type of creditor and (b) experience with debt servicing.

(a) Within the classification by *predominant type of creditor* (sources of borrowing), three subgroups are identified: market borrowers, official borrowers, and diversified borrowers. *Market borrowers* (23 countries) are defined as net debtor countries with more than two thirds of their total liabilities outstanding at the end of 1989 owed to commercial creditors. This group comprises

| | | |
|---|---|---|
| Algeria | Iran, Islamic Rep. of | Peru |
| Antigua and Barbuda | Israel | Singapore |
| Argentina | Kiribati | Suriname |
| Bahamas, The | Korea | Thailand |
| Brazil | Malaysia | Trinidad and Tobago |
| Chile | Mexico | Uruguay |
| China | Panama | Venezuela |
| Hong Kong | Papua New Guinea | |

*Official borrowers* (69 countries) are defined as net debtor countries with more than two thirds of their total liabilities outstanding at the end of 1989 owed to official creditors. This group comprises

| | | |
|---|---|---|
| Afghanistan, Islamic State of | Ghana | Nicaragua |
| Aruba | Grenada | Niger |
| Bangladesh | Guinea | Nigeria |
| Belize | Guinea-Bissau | Pakistan |
| Bhutan | Guyana | Rwanda |
| Bolivia | Haiti | São Tomé and Principe |
| Botswana | Honduras | Somalia |
| Burkina Faso | Jamaica | St. Kitts and Nevis |
| Burundi | Lao People's Dem. Rep. | St. Lucia |
| Cambodia | Lesotho | St. Vincent and the Grenadines |
| Cameroon | Madagascar | Sudan |
| Cape Verde | Malawi | Swaziland |
| Central African Rep. | Maldives | Tanzania |
| Chad | Mali | Togo |
| Comoros | Malta | Tonga |
| Djibouti | Mauritania | Tunisia |
| Dominica | Mauritius | Uganda |
| Dominican Rep. | Morocco | Vietnam |
| Egypt | Mozambique, Rep. of | Western Samoa |
| El Salvador | Myanmar | Yemen, Rep. of |
| Equatorial Guinea | Namibia | Zaïre |
| Ethiopia | Nepal | Zambia |
| Gabon | Netherlands Antilles | |
| Gambia, The | | |

*Diversified borrowers* (33 countries) consist of those net debtor developing countries that are classified neither as market nor as official borrowers.

(b) Within the classification by *experience with debt servicing*, a further distinction is made. *Countries with recent debt-servicing* difficulties (72 countries) are defined as those countries that incurred external payments arrears or entered into official or commercial bank debt-rescheduling agreements during 1986–90. Information on these developments is taken from relevant issues of the IMF's *Annual Report on Exchange Arrangements and Exchange Restrictions.*

All other net debtor countries are classified as *countries without debt-servicing difficulties* (53 countries).

## Other Groups

The countries classified by the World Bank as *small low-income economies* (50 countries) are those whose GNP per capita (as estimated by the World Bank) did not exceed the equivalent of $695 in 1993. This group comprises

| | | |
|---|---|---|
| Afghanistan, Islamic State of | Guinea-Bissau | Nigeria |
| Bangladesh | Guyana | Pakistan |
| Benin | Haiti | Rwanda |
| Bhutan | Honduras | São Tomé and Principe |
| Burkina Faso | Kenya | Sierra Leone |
| Burundi | Lao People's Dem. Rep. | Somalia |
| Cambodia | Lesotho | Sri Lanka |
| Central African Rep. | Liberia | Sudan |
| Chad | Madagascar | Tanzania |
| Comoros | Malawi | Togo |
| Côte d'Ivoire | Mali | Uganda |
| Egypt | Mauritania | Vietnam |
| Equatorial Guinea | Mozambique, Rep. of | Yemen, Rep. of |
| Ethiopia | Myanmar | Zaïre |
| Gambia, The | Nepal | Zambia |
| Ghana | Nicaragua | Zimbabwe |
| Guinea | Niger | |

The countries currently classified by the United Nations as the *least developed countries* (46 countries) are[9]

| | | |
|---|---|---|
| Afghanistan, Islamic State of | Guinea | Rwanda |
| Bangladesh | Guinea-Bissau | São Tomé and Principe |
| Benin | Haiti | Sierra Leone |
| Bhutan | Kiribati | Solomon Islands |
| Botswana | Lao People's Dem. Rep. | Somalia |
| Burkina Faso | Lesotho | Sudan |
| Burundi | Liberia | Tanzania |
| Cambodia | Madagascar | Togo |
| Cape Verde | Malawi | Uganda |
| Central African Rep. | Maldives | Vanuatu |
| Chad | Mali | Western Samoa |
| Comoros | Mauritania | Yemen, Rep. of |
| Djibouti | Mozambique, Rep. of | Zaïre |
| Equatorial Guinea | Myanmar | Zambia |
| Ethiopia | Nepal | |
| Gambia, The | Niger | |

_____

[9]The United Nations classification also covers Tuvalu, which is not included in the *World Economic Outlook* classification.

## List of Tables

## Table A1. Summary of World Output[1]

*(Annual percent change)*

| | Average 1977–86 | 1987 | 1988 | 1989 | 1990 | 1991 | 1992 | 1993 | 1994 | 1995 | 1996 |
|---|---|---|---|---|---|---|---|---|---|---|---|
| **World** | **3.3** | **4.0** | **4.6** | **3.5** | **2.4** | **1.3** | **2.0** | **2.5** | **3.6** | **3.7** | **4.1** |
| **Industrial countries** | **2.7** | **3.2** | **4.4** | **3.3** | **2.4** | **0.8** | **1.5** | **1.1** | **3.1** | **2.5** | **2.4** |
| United States | 2.7 | 3.1 | 3.9 | 2.5 | 1.2 | −0.6 | 2.3 | 3.1 | 4.1 | 2.9 | 2.0 |
| European Union | 2.1 | 2.9 | 4.2 | 3.5 | 3.0 | 1.1 | 1.0 | −0.6 | 2.8 | 2.9 | 2.8 |
| Japan | 4.0 | 4.1 | 6.2 | 4.7 | 4.8 | 4.3 | 1.1 | −0.2 | 0.5 | 0.5 | 2.2 |
| Other industrial countries | 2.7 | 3.5 | 3.9 | 3.1 | 1.0 | −1.2 | 0.7 | 1.5 | 4.0 | 2.8 | 2.9 |
| **Developing countries** | **4.5** | **5.7** | **5.2** | **4.2** | **4.0** | **4.9** | **5.9** | **6.1** | **6.2** | **6.0** | **6.3** |
| **By region** | | | | | | | | | | | |
| Africa | 2.1 | 1.6 | 3.6 | 3.4 | 2.1 | 1.7 | 0.7 | 0.8 | 2.6 | 3.0 | 5.2 |
| Asia | 6.7 | 8.1 | 9.1 | 6.0 | 5.7 | 6.4 | 8.2 | 8.7 | 8.5 | 8.7 | 7.9 |
| Middle East and Europe | 2.6 | 5.0 | −0.5 | 2.7 | 4.8 | 3.2 | 5.5 | 3.6 | 0.3 | 2.4 | 3.2 |
| Western Hemisphere | 3.2 | 3.4 | 1.1 | 1.6 | 0.6 | 3.5 | 2.7 | 3.3 | 4.6 | 1.8 | 4.0 |
| **By analytical criteria** | | | | | | | | | | | |
| Fuel exporters | 1.0 | 1.3 | −0.5 | 3.2 | 5.3 | 5.1 | 3.9 | 0.4 | 0.1 | 1.9 | 2.6 |
| Nonfuel exporters | 5.1 | 6.3 | 5.9 | 4.4 | 3.8 | 4.9 | 6.1 | 6.8 | 6.8 | 6.5 | 6.7 |
| Net creditor countries | 2.9 | 3.2 | 4.2 | 6.5 | 4.6 | 4.5 | 6.5 | 3.8 | 3.0 | 3.3 | 3.8 |
| Net debtor countries | 4.6 | 5.9 | 5.3 | 4.1 | 4.0 | 4.9 | 5.9 | 6.3 | 6.3 | 6.2 | 6.4 |
| Market borrowers | 5.1 | 6.4 | 5.5 | 3.8 | 3.7 | 6.5 | 7.5 | 7.9 | 7.9 | 7.2 | 6.9 |
| Official borrowers | 3.4 | 4.0 | 3.8 | 3.6 | 3.6 | 3.8 | 2.7 | 2.5 | 3.4 | 3.6 | 5.5 |
| Countries with recent debt-servicing difficulties | 3.0 | 3.8 | 1.8 | 2.1 | 0.5 | 2.5 | 2.2 | 2.7 | 4.1 | 2.4 | 4.2 |
| Countries without debt-servicing difficulties | 5.8 | 7.3 | 7.5 | 5.4 | 6.0 | 6.2 | 7.8 | 8.0 | 7.4 | 8.0 | 7.5 |
| **Countries in transition** | **3.3** | **2.5** | **4.0** | **2.0** | **−3.9** | **−11.6** | **−15.2** | **−9.1** | **−9.5** | **−2.1** | **3.4** |
| Central and eastern Europe | ... | ... | ... | ... | ... | −11.1 | −11.3 | −6.1 | −3.8 | 0.2 | 4.3 |
| Excluding Belarus and Ukraine | ... | ... | ... | ... | ... | −11.9 | −9.2 | −1.9 | 2.8 | 4.0 | 4.4 |
| Russia, Transcaucasus, and central Asia | ... | ... | ... | ... | ... | −12.0 | −18.7 | −11.8 | −15.2 | −4.6 | 2.4 |
| *Memorandum* | | | | | | | | | | | |
| **Median growth rate** | | | | | | | | | | | |
| Industrial countries | 2.6 | 3.1 | 4.1 | 3.8 | 2.1 | 1.3 | 1.1 | −0.1 | 2.8 | 2.9 | 2.7 |
| Developing countries | 3.7 | 3.6 | 3.5 | 3.9 | 3.2 | 3.1 | 3.6 | 3.4 | 3.5 | 4.4 | 4.8 |
| Countries in transition | 3.6 | 2.8 | 5.3 | 3.0 | −2.3 | −11.9 | −15.5 | −10.3 | −1.0 | 1.7 | 4.6 |
| **Output per capita** | | | | | | | | | | | |
| Industrial countries | 2.0 | 2.6 | 3.7 | 2.5 | 1.6 | — | 0.8 | 0.5 | 2.4 | 1.9 | 1.8 |
| Developing countries | 2.0 | 3.5 | 4.8 | 0.9 | 2.2 | 3.1 | 3.5 | 4.3 | 4.2 | 3.9 | 4.4 |
| Countries in transition | 2.6 | 1.8 | 3.4 | 1.6 | −4.5 | −11.8 | −15.4 | −9.3 | −9.6 | −2.3 | 3.2 |
| **Value of world output in billions of U.S. dollars** | | | | | | | | | | | |
| At market exchange rates | 11,389 | 17,025 | 18,991 | 19,834 | 22,208 | 23,203 | 23,236 | 23,930 | 25,843 | 28,988 | 30,628 |
| At purchasing power parities | 13,886 | 20,369 | 22,054 | 23,935 | 25,660 | 26,969 | 28,482 | 29,662 | 31,335 | 33,485 | 35,906 |

[1]Real GDP. For most countries included in the group "countries in transition," total output is measured by real net material product (NMP) or by NMP-based estimates of GDP.

## Table A2. Industrial Countries: Real GDP and Total Domestic Demand

*(Annual percent change)*

| | Average 1977–86 | 1987 | 1988 | 1989 | 1990 | 1991 | 1992 | 1993 | 1994 | 1995 | 1996 | Fourth Quarter[1] 1994 | 1995 | 1996 |
|---|---|---|---|---|---|---|---|---|---|---|---|---|---|---|
| **Real GDP** | | | | | | | | | | | | | | |
| **Industrial countries** | **2.7** | **3.2** | **4.4** | **3.3** | **2.4** | **0.8** | **1.5** | **1.1** | **3.1** | **2.5** | **2.4** | ... | ... | ... |
| Major industrial countries | 2.8 | 3.2 | 4.5 | 3.2 | 2.4 | 0.8 | 1.6 | 1.3 | 3.1 | 2.4 | 2.3 | 3.4 | 2.0 | 2.5 |
| United States | 2.7 | 3.1 | 3.9 | 2.5 | 1.2 | −0.6 | 2.3 | 3.1 | 4.1 | 2.9 | 2.0 | 4.1 | 1.9 | 2.2 |
| Japan | 4.0 | 4.1 | 6.2 | 4.7 | 4.8 | 4.3 | 1.1 | −0.2 | 0.5 | 0.5 | 2.2 | 0.8 | 1.4 | 2.5 |
| Germany[2] | 1.9 | 1.5 | 3.7 | 3.6 | 5.7 | 2.8 | 2.2 | −1.2 | 2.9 | 2.6 | 2.9 | 3.7 | 3.0 | 2.5 |
| France | 2.2 | 2.3 | 4.4 | 4.3 | 2.5 | 0.8 | 1.3 | −1.5 | 2.9 | 2.9 | 2.7 | 4.1 | 2.2 | 3.0 |
| Italy | 2.7 | 3.1 | 4.1 | 2.9 | 2.1 | 1.2 | 0.7 | −1.2 | 2.2 | 3.0 | 2.8 | 2.9 | 2.4 | 2.8 |
| United Kingdom[3] | 2.1 | 4.8 | 5.0 | 2.2 | 0.4 | −2.0 | −0.5 | 2.2 | 3.8 | 2.7 | 2.9 | 4.0 | 2.2 | 3.2 |
| Canada | 3.1 | 4.2 | 5.0 | 2.4 | −0.2 | −1.8 | 0.8 | 2.2 | 4.6 | 2.2 | 2.7 | 5.4 | 0.7 | 3.4 |
| Other industrial countries | 2.1 | 3.2 | 3.8 | 4.0 | 2.7 | 0.9 | 1.0 | 0.2 | 2.9 | 3.2 | 3.0 | ... | ... | ... |
| Spain | 1.7 | 5.7 | 5.2 | 4.7 | 3.6 | 2.2 | 0.9 | −1.2 | 2.0 | 3.2 | 3.2 | ... | ... | ... |
| Netherlands | 1.6 | 1.2 | 2.6 | 4.7 | 4.1 | 2.3 | 1.3 | 0.4 | 2.5 | 3.3 | 2.4 | ... | ... | ... |
| Belgium | 1.2 | 2.0 | 4.9 | 3.5 | 3.2 | 2.3 | 1.9 | −1.7 | 2.4 | 2.5 | 2.5 | ... | ... | ... |
| Sweden | 1.7 | 3.5 | 2.1 | 2.5 | 1.1 | −1.4 | −1.4 | −2.6 | 2.2 | 2.5 | 2.6 | ... | ... | ... |
| Austria | 2.0 | 1.7 | 4.1 | 3.8 | 4.2 | 3.0 | 1.8 | −0.1 | 2.7 | 2.8 | 2.5 | ... | ... | ... |
| Denmark | 2.3 | 0.3 | 1.2 | 0.6 | 1.4 | 1.3 | 0.8 | 1.5 | 4.4 | 3.3 | 2.5 | ... | ... | ... |
| Finland | 3.2 | 4.1 | 4.9 | 5.7 | −0.1 | −7.0 | −3.6 | −1.6 | 3.9 | 5.2 | 4.6 | ... | ... | ... |
| Greece[4] | 2.3 | −0.5 | 4.5 | 4.0 | −1.0 | 3.2 | 0.8 | −0.5 | 1.5 | 1.9 | 2.3 | ... | ... | ... |
| Portugal | 2.8 | 5.1 | 5.4 | 5.7 | 4.1 | 2.3 | 1.7 | −1.2 | 1.0 | 2.8 | 3.2 | ... | ... | ... |
| Ireland | 3.2 | 4.6 | 4.3 | 7.4 | 8.6 | 2.9 | 5.0 | 4.0 | 5.2 | 6.2 | 4.9 | ... | ... | ... |
| Luxembourg | 3.1 | 4.2 | 6.4 | 7.8 | 4.6 | 2.7 | 2.8 | 2.8 | 2.8 | 3.0 | 3.3 | ... | ... | ... |
| Switzerland | 2.0 | 2.0 | 2.9 | 3.9 | 2.3 | — | −0.3 | −0.9 | 1.2 | 1.5 | 2.0 | ... | ... | ... |
| Norway | 3.8 | 2.0 | −0.5 | 0.6 | 1.7 | 1.6 | 3.4 | 2.3 | 5.1 | 5.0 | 3.5 | ... | ... | ... |
| Iceland | 4.5 | 8.6 | −0.1 | 0.3 | 1.1 | 1.3 | −3.3 | 1.1 | 2.8 | 3.0 | 2.6 | ... | ... | ... |
| Australia | 2.9 | 4.7 | 4.1 | 4.4 | 1.4 | −1.5 | 2.0 | 3.9 | 5.4 | 3.8 | 3.6 | ... | ... | ... |
| New Zealand | 1.8 | −0.7 | 3.9 | −1.4 | — | −3.7 | 0.5 | 5.0 | 4.3 | 2.2 | 3.2 | ... | ... | ... |
| *Memorandum* | | | | | | | | | | | | | | |
| European Union | 2.1 | 2.9 | 4.2 | 3.5 | 3.0 | 1.1 | 1.0 | −0.6 | 2.8 | 2.9 | 2.8 | ... | ... | ... |
| **Real total domestic demand** | | | | | | | | | | | | | | |
| **Industrial countries** | **2.6** | **3.6** | **4.5** | **3.3** | **2.2** | **0.5** | **1.5** | **0.9** | **3.3** | **2.6** | **2.5** | ... | ... | ... |
| Major industrial countries | 2.7 | 3.5 | 4.5 | 3.1 | 2.1 | 0.5 | 1.6 | 1.3 | 3.3 | 2.5 | 2.4 | 3.6 | 2.1 | 2.6 |
| United States | 3.0 | 2.7 | 3.0 | 1.8 | 0.8 | −1.3 | 2.6 | 3.9 | 4.7 | 3.0 | 1.8 | 4.5 | 1.8 | 2.1 |
| Japan | 3.5 | 5.1 | 7.6 | 5.8 | 5.0 | 2.9 | 0.3 | — | 0.9 | 1.5 | 3.1 | 0.9 | 2.8 | 2.9 |
| Germany | 1.6 | 2.4 | 3.6 | 2.9 | 5.2 | 6.1 | 2.8 | −1.3 | 2.8 | 2.3 | 3.2 | 4.0 | 2.4 | 3.1 |
| France | 2.0 | 3.3 | 4.6 | 3.9 | 2.8 | 0.6 | 0.4 | −2.3 | 3.1 | 2.5 | 2.9 | 4.8 | 2.4 | 2.8 |
| Italy | 2.4 | 4.2 | 4.4 | 2.8 | 2.5 | 1.9 | 0.8 | −5.5 | 1.9 | 2.7 | 2.9 | 3.8 | 2.7 | 2.9 |
| United Kingdom | 2.0 | 5.3 | 7.9 | 2.9 | −0.6 | −3.1 | 0.3 | 2.0 | 3.3 | 2.0 | 2.6 | 3.4 | 1.3 | 3.0 |
| Canada | 2.9 | 5.3 | 5.5 | 4.3 | −0.5 | −1.2 | 0.4 | 2.0 | 3.2 | 1.8 | 2.3 | 2.7 | 1.2 | 3.2 |
| Other industrial countries | 1.7 | 3.8 | 4.5 | 5.0 | 2.5 | 0.5 | 0.7 | −1.2 | 2.9 | 3.3 | 3.2 | ... | ... | ... |
| *Memorandum* | | | | | | | | | | | | | | |
| European Union | 1.8 | 3.9 | 5.0 | 3.7 | 2.9 | 1.8 | 1.1 | −1.9 | 2.5 | 2.6 | 3.0 | ... | ... | ... |

[1]From fourth quarter of preceding year.
[2]Data through 1990 apply to west Germany only.
[3]Average of expenditure, income, and output estimates of GDP at market prices.
[4]Based on revised national accounts for 1988 onward.

## Table A3. Industrial Countries: Components of Real GDP

*(Annual percent change)*

| | Average 1977–86 | 1987 | 1988 | 1989 | 1990 | 1991 | 1992 | 1993 | 1994 | 1995 | 1996 |
|---|---|---|---|---|---|---|---|---|---|---|---|
| **Private consumer expenditure** | | | | | | | | | | | |
| **Industrial countries** | **2.8** | **3.4** | **4.0** | **2.9** | **2.5** | **1.1** | **2.0** | **1.5** | **2.6** | **2.2** | **2.4** |
| Major industrial countries | 2.9 | 3.5 | 4.2 | 2.8 | 2.4 | 0.9 | 2.1 | 1.8 | 2.6 | 2.2 | 2.3 |
| United States | 3.0 | 2.8 | 3.6 | 1.9 | 1.5 | −0.4 | 2.8 | 3.3 | 3.5 | 2.6 | 1.6 |
| Japan | 3.6 | 4.2 | 5.2 | 4.3 | 3.9 | 2.2 | 1.7 | 1.0 | 2.2 | 1.2 | 3.0 |
| Germany[1] | 1.9 | 3.4 | 2.7 | 2.8 | 5.4 | 5.4 | 2.8 | 0.5 | 0.9 | 1.8 | 3.3 |
| France | 2.4 | 2.9 | 3.3 | 3.0 | 2.7 | 1.4 | 1.4 | 0.2 | 1.5 | 2.5 | 2.7 |
| Italy | 3.2 | 4.2 | 4.2 | 3.5 | 2.5 | 2.7 | 1.1 | −2.5 | 1.6 | 2.6 | 3.2 |
| United Kingdom | 2.7 | 5.3 | 7.5 | 3.2 | 0.6 | −2.2 | — | 2.5 | 3.0 | 2.0 | 2.8 |
| Canada | 2.9 | 4.4 | 4.5 | 3.4 | 1.0 | −1.6 | 1.3 | 1.6 | 3.0 | 1.8 | 2.5 |
| Other industrial countries | 1.8 | 3.3 | 3.1 | 3.7 | 2.7 | 2.0 | 1.7 | −0.4 | 2.1 | 2.5 | 2.8 |
| *Memorandum* | | | | | | | | | | | |
| European Union | 2.3 | 3.9 | 4.1 | 3.4 | 3.0 | 2.3 | 1.5 | −0.1 | 1.6 | 2.2 | 3.0 |
| **Public consumption** | | | | | | | | | | | |
| **Industrial countries** | **2.6** | **2.4** | **1.7** | **1.7** | **2.6** | **1.7** | **1.2** | **0.3** | **0.6** | **0.6** | **0.9** |
| Major industrial countries | 2.6 | 2.3 | 1.6 | 1.5 | 2.5 | 1.5 | 1.1 | 0.2 | 0.5 | 0.6 | 0.9 |
| United States | 2.6 | 3.0 | 0.6 | 2.0 | 3.1 | 1.2 | −0.7 | −0.8 | −0.7 | −0.3 | 0.5 |
| Japan | 3.5 | 0.4 | 2.2 | 2.0 | 1.9 | 1.6 | 2.7 | 1.7 | 2.8 | 3.6 | 2.7 |
| Germany[1] | 1.9 | 1.5 | 2.1 | −1.6 | 2.2 | 0.6 | 5.0 | −0.5 | 1.2 | 1.6 | 0.7 |
| France | 2.7 | 2.8 | 3.5 | 0.4 | 2.1 | 2.8 | 3.4 | 3.3 | 1.1 | 1.8 | 1.2 |
| Italy | 2.8 | 3.4 | 2.8 | 0.8 | 1.2 | 1.6 | 1.0 | 0.7 | — | −3.2 | 0.1 |
| United Kingdom | 1.0 | 1.0 | 0.7 | 1.4 | 2.5 | 2.6 | — | 0.2 | 2.0 | 0.5 | 0.5 |
| Canada | 2.2 | 1.7 | 4.1 | 4.0 | 3.2 | 2.7 | 1.0 | 0.5 | −1.7 | −0.1 | −0.4 |
| Other industrial countries | 2.9 | 3.3 | 2.1 | 3.3 | 3.1 | 2.9 | 1.7 | 0.9 | 1.6 | 0.9 | 1.0 |
| *Memorandum* | | | | | | | | | | | |
| European Union | 2.3 | 2.6 | 2.1 | 1.1 | 2.2 | 2.2 | 2.4 | 0.9 | 1.1 | 0.4 | 0.7 |
| **Gross fixed capital formation** | | | | | | | | | | | |
| **Industrial countries** | **2.7** | **3.9** | **7.4** | **4.6** | **1.8** | **−2.4** | **1.4** | **1.7** | **5.9** | **6.2** | **4.6** |
| Major industrial countries | 2.9 | 3.6 | 7.2 | 3.9 | 1.8 | −2.4 | 2.1 | 2.8 | 6.3 | 6.0 | 4.4 |
| United States | 3.9 | −0.5 | 4.2 | 0.1 | −1.7 | −7.6 | 5.5 | 11.3 | 12.3 | 9.9 | 4.4 |
| Japan | 3.2 | 9.6 | 11.9 | 9.3 | 8.8 | 3.7 | −1.1 | −1.8 | −2.4 | 0.9 | 3.2 |
| Germany[1] | 1.1 | 1.8 | 4.4 | 6.3 | 8.5 | 9.8 | 3.5 | −5.6 | 4.3 | 3.3 | 4.3 |
| France | 0.4 | 4.8 | 9.6 | 7.9 | 2.8 | — | −3.1 | −5.8 | 1.6 | 3.3 | 4.6 |
| Italy | 1.3 | 5.0 | 6.9 | 4.3 | 3.8 | 0.6 | −1.7 | −13.1 | −0.1 | 6.6 | 4.0 |
| United Kingdom | 1.4 | 10.2 | 14.0 | 6.0 | −3.5 | −9.5 | −1.2 | 0.3 | 3.7 | 2.2 | 6.1 |
| Canada | 3.9 | 10.8 | 10.3 | 6.1 | −3.5 | −2.9 | −1.5 | 0.6 | 7.2 | 3.4 | 7.3 |
| Other industrial countries | 1.3 | 5.6 | 8.8 | 8.8 | 1.9 | −2.8 | −2.4 | −4.4 | 3.9 | 7.1 | 5.9 |
| *Memorandum* | | | | | | | | | | | |
| European Union | 1.0 | 5.6 | 8.8 | 7.1 | 3.8 | 0.5 | −1.0 | −6.4 | 2.3 | 4.8 | 5.1 |

## Table A3  *(concluded)*

| | Average 1977–86 | 1987 | 1988 | 1989 | 1990 | 1991 | 1992 | 1993 | 1994 | 1995 | 1996 |
|---|---|---|---|---|---|---|---|---|---|---|---|
| **Final domestic demand** | | | | | | | | | | | |
| **Industrial countries** | **2.7** | **3.5** | **4.4** | **3.2** | **2.5** | **0.7** | **1.6** | **1.0** | **2.6** | **2.6** | **2.6** |
| Major industrial countries | 2.8 | 3.4 | 4.4 | 3.0 | 2.5 | 0.6 | 1.7 | 1.4 | 2.7 | 2.5 | 2.5 |
| United States | 3.1 | 2.3 | 3.1 | 1.7 | 1.3 | −1.2 | 2.5 | 3.7 | 4.1 | 3.3 | 1.9 |
| Japan | 3.5 | 5.4 | 7.0 | 5.7 | 5.3 | 2.6 | 0.8 | 0.1 | 0.7 | 1.3 | 3.1 |
| Germany[1] | 1.8 | 2.7 | 3.0 | 2.6 | 5.4 | 5.4 | 3.4 | −1.1 | 1.7 | 2.1 | 3.0 |
| France | 2.0 | 3.3 | 4.6 | 3.6 | 2.6 | 1.3 | 0.8 | −0.5 | 1.4 | 2.5 | 2.8 |
| Italy | 2.7 | 4.2 | 4.5 | 3.3 | 2.6 | 2.1 | 0.5 | −4.2 | 1.0 | 2.4 | 2.9 |
| United Kingdom | 2.1 | 5.2 | 7.2 | 3.4 | 0.2 | −2.6 | −0.2 | 1.6 | 2.9 | 1.7 | 2.9 |
| Canada | 2.9 | 5.1 | 5.6 | 4.1 | 0.4 | −1.0 | 0.6 | 1.1 | 2.9 | 1.8 | 3.0 |
| Other industrial countries | 1.8 | 3.8 | 4.1 | 4.8 | 2.5 | 1.1 | 0.8 | −1.0 | 2.4 | 3.2 | 3.2 |
| *Memorandum* | | | | | | | | | | | |
| European Union | 2.0 | 3.9 | 4.6 | 3.7 | 3.0 | 1.9 | 1.2 | −1.3 | 1.7 | 2.4 | 3.0 |
| **Stock building[2]** | | | | | | | | | | | |
| **Industrial countries** | **−0.1** | **0.1** | **0.2** | **0.1** | **−0.3** | **−0.1** | **−0.1** | **−0.1** | **0.6** | **—** | **—** |
| Major industrial countries | −0.1 | 0.1 | 0.1 | 0.1 | −0.4 | −0.1 | −0.1 | −0.1 | 0.7 | — | −0.1 |
| United States | — | 0.4 | −0.1 | 0.2 | −0.5 | −0.1 | 0.1 | 0.3 | 0.6 | −0.3 | −0.1 |
| Japan | — | −0.3 | 0.6 | 0.2 | −0.3 | 0.3 | −0.5 | −0.2 | 0.2 | 0.1 | 0.1 |
| Germany[1] | −0.1 | −0.2 | 0.6 | 0.3 | −0.1 | 0.7 | −0.6 | −0.2 | 1.1 | 0.2 | 0.2 |
| France | — | 0.1 | — | 0.4 | 0.2 | −0.7 | −0.4 | −1.8 | 1.7 | — | 0.1 |
| Italy | −0.3 | — | — | −0.4 | — | −0.1 | 0.3 | −1.4 | 0.8 | 0.3 | — |
| United Kingdom | — | 0.1 | 0.7 | −0.4 | −0.8 | −0.5 | 0.5 | 0.4 | 0.4 | 0.2 | −0.3 |
| Canada | — | 0.1 | −0.1 | 0.2 | −1.0 | −0.1 | −0.2 | 0.9 | 0.3 | 0.1 | −0.7 |
| Other industrial countries | — | 0.1 | 0.4 | 0.2 | — | −0.5 | −0.1 | −0.2 | 0.4 | 0.1 | 0.1 |
| *Memorandum* | | | | | | | | | | | |
| European Union | −0.1 | — | 0.4 | — | −0.1 | −0.1 | −0.1 | −0.6 | 0.9 | 0.2 | — |
| **Foreign balance[2]** | | | | | | | | | | | |
| **Industrial countries** | **—** | **−0.4** | **−0.2** | **−0.1** | **0.2** | **0.3** | **—** | **0.2** | **−0.2** | **−0.1** | **−0.1** |
| Major industrial countries | −0.1 | −0.3 | −0.1 | 0.1 | 0.2 | 0.3 | — | — | −0.3 | −0.1 | −0.1 |
| United States | −0.4 | 0.3 | 0.9 | 0.6 | 0.4 | 0.7 | −0.3 | −0.8 | −0.7 | −0.1 | 0.2 |
| Japan | 0.5 | −0.9 | −1.2 | −1.1 | −0.2 | 1.3 | 0.8 | −0.2 | −0.4 | −1.0 | −1.0 |
| Germany[1] | 0.3 | −0.8 | 0.3 | 0.9 | 0.8 | −3.1 | −0.6 | 0.2 | 0.1 | 0.2 | −0.3 |
| France | 0.1 | −1.1 | −0.3 | 0.3 | −0.3 | 0.2 | 1.0 | 0.8 | −0.2 | 0.3 | −0.3 |
| Italy | — | −1.1 | −0.5 | — | −0.5 | −0.8 | −0.1 | 4.6 | 0.3 | 0.3 | — |
| United Kingdom | −0.1 | −0.5 | −2.9 | −0.8 | 1.0 | 1.3 | −0.9 | 0.2 | 0.4 | 0.7 | 0.3 |
| Canada | 0.2 | −0.9 | −1.2 | −1.6 | 0.6 | −0.6 | 0.5 | 0.3 | 1.1 | 0.3 | 0.3 |
| Other industrial countries | 0.3 | −0.7 | −0.6 | −1.3 | 0.2 | 0.5 | 0.3 | 1.3 | 0.1 | −0.1 | −0.2 |
| *Memorandum* | | | | | | | | | | | |
| European Union | 0.2 | −0.9 | −0.8 | −0.3 | 0.1 | −0.6 | −0.1 | 1.4 | 0.2 | 0.3 | −0.2 |

[1]Data through 1990 apply to west Germany only.
[2]Changes expressed as percent of GDP in the preceding period.

## Table A4. Industrial Countries: Unemployment, Employment, and Real Per Capita GDP

*(In percent)*

| | Average[1] 1977–86 | 1987 | 1988 | 1989 | 1990 | 1991 | 1992 | 1993 | 1994 | 1995 | 1996 |
|---|---|---|---|---|---|---|---|---|---|---|---|
| **Unemployment rate** | | | | | | | | | | | |
| **Industrial countries** | **6.7** | **7.3** | **6.8** | **6.2** | **6.0** | **6.8** | **7.7** | **8.1** | **8.1** | **7.6** | **7.5** |
| Major industrial countries | 6.4 | 6.8 | 6.2 | 5.7 | 5.6 | 6.4 | 7.2 | 7.3 | 7.2 | 6.8 | 6.8 |
| United States[2] | 7.5 | 6.2 | 5.5 | 5.3 | 5.5 | 6.7 | 7.4 | 6.8 | 6.1 | 5.7 | 5.9 |
| Japan | 2.4 | 2.8 | 2.5 | 2.3 | 2.1 | 2.1 | 2.2 | 2.5 | 2.9 | 3.1 | 3.2 |
| Germany[3] | 5.8 | 7.9 | 7.8 | 6.8 | 6.2 | 6.6 | 7.7 | 8.8 | 9.6 | 9.1 | 8.7 |
| France | 7.6 | 10.5 | 10.0 | 9.4 | 8.9 | 9.4 | 10.3 | 11.6 | 12.4 | 11.7 | 11.0 |
| Italy[4] | 8.2 | 10.2 | 10.4 | 10.2 | 9.1 | 8.6 | 10.7 | 10.4 | 11.3 | 11.2 | 10.5 |
| United Kingdom | 7.8 | 10.0 | 8.0 | 6.3 | 5.8 | 8.1 | 9.7 | 10.3 | 9.3 | 8.3 | 8.1 |
| Canada | 9.3 | 8.8 | 7.8 | 7.5 | 8.1 | 10.4 | 11.3 | 11.2 | 10.4 | 9.7 | 9.4 |
| Other industrial countries | 7.9 | 9.8 | 9.5 | 8.5 | 8.1 | 8.9 | 10.2 | 12.2 | 12.5 | 11.8 | 11.2 |
| Spain | 14.5 | 20.5 | 19.5 | 17.3 | 16.3 | 16.3 | 18.4 | 22.7 | 24.2 | 23.1 | 22.0 |
| Netherlands | 6.6 | 8.5 | 8.4 | 7.7 | 7.0 | 6.6 | 6.7 | 7.7 | 8.7 | 8.6 | 8.5 |
| Belgium | 9.6 | 11.0 | 9.8 | 8.1 | 7.2 | 7.1 | 7.9 | 9.5 | 10.3 | 9.8 | 9.4 |
| Sweden | 2.6 | 1.9 | 1.6 | 1.4 | 1.5 | 2.9 | 5.3 | 8.2 | 8.0 | 7.3 | 6.9 |
| Austria | 3.3 | 5.6 | 5.3 | 3.1 | 3.2 | 3.5 | 3.6 | 4.2 | 4.4 | 4.2 | 4.2 |
| Denmark | 8.3 | 7.8 | 8.6 | 9.3 | 9.6 | 10.5 | 11.2 | 12.3 | 12.1 | 10.0 | 9.7 |
| Finland | 5.5 | 4.7 | 4.5 | 3.5 | 3.5 | 7.6 | 13.1 | 17.9 | 18.4 | 16.8 | 14.7 |
| Greece | 6.5 | 7.4 | 7.7 | 7.5 | 7.0 | 7.7 | 8.7 | 9.7 | 9.6 | 9.5 | 9.3 |
| Portugal | 8.1 | 7.1 | 7.0 | 5.8 | 4.7 | 4.1 | 4.1 | 5.5 | 6.8 | 7.0 | 6.6 |
| Ireland | 11.6 | 16.7 | 16.1 | 14.7 | 13.4 | 14.7 | 15.5 | 15.7 | 14.8 | 13.8 | 13.5 |
| Luxembourg | 1.2 | 1.7 | 1.5 | 1.4 | 1.3 | 1.4 | 1.6 | 2.1 | 2.8 | 3.0 | 2.6 |
| Switzerland | 0.6 | 0.7 | 0.6 | 0.5 | 0.5 | 1.1 | 2.6 | 4.6 | 4.8 | 4.3 | 4.0 |
| Norway | 2.3 | 2.1 | 3.2 | 4.9 | 5.2 | 5.5 | 5.9 | 6.0 | 5.4 | 5.0 | 4.5 |
| Iceland | 0.6 | 0.4 | 0.6 | 1.7 | 1.8 | 1.5 | 3.1 | 4.4 | 4.8 | 4.5 | 4.3 |
| Australia | 7.3 | 8.1 | 7.2 | 6.2 | 7.0 | 9.6 | 10.8 | 10.9 | 9.7 | 8.4 | 7.6 |
| New Zealand | 4.3 | 4.4 | 6.8 | 7.3 | 8.6 | 10.6 | 10.3 | 9.2 | 7.4 | 6.5 | 6.3 |
| *Memorandum* | | | | | | | | | | | |
| European Union | 7.8 | 10.1 | 9.6 | 8.5 | 7.9 | 8.4 | 9.8 | 11.1 | 11.6 | 11.0 | 10.4 |
| **Growth in employment** | | | | | | | | | | | |
| **Industrial countries** | **1.0** | **1.7** | **1.9** | **1.9** | **1.2** | **–0.5** | **–0.3** | **–0.2** | **1.0** | **1.2** | **0.9** |
| Major industrial countries | 1.2 | 1.7 | 2.0 | 1.8 | 1.1 | –0.5 | –0.1 | 0.2 | 1.2 | 1.0 | 0.7 |
| United States | 2.1 | 2.6 | 2.3 | 2.0 | 0.5 | –0.9 | 0.6 | 1.5 | 3.1 | 1.5 | 0.7 |
| Japan | 1.1 | 1.0 | 1.7 | 1.9 | 2.0 | 1.9 | 1.1 | 0.2 | 0.1 | 0.1 | 0.2 |
| Germany[3] | 0.4 | 0.7 | 0.8 | 1.5 | 3.0 | –2.2 | –1.6 | –1.8 | –0.9 | 0.8 | 0.7 |
| France | — | 0.4 | 0.9 | 1.5 | 1.1 | 0.2 | –0.6 | –1.0 | 0.1 | 1.7 | 1.5 |
| Italy | 0.5 | –0.3 | 0.5 | –0.1 | 1.2 | 0.8 | –0.9 | –2.5 | –1.7 | 1.0 | 1.0 |
| United Kingdom | –0.1 | 2.3 | 4.2 | 2.7 | 0.4 | –3.1 | –2.5 | –0.6 | 0.3 | 0.6 | 0.6 |
| Canada | 2.1 | 2.7 | 3.2 | 2.1 | 0.6 | –1.9 | –0.6 | 1.4 | 2.1 | 1.7 | 1.9 |
| Other industrial countries | 0.3 | 1.6 | 1.7 | 2.2 | 1.7 | –0.4 | –1.3 | –1.8 | 0.3 | 1.8 | 1.7 |
| *Memorandum* | | | | | | | | | | | |
| European Union | 0.1 | 1.1 | 1.7 | 1.7 | 1.6 | –0.9 | –1.5 | –1.7 | –0.4 | 1.2 | 1.2 |

Table A4 *(concluded)*

| | Average[1] 1977–86 | 1987 | 1988 | 1989 | 1990 | 1991 | 1992 | 1993 | 1994 | 1995 | 1996 |
|---|---|---|---|---|---|---|---|---|---|---|---|
| **Growth in real per capita GDP** | | | | | | | | | | | |
| **Industrial countries** | **2.0** | **2.6** | **3.7** | **2.5** | **1.6** | **—** | **0.8** | **0.5** | **2.4** | **1.9** | **1.8** |
| Major industrial countries | 2.1 | 2.6 | 3.8 | 2.4 | 1.5 | — | 0.9 | 0.7 | 2.4 | 1.7 | 1.7 |
| United States | 1.7 | 2.2 | 3.0 | 1.6 | 0.2 | −1.7 | 1.2 | 2.0 | 3.0 | 1.9 | 1.0 |
| Japan | 3.2 | 3.6 | 5.8 | 4.3 | 4.5 | 3.9 | 0.8 | −0.5 | 0.3 | 0.2 | 1.9 |
| Germany[3] | 2.0 | 1.5 | 3.1 | 2.6 | 3.8 | 2.0 | 1.4 | −1.9 | 2.6 | 2.0 | 2.3 |
| France | 1.7 | 1.8 | 4.0 | 3.8 | 2.0 | 0.4 | 0.9 | −1.9 | 2.5 | 2.5 | 2.2 |
| Italy | 2.5 | 3.0 | 3.9 | 2.8 | 2.0 | 0.9 | 1.1 | 0.2 | 2.1 | 2.9 | 2.8 |
| United Kingdom | 2.0 | 4.5 | 4.8 | 1.9 | 0.1 | −2.6 | −0.8 | 2.0 | 3.6 | 2.5 | 2.6 |
| Canada | 2.0 | 2.9 | 3.6 | 0.7 | −1.7 | −3.0 | −0.4 | 1.1 | 3.2 | 1.1 | 1.6 |
| Other industrial countries | 1.6 | 2.8 | 3.5 | 3.4 | 2.1 | 0.3 | 0.4 | −0.5 | 2.3 | 2.6 | 2.4 |
| *Memorandum* | | | | | | | | | | | |
| European Union | 1.9 | 2.7 | 3.9 | 3.1 | 2.3 | 0.6 | 0.7 | −0.7 | 2.5 | 2.5 | 2.5 |

[1]Compound annual rate of change for employment and per capita GDP; arithmetic average for unemployment rate.
[2]The projections for unemployment have been adjusted to reflect the new survey techniques adopted by the U.S. Bureau of Labor Statistics in January 1994.
[3]Data through 1990 apply to west Germany only.
[4]New series starting in 1993, reflecting revisions in the labor force surveys and the definition of unemployment to bring data in line with those of other industrial countries.

## Table A5. Developing Countries: Real GDP

*(Annual percent change)*

| | Average 1977–86 | 1987 | 1988 | 1989 | 1990 | 1991 | 1992 | 1993 | 1994 | 1995 | 1996 |
|---|---|---|---|---|---|---|---|---|---|---|---|
| **Developing countries** | **4.5** | **5.7** | **5.2** | **4.2** | **4.0** | **4.9** | **5.9** | **6.1** | **6.2** | **6.0** | **6.3** |
| **By region** | | | | | | | | | | | |
| Africa | 2.1 | 1.6 | 3.6 | 3.4 | 2.1 | 1.7 | 0.7 | 0.8 | 2.6 | 3.0 | 5.2 |
| Asia | 6.7 | 8.1 | 9.1 | 6.0 | 5.7 | 6.4 | 8.2 | 8.7 | 8.5 | 8.7 | 7.9 |
| Middle East and Europe | 2.6 | 5.0 | –0.5 | 2.7 | 4.8 | 3.2 | 5.5 | 3.6 | 0.3 | 2.4 | 3.2 |
| Western Hemisphere | 3.2 | 3.4 | 1.1 | 1.6 | 0.6 | 3.5 | 2.7 | 3.3 | 4.6 | 1.8 | 4.0 |
| Sub-Saharan Africa | 2.8 | 3.2 | 2.5 | 2.3 | 1.1 | 1.6 | 0.9 | 1.5 | 2.1 | 5.0 | 5.5 |
| Four newly industrializing Asian economies | 8.1 | 11.9 | 9.5 | 6.4 | 7.1 | 7.8 | 5.7 | 5.9 | 7.5 | 8.1 | 7.0 |
| **By predominant export** | | | | | | | | | | | |
| Fuel | 1.0 | 1.3 | –0.5 | 3.2 | 5.3 | 5.1 | 3.9 | 0.4 | 0.1 | 1.9 | 2.6 |
| Nonfuel exports | 5.1 | 6.3 | 5.9 | 4.4 | 3.8 | 4.9 | 6.1 | 6.8 | 6.8 | 6.5 | 6.7 |
| Manufactures | 8.6 | 11.0 | 10.4 | 4.5 | 4.6 | 8.2 | 11.0 | 11.5 | 10.4 | 10.5 | 8.7 |
| Primary products | 1.9 | 3.4 | 0.3 | –0.3 | 0.7 | 4.6 | 4.9 | 4.3 | 5.1 | 4.5 | 4.9 |
| Agricultural products | 1.6 | 2.1 | 0.2 | –0.6 | 1.0 | 4.9 | 5.5 | 4.3 | 4.5 | 3.9 | 4.6 |
| Minerals | 2.5 | 6.1 | 0.7 | 0.5 | –0.1 | 3.9 | 3.6 | 4.5 | 6.4 | 5.8 | 5.5 |
| Services, income, and private transfers | 4.2 | 6.6 | 1.6 | 4.3 | –0.6 | –1.2 | 5.5 | 4.5 | 2.5 | 2.4 | 4.1 |
| Diversified export base | 4.4 | 4.4 | 4.8 | 5.0 | 4.2 | 3.4 | 3.4 | 4.2 | 4.9 | 4.2 | 5.7 |
| **By financial criteria** | | | | | | | | | | | |
| Net creditor countries | 2.9 | 3.2 | 4.2 | 6.5 | 4.6 | 4.5 | 6.5 | 3.8 | 3.0 | 3.3 | 3.8 |
| Net debtor countries | 4.6 | 5.9 | 5.3 | 4.1 | 4.0 | 4.9 | 5.9 | 6.3 | 6.3 | 6.2 | 6.4 |
| Market borrowers | 5.1 | 6.4 | 5.5 | 3.8 | 3.7 | 6.5 | 7.5 | 7.9 | 7.9 | 7.2 | 6.9 |
| Diversified borrowers | 4.2 | 5.7 | 5.6 | 5.0 | 4.6 | 2.2 | 4.1 | 4.5 | 4.1 | 5.2 | 5.9 |
| Official borrowers | 3.4 | 4.0 | 3.8 | 3.6 | 3.6 | 3.8 | 2.7 | 2.5 | 3.4 | 3.6 | 5.5 |
| Countries with recent debt-servicing difficulties | 3.0 | 3.8 | 1.8 | 2.1 | 0.5 | 2.5 | 2.2 | 2.7 | 4.1 | 2.4 | 4.2 |
| Countries without debt-servicing difficulties | 5.8 | 7.3 | 7.5 | 5.4 | 6.0 | 6.2 | 7.8 | 8.0 | 7.4 | 8.0 | 7.5 |
| **Other groups** | | | | | | | | | | | |
| Small low-income economies | 3.3 | 4.0 | 3.8 | 3.7 | 3.8 | 3.7 | 2.7 | 2.8 | 3.0 | 4.4 | 5.2 |
| Least developed countries | 2.8 | 2.6 | 2.5 | 3.0 | 2.5 | 2.4 | 3.0 | 3.3 | 3.2 | 5.4 | 5.3 |
| *Memorandum* | | | | | | | | | | | |
| **Real per capita GDP** | | | | | | | | | | | |
| Developing countries | 2.0 | 3.5 | 4.8 | 0.9 | 2.2 | 3.1 | 3.5 | 4.3 | 4.2 | 3.9 | 4.4 |
| By region | | | | | | | | | | | |
| Africa | –0.5 | –1.1 | 0.7 | 0.7 | –0.8 | –1.0 | –1.9 | –1.8 | –0.1 | 0.4 | 2.4 |
| Asia | 4.6 | 6.2 | 10.5 | 1.8 | 4.0 | 4.7 | 6.5 | 7.0 | 6.8 | 7.0 | 6.2 |
| Middle East and Europe | –1.2 | 1.2 | –3.4 | 1.0 | 3.2 | 2.0 | –0.3 | 1.4 | –2.4 | –0.3 | 0.2 |
| Western Hemisphere | 0.9 | 1.3 | –0.7 | –0.8 | –1.4 | 1.6 | 0.7 | 1.3 | 2.7 | –0.9 | 2.2 |

## Table A6. Developing Countries—by Country: Real GDP[1]

*(Annual percent change)*

| | Average 1977–86 | 1987 | 1988 | 1989 | 1990 | 1991 | 1992 | 1993 | 1994 |
|---|---|---|---|---|---|---|---|---|---|
| **Africa** | **2.1** | **1.6** | **3.6** | **3.4** | **2.1** | **1.7** | **0.7** | **0.8** | **2.6** |
| Algeria | 2.5 | −0.7 | −1.9 | 4.8 | — | −1.3 | 1.6 | −2.2 | −0.2 |
| Angola | ... | 9.4 | −8.4 | 4.4 | −5.3 | −1.6 | 1.3 | −23.8 | 2.7 |
| Benin | 4.0 | −1.8 | 1.1 | −2.5 | 3.1 | 4.7 | 4.1 | 3.2 | 3.4 |
| Botswana | 10.8 | 12.2 | 14.1 | 9.2 | 7.3 | 7.6 | 2.3 | 0.4 | 2.8 |
| Burkina Faso | 3.6 | −1.4 | 6.6 | 0.9 | −1.5 | 10.0 | 2.5 | −0.8 | 1.2 |
| Burundi | 3.6 | 5.5 | 5.0 | 1.3 | 3.5 | 5.0 | 2.7 | −5.7 | −6.7 |
| Cameroon | 8.0 | 0.5 | −12.9 | −3.5 | −4.5 | −6.7 | −4.8 | −2.2 | −3.8 |
| Cape Verde | 4.6 | 7.6 | 7.6 | 6.9 | 2.4 | 1.0 | 2.9 | 4.3 | 4.5 |
| Central African Republic | 2.0 | −5.0 | 1.3 | 3.4 | −1.0 | −0.6 | −2.5 | −2.2 | 6.7 |
| Chad | 0.9 | −1.8 | 13.8 | 5.8 | −2.3 | 13.2 | 8.1 | −12.0 | 4.1 |
| Comoros | 4.5 | 1.6 | 2.7 | −3.2 | 2.5 | 2.1 | 1.6 | 1.3 | 0.8 |
| Congo | 7.1 | 0.2 | 1.8 | 2.9 | 0.7 | 2.2 | 2.4 | −1.2 | −6.7 |
| Côte d'Ivoire | 2.9 | −1.6 | −2.0 | −1.1 | −2.1 | −0.8 | — | −0.8 | 1.7 |
| Djibouti | 0.4 | 0.5 | 1.2 | −2.6 | −0.6 | 1.3 | 2.4 | −2.3 | −4.5 |
| Equatorial Guinea | 1.5 | 4.4 | 2.7 | −1.2 | 3.3 | −1.1 | 13.0 | 7.1 | 2.5 |
| Ethiopia | 1.6 | 9.9 | 2.4 | 1.2 | −2.2 | −1.0 | −3.2 | −12.3 | 1.3 |
| Gabon | −4.5 | −15.4 | 3.5 | 5.0 | 5.4 | 5.0 | 0.7 | 3.2 | 1.7 |
| Gambia, The | 3.5 | 2.8 | 1.7 | 4.3 | 5.7 | 2.2 | 4.4 | 2.1 | — |
| Ghana | 1.1 | 4.8 | 5.6 | 5.1 | 3.3 | 5.3 | 3.9 | 5.0 | 3.8 |
| Guinea | 1.8 | 3.3 | 6.3 | 4.0 | 4.3 | 2.4 | 3.0 | 4.7 | 4.0 |
| Guinea-Bissau | 6.5 | 5.6 | 6.9 | 4.5 | 3.2 | 3.0 | 2.8 | 2.7 | 6.3 |
| Kenya | 5.1 | 5.9 | 6.0 | 4.6 | 4.8 | 1.9 | −1.5 | −0.6 | 3.2 |
| Lesotho | −0.7 | 5.1 | 12.9 | 11.9 | 4.6 | 1.7 | 2.6 | 5.6 | 16.7 |
| Liberia | 0.5 | 1.3 | 3.1 | −10.8 | 0.3 | 2.9 | 1.9 | 2.2 | 2.2 |
| Madagascar | 0.4 | 1.2 | 3.4 | 4.1 | 3.1 | −6.3 | 1.1 | 2.1 | 0.2 |
| Malawi | 2.9 | 1.6 | 3.3 | 4.1 | 4.8 | 7.8 | −7.9 | 10.8 | −12.4 |
| Mali | 1.6 | 1.2 | −0.2 | 11.8 | 0.4 | −2.5 | 7.8 | −0.7 | 2.4 |
| Mauritania | 4.2 | 2.9 | 3.1 | 4.8 | −1.8 | 2.6 | 1.7 | 4.9 | 4.6 |
| Mauritius | 3.1 | 10.8 | 8.7 | 5.7 | 4.7 | 6.3 | 4.7 | 6.7 | 4.7 |
| Morocco | 4.2 | −2.7 | 10.4 | 2.5 | 3.9 | 6.9 | −4.1 | −1.1 | 11.5 |
| Mozambique, Rep. of | −2.3 | 14.6 | 8.2 | 6.5 | 0.9 | 4.9 | −0.8 | 19.3 | 5.4 |
| Namibia | ... | 4.3 | 0.2 | 2.1 | 0.3 | 6.6 | 7.5 | −1.9 | 5.4 |
| Niger | 2.1 | −3.6 | 6.9 | 0.9 | −1.3 | 2.5 | −6.5 | 1.4 | 4.0 |
| Nigeria | −1.2 | −0.7 | 9.9 | 7.2 | 8.2 | 4.8 | 2.9 | 2.3 | 1.3 |
| Rwanda | 3.8 | −0.3 | 3.8 | 1.0 | 0.4 | 0.3 | 0.4 | −10.9 | ... |
| São Tomé and Principe | 0.5 | −1.5 | 2.0 | 3.1 | −2.2 | 1.5 | 1.5 | 1.3 | 1.5 |
| Senegal | 2.0 | 4.0 | 5.1 | −1.4 | 4.5 | 0.7 | 2.9 | −2.0 | 2.0 |
| Seychelles | 3.5 | 4.9 | 5.3 | 10.3 | 7.5 | 2.7 | 6.9 | 5.8 | −1.1 |
| Sierra Leone | 0.3 | 4.0 | 2.5 | 2.4 | −0.1 | 0.7 | −0.8 | 1.5 | 3.5 |
| Somalia | 2.9 | 4.1 | −5.0 | 2.4 | −0.2 | ... | ... | ... | ... |
| South Africa | 2.0 | 2.1 | 4.2 | 2.4 | −0.3 | −1.0 | −2.2 | 1.1 | 2.3 |
| Sudan | 1.0 | 1.3 | 1.4 | 1.5 | — | 6.1 | 8.6 | 7.6 | 5.5 |
| Swaziland | 3.8 | 16.9 | 10.0 | 3.5 | 8.8 | 3.8 | 3.8 | 4.1 | 3.5 |
| Tanzania | 1.8 | 5.1 | 4.2 | 4.0 | 4.8 | 5.7 | 3.5 | 3.7 | 3.1 |
| Togo | 1.8 | 0.5 | 6.2 | 3.9 | 0.1 | −0.9 | −3.7 | −13.5 | 10.7 |
| Tunisia | 4.5 | 6.7 | 0.1 | 3.7 | 7.1 | 3.9 | 7.8 | 2.3 | 3.4 |
| Uganda | 1.3 | 7.6 | 6.0 | 5.7 | 5.1 | 3.1 | 8.4 | 5.5 | 10.0 |
| Zaïre | 1.1 | 2.5 | 0.6 | −1.4 | −6.6 | −8.4 | −10.5 | −16.2 | −7.6 |
| Zambia | 0.3 | 2.8 | 1.9 | 1.0 | −0.5 | −0.2 | −5.2 | 9.2 | 1.4 |
| Zimbabwe | 2.5 | −0.5 | 7.3 | 4.5 | 2.2 | 4.3 | −6.2 | 2.1 | 4.5 |

## Table A6 (continued)

| | Average 1977–86 | 1987 | 1988 | 1989 | 1990 | 1991 | 1992 | 1993 | 1994 |
|---|---|---|---|---|---|---|---|---|---|
| **Asia** | **6.7** | **8.1** | **9.1** | **6.0** | **5.7** | **6.4** | **8.2** | **8.7** | **8.5** |
| Afghanistan, Islamic State of | 0.5 | −10.3 | −8.3 | −7.1 | −2.6 | 0.8 | 1.0 | −3.1 | −3.0 |
| Bangladesh | 4.2 | 4.3 | 3.5 | 5.0 | 5.1 | 4.1 | 4.8 | 4.9 | 4.4 |
| Bhutan | 6.9 | 17.8 | 1.0 | 4.7 | 6.6 | 3.5 | 3.7 | 5.2 | 5.0 |
| Cambodia | . . . | . . . | 9.9 | 3.5 | 1.2 | 7.6 | 7.0 | 3.9 | 5.2 |
| China | 9.0 | 10.9 | 11.3 | 4.3 | 3.8 | 8.2 | 13.1 | 13.7 | 11.5 |
| Fiji | 2.1 | −5.9 | 3.5 | 13.4 | 5.6 | −0.2 | 4.4 | 2.7 | 3.3 |
| Hong Kong | 8.3 | 13.0 | 8.0 | 2.6 | 3.4 | 5.1 | 6.0 | 5.8 | 5.7 |
| India | 4.8 | 4.8 | 8.7 | 7.4 | 5.9 | 1.7 | 3.6 | 3.7 | 4.9 |
| Indonesia | 5.6 | 4.9 | 5.8 | 7.5 | 7.2 | 6.9 | 6.5 | 6.5 | 7.3 |
| Kiribati | −5.8 | 0.3 | 10.2 | −2.2 | −2.9 | 2.8 | 3.1 | 2.9 | 3.5 |
| Korea | 7.8 | 11.5 | 11.3 | 6.4 | 9.5 | 9.1 | 5.1 | 5.3 | 8.4 |
| Lao P.D. Republic | 4.9 | −1.0 | −2.1 | 9.9 | 6.7 | 4.0 | 7.0 | 6.1 | 8.4 |
| Malaysia | 5.8 | 5.4 | 8.9 | 9.2 | 9.7 | 8.7 | 7.8 | 8.3 | 8.7 |
| Maldives | 8.4 | 8.9 | 8.7 | 9.3 | 16.2 | 7.6 | 6.3 | 6.2 | 6.6 |
| Marshall Islands | . . . | 15.4 | 5.1 | −1.7 | 3.2 | 0.1 | 0.1 | 2.5 | 2.0 |
| Micronesia, Fed. States of | . . . | 9.6 | 12.4 | −1.7 | −2.7 | 4.3 | −1.2 | 5.2 | −0.4 |
| Myanmar | 4.9 | −3.3 | −9.5 | −0.4 | 3.0 | 0.2 | 6.8 | 6.7 | 6.3 |
| Nepal | 3.2 | 3.9 | 7.2 | 3.9 | 8.0 | 4.6 | 2.1 | 4.8 | 5.1 |
| Pakistan | 6.3 | 6.4 | 4.8 | 4.7 | 5.6 | 8.2 | 4.8 | 2.5 | 3.9 |
| Papua New Guinea | 1.5 | 2.8 | 2.9 | −1.4 | −3.0 | 9.5 | 11.8 | 16.6 | 3.0 |
| Philippines | 2.0 | 4.3 | 6.8 | 6.2 | 2.7 | −0.2 | 0.3 | 2.1 | 4.3 |
| Singapore | 6.8 | 9.5 | 11.1 | 9.6 | 8.8 | 6.7 | 6.0 | 10.1 | 10.1 |
| Solomon Islands | 2.5 | 8.4 | 1.3 | 4.3 | 1.0 | 1.7 | 10.5 | 0.5 | 3.7 |
| Sri Lanka | 5.2 | 1.5 | 2.7 | 2.3 | 6.2 | 4.6 | 4.3 | 6.9 | 5.6 |
| Taiwan Province of China | 8.4 | 12.3 | 7.3 | 7.6 | 4.9 | 7.2 | 6.5 | 6.1 | 6.5 |
| Thailand | 6.2 | 9.5 | 13.3 | 12.2 | 11.6 | 8.4 | 7.9 | 8.2 | 8.5 |
| Vanuatu | 3.5 | 0.4 | 0.6 | 4.5 | 5.2 | 6.5 | 0.6 | 4.4 | 2.0 |
| Vietnam | 5.6 | 2.5 | 5.1 | 7.8 | 4.9 | 6.0 | 8.6 | 8.1 | 8.8 |
| Western Samoa | 2.2 | 0.5 | −1.5 | 6.4 | −9.4 | −1.9 | −1.3 | 5.4 | −5.5 |
| **Middle East and Europe** | **2.6** | **5.0** | **−0.5** | **2.7** | **4.8** | **3.2** | **5.5** | **3.6** | **0.3** |
| Bahrain | 4.8 | −1.2 | 10.9 | 1.2 | 1.3 | 4.6 | 7.8 | 8.2 | 2.3 |
| Cyprus | 7.0 | 7.0 | 8.7 | 8.0 | 7.3 | 1.2 | 10.3 | 1.3 | 4.0 |
| Egypt | 6.2 | 8.7 | 3.5 | 2.7 | 2.3 | 1.2 | 0.4 | 1.5 | 1.3 |
| Iran, Islamic Republic of | −0.8 | −2.2 | −9.7 | 4.5 | 11.2 | 10.7 | 6.1 | 2.3 | 1.6 |
| Iraq | 1.1 | 28.3 | −10.2 | 12.0 | −26.0 | −61.3 | — | — | 1.0 |
| Israel | 3.0 | 6.1 | 3.1 | 1.3 | 5.8 | 6.2 | 6.6 | 3.5 | 6.5 |
| Jordan | 7.2 | 2.9 | −1.9 | −13.4 | 1.0 | 1.8 | 16.1 | 5.8 | 5.7 |
| Kuwait | −2.2 | 8.1 | −10.0 | 25.0 | −25.7 | −41.0 | 76.3 | 29.3 | 1.1 |
| Lebanon | 11.7 | 16.7 | −28.2 | −42.2 | −13.4 | 38.2 | 4.5 | 7.0 | 8.0 |
| Libya | −2.6 | −23.6 | −10.2 | 7.2 | 5.6 | 3.6 | −3.0 | −6.1 | −3.0 |
| Malta | 4.3 | 4.1 | 8.4 | 8.2 | 6.3 | 6.2 | 4.7 | 4.5 | 4.3 |
| Oman | 7.7 | −3.7 | 6.1 | 3.3 | 7.5 | 9.2 | 6.0 | 6.4 | 3.5 |
| Qatar | −0.8 | 0.9 | 4.7 | 5.3 | 2.7 | −0.8 | 9.7 | −0.6 | 0.2 |
| Saudi Arabia | 2.5 | −1.4 | 8.4 | −0.2 | 8.9 | 9.7 | 3.1 | −0.5 | −0.1 |
| Syrian Arab Republic | 3.1 | 1.9 | 13.3 | −9.0 | 7.6 | 7.1 | 10.5 | 3.9 | 5.5 |
| Turkey | 3.9 | 9.6 | 1.9 | 0.6 | 9.3 | 0.8 | 6.1 | 7.5 | −5.5 |
| United Arab Emirates | −1.2 | 5.5 | −2.6 | 13.3 | 17.5 | 0.2 | 2.8 | −1.5 | 1.1 |
| Yemen Arab Republic, former | 7.9 | 4.4 | 6.7 | 3.4 | 1.7 | . . . | . . . | . . . | . . . |
| Yemen, former P.D. Republic of | 0.8 | 1.4 | 1.0 | 2.5 | 3.0 | . . . | . . . | . . . | . . . |
| Yemen, Republic of | . . . | . . . | . . . | . . . | . . . | — | 4.2 | 5.9 | 6.0 |

## Table A6 *(concluded)*

| | Average 1977–86 | 1987 | 1988 | 1989 | 1990 | 1991 | 1992 | 1993 | 1994 |
|---|---|---|---|---|---|---|---|---|---|
| **Western Hemisphere** | **3.2** | **3.4** | **1.1** | **1.6** | **0.6** | **3.5** | **2.7** | **3.3** | **4.6** |
| Antigua and Barbuda | 6.8 | 9.0 | 7.7 | 6.3 | 3.5 | 4.4 | 1.1 | 3.4 | 4.2 |
| Argentina | 0.5 | 2.6 | −1.9 | −6.2 | 0.1 | 8.9 | 8.7 | 6.0 | 7.4 |
| Aruba | ... | 15.9 | 16.7 | 9.1 | 11.7 | 3.8 | 3.8 | 3.8 | 3.8 |
| Bahamas, The | 5.0 | 3.7 | 2.3 | 2.3 | 1.2 | −3.1 | 0.1 | 2.0 | 2.3 |
| Barbados | 2.8 | 3.8 | 3.1 | 3.7 | −3.3 | −3.9 | −5.6 | 0.4 | 3.7 |
| Belize | 2.7 | 11.6 | 9.0 | 13.0 | 9.3 | 4.6 | 9.0 | 4.2 | 1.5 |
| Bolivia | −0.4 | 2.6 | 3.0 | 3.6 | 4.4 | 4.6 | 2.8 | 4.1 | 4.2 |
| Brazil | 3.8 | 3.6 | 0.3 | 3.3 | −4.4 | 1.1 | −0.9 | 4.3 | 5.7 |
| Chile | 3.7 | 6.6 | 7.3 | 9.9 | 3.3 | 7.3 | 11.0 | 6.3 | 4.2 |
| Colombia | 3.9 | 5.4 | 4.1 | 3.4 | 4.3 | 2.0 | 4.0 | 5.3 | 5.7 |
| Costa Rica | 3.1 | 4.8 | 3.4 | 5.6 | 3.6 | 2.2 | 7.3 | 6.0 | 3.5 |
| Dominica | 3.7 | 6.8 | 7.4 | −1.1 | 6.3 | 2.3 | 2.9 | 2.1 | 1.0 |
| Dominican Republic | 3.1 | 10.0 | 2.2 | 4.8 | −6.0 | 0.8 | 7.8 | 3.0 | 4.3 |
| Ecuador | 3.7 | −5.9 | 10.4 | 0.3 | 3.0 | 5.0 | 3.6 | 2.0 | 4.0 |
| El Salvador | −0.8 | 2.7 | 1.6 | 1.0 | 3.4 | 3.5 | 5.0 | 5.3 | 5.8 |
| Grenada | 4.5 | 7.7 | 6.8 | 5.0 | 6.8 | 2.1 | — | 1.0 | 1.4 |
| Guatemala | 1.5 | 3.5 | 4.0 | 3.9 | 3.1 | 3.7 | 4.8 | 3.9 | 4.0 |
| Guyana | −2.6 | 0.9 | −2.6 | −3.3 | −2.5 | 6.1 | 7.8 | 8.2 | 8.5 |
| Haiti | 1.4 | −0.8 | 0.8 | 1.1 | −0.1 | −3.0 | −14.8 | −2.6 | −10.6 |
| Honduras | 3.5 | 6.1 | 4.5 | 4.3 | 0.1 | 3.3 | 5.6 | 6.0 | −1.5 |
| Jamaica | 1.6 | 7.7 | −4.0 | 4.7 | 4.1 | 0.8 | 1.8 | 2.0 | 3.0 |
| Mexico | 3.8 | 1.9 | 1.2 | 3.3 | 4.4 | 3.6 | 2.8 | 0.6 | 3.5 |
| Netherlands Antilles | 1.4 | 0.2 | 2.6 | 3.1 | 0.6 | 5.8 | 5.2 | −1.8 | 3.0 |
| Nicaragua | −2.4 | −0.7 | −12.5 | −1.7 | −0.1 | −0.2 | 0.4 | −0.2 | 3.2 |
| Panama | 4.7 | 2.4 | −15.6 | −0.4 | 4.6 | 9.5 | 8.6 | 5.6 | 4.7 |
| Paraguay | 5.7 | 4.3 | 6.4 | 5.8 | 3.1 | 2.5 | 1.8 | 4.1 | 3.5 |
| Peru | 1.9 | 8.3 | −8.2 | −11.8 | −4.3 | 2.8 | −2.4 | 6.5 | 12.9 |
| St. Kitts and Nevis | 4.8 | 7.4 | 9.8 | 6.7 | 3.0 | 3.9 | 3.0 | 4.5 | 3.2 |
| St. Lucia | 6.6 | 1.9 | 12.2 | 9.1 | 4.1 | 2.3 | 7.1 | 2.3 | 2.2 |
| St. Vincent and the Grenadines | 5.9 | 6.3 | 8.9 | 6.5 | 5.4 | 3.1 | 4.9 | 1.4 | 1.6 |
| Suriname | 0.2 | −7.3 | 8.5 | 4.0 | 0.1 | 2.9 | 4.3 | −6.8 | −1.0 |
| Trinidad and Tobago | −0.9 | −4.6 | −4.0 | −0.7 | 1.5 | 2.7 | −1.7 | −1.4 | 4.6 |
| Uruguay | 1.3 | 7.9 | — | 1.3 | 0.9 | 3.2 | 7.9 | 2.5 | 5.1 |
| Venezuela | 1.0 | 3.6 | 5.8 | −8.6 | 6.5 | 9.7 | 6.1 | −0.4 | −3.3 |

[1]For many countries, figures for recent years are IMF staff estimates. Data for some countries are for fiscal years.

## Table A7. Countries in Transition: Real GDP[1]

*(Annual percent change)*

| | Average 1977–86 | 1987 | 1988 | 1989 | 1990 | 1991 | 1992 | 1993 | 1994 |
|---|---|---|---|---|---|---|---|---|---|
| **Central and eastern Europe** | ... | ... | ... | ... | ... | **−11.1** | **−11.3** | **−6.1** | **−3.8** |
| Albania | 2.6 | −0.8 | −1.4 | 9.8 | −10.0 | −28.0 | −7.2 | 9.6 | 9.4 |
| Belarus | ... | ... | ... | ... | ... | −1.2 | −9.7 | −10.6 | −20.2 |
| Bulgaria | 4.8 | 4.7 | 2.4 | −0.5 | −9.1 | −11.7 | −7.3 | −2.4 | 1.4 |
| Croatia | ... | ... | ... | ... | ... | ... | ... | −3.7 | 0.8 |
| Czech Republic | ... | ... | ... | ... | ... | ... | ... | −0.9 | 2.6 |
| Czechoslovakia, former | 2.7 | 2.1 | 2.5 | 4.5 | −0.4 | −15.9 | −8.5 | ... | ... |
| Estonia | ... | ... | ... | ... | ... | −7.9 | −21.6 | −6.6 | 6.0 |
| Hungary | 2.5 | 4.1 | −0.1 | 0.7 | −3.5 | −11.9 | −3.0 | −0.8 | 2.0 |
| Latvia | ... | ... | ... | ... | ... | −11.1 | −35.2 | −14.8 | 1.9 |
| Lithuania | ... | ... | ... | ... | ... | −13.1 | −56.6 | −24.2 | 1.7 |
| Macedonia, former Yugoslav Rep. of | ... | ... | ... | ... | ... | ... | ... | −15.5 | −7.2 |
| Moldova | ... | ... | ... | ... | ... | −18.1 | −20.6 | −8.7 | −22.1 |
| Poland | 1.4 | 2.0 | 4.1 | 0.2 | −11.6 | −7.0 | 2.6 | 3.8 | 6.0 |
| Romania | 4.0 | 0.8 | −0.5 | −5.8 | −5.6 | −12.9 | −8.8 | 1.3 | 3.5 |
| Slovak Republic | ... | ... | ... | ... | ... | ... | ... | −4.1 | 4.8 |
| Slovenia | ... | ... | ... | ... | ... | ... | ... | 1.3 | 5.0 |
| Ukraine | ... | ... | ... | ... | ... | −11.9 | −17.0 | −16.8 | −23.7 |
| Yugoslavia, former | 3.1 | −1.0 | −2.0 | 0.8 | −7.5 | −17.0 | −34.0 | ... | ... |
| **Russia** | ... | ... | ... | ... | ... | **−13.0** | **−19.0** | **−12.0** | **−15.0** |
| **Transcaucasus and central Asia** | ... | ... | ... | ... | ... | **−7.7** | **−17.6** | **−11.2** | **−16.2** |
| Armenia | ... | ... | ... | ... | ... | −12.4 | −52.6 | −14.1 | 5.3 |
| Azerbaijan | ... | ... | ... | ... | ... | −0.7 | −22.1 | −23.1 | −22.0 |
| Georgia | ... | ... | ... | ... | ... | −20.6 | −42.7 | −39.2 | −35.0 |
| Kazakhstan | ... | ... | ... | ... | ... | −13.0 | −14.0 | −12.0 | −25.0 |
| Kyrgyz Republic | ... | ... | ... | ... | ... | −5.0 | −19.1 | −16.0 | −26.5 |
| Mongolia | 6.9 | 3.5 | 8.5 | 4.2 | −5.6 | −9.2 | −9.5 | −3.0 | 2.1 |
| Tajikistan | ... | ... | ... | ... | ... | −7.1 | −28.9 | −11.1 | −21.4 |
| Turkmenistan | ... | ... | ... | ... | ... | −4.7 | −5.3 | −10.0 | −20.0 |
| Uzbekistan | ... | ... | ... | ... | ... | −0.9 | −11.1 | −2.4 | −3.4 |

[1]Data for some countries refer to real net material product (NMP) or are estimates based on NMP. For many countries, figures for recent years are IMF staff estimates. The figures should be interpreted only as indicative of broad orders of magnitude because reliable, comparable data are not generally available. In particular, the growth of output of new private enterprises or of the informal economy is not fully reflected in the recent figures.

## Table A8. Summary of Inflation

*(In percent)*

| | Average 1977–86 | 1987 | 1988 | 1989 | 1990 | 1991 | 1992 | 1993 | 1994 | 1995 | 1996 |
|---|---|---|---|---|---|---|---|---|---|---|---|
| **GDP deflators** | | | | | | | | | | | |
| **Industrial countries** | **7.1** | **3.2** | **3.6** | **4.4** | **4.3** | **4.2** | **3.2** | **2.5** | **1.9** | **2.0** | **2.5** |
| United States | 6.4 | 3.1 | 3.9 | 4.6 | 4.3 | 3.8 | 2.8 | 2.2 | 2.1 | 1.9 | 2.8 |
| European Union | 9.1 | 4.0 | 4.3 | 4.9 | 5.1 | 5.6 | 4.4 | 3.7 | 2.7 | 3.0 | 2.9 |
| Japan | 3.1 | — | 0.4 | 1.8 | 2.2 | 2.0 | 1.5 | 0.9 | 0.2 | –0.1 | 0.5 |
| Other industrial countries | 7.2 | 5.3 | 5.3 | 5.7 | 4.6 | 3.6 | 1.6 | 1.8 | 1.4 | 2.4 | 2.5 |
| **Consumer prices** | | | | | | | | | | | |
| **Industrial countries** | **7.3** | **3.1** | **3.4** | **4.4** | **5.0** | **4.5** | **3.3** | **2.9** | **2.3** | **2.5** | **2.5** |
| United States | 6.8 | 3.7 | 4.1 | 4.8 | 5.4 | 4.2 | 3.0 | 3.0 | 2.6 | 3.0 | 3.2 |
| European Union | 8.9 | 3.2 | 3.5 | 4.7 | 5.4 | 5.1 | 4.5 | 3.8 | 3.0 | 3.1 | 2.8 |
| Japan | 3.8 | 0.1 | 0.7 | 2.3 | 2.8 | 3.3 | 1.7 | 1.3 | 0.7 | –0.2 | 0.1 |
| Other industrial countries | 7.6 | 5.2 | 4.8 | 5.2 | 5.9 | 5.1 | 2.1 | 2.5 | 1.2 | 2.7 | 2.4 |
| **Developing countries** | **26.1** | **33.3** | **51.2** | **59.6** | **62.0** | **33.5** | **35.8** | **43.1** | **48.1** | **19.5** | **13.0** |
| **By region** | | | | | | | | | | | |
| Africa | 15.8 | 14.0 | 17.1 | 19.4 | 20.1 | 25.0 | 28.2 | 27.9 | 32.9 | 20.8 | 9.3 |
| Asia | 7.5 | 7.0 | 11.5 | 11.1 | 6.5 | 7.6 | 7.1 | 9.4 | 13.5 | 12.0 | 9.6 |
| Middle East and Europe | 20.3 | 23.0 | 27.1 | 22.2 | 22.0 | 25.9 | 25.7 | 24.5 | 32.3 | 25.3 | 15.2 |
| Western Hemisphere | 69.3 | 120.9 | 233.3 | 340.0 | 438.6 | 129.4 | 152.7 | 212.2 | 226.7 | 38.2 | 23.3 |
| **By analytical criteria** | | | | | | | | | | | |
| Fuel exporters | 12.2 | 14.4 | 17.4 | 22.6 | 19.0 | 19.4 | 21.0 | 24.8 | 30.5 | 26.7 | 20.3 |
| Nonfuel exporters | 28.8 | 36.1 | 55.9 | 64.7 | 67.9 | 35.2 | 37.6 | 45.3 | 50.0 | 18.8 | 12.3 |
| Market borrowers | 38.0 | 51.9 | 87.7 | 108.1 | 112.6 | 45.8 | 52.5 | 68.4 | 74.7 | 23.0 | 15.5 |
| Official borrowers | 16.9 | 17.3 | 22.2 | 23.3 | 20.1 | 26.1 | 22.2 | 20.4 | 23.6 | 18.0 | 9.7 |
| Countries with recent debt-servicing difficulties | 49.5 | 83.1 | 144.1 | 195.6 | 239.6 | 91.9 | 106.4 | 140.0 | 150.8 | 32.5 | 18.9 |
| Countries without debt-servicing difficulties | 11.7 | 10.5 | 15.4 | 13.9 | 10.1 | 11.4 | 11.2 | 13.2 | 18.0 | 15.0 | 11.1 |
| **Countries in transition** | **6.4** | **9.4** | **13.6** | **37.1** | **44.1** | **95.1** | **722.3** | **675.2** | **301.3** | **147.7** | **25.4** |
| Central and eastern Europe | ... | ... | ... | ... | ... | 97.2 | 368.4 | 458.8 | 203.2 | 115.8 | 25.0 |
| Excluding Belarus and Ukraine | ... | ... | ... | ... | ... | 101.2 | 183.2 | 139.2 | 87.1 | 63.6 | 24.8 |
| Russia | ... | ... | ... | ... | ... | 92.7 | 1,353.0 | 896.0 | 302.0 | 180.8 | 25.4 |
| Transcaucasus and central Asia | ... | ... | ... | ... | ... | 95.7 | 914.9 | 1,241.3 | 1,582.7 | 214.2 | 27.6 |
| *Memorandum* | | | | | | | | | | | |
| **Median inflation rate** | | | | | | | | | | | |
| Industrial countries | 7.9 | 4.1 | 4.6 | 4.8 | 5.4 | 3.6 | 3.1 | 3.0 | 2.3 | 2.5 | 2.5 |
| Developing countries | 10.7 | 7.5 | 8.2 | 9.2 | 9.9 | 11.7 | 9.8 | 8.5 | 11.5 | 8.0 | 5.1 |
| Countries in transition | 1.0 | 1.3 | 0.6 | 2.0 | 5.6 | 96.5 | 883.6 | 685.6 | 207.4 | 53.1 | 20.1 |

## Table A9. Industrial Countries: GDP Deflators and Consumer Prices

*(Annual percent change)*

| | Average 1977–86 | 1987 | 1988 | 1989 | 1990 | 1991 | 1992 | 1993 | 1994 | 1995 | 1996 | Fourth Quarter[1] 1994 | 1995 | 1996 |
|---|---|---|---|---|---|---|---|---|---|---|---|---|---|---|
| **GDP deflators** | | | | | | | | | | | | | | |
| **Industrial countries** | **7.1** | **3.2** | **3.6** | **4.4** | **4.3** | **4.2** | **3.2** | **2.5** | **1.9** | **2.0** | **2.5** | ... | ... | ... |
| Major industrial countries | 6.7 | 2.9 | 3.4 | 4.1 | 4.0 | 4.0 | 3.0 | 2.3 | 1.7 | 1.8 | 2.3 | 1.7 | 2.2 | 2.3 |
| United States | 6.4 | 3.1 | 3.9 | 4.6 | 4.3 | 3.8 | 2.8 | 2.2 | 2.1 | 1.9 | 2.8 | 2.3 | 2.1 | 3.1 |
| Japan | 3.1 | — | 0.4 | 1.8 | 2.2 | 2.0 | 1.5 | 0.9 | 0.2 | −0.1 | 0.5 | −0.6 | 0.5 | 0.3 |
| Germany[2] | 3.6 | 1.8 | 1.6 | 2.4 | 2.1 | 4.9 | 5.5 | 3.8 | 2.3 | 2.2 | 1.9 | 2.1 | 2.2 | 2.0 |
| France | 9.2 | 3.0 | 2.8 | 3.0 | 3.1 | 3.3 | 2.1 | 2.5 | 1.3 | 2.0 | 2.2 | 1.7 | 2.4 | 1.9 |
| Italy | 14.4 | 6.0 | 6.7 | 6.2 | 7.7 | 7.7 | 4.5 | 4.3 | 3.6 | 5.1 | 3.9 | 4.0 | 5.6 | 2.8 |
| United Kingdom | 9.6 | 5.0 | 6.0 | 7.1 | 6.4 | 6.5 | 4.3 | 3.3 | 2.1 | 1.9 | 3.2 | 1.8 | 2.4 | 3.2 |
| Canada | 6.5 | 4.7 | 4.6 | 4.8 | 3.1 | 2.9 | 1.2 | 1.0 | 0.6 | 2.0 | 2.1 | 0.4 | 2.6 | 1.9 |
| Other industrial countries | 9.5 | 5.1 | 5.3 | 6.1 | 6.1 | 5.3 | 4.2 | 3.5 | 3.0 | 3.3 | 3.3 | ... | ... | ... |
| Spain | 14.2 | 5.8 | 5.7 | 7.0 | 7.4 | 7.0 | 6.7 | 4.5 | 4.1 | 5.2 | 4.8 | ... | ... | ... |
| Netherlands | 3.8 | −0.5 | 1.2 | 1.2 | 2.3 | 2.7 | 2.5 | 1.6 | 2.0 | 1.2 | 1.6 | ... | ... | ... |
| Belgium | 5.3 | 2.3 | 1.8 | 4.8 | 3.1 | 2.7 | 3.4 | 4.4 | 2.2 | 2.4 | 2.5 | ... | ... | ... |
| Sweden | 8.8 | 4.4 | 6.7 | 7.9 | 9.1 | 7.9 | 1.0 | 2.7 | 3.0 | 3.4 | 3.4 | ... | ... | ... |
| Austria | 4.9 | 2.4 | 1.7 | 2.9 | 3.3 | 4.0 | 4.2 | 3.6 | 3.2 | 2.7 | 2.6 | ... | ... | ... |
| Denmark | 7.8 | 4.7 | 3.4 | 4.2 | 2.7 | 2.2 | 2.0 | 1.1 | 2.0 | 2.0 | 3.0 | ... | ... | ... |
| Finland | 8.3 | 4.7 | 7.0 | 6.1 | 5.8 | 2.5 | 0.7 | 2.4 | 2.5 | 3.1 | 2.8 | ... | ... | ... |
| Greece | 18.1 | 13.5 | 14.3 | 14.5 | 23.9 | 18.4 | 14.2 | 13.6 | 10.9 | 9.1 | 7.2 | ... | ... | ... |
| Portugal | 21.7 | 11.3 | 11.8 | 12.0 | 12.9 | 14.7 | 13.1 | 6.9 | 5.1 | 4.4 | 3.7 | ... | ... | ... |
| Ireland | 11.9 | 2.2 | 3.1 | 4.4 | −1.7 | 1.1 | 1.3 | 3.6 | 3.2 | 2.3 | 1.7 | ... | ... | ... |
| Luxembourg | 6.0 | −3.1 | 1.0 | 0.2 | 1.3 | 3.8 | 3.8 | 0.6 | 3.2 | 2.1 | 2.3 | ... | ... | ... |
| Switzerland | 3.5 | 2.6 | 2.4 | 4.2 | 5.7 | 5.5 | 2.6 | 2.1 | 1.8 | 1.4 | 1.6 | ... | ... | ... |
| Norway | 7.5 | 7.1 | 4.5 | 5.9 | 4.5 | 2.5 | −1.0 | 2.1 | 0.3 | 2.4 | 2.5 | ... | ... | ... |
| Iceland | 43.1 | 19.5 | 22.8 | 19.8 | 16.8 | 7.6 | 3.7 | 2.2 | 2.6 | 2.9 | 3.0 | ... | ... | ... |
| Australia | 8.5 | 7.4 | 8.4 | 7.4 | 4.6 | 1.9 | 1.5 | 1.3 | 1.2 | 2.6 | 3.6 | ... | ... | ... |
| New Zealand | 14.7 | 15.9 | 4.9 | 8.0 | 3.3 | 4.3 | 2.0 | 1.6 | 0.9 | 4.3 | 0.1 | ... | ... | ... |
| *Memorandum* | | | | | | | | | | | | | | |
| European Union | 9.1 | 4.0 | 4.3 | 4.9 | 5.1 | 5.6 | 4.4 | 3.7 | 2.7 | 3.0 | 2.9 | ... | ... | ... |
| **Consumer prices** | | | | | | | | | | | | | | |
| **Industrial countries** | **7.3** | **3.1** | **3.4** | **4.4** | **5.0** | **4.5** | **3.3** | **2.9** | **2.3** | **2.5** | **2.5** | ... | ... | ... |
| Major industrial countries | 7.0 | 2.8 | 3.2 | 4.3 | 4.8 | 4.3 | 3.2 | 2.8 | 2.2 | 2.4 | 2.4 | 2.2 | 2.4 | 2.4 |
| United States | 6.8 | 3.7 | 4.1 | 4.8 | 5.4 | 4.2 | 3.0 | 3.0 | 2.6 | 3.0 | 3.2 | 2.6 | 3.1 | 3.3 |
| Japan | 3.8 | 0.1 | 0.7 | 2.3 | 2.8 | 3.3 | 1.7 | 1.3 | 0.7 | −0.2 | 0.1 | 0.9 | −0.6 | 0.4 |
| Germany[2,3] | 3.5 | 0.2 | 1.3 | 2.8 | 2.7 | 3.6 | 5.1 | 4.5 | 2.7 | 1.8 | 1.7 | 2.6 | 1.9 | 1.7 |
| France | 9.3 | 3.3 | 2.7 | 3.5 | 3.4 | 3.2 | 2.4 | 2.1 | 1.7 | 2.1 | 2.3 | 1.6 | 2.6 | 1.9 |
| Italy | 14.2 | 4.7 | 5.1 | 6.3 | 6.5 | 6.3 | 5.2 | 4.5 | 4.0 | 5.4 | 4.0 | 3.9 | 5.9 | 3.3 |
| United Kingdom[4] | 9.2 | 4.1 | 4.6 | 5.9 | 8.1 | 6.8 | 4.7 | 3.0 | 2.4 | 2.9 | 3.0 | 2.2 | 3.2 | 2.7 |
| Canada | 7.5 | 4.4 | 4.0 | 5.0 | 4.8 | 5.6 | 1.5 | 1.8 | 0.2 | 2.1 | 2.0 | — | 2.5 | 1.9 |
| Other industrial countries | 9.1 | 4.9 | 4.7 | 5.6 | 6.4 | 5.4 | 4.2 | 3.7 | 3.2 | 3.5 | 3.0 | ... | ... | ... |
| *Memorandum* | | | | | | | | | | | | | | |
| European Union | 8.9 | 3.2 | 3.5 | 4.7 | 5.4 | 5.1 | 4.5 | 3.8 | 3.0 | 3.1 | 2.8 | ... | ... | ... |

[1]From fourth quarter of preceding year.
[2]Data through 1990 apply to west Germany only.
[3]Based on the revised consumer price index for united Germany introduced in September 1995.
[4]Retail price index excluding mortgage interest.

## Table A10. Industrial Countries: Hourly Earnings, Productivity, and Unit Labor Costs in Manufacturing

*(Annual percent change)*

| | Average 1977–86 | 1987 | 1988 | 1989 | 1990 | 1991 | 1992 | 1993 | 1994 | 1995 | 1996 |
|---|---|---|---|---|---|---|---|---|---|---|---|
| **Hourly earnings** | | | | | | | | | | | |
| **Industrial countries** | **8.5** | **3.8** | **4.6** | **5.5** | **6.3** | **6.4** | **5.3** | **3.6** | **2.6** | **3.2** | **3.5** |
| Major industrial countries | 8.1 | 3.4 | 4.4 | 5.4 | 6.0 | 6.3 | 5.2 | 3.5 | 2.4 | 3.1 | 3.3 |
| United States | 7.1 | 2.2 | 4.0 | 3.9 | 5.2 | 5.5 | 4.1 | 2.8 | 1.8 | 2.3 | 2.9 |
| Japan | 4.9 | 1.0 | 3.2 | 6.7 | 6.5 | 5.9 | 4.6 | 2.6 | 2.7 | 2.7 | 2.1 |
| Germany[1] | 5.9 | 5.2 | 3.9 | 4.2 | 5.8 | 7.2 | 8.7 | 6.8 | 2.4 | 4.8 | 4.7 |
| France | 11.6 | 4.6 | 3.9 | 4.8 | 4.8 | 5.4 | 5.2 | 2.7 | 2.1 | 3.2 | 3.7 |
| Italy | 16.1 | 7.6 | 7.5 | 9.7 | 8.6 | 9.4 | 7.3 | 4.6 | 3.9 | 4.5 | 5.9 |
| United Kingdom | 11.8 | 7.4 | 7.9 | 9.0 | 9.6 | 9.3 | 6.4 | 5.4 | 4.3 | 5.8 | 4.8 |
| Canada | 7.6 | 3.4 | 3.9 | 5.3 | 5.2 | 4.7 | 3.5 | 2.1 | 1.6 | 0.9 | 1.8 |
| Other industrial countries | 11.0 | 6.7 | 6.1 | 6.2 | 7.8 | 7.4 | 6.0 | 4.3 | 3.9 | 3.9 | 4.4 |
| *Memorandum* | | | | | | | | | | | |
| European Union | 11.0 | 6.3 | 5.8 | 6.6 | 7.3 | 7.8 | 7.0 | 5.1 | 3.5 | 4.5 | 4.7 |
| **Productivity** | | | | | | | | | | | |
| **Industrial countries** | **2.8** | **4.6** | **4.1** | **2.4** | **2.0** | **2.0** | **1.9** | **2.6** | **5.3** | **3.0** | **2.2** |
| Major industrial countries | 2.5 | 5.1 | 4.2 | 2.4 | 2.2 | 2.1 | 1.9 | 2.4 | 5.4 | 3.0 | 2.2 |
| United States | 1.7 | 6.4 | 2.4 | 0.6 | 1.7 | 2.5 | 1.9 | 3.7 | 4.6 | 2.3 | 2.2 |
| Japan | 3.3 | 4.1 | 7.4 | 4.5 | 2.8 | 1.5 | −3.7 | −1.6 | 3.5 | 4.5 | 1.4 |
| Germany[1] | 2.9 | 1.9 | 4.2 | 3.4 | 3.6 | 2.8 | 4.4 | 4.7 | 9.8 | 6.1 | 3.4 |
| France | 4.0 | 5.0 | 7.3 | 5.1 | 1.5 | 1.3 | 5.0 | 0.1 | 8.8 | 1.8 | 1.6 |
| Italy | 3.6 | 5.3 | 5.7 | 2.9 | 1.6 | 1.8 | 4.3 | 1.9 | 6.8 | 2.0 | 1.8 |
| United Kingdom | 2.9 | 4.9 | 5.1 | 4.4 | 2.2 | 2.2 | 4.4 | 4.5 | 4.6 | 3.8 | 4.3 |
| Canada | 2.0 | 2.5 | 0.4 | 0.5 | 3.4 | 0.9 | 4.4 | 3.1 | 3.2 | −0.6 | 0.2 |
| Other industrial countries | 4.2 | 2.0 | 3.9 | 2.4 | 0.9 | 1.6 | 2.3 | 3.3 | 5.2 | 2.7 | 2.0 |
| *Memorandum* | | | | | | | | | | | |
| European Union | 3.7 | 3.6 | 5.1 | 3.6 | 1.9 | 2.0 | 4.0 | 3.2 | 7.3 | 3.5 | 2.6 |
| **Unit labor costs** | | | | | | | | | | | |
| **Industrial countries** | **5.6** | **−0.7** | **0.6** | **3.1** | **4.2** | **4.3** | **3.4** | **1.0** | **−2.6** | **0.2** | **1.3** |
| Major industrial countries | 5.5 | −1.6 | 0.3 | 3.0 | 3.8 | 4.1 | 3.3 | 1.0 | −2.8 | 0.1 | 1.1 |
| United States | 5.3 | −3.9 | 1.6 | 3.3 | 3.4 | 3.0 | 2.1 | −0.9 | −2.7 | — | 0.6 |
| Japan | 1.5 | −3.0 | −3.9 | 2.0 | 3.5 | 4.3 | 8.6 | 4.3 | −0.7 | −1.7 | 0.7 |
| Germany[1] | 2.9 | 3.3 | −0.2 | 0.8 | 2.1 | 4.3 | 4.1 | 2.1 | −6.7 | −1.2 | 1.2 |
| France | 7.3 | −0.4 | −3.2 | −0.3 | 3.3 | 4.0 | 0.1 | 2.7 | −6.1 | 1.3 | 2.0 |
| Italy | 12.2 | 2.1 | 1.7 | 6.6 | 6.9 | 7.4 | 2.9 | 2.7 | −2.8 | 2.5 | 4.1 |
| United Kingdom | 8.6 | 2.5 | 2.7 | 4.4 | 7.3 | 7.0 | 1.9 | 0.8 | −0.2 | 2.0 | 0.5 |
| Canada | 5.5 | 0.8 | 3.4 | 4.8 | 1.7 | 3.8 | −0.9 | −1.0 | −1.5 | 1.5 | 1.6 |
| Other industrial countries | 6.6 | 4.7 | 2.3 | 3.8 | 6.8 | 5.8 | 3.7 | 1.1 | −1.2 | 1.2 | 2.4 |
| *Memorandum* | | | | | | | | | | | |
| European Union | 7.1 | 2.7 | 0.7 | 2.9 | 5.3 | 5.7 | 3.0 | 1.9 | −3.5 | 0.9 | 2.0 |

[1]Data through 1990 apply to west Germany only.

## Table A11. Developing Countries: Consumer Prices

*(Annual percent change)*

| | Average 1977–86 | 1987 | 1988 | 1989 | 1990 | 1991 | 1992 | 1993 | 1994 | 1995 | 1996 |
|---|---|---|---|---|---|---|---|---|---|---|---|
| **Developing countries** | **26.1** | **33.3** | **51.2** | **59.6** | **62.0** | **33.5** | **35.8** | **43.1** | **48.1** | **19.5** | **13.0** |
| **By region** | | | | | | | | | | | |
| Africa | 15.8 | 14.0 | 17.1 | 19.4 | 20.1 | 25.0 | 28.2 | 27.9 | 32.9 | 20.8 | 9.3 |
| Asia | 7.5 | 7.0 | 11.5 | 11.1 | 6.5 | 7.6 | 7.1 | 9.4 | 13.5 | 12.0 | 9.6 |
| Middle East and Europe | 20.3 | 23.0 | 27.1 | 22.2 | 22.0 | 25.9 | 25.7 | 24.5 | 32.3 | 25.3 | 15.2 |
| Western Hemisphere | 69.3 | 120.9 | 233.3 | 340.0 | 438.6 | 129.4 | 152.7 | 212.2 | 226.7 | 38.2 | 23.3 |
| Sub-Saharan Africa | 20.7 | 20.7 | 23.3 | 22.3 | 22.0 | 37.4 | 40.6 | 34.6 | 52.1 | 25.4 | 9.3 |
| Four newly industrializing Asian economies | 8.4 | 2.5 | 5.0 | 5.8 | 7.0 | 7.5 | 5.9 | 4.6 | 5.6 | 5.0 | 4.6 |
| **By predominant export** | | | | | | | | | | | |
| Fuel | 12.2 | 14.4 | 17.4 | 22.6 | 19.0 | 19.4 | 21.0 | 24.8 | 30.5 | 26.7 | 20.3 |
| Nonfuel exports | 28.8 | 36.1 | 55.9 | 64.7 | 67.9 | 35.2 | 37.6 | 45.3 | 50.0 | 18.8 | 12.3 |
| Manufactures | 8.0 | 7.5 | 15.3 | 14.9 | 4.0 | 4.5 | 6.1 | 10.9 | 17.4 | 14.6 | 10.9 |
| Primary products | 70.8 | 58.9 | 129.7 | 306.6 | 310.8 | 100.3 | 36.7 | 26.4 | 26.6 | 14.7 | 7.4 |
| Agricultural products | 79.2 | 64.8 | 125.7 | 325.4 | 291.2 | 87.3 | 25.6 | 19.0 | 17.3 | 12.7 | 6.6 |
| Minerals | 54.0 | 47.1 | 138.3 | 270.2 | 355.1 | 131.0 | 64.1 | 44.1 | 49.0 | 18.9 | 9.1 |
| Services, income, and private transfers | 12.0 | 12.2 | 13.8 | 16.2 | 16.5 | 19.7 | 14.8 | 11.6 | 11.9 | 9.0 | 6.9 |
| Diversified export base | 32.7 | 52.0 | 77.0 | 80.8 | 99.1 | 49.5 | 63.5 | 80.1 | 86.3 | 23.4 | 14.5 |
| **By financial criteria** | | | | | | | | | | | |
| Net creditor countries | 5.6 | 0.7 | 1.6 | 2.9 | 3.5 | 5.3 | 3.4 | 3.0 | 4.2 | 4.9 | 4.1 |
| Net debtor countries | 27.5 | 35.5 | 54.5 | 63.4 | 66.0 | 35.3 | 37.9 | 45.7 | 50.9 | 20.3 | 13.5 |
| Market borrowers | 38.0 | 51.9 | 87.7 | 108.1 | 112.6 | 45.8 | 52.5 | 68.4 | 74.7 | 23.0 | 15.5 |
| Diversified borrowers | 15.1 | 15.7 | 17.9 | 15.2 | 18.1 | 19.8 | 18.1 | 16.4 | 19.3 | 15.5 | 10.8 |
| Official borrowers | 16.9 | 17.3 | 22.2 | 23.3 | 20.1 | 26.1 | 22.2 | 20.4 | 23.6 | 18.0 | 9.7 |
| Countries with recent debt-servicing difficulties | 49.5 | 83.1 | 144.1 | 195.6 | 239.6 | 91.9 | 106.4 | 140.0 | 150.8 | 32.5 | 18.9 |
| Countries without debt-servicing difficulties | 11.7 | 10.5 | 15.4 | 13.9 | 10.1 | 11.4 | 11.2 | 13.2 | 18.0 | 15.0 | 11.1 |
| **Other groups** | | | | | | | | | | | |
| Small low-income economies | 16.0 | 18.8 | 23.9 | 24.8 | 21.3 | 27.8 | 25.0 | 23.5 | 26.5 | 18.7 | 10.2 |
| Least developed countries | 17.1 | 20.9 | 23.1 | 25.4 | 25.7 | 39.3 | 37.7 | 28.9 | 38.6 | 19.9 | 10.5 |
| ***Memorandum*** | | | | | | | | | | | |
| **Median** | | | | | | | | | | | |
| Developing countries | 10.7 | 7.5 | 8.2 | 9.2 | 9.9 | 11.7 | 9.8 | 8.5 | 11.5 | 8.0 | 5.1 |
| By region | | | | | | | | | | | |
| Africa | 11.4 | 7.0 | 7.6 | 9.7 | 8.9 | 9.5 | 10.0 | 9.1 | 24.8 | 10.2 | 4.9 |
| Asia | 8.3 | 6.9 | 8.4 | 7.2 | 8.6 | 9.6 | 8.8 | 7.0 | 8.5 | 7.3 | 5.6 |
| Middle East and Europe | 9.0 | 5.0 | 5.8 | 6.9 | 9.5 | 10.4 | 8.9 | 7.9 | 6.8 | 6.0 | 4.4 |
| Western Hemisphere | 12.6 | 13.5 | 12.1 | 14.3 | 21.8 | 22.7 | 12.1 | 10.7 | 8.8 | 8.0 | 5.6 |

## Table A12.  Developing Countries—by Country: Consumer Prices[1]

*(Annual percent change)*

| | Average 1977–86 | 1987 | 1988 | 1989 | 1990 | 1991 | 1992 | 1993 | 1994 |
|---|---|---|---|---|---|---|---|---|---|
| **Africa** | **15.8** | **14.0** | **17.1** | **19.4** | **20.1** | **25.0** | **28.2** | **27.9** | **32.9** |
| Algeria | 11.0 | 5.9 | 5.9 | 9.2 | 46.9 | 31.7 | 20.5 | 29.0 | 22.5 |
| Angola | ... | ... | ... | ... | ... | 80.1 | 299.0 | 1,379.0 | 950.0 |
| Benin | 9.3 | 3.0 | 4.3 | 0.9 | 1.1 | 2.1 | 5.9 | 0.5 | 38.6 |
| Botswana | 11.9 | 9.8 | 8.0 | 11.6 | 11.4 | 12.6 | 15.0 | 14.2 | 11.1 |
| Burkina Faso | 8.3 | −2.9 | 4.2 | −0.3 | −0.8 | 2.5 | −2.0 | 0.6 | 24.7 |
| Burundi | 10.0 | 7.0 | 4.5 | 11.5 | 7.1 | 8.7 | 5.0 | 9.7 | 14.7 |
| Cameroon | 11.0 | 2.8 | 1.7 | 1.6 | 1.5 | −0.6 | 1.9 | −3.7 | 12.7 |
| Cape Verde | 14.2 | 4.0 | 3.7 | 6.9 | 6.6 | 7.0 | 5.2 | 4.4 | 4.6 |
| Central African Republic | 11.6 | −7.0 | −3.9 | 0.6 | −0.2 | −2.8 | −0.8 | −2.9 | 24.5 |
| Chad | 6.7 | −2.7 | 14.9 | −4.9 | 0.5 | 4.0 | −3.8 | −7.0 | 41.3 |
| Comoros | 7.4 | 4.0 | 1.1 | 5.7 | 1.6 | 1.7 | −1.4 | 1.9 | 25.0 |
| Congo | 9.8 | −1.0 | 4.4 | 4.0 | 2.6 | 1.5 | 2.0 | 0.3 | 56.9 |
| Côte d'Ivoire | 11.0 | 7.0 | 6.9 | 1.0 | −0.7 | 1.6 | 4.2 | 2.1 | 26.0 |
| Djibouti | 8.9 | 4.2 | 6.4 | 3.0 | 7.8 | 6.8 | 5.0 | 5.8 | 4.0 |
| Equatorial Guinea | 18.1 | −9.0 | −3.4 | 5.2 | 2.7 | −0.9 | 0.9 | 1.6 | 40.6 |
| Ethiopia | 9.5 | −9.5 | 2.2 | 9.6 | 5.2 | 20.9 | 21.0 | 10.0 | 1.5 |
| Gabon | 10.0 | −1.0 | −9.8 | 6.6 | 6.0 | 3.3 | −10.8 | 0.6 | 36.1 |
| Gambia, The | 13.0 | 46.2 | 12.4 | 10.8 | 10.2 | 9.1 | 12.0 | 5.9 | 4.0 |
| Ghana | 58.2 | 39.8 | 31.4 | 25.2 | 37.2 | 18.0 | 10.1 | 25.0 | 24.9 |
| Guinea | 25.6 | 36.7 | 27.4 | 28.3 | 19.4 | 19.6 | 16.6 | 7.1 | 4.1 |
| Guinea-Bissau | 30.2 | 86.8 | 60.3 | 80.8 | 33.0 | 57.6 | 69.6 | 48.1 | 15.2 |
| Kenya | 12.4 | 5.1 | 8.3 | 9.9 | 15.7 | 19.6 | 27.3 | 46.0 | 28.8 |
| Lesotho | 14.4 | 11.6 | 14.9 | 14.4 | 15.8 | 14.0 | 18.8 | 12.0 | 9.5 |
| Liberia | 5.9 | 5.0 | 9.7 | 25.3 | 10.0 | 10.0 | 10.0 | 10.0 | 10.0 |
| Madagascar | 15.7 | 15.5 | 26.3 | 9.0 | 11.8 | 8.5 | 15.3 | 9.2 | 39.1 |
| Malawi | 12.0 | 26.8 | 28.0 | 7.5 | 14.0 | 8.3 | 23.0 | 22.8 | 34.6 |
| Mali | 11.4 | −15.0 | 8.5 | −0.2 | 1.6 | 1.5 | −4.2 | 0.9 | 33.8 |
| Mauritania | 4.4 | 8.2 | 6.3 | 13.0 | 6.4 | 5.6 | 10.1 | 9.3 | 4.1 |
| Mauritius | 12.3 | 0.7 | 1.5 | 16.0 | 10.7 | 12.8 | 2.9 | 8.9 | 9.4 |
| Morocco | 9.8 | 2.7 | 2.4 | 3.1 | 7.0 | 8.0 | 5.7 | 5.2 | 5.1 |
| Mozambique, Rep. of | 15.0 | 164.1 | 58.5 | 42.1 | 43.7 | 33.3 | 45.1 | 42.3 | 63.1 |
| Namibia | ... | 12.6 | 12.5 | 15.5 | 12.0 | 11.9 | 17.7 | 8.5 | 10.8 |
| Niger | 8.7 | −6.6 | 0.6 | −0.8 | −2.0 | −1.8 | −1.6 | −0.5 | 35.6 |
| Nigeria | 15.8 | 10.2 | 34.5 | 50.5 | 7.4 | 13.0 | 44.6 | 57.2 | 57.0 |
| Rwanda | 8.0 | 4.1 | 3.0 | 1.0 | 4.2 | 19.6 | 9.5 | 12.5 | 64.0 |
| São Tomé and Principe | 5.7 | 23.8 | 41.2 | 44.8 | 40.5 | 36.1 | 27.4 | 21.8 | 37.7 |
| Senegal | 9.8 | −4.1 | −1.8 | 0.4 | 0.3 | −1.8 | — | −0.7 | 32.0 |
| Seychelles | 7.2 | 2.6 | 1.8 | 1.6 | 3.9 | 2.0 | 3.2 | 1.3 | 1.0 |
| Sierra Leone | 36.9 | 178.7 | 32.7 | 62.8 | 111.0 | 102.7 | 65.5 | 17.6 | 18.4 |
| Somalia | 35.5 | 28.1 | 82.0 | 111.0 | 216.8 | ... | ... | ... | ... |
| South Africa | 13.9 | 16.2 | 12.7 | 14.7 | 14.4 | 15.3 | 13.9 | 9.7 | 9.0 |
| Sudan | 27.9 | 21.5 | 62.9 | 65.3 | 56.0 | 111.0 | 106.5 | 111.5 | 102.0 |
| Swaziland | 15.4 | 13.2 | 12.2 | 12.9 | 13.5 | 13.0 | 9.0 | 8.0 | 8.0 |
| Tanzania | 24.7 | 29.9 | 31.2 | 25.8 | 19.7 | 22.3 | 22.2 | 26.1 | 29.0 |
| Togo | 8.0 | 0.1 | 0.2 | −1.2 | 1.0 | 0.4 | 3.7 | −3.6 | 41.4 |
| Tunisia | 8.3 | 8.2 | 7.2 | 7.7 | 6.5 | 8.2 | 5.8 | 4.0 | 4.7 |
| Uganda | 89.7 | 166.7 | 130.8 | 45.4 | 24.5 | 42.2 | 28.3 | 6.5 | 6.1 |
| Zaïre | 52.5 | 90.4 | 82.7 | 104.1 | 81.3 | 2,154.4 | 4,129.2 | 1,893.1 | 23,759.7 |
| Zambia | 22.2 | 47.0 | 54.0 | 128.3 | 109.6 | 93.4 | 191.3 | 187.3 | 53.0 |
| Zimbabwe | 12.5 | 11.9 | 7.1 | 11.6 | 15.5 | 23.9 | 42.7 | 25.4 | 23.2 |

## Table A12 *(continued)*

| | Average 1977–86 | 1987 | 1988 | 1989 | 1990 | 1991 | 1992 | 1993 | 1994 |
|---|---|---|---|---|---|---|---|---|---|
| **Asia** | **7.5** | **7.0** | **11.5** | **11.1** | **6.5** | **7.6** | **7.1** | **9.4** | **13.5** |
| Afghanistan, Islamic State of | 10.9 | 18.2 | 29.2 | 89.8 | 157.8 | 166.0 | 58.2 | 34.0 | 20.0 |
| Bangladesh | 12.3 | 10.9 | 9.6 | 8.7 | 9.1 | 6.9 | 3.2 | 1.6 | 3.2 |
| Bhutan | 5.9 | 11.1 | 7.9 | 6.4 | 6.7 | 6.7 | 11.4 | 9.0 | 8.0 |
| Cambodia | ... | ... | ... | 90.5 | 152.3 | 87.9 | 176.8 | 31.0 | 26.0 |
| China | 3.4 | 7.3 | 18.5 | 17.8 | 2.1 | 2.7 | 5.4 | 13.0 | 21.7 |
| Fiji | 7.1 | 5.7 | 11.9 | 6.1 | 8.1 | 6.5 | 4.9 | 5.2 | 1.5 |
| Hong Kong | 8.6 | 5.5 | 7.5 | 10.1 | 9.7 | 11.6 | 9.3 | 8.5 | 8.0 |
| India | 8.4 | 9.0 | 8.9 | 6.5 | 9.9 | 13.0 | 10.7 | 8.1 | 10.2 |
| Indonesia | 11.3 | 9.3 | 8.1 | 6.4 | 7.8 | 9.4 | 7.5 | 9.7 | 8.5 |
| Kiribati | 7.4 | 6.5 | 3.1 | 5.3 | 3.8 | 5.7 | 4.0 | 6.5 | 4.0 |
| Korea | 10.8 | 3.1 | 7.1 | 5.7 | 8.6 | 9.3 | 6.2 | 4.8 | 6.3 |
| Lao P.D. Republic | 55.9 | 6.1 | 14.8 | 59.7 | 35.7 | 13.4 | 9.8 | 6.3 | 6.8 |
| Malaysia | 4.4 | 0.8 | 2.5 | 2.8 | 3.1 | 4.4 | 4.7 | 3.6 | 3.7 |
| Maldives | 10.5 | 11.7 | 6.5 | 7.2 | 3.6 | 14.7 | 16.8 | 20.2 | 16.5 |
| Marshall Islands | ... | −0.6 | 2.6 | 2.2 | 0.7 | 4.0 | 10.3 | 5.0 | 2.8 |
| Micronesia, Fed. States of | ... | −3.1 | 3.7 | 4.5 | 3.5 | 4.0 | 5.0 | 6.0 | 5.0 |
| Myanmar | 3.3 | 23.3 | 17.3 | 27.5 | 17.6 | 32.3 | 21.9 | 31.7 | 22.2 |
| Nepal | 10.3 | 13.3 | 11.0 | 8.1 | 9.7 | 9.8 | 20.8 | 8.0 | 7.0 |
| Pakistan | 7.6 | 4.9 | 3.3 | 7.2 | 9.7 | 11.0 | 9.2 | 10.5 | 12.8 |
| Papua New Guinea | 6.6 | 3.3 | 5.4 | 4.5 | 7.0 | 7.0 | 4.3 | 5.0 | 2.9 |
| Philippines | 15.3 | 3.8 | 9.1 | 10.6 | 12.7 | 18.7 | 8.9 | 7.6 | 9.1 |
| Singapore | 3.6 | 0.5 | 1.6 | 2.3 | 3.5 | 3.4 | 2.3 | 2.2 | 3.1 |
| Solomon Islands | 10.3 | 11.5 | 16.8 | 14.9 | 8.6 | 15.2 | 10.7 | 9.2 | 13.7 |
| Sri Lanka | 11.4 | 7.7 | 14.0 | 11.6 | 21.5 | 12.2 | 11.4 | 11.7 | 8.4 |
| Taiwan Province of China | 6.1 | 0.5 | 1.3 | 4.4 | 4.1 | 3.6 | 4.5 | 2.9 | 4.1 |
| Thailand | 7.1 | 2.5 | 3.9 | 5.5 | 6.0 | 5.7 | 4.1 | 3.3 | 5.0 |
| Vanuatu | 7.2 | 14.7 | 8.4 | 7.5 | 5.0 | 6.4 | 5.1 | 1.7 | 3.5 |
| Vietnam | 62.8 | 316.7 | 394.0 | 35.0 | 67.0 | 68.1 | 17.5 | 5.2 | 14.5 |
| Western Samoa | 14.0 | 4.7 | 8.5 | 6.4 | 15.2 | −1.3 | 8.5 | 1.7 | 18.4 |
| **Middle East and Europe** | **20.3** | **23.0** | **27.1** | **22.2** | **22.0** | **25.9** | **25.7** | **24.5** | **32.3** |
| Bahrain | 5.5 | −1.7 | 0.2 | 1.2 | 1.3 | 0.8 | −0.2 | 2.5 | 0.9 |
| Cyprus | 7.2 | 2.8 | 3.4 | 3.8 | 4.5 | 5.0 | 6.5 | 4.9 | 4.7 |
| Egypt | 14.7 | 18.8 | 18.0 | 19.3 | 16.7 | 19.8 | 13.6 | 12.0 | 8.1 |
| Iran, Islamic Republic of | 17.1 | 27.7 | 28.9 | 17.4 | 9.0 | 20.7 | 24.4 | 22.9 | 35.2 |
| Iraq | 16.0 | 18.0 | 15.0 | 15.0 | 50.0 | 50.0 | 50.0 | 75.0 | 60.0 |
| Israel | 121.1 | 19.9 | 16.3 | 20.2 | 17.2 | 19.0 | 11.9 | 10.9 | 12.3 |
| Jordan | 7.3 | −0.2 | 6.7 | 25.6 | 16.2 | 8.2 | 4.0 | 3.3 | 3.6 |
| Kuwait | 4.7 | 0.6 | 1.5 | 3.3 | 2.1 | 17.4 | 0.4 | −1.2 | 4.7 |
| Lebanon | 30.5 | 487.2 | 155.0 | 72.2 | 68.8 | 51.5 | 120.0 | 29.1 | 8.3 |
| Libya | 10.9 | 4.4 | 3.1 | 1.3 | 8.6 | 11.7 | 15.0 | 20.0 | 30.0 |
| Malta | 5.4 | 0.4 | 1.0 | 0.9 | 3.0 | 2.6 | 1.6 | 4.1 | 5.4 |
| Oman | 3.2 | 2.5 | 1.6 | 1.3 | 10.0 | 4.6 | 1.0 | 1.1 | −0.7 |
| Qatar | 6.3 | 4.5 | 4.6 | 3.3 | 3.0 | 4.4 | 3.0 | 3.1 | 3.0 |
| Saudi Arabia | 2.7 | −1.6 | 0.9 | 1.0 | 2.1 | 4.6 | −0.4 | 0.8 | 0.6 |
| Syrian Arab Republic | 13.8 | 59.5 | 34.6 | 10.0 | 11.1 | 9.0 | 11.0 | 13.2 | 15.0 |
| Turkey | 45.9 | 38.8 | 73.7 | 63.3 | 60.3 | 66.0 | 70.1 | 66.1 | 106.3 |
| United Arab Emirates | 8.2 | 5.5 | 5.0 | 3.3 | 0.6 | 5.5 | 6.8 | 4.7 | 4.6 |
| Yemen Arab Republic, former | 14.5 | 20.7 | 13.9 | 19.4 | 14.0 | ... | ... | ... | ... |
| Yemen, former P.D. Republic of | 6.3 | 2.5 | 0.5 | — | 2.1 | ... | ... | ... | ... |
| Yemen, Republic of | ... | ... | ... | ... | ... | 44.9 | 50.6 | 62.3 | 71.8 |

**Table A12** *(concluded)*

| | Average 1977–86 | 1987 | 1988 | 1989 | 1990 | 1991 | 1992 | 1993 | 1994 |
|---|---|---|---|---|---|---|---|---|---|
| **Western Hemisphere** | **69.3** | **120.9** | **233.3** | **340.0** | **438.6** | **129.4** | **152.7** | **212.2** | **226.7** |
| Antigua and Barbuda | 10.8 | 3.6 | 6.8 | 3.7 | 7.0 | 5.7 | 3.0 | 3.1 | 3.5 |
| Argentina | 216.7 | 131.3 | 343.0 | 3,080.5 | 2,314.7 | 171.7 | 24.9 | 10.6 | 4.3 |
| Aruba | . . . | 3.6 | 3.1 | 4.0 | 5.8 | 5.6 | 3.9 | 5.2 | 5.2 |
| Bahamas, The | 6.5 | 6.0 | 4.1 | 5.4 | 4.6 | 7.3 | 5.7 | 2.7 | 3.2 |
| Barbados | 8.8 | 3.6 | 4.7 | 6.3 | 3.0 | 6.3 | 6.0 | 1.1 | — |
| Belize | 4.1 | 2.0 | 3.2 | 2.1 | 3.0 | 5.6 | 2.8 | 1.6 | 2.3 |
| Bolivia | 227.9 | 14.6 | 16.0 | 15.2 | 17.1 | 21.4 | 12.1 | 8.5 | 7.7 |
| Brazil[2] | 109.4 | 224.8 | 684.6 | 1,319.9 | 2,740.0 | 413.3 | 991.4 | 2,103.3 | 2,407.6 |
| Chile | 31.3 | 19.9 | 14.7 | 17.0 | 26.0 | 21.8 | 15.4 | 12.7 | 11.4 |
| Colombia | 23.6 | 23.3 | 28.1 | 25.9 | 29.1 | 30.5 | 27.0 | 22.4 | 22.6 |
| Costa Rica | 21.6 | 16.8 | 20.8 | 16.5 | 19.0 | 28.7 | 21.8 | 9.8 | 13.5 |
| Dominica | 9.6 | 4.7 | 2.2 | 6.9 | 2.0 | 6.2 | 5.3 | 1.4 | 1.6 |
| Dominican Republic | 13.1 | 13.5 | 43.9 | 40.7 | 50.4 | 47.1 | 4.3 | 5.2 | 8.3 |
| Ecuador | 20.2 | 29.5 | 58.2 | 75.7 | 48.4 | 48.8 | 54.6 | 45.0 | 27.3 |
| El Salvador | 15.8 | 25.3 | 19.9 | 17.6 | 24.0 | 14.4 | 11.2 | 18.5 | 10.8 |
| Grenada | 11.8 | −4.4 | 4.0 | 5.6 | 2.7 | 2.7 | 3.8 | 2.8 | 2.6 |
| Guatemala | 12.1 | 12.3 | 10.8 | 13.0 | 41.0 | 35.1 | 10.2 | 13.4 | 12.5 |
| Guyana | 16.0 | 28.7 | 39.9 | 89.7 | 63.6 | 101.5 | 28.2 | 11.3 | 14.0 |
| Haiti | 8.1 | −5.0 | 2.9 | 11.0 | 20.4 | 19.5 | 17.7 | 20.2 | 42.6 |
| Honduras | 8.2 | 2.8 | 6.6 | 7.0 | 21.2 | 26.0 | 9.1 | 10.7 | 22.5 |
| Jamaica | 20.7 | 11.2 | 8.2 | 14.3 | 21.9 | 51.0 | 77.3 | 22.1 | 30.0 |
| Mexico | 46.4 | 131.8 | 114.2 | 20.0 | 26.7 | 22.7 | 15.5 | 9.8 | 7.0 |
| Netherlands Antilles | 6.3 | 3.8 | 2.6 | 3.8 | 3.7 | 3.9 | 1.5 | 1.9 | 3.5 |
| Nicaragua | 69.0 | 911.9 | 14,315.8 | 4,709.3 | 3,127.5 | 7,755.3 | 40.5 | 20.4 | 7.7 |
| Panama | 4.3 | 1.0 | 1.0 | 0.2 | 0.8 | 1.4 | 1.8 | 0.5 | 1.3 |
| Paraguay | 17.9 | 21.8 | 23.0 | 26.0 | 38.2 | 24.3 | 15.1 | 18.3 | 20.6 |
| Peru | 79.6 | 85.8 | 667.0 | 3,398.6 | 7,481.6 | 409.2 | 73.2 | 48.6 | 23.7 |
| St. Kitts and Nevis | 9.3 | 0.9 | 0.2 | 5.1 | 4.2 | 4.2 | 2.9 | 1.8 | 2.6 |
| St. Lucia | 7.1 | 7.0 | 0.8 | 4.4 | 3.8 | 6.1 | 5.7 | 0.8 | 2.7 |
| St. Vincent and the Grenadines | 8.9 | 2.9 | 0.3 | 2.7 | 7.3 | 6.0 | 3.7 | 4.3 | 0.5 |
| Suriname | 10.0 | 53.4 | 7.3 | 0.8 | 21.8 | 26.0 | 43.7 | 143.4 | 368.5 |
| Trinidad and Tobago | 12.4 | 13.4 | 12.1 | 4.6 | 11.0 | 3.8 | 6.5 | 10.8 | 8.8 |
| Uruguay | 53.5 | 63.6 | 62.2 | 80.4 | 112.5 | 102.0 | 68.5 | 54.1 | 44.7 |
| Venezuela | 11.5 | 28.1 | 29.4 | 84.5 | 40.7 | 34.2 | 31.4 | 38.1 | 60.8 |

[1]For many countries, figures for recent years are IMF staff estimates. Data for some countries are for fiscal years.

[2]From December 1993 to June 1994, consumer prices in Brazil rose 763 percent. Following the introduction of the real on July 1, 1994, monthly inflation fell to 5½ percent in July. From June 1994 to December 1994, consumer prices increased by 17 percent. These figures differ from the year-on-year changes reported in the table.

## Table A13. Countries in Transition: Consumer Prices[1]

*(Annual percent change)*

| | Average 1977–86 | 1987 | 1988 | 1989 | 1990 | 1991 | 1992 | 1993 | 1994 |
|---|---|---|---|---|---|---|---|---|---|
| **Central and eastern Europe** | ... | ... | ... | ... | ... | 97.2 | 368.4 | 458.8 | 203.2 |
| Albania | — | — | — | — | — | 35.8 | 225.2 | 85.0 | 22.6 |
| Belarus | ... | ... | ... | ... | ... | 83.5 | 969.0 | 1,188.0 | 2,220.0 |
| Bulgaria | 1.4 | 2.7 | 2.5 | 6.4 | 23.9 | 333.5 | 82.0 | 72.8 | 96.0 |
| Croatia | ... | ... | ... | ... | ... | ... | ... | 1,516.0 | 97.5 |
| Czech Republic | ... | ... | ... | ... | ... | ... | ... | 20.8 | 10.0 |
| Czechoslovakia, former | ... | 0.1 | 0.2 | 1.4 | 10.8 | 59.0 | 11.0 | ... | ... |
| Estonia | ... | ... | ... | ... | ... | 210.6 | 1,069.0 | 89.0 | 47.8 |
| Hungary | 6.5 | 8.6 | 15.7 | 16.9 | 29.0 | 34.2 | 23.0 | 22.5 | 18.8 |
| Latvia | ... | ... | ... | ... | ... | 124.4 | 951.2 | 109.0 | 35.6 |
| Lithuania | ... | ... | ... | ... | ... | 224.7 | 1,020.5 | 410.4 | 72.1 |
| Macedonia, former Yugoslav Rep. of | ... | ... | ... | ... | ... | ... | ... | 247.6 | 55.0 |
| Moldova | ... | ... | ... | ... | ... | 162.0 | 1,276.0 | 837.0 | 111.1 |
| Poland | 20.4 | 25.2 | 60.2 | 251.1 | 585.8 | 70.3 | 43.0 | 35.3 | 32.2 |
| Romania | 2.9 | 1.1 | 2.6 | 0.9 | 4.7 | 161.1 | 210.3 | 256.0 | 136.8 |
| Slovak Republic | ... | ... | ... | ... | ... | ... | ... | 23.1 | 13.4 |
| Slovenia | ... | ... | ... | ... | ... | ... | ... | 32.3 | 19.8 |
| Ukraine | ... | ... | ... | ... | ... | 91.2 | 1,209.7 | 4,734.9 | 891.0 |
| Yugoslavia, former | 39.0 | 120.8 | 194.1 | 1,239.9 | 583.1 | 117.4 | 6,146.6 | ... | ... |
| **Russia** | ... | ... | ... | ... | ... | 92.7 | 1,353.0 | 896.0 | 302.0 |
| **Transcaucasus and central Asia** | ... | ... | ... | ... | ... | 95.7 | 914.9 | 1,241.3 | 1,582.7 |
| Armenia | ... | ... | ... | ... | ... | 100.3 | 824.5 | 3,731.8 | 5,273.4 |
| Azerbaijan | ... | ... | ... | ... | ... | 105.6 | 912.6 | 1,129.7 | 1,664.4 |
| Georgia | ... | ... | ... | ... | ... | 78.5 | 913.0 | 3,421.5 | 7,379.8 |
| Kazakhstan | ... | ... | ... | ... | ... | 91.0 | 1,381.0 | 1,662.3 | 1,879.9 |
| Kyrgyz Republic | ... | ... | ... | ... | ... | 85.0 | 854.6 | 1,208.8 | 278.1 |
| Mongolia | 0.2 | — | — | — | — | 20.2 | 202.6 | 268.4 | 87.6 |
| Tajikistan | ... | ... | ... | ... | ... | 111.6 | 1,156.7 | 2,194.9 | 350.4 |
| Turkmenistan | ... | ... | ... | ... | ... | 102.5 | 492.9 | 3,102.4 | 2,610.7 |
| Uzbekistan | ... | ... | ... | ... | ... | 105.0 | 644.7 | 534.2 | 1,432.5 |

[1]For many countries, inflation for the earlier years is measured based on a retail price index. Consumer price indices with a broader and more up-to-date coverage are typically used for more recent years.

## Table A14. Summary Financial Indicators

*(In percent)*

| | 1987 | 1988 | 1989 | 1990 | 1991 | 1992 | 1993 | 1994 | 1995 | 1996 |
|---|---|---|---|---|---|---|---|---|---|---|
| **Industrial countries** | | | | | | | | | | |
| **Central government fiscal balance[1]** | | | | | | | | | | |
| Industrial countries | −3.2 | −2.6 | −2.3 | −2.7 | −3.1 | −4.2 | −4.5 | −3.8 | −3.4 | −3.1 |
| United States | −3.3 | −2.8 | −2.3 | −2.9 | −3.5 | −4.7 | −3.8 | −2.4 | −2.3 | −2.3 |
| European Union | −3.8 | −3.3 | −2.9 | −3.5 | −3.9 | −4.8 | −6.0 | −5.3 | −4.4 | −3.6 |
| Japan | −2.2 | −1.3 | −1.2 | −0.5 | −0.2 | −1.6 | −2.8 | −3.8 | −4.4 | −4.7 |
| Other industrial countries | −1.5 | −0.9 | −0.6 | −1.2 | −3.0 | −4.2 | −5.5 | −4.4 | −3.6 | −1.9 |
| **General government fiscal balance[1]** | | | | | | | | | | |
| Industrial countries | −2.5 | −1.9 | −1.2 | −2.0 | −2.8 | −3.8 | −4.4 | −3.7 | −3.4 | −3.0 |
| United States | −2.5 | −2.0 | −1.5 | −2.5 | −3.2 | −4.3 | −3.4 | −2.0 | −1.9 | −2.0 |
| European Union | −3.8 | −3.2 | −2.4 | −3.6 | −4.4 | −5.2 | −6.5 | −5.7 | −4.9 | −4.0 |
| Japan | 0.5 | 1.5 | 2.5 | 2.9 | 3.0 | 1.5 | −1.4 | −3.0 | −3.7 | −3.9 |
| Other industrial countries | −1.2 | −0.3 | −0.1 | −0.9 | −3.7 | −5.4 | −6.2 | −4.7 | −3.7 | −2.4 |
| **Growth of broad money** | | | | | | | | | | |
| Industrial countries | 8.0 | 8.8 | 9.0 | 8.0 | 5.7 | 3.4 | 4.1 | 2.4 | ... | ... |
| United States | 4.3 | 5.3 | 4.9 | 4.0 | 2.9 | 2.0 | 1.7 | 1.0 | ... | ... |
| European Union | 10.1 | 10.1 | 11.0 | 12.2 | 10.0 | 5.6 | 6.4 | 2.7 | ... | ... |
| Japan | 10.8 | 10.2 | 12.0 | 7.4 | 2.3 | −0.2 | 2.2 | 2.8 | ... | ... |
| Other industrial countries | 11.7 | 15.9 | 11.6 | 7.8 | 19.1 | 6.7 | 6.2 | 5.1 | ... | ... |
| **Short-term interest rates[2]** | | | | | | | | | | |
| United States | 5.8 | 6.7 | 8.1 | 7.5 | 5.4 | 3.4 | 3.0 | 4.2 | 5.6 | 5.6 |
| Japan | 3.9 | 4.0 | 4.7 | 6.9 | 7.0 | 4.1 | 2.7 | 1.9 | 1.1 | 1.0 |
| Germany | 4.0 | 4.3 | 7.1 | 8.4 | 9.2 | 9.5 | 7.2 | 5.3 | 4.5 | 4.9 |
| LIBOR | 7.3 | 8.1 | 9.3 | 8.4 | 6.1 | 3.9 | 3.4 | 5.1 | 6.2 | 6.2 |
| **Developing countries** | | | | | | | | | | |
| **Central government fiscal balance[1]** | | | | | | | | | | |
| Weighted average | −5.8 | −5.3 | −4.2 | −3.1 | −3.3 | −2.7 | −3.0 | −2.5 | −2.0 | −1.2 |
| Median | −5.3 | −5.3 | −4.7 | −4.2 | −4.4 | −4.0 | −4.3 | −4.2 | −3.0 | −2.4 |
| **Growth of broad money** | | | | | | | | | | |
| Weighted average | 44.2 | 74.2 | 84.5 | 79.2 | 57.9 | 66.2 | 73.4 | 55.6 | 25.7 | 20.3 |
| Median | 16.1 | 18.4 | 16.5 | 17.2 | 18.1 | 15.6 | 14.5 | 15.7 | 12.4 | 11.1 |
| **Countries in transition** | | | | | | | | | | |
| Central government fiscal balance[1,3] | −1.9 | −2.3 | −2.1 | −4.9 | −9.8 | −12.9 | −7.3 | −8.3 | −4.4 | −3.2 |
| Growth of broad money | 18.4 | 22.9 | 34.8 | 21.6 | 116.7 | 654.6 | 409.3 | 207.7 | 40.2 | 27.2 |

[1]In percent of GDP.

[2]For the United States, three-month treasury bills; for Japan, three-month certificates of deposit; for Germany, three-month interbank deposits; for LIBOR, London interbank offered rate on six-month U.S. dollar deposits.

[3]Because of country differences in definition and coverage, the estimates for this group of countries should be interpreted only as indicative of broad orders of magnitude.

**Table A15. Industrial Countries: General and Central Government Fiscal Balances and Balances Excluding Social Security Transactions[1]**

*(In percent of GDP)*

| | 1987 | 1988 | 1989 | 1990 | 1991 | 1992 | 1993 | 1994 | 1995 | 1996 |
|---|---|---|---|---|---|---|---|---|---|---|
| **General government fiscal balance** | | | | | | | | | | |
| **Industrial countries** | **−2.5** | **−1.9** | **−1.2** | **−2.0** | **−2.8** | **−3.8** | **−4.4** | **−3.7** | **−3.4** | **−3.0** |
| Major industrial countries | −2.5 | −1.8 | −1.1 | −2.0 | −2.6 | −3.7 | −4.1 | −3.5 | −3.3 | −3.0 |
| United States | −2.5 | −2.0 | −1.5 | −2.5 | −3.2 | −4.3 | −3.4 | −2.0 | −1.9 | −2.0 |
| Japan | 0.5 | 1.5 | 2.5 | 2.9 | 3.0 | 1.5 | −1.4 | −3.0 | −3.7 | −3.9 |
| Germany[2] | −1.9 | −2.1 | 0.1 | −1.9 | −3.3 | −2.9 | −3.3 | −2.5 | −2.5 | −2.1 |
| France[3] | −1.9 | −1.7 | −1.2 | −1.6 | −2.2 | −4.0 | −6.1 | −6.0 | −5.2 | −4.5 |
| Italy[4] | −11.0 | −10.7 | −9.9 | −10.9 | −10.2 | −9.5 | −9.6 | −9.0 | −7.7 | −6.5 |
| United Kingdom[5] | −1.4 | 1.0 | 0.9 | −1.2 | −2.6 | −6.1 | −7.8 | −6.8 | −4.9 | −3.2 |
| Canada | −3.8 | −2.5 | −2.9 | −4.1 | −6.6 | −7.4 | −7.3 | −5.3 | −4.6 | −3.4 |
| Other industrial countries | −2.6 | −2.0 | −1.7 | −2.3 | −3.7 | −4.6 | −6.0 | −5.1 | −4.1 | −3.3 |
| Spain[6] | −3.1 | −3.3 | −2.8 | −3.9 | −5.0 | −4.4 | −7.5 | −6.6 | −5.9 | −5.5 |
| Netherlands | −5.9 | −4.6 | −4.7 | −5.1 | −2.9 | −3.9 | −3.3 | −3.4 | −3.2 | −2.7 |
| Belgium | −7.4 | −6.6 | −6.2 | −5.4 | −6.5 | −6.7 | −6.6 | −5.4 | −4.5 | −4.4 |
| Sweden | 4.2 | 3.5 | 5.4 | 4.2 | −1.1 | −7.8 | −13.4 | −10.4 | −8.9 | −5.3 |
| Austria | −4.3 | −3.0 | −2.8 | −2.2 | −2.4 | −2.0 | −4.1 | −4.0 | −4.8 | −4.1 |
| Denmark | 2.4 | 0.6 | −0.5 | −1.5 | −2.1 | −2.9 | −4.5 | −3.8 | −1.9 | −1.3 |
| Finland | 1.1 | 4.1 | 6.3 | 5.3 | −1.5 | −5.9 | −8.0 | −5.8 | −5.3 | −1.3 |
| Greece | −11.8 | −11.9 | −14.7 | −14.0 | −11.4 | −11.7 | −12.1 | −11.4 | −9.0 | −7.7 |
| Portugal | −6.1 | −3.6 | −2.3 | −5.4 | −6.5 | −3.3 | −7.0 | −5.8 | −5.3 | −4.6 |
| Ireland | −9.8 | −3.3 | −2.6 | −2.5 | −2.9 | −2.9 | −2.7 | −2.5 | −2.5 | −2.5 |
| Luxembourg | 1.0 | 1.8 | 5.2 | 5.7 | −0.5 | −0.9 | −0.5 | 0.5 | 1.0 | 1.0 |
| Switzerland | 1.2 | 1.0 | 0.8 | — | −2.1 | −3.4 | −4.3 | −4.2 | −3.7 | −3.1 |
| Norway | 2.4 | 1.0 | 0.5 | 2.0 | −0.9 | −3.2 | −4.1 | −2.1 | −0.2 | 1.6 |
| Iceland | −0.9 | −2.0 | −4.6 | −3.3 | −2.9 | −2.8 | −4.5 | −4.1 | −4.3 | −4.9 |
| Australia | −0.7 | 1.0 | 1.5 | 0.4 | −2.6 | −4.6 | −3.9 | −3.1 | −0.8 | −0.6 |
| New Zealand | −2.0 | −1.4 | −1.8 | −2.3 | −2.2 | −2.1 | −0.7 | 1.5 | 2.8 | 4.3 |
| *Memorandum* | | | | | | | | | | |
| European Union | −3.8 | −3.2 | −2.4 | −3.6 | −4.4 | −5.2 | −6.5 | −5.7 | −4.9 | −4.0 |
| **Fiscal balance excluding social security transactions** | | | | | | | | | | |
| United States | −4.3 | −4.2 | −3.8 | −4.7 | −5.2 | −5.9 | −5.0 | −3.7 | −3.7 | −3.7 |
| Japan | −2.3 | −1.6 | −0.7 | −0.6 | −0.7 | −2.0 | −4.9 | −6.5 | −7.0 | −7.0 |
| Germany[2] | −2.2 | −2.2 | −0.6 | −2.6 | −4.0 | −2.9 | −3.6 | −2.7 | −2.6 | −2.3 |
| France | −2.1 | −1.9 | −1.5 | −1.6 | −1.9 | −3.3 | −4.7 | −5.0 | −4.4 | −3.6 |
| Italy[4] | −6.6 | −5.8 | −4.9 | −5.3 | −5.1 | −4.0 | −4.5 | −3.7 | −3.6 | −3.1 |
| Canada | −2.2 | −0.9 | −1.3 | −2.4 | −4.8 | −5.3 | −5.0 | −2.9 | −2.4 | −1.2 |

## Table A15 *(concluded)*

| | 1987 | 1988 | 1989 | 1990 | 1991 | 1992 | 1993 | 1994 | 1995 | 1996 |
|---|---|---|---|---|---|---|---|---|---|---|
| **Central government fiscal balance** | | | | | | | | | | |
| **Industrial countries** | **−3.2** | **−2.6** | **−2.3** | **−2.7** | **−3.1** | **−4.2** | **−4.5** | **−3.8** | **−3.4** | **−3.1** |
| Major industrial countries | −3.3 | −2.7 | −2.3 | −2.7 | −3.1 | −4.2 | −4.3 | −3.6 | −3.3 | −3.1 |
| United States[7] | −3.3 | −2.8 | −2.3 | −2.9 | −3.5 | −4.7 | −3.8 | −2.4 | −2.3 | −2.3 |
| Japan[8] | −2.2 | −1.3 | −1.2 | −0.5 | −0.2 | −1.6 | −2.8 | −3.8 | −4.4 | −4.7 |
| Germany[9,10] | −1.4 | −1.7 | −0.9 | −1.8 | −1.9 | −1.3 | −2.1 | −1.5 | −1.4 | −1.6 |
| France[10] | −1.9 | −1.7 | −1.4 | −1.6 | −1.7 | −3.0 | −4.5 | −4.9 | −4.2 | −3.5 |
| Italy[11] | −11.2 | −11.0 | −10.7 | −10.1 | −10.3 | −10.4 | −10.0 | −9.5 | −7.4 | −6.2 |
| United Kingdom | −1.1 | 1.1 | 1.2 | −1.1 | −2.3 | −6.9 | −8.0 | −6.5 | −4.6 | −2.9 |
| Canada | −3.8 | −3.2 | −3.2 | −3.9 | −4.5 | −4.2 | −4.9 | −3.8 | −3.7 | −2.2 |
| Other industrial countries | −2.8 | −2.3 | −2.0 | −2.3 | −3.3 | −4.0 | −5.8 | −4.8 | −4.0 | −3.1 |
| *Memorandum* | | | | | | | | | | |
| European Union | −3.8 | −3.3 | −2.9 | −3.5 | −3.9 | −4.8 | −6.0 | −5.3 | −4.4 | −3.6 |

[1]On a national income accounts basis except as indicated in footnotes. The projections are based on "unchanged fiscal policies" which may differ from countries' stated fiscal objectives. For a summary of medium-term fiscal objectives see the May 1995 *World Economic Outlook* , Table 5, p. 28.

[2]Data through 1990 apply to west Germany only.

[3]Adjusted for valuation changes of the foreign exchange stabilization fund.

[4]Includes interest accruing on zero coupon bonds.

[5]Excludes asset sales.

[6]The authorities have indicated their intention to present a budget for 1996 limiting the general government's deficit in that year to 4.4 percent, in accordance with the objective in the government's Maastricht convergence plan.

[7]Data are on a budget basis.

[8]Data are on a national income basis and exclude social security transactions.

[9]Data through June 1990 apply to west Germany only.

[10]Data are on an administrative basis and exclude social security transactions.

[11]Data refer to the state sector and cover the transactions of the state budget as well as those of several autonomous entities operating at the same level; data do not include the gross transactions of social security institutions, only their deficits. Includes interest accruing on zero coupon bonds.

## Table A16. Industrial Countries: General Government Structural Balances and Fiscal Impulses[1]

*(In percent of GDP)*

| | 1987 | 1988 | 1989 | 1990 | 1991 | 1992 | 1993 | 1994 | 1995 | 1996 |
|---|---|---|---|---|---|---|---|---|---|---|
| **Structural balance[2]** | | | | | | | | | | |
| **Major industrial countries** | **−2.6** | **−2.7** | **−2.3** | **−3.1** | **−2.9** | **−3.3** | **−3.0** | **−2.6** | **−2.5** | **−2.2** |
| United States | −2.9 | −3.0 | −2.5 | −3.2 | −2.8 | −3.6 | −2.9 | −2.0 | −2.1 | −2.1 |
| Japan | 0.6 | 0.9 | 1.7 | 1.8 | 1.9 | 1.2 | −0.5 | −1.4 | −1.5 | −1.6 |
| Germany[3] | −0.9 | −1.7 | — | −3.3 | −5.2 | −3.9 | −2.2 | −1.2 | −1.2 | −1.0 |
| France | −1.0 | −1.7 | −2.3 | −2.8 | −2.4 | −3.7 | −3.8 | −3.6 | −3.5 | −3.2 |
| Italy[4] | −11.3 | −11.6 | −11.4 | −12.4 | −11.2 | −9.6 | −7.9 | −7.3 | −6.5 | −5.6 |
| United Kingdom | −1.3 | −0.8 | −2.0 | −3.6 | −2.7 | −3.7 | −4.4 | −4.1 | −3.1 | −2.0 |
| Canada | −4.9 | −4.7 | −5.1 | −4.9 | −4.9 | −4.8 | −4.6 | −3.8 | −3.3 | −2.3 |
| **Other industrial countries** | **−2.5** | **−2.4** | **−2.6** | **−3.3** | **−3.7** | **−3.7** | **−3.4** | **−2.8** | **−2.6** | **−2.2** |
| Spain[5] | −3.0 | −4.0 | −4.2 | −5.1 | −5.6 | −3.6 | −4.1 | −3.0 | −3.0 | −3.2 |
| Netherlands | −4.8 | −3.5 | −5.1 | −6.7 | −4.5 | −4.7 | −2.5 | −2.5 | −3.0 | −2.7 |
| Belgium | −5.0 | −6.1 | −7.0 | −7.1 | −8.3 | −8.0 | −5.3 | −4.1 | −3.6 | −4.0 |
| Sweden | — | −0.4 | 1.5 | 0.7 | −1.9 | −6.2 | −8.1 | −7.3 | −7.2 | −4.5 |
| Austria | −3.1 | −2.8 | −3.9 | −3.6 | −3.6 | −2.6 | −3.3 | −3.4 | −4.4 | −3.9 |
| Denmark | 0.8 | −0.3 | −0.5 | −1.0 | −0.4 | −0.4 | −1.0 | −1.3 | −1.0 | −0.7 |
| Finland | 0.7 | 2.6 | 3.3 | 2.4 | 0.1 | −1.1 | −1.1 | −0.1 | −1.5 | 0.8 |
| Ireland | −6.7 | −0.2 | −2.0 | −3.4 | −2.7 | −2.8 | −2.4 | −2.5 | −2.6 | −2.5 |
| Norway | −1.1 | −0.7 | 1.4 | 3.5 | 1.9 | −0.4 | −1.7 | −1.0 | −0.3 | 1.1 |
| Australia | −0.9 | 0.3 | 0.2 | −0.4 | −1.6 | −2.6 | −2.0 | −2.1 | −0.3 | −0.5 |
| New Zealand | −5.1 | −6.4 | −7.1 | −8.0 | −2.8 | 0.1 | 0.2 | 1.1 | 3.0 | 5.1 |
| *Memorandum* | | | | | | | | | | |
| European Union[6] | −3.3 | −3.5 | −3.5 | −5.0 | −5.1 | −4.9 | −4.2 | −3.6 | −3.4 | −2.8 |
| **Fiscal impulse[7]** | | | | | | | | | | |
| **Major industrial countries** | **−0.6** | **—** | **−0.4** | **0.6** | **0.2** | **0.2** | **−0.3** | **−0.4** | **−0.2** | **−0.3** |
| United States[8] | −0.7 | — | −0.5 | 0.7 | — | — | −0.6 | −0.8 | — | — |
| Japan[8] | −1.6 | −0.4 | — | −1.2 | — | 0.6 | 0.8 | 0.6 | −0.4 | — |
| Germany[3,8] | 0.4 | 0.7 | −1.7 | 3.0 | 1.2 | −0.8 | −1.7 | −0.9 | — | — |
| France[8] | −1.0 | 0.6 | 0.5 | — | — | 1.1 | — | 0.4 | — | −0.4 |
| Italy | — | 0.5 | — | 0.8 | −1.3 | −1.6 | −1.9 | −0.6 | −0.7 | −0.8 |
| United Kingdom | — | −1.0 | — | 1.1 | −0.5 | 2.0 | 1.7 | — | −1.3 | −1.2 |
| Canada | −0.9 | — | — | — | — | — | — | −0.7 | −0.4 | −0.9 |

[1]On a national income accounts basis.

[2]The structural budget position is defined as the actual budget deficit (or surplus) less the effects of cyclical deviations of output from potential output. Because of the margin of uncertainty that attaches to estimates of cyclical gaps and to tax and expenditure elasticities with respect to national income, indicators of structural budget positions should be interpreted as broad orders of magnitude. Moreover, it is important to note that changes in structural budget balances are not necessarily attributable to policy changes but may reflect the built-in momentum of existing expenditure programs. In the period beyond that for which specific consolidation programs exist, it is assumed that the structural deficit remains unchanged.

[3]Data through 1990 apply to west Germany only. The estimate of the fiscal impulse for 1995 is affected by the assumption by the federal government of the debt of the Treuhandanstalt and various other agencies, which were formerly held outside the general government sector. At the public sector level, there would be an estimated withdrawal of fiscal impulse amounting to just over 1 percent of GDP.

[4]Includes interest accruing on zero coupon bonds.

[5]See footnote 6 on Table A15.

[6]Excludes Greece, Luxembourg, and Portugal.

[7]For a definition of the fiscal impulse measure, see *The New Palgrave Dictionary of Money and Finance*, edited by Peter Newman, Murray Milgate, and John Eatwell (London: Macmillan, 1992; New York: Stockton, 1992). Impulse estimates equal to or less than ±0.3 percent of GDP are indicated by "—."

[8]For relevant years, the fiscal impulse is calculated on the basis of data adjusted for net international financial transfers related to the 1990–91 regional conflict in the Middle East.

## Table A17. Industrial Countries: Monetary Aggregates

*(Annual percent change)*[1]

| | 1987 | 1988 | 1989 | 1990 | 1991 | 1992 | 1993 | 1994 |
|---|---|---|---|---|---|---|---|---|
| **Narrow money[2]** | | | | | | | | |
| **Industrial countries** | **6.8** | **6.8** | **4.6** | **7.8** | **6.4** | **7.4** | **8.1** | **4.0** |
| Major industrial countries | 6.0 | 6.3 | 3.1 | 6.6 | 6.5 | 8.2 | 8.4 | 3.7 |
| United States | 6.3 | 4.3 | 0.6 | 4.2 | 7.9 | 14.3 | 10.5 | 2.4 |
| Japan | 4.8 | 8.6 | 2.4 | 4.5 | 9.5 | 3.9 | 7.0 | 4.2 |
| Germany[3] | 7.4 | 10.9 | 5.6 | 29.6 | 3.4 | 10.8 | 8.5 | 5.2 |
| France | 4.3 | 4.1 | 7.7 | 3.9 | −4.7 | −0.2 | 1.5 | 3.0 |
| Italy | 7.8 | 7.3 | 10.2 | 6.6 | 10.5 | 0.7 | 7.6 | 3.5 |
| United Kingdom | 4.2 | 7.7 | 5.7 | 2.7 | 3.0 | 2.8 | 6.0 | 6.7 |
| Canada | 8.2 | 7.4 | 3.3 | −1.0 | 5.5 | 5.7 | 14.7 | 7.0 |
| Other industrial countries | 12.2 | 10.0 | 13.5 | 15.5 | 5.2 | 2.7 | 6.4 | 5.4 |
| *Memorandum* | | | | | | | | |
| European Union | 6.8 | 8.5 | 8.0 | 11.7 | 3.8 | 3.8 | 6.4 | 4.7 |
| **Broad money[4]** | | | | | | | | |
| **Industrial countries** | **8.0** | **8.8** | **9.0** | **8.0** | **5.7** | **3.4** | **4.1** | **2.4** |
| Major industrial countries | 7.3 | 8.0 | 8.6 | 7.8 | 3.7 | 2.7 | 3.3 | 1.9 |
| United States | 4.3 | 5.3 | 4.9 | 4.0 | 2.9 | 2.0 | 1.7 | 1.0 |
| Japan | 10.8 | 10.2 | 12.0 | 7.4 | 2.3 | −0.2 | 2.2 | 2.8 |
| Germany[3] | 5.9 | 6.9 | 5.5 | 19.7 | 6.3 | 7.6 | 10.9 | 1.6 |
| France | 11.2 | 8.1 | 9.9 | 9.0 | 2.0 | 5.1 | −3.1 | 2.0 |
| Italy | 7.1 | 9.5 | 10.7 | 9.4 | 9.1 | 4.7 | 8.1 | 1.9 |
| United Kingdom | 17.9 | 17.7 | 19.0 | 12.3 | 5.6 | 3.1 | 5.1 | 4.2 |
| Canada | 8.4 | 12.7 | 14.3 | 8.1 | 4.6 | 3.1 | 3.2 | 2.8 |
| Other industrial countries | 12.6 | 14.2 | 11.6 | 8.8 | 17.2 | 7.7 | 8.5 | 5.0 |
| *Memorandum* | | | | | | | | |
| European Union | 10.1 | 10.1 | 11.0 | 12.2 | 10.0 | 5.6 | 6.4 | 2.7 |

[1]Based on end-of-period data.

[2]M1 except for the United Kingdom, where M0 is used here as a measure of narrow money; it comprises notes in circulation plus bankers' operational deposits. M1 is generally currency in circulation plus private demand deposits. In addition, the United States includes traveler's checks of nonbank issues and other checkable deposits and excludes private sector float and demand deposits of banks. Japan includes government demand deposits and excludes float. Germany includes demand deposits at fixed interest rates. Canada excludes private sector float.

[3]Data through 1989 apply to west Germany only. The growth rates for the monetary aggregates in 1990 are affected by the extension of the currency area.

[4]M2, defined as M1 plus quasi-money, except for Japan, Germany, and the United Kingdom, for which the data are based on M2 plus certificates of deposit (CDs), M3, and M4, respectively. Quasi-money is essentially private term deposits and other notice deposits. The United States also includes money market mutual fund balances, money market deposit accounts, overnight repurchase agreements, and overnight Eurodollars issued to U.S. residents by foreign branches of U.S. banks. For Japan, M2 plus CDs is currency in circulation plus total private and public sector deposits and installments of Sogo Banks plus CDs. For Germany, M3 is M1 plus private time deposits with maturities of less than four years plus savings deposits at statutory notice. For the United Kingdom, M4 is composed of non-interest-bearing M1, private sector interest-bearing sterling sight bank deposits, private sector sterling time bank deposits, private sector holdings of sterling bank CDs, private sector holdings of building society shares and deposits, and sterling CDs less building society holdings of bank deposits and bank CDs, and notes and coins.

## Table A18. Industrial Countries: Interest Rates
*(In percent a year)*

| | 1987 | 1988 | 1989 | 1990 | 1991 | 1992 | 1993 | 1994 | August 1995 |
|---|---|---|---|---|---|---|---|---|---|
| **Policy-related interest rate[1]** | | | | | | | | | |
| Major industrial countries | 6.4 | 6.9 | 8.6 | 9.0 | 7.8 | 6.3 | 4.9 | 4.4 | 4.8 |
| United States | 6.7 | 7.6 | 9.2 | 8.1 | 5.7 | 3.5 | 3.0 | 4.2 | 5.7 |
| Japan | 3.5 | 3.6 | 4.9 | 7.2 | 7.5 | 4.6 | 3.0 | 2.1 | 0.8 |
| Germany | 3.7 | 3.8 | 6.6 | 8.0 | 8.9 | 9.4 | 7.4 | 5.3 | 4.5 |
| France | 8.0 | 7.6 | 9.4 | 10.0 | 9.5 | 10.7 | 8.6 | 5.6 | 5.8 |
| Italy | 11.1 | 11.2 | 12.7 | 12.3 | 12.7 | 14.5 | 10.5 | 8.8 | 10.6 |
| United Kingdom | 9.6 | 10.3 | 13.9 | 14.8 | 11.5 | 9.4 | 5.9 | 5.5 | 6.8 |
| Canada | 8.0 | 9.2 | 11.9 | 12.9 | 9.0 | 6.6 | 4.6 | 5.1 | 6.4 |
| **Short-term interest rate[2]** | | | | | | | | | |
| **Industrial countries** | **6.7** | **7.1** | **8.8** | **9.2** | **8.0** | **6.8** | **5.2** | **4.9** | ... |
| Major industrial countries | 6.7 | 7.2 | 8.7 | 9.2 | 7.8 | 6.4 | 4.9 | 4.6 | 4.7 |
| United States | 6.9 | 7.7 | 9.1 | 8.2 | 5.8 | 3.7 | 3.2 | 4.6 | 5.8 |
| Japan | 4.1 | 4.4 | 5.3 | 7.6 | 7.2 | 4.3 | 2.8 | 2.1 | 0.7 |
| Germany | 4.0 | 4.3 | 7.1 | 8.4 | 9.2 | 9.5 | 7.2 | 5.3 | 4.4 |
| France | 8.2 | 7.9 | 9.3 | 10.3 | 9.7 | 10.4 | 8.4 | 5.8 | 6.0 |
| Italy | 11.1 | 11.2 | 12.7 | 12.3 | 12.7 | 14.5 | 10.5 | 8.8 | 10.6 |
| United Kingdom | 9.7 | 10.3 | 13.9 | 14.8 | 11.5 | 9.6 | 5.9 | 5.5 | 6.8 |
| Canada | 8.4 | 9.6 | 12.2 | 13.0 | 9.0 | 6.7 | 5.0 | 5.6 | 6.6 |
| Other industrial countries | 9.5 | 8.9 | 10.9 | 11.4 | 10.7 | 10.5 | 8.4 | 6.8 | ... |
| *Memorandum* | | | | | | | | | |
| European Union | 8.1 | 8.2 | 10.3 | 11.1 | 10.7 | 11.0 | 8.3 | 6.6 | ... |
| **Long-term interest rate[3]** | | | | | | | | | |
| **Industrial countries** | **8.4** | **8.6** | **8.7** | **9.6** | **8.7** | **8.0** | **6.6** | **7.2** | ... |
| Major industrial countries | 8.0 | 8.1 | 8.1 | 9.0 | 8.3 | 7.5 | 6.2 | 6.8 | 6.2 |
| United States | 8.4 | 8.8 | 8.5 | 8.6 | 7.9 | 7.0 | 5.9 | 7.1 | 6.5 |
| Japan | 5.0 | 4.8 | 5.1 | 7.0 | 6.3 | 5.1 | 4.0 | 4.2 | 3.1 |
| Germany | 6.2 | 6.5 | 7.0 | 8.7 | 8.5 | 7.9 | 6.5 | 6.9 | 6.8 |
| France | 9.4 | 9.1 | 8.8 | 10.0 | 9.0 | 8.6 | 6.9 | 7.4 | 7.3 |
| Italy[4] | 11.6 | 12.0 | 13.3 | 13.6 | 13.1 | 13.1 | 11.3 | 10.3 | 11.3 |
| United Kingdom | 9.6 | 9.7 | 10.2 | 11.8 | 10.1 | 9.1 | 7.5 | 8.2 | 8.2 |
| Canada | 9.9 | 10.2 | 9.9 | 10.8 | 9.8 | 8.8 | 7.9 | 8.6 | 8.5 |
| Other industrial countries | 10.9 | 10.3 | 11.2 | 12.2 | 10.8 | 10.3 | 8.5 | 8.6 | ... |
| *Memorandum* | | | | | | | | | |
| European Union | 9.4 | 9.5 | 10.0 | 11.3 | 10.4 | 10.0 | 8.2 | 8.4 | ... |

[1]For the United States, federal funds rate; for Japan, overnight call rate; for Germany, repurchase rate; for France, day-to-day money rate; for Italy, three-month treasury bill rate; for the United Kingdom, base lending rate; and for Canada, overnight money market financing rate.

[2]For the United States, three-month certificates of deposit (CDs) in secondary markets; for Japan, three-month CDs; for Germany, France, and the United Kingdom, three-month interbank deposits; for Italy, three-month treasury bills; and for Canada, three-month prime corporate paper.

[3]For the United States, yield on ten-year treasury bonds; for Japan, over-the-counter sales yield on ten-year government bonds with longest residual maturity; for Germany, yield on government bonds with maturities of nine to ten years; for France, long-term (seven- to ten-year) government bond yield (Emprunts d'Etat à long terme TME); for Italy, secondary market yield on fixed-coupon (BTP) government bonds with two to four years' residual maturity; for the United Kingdom, yield on medium-dated (ten-year) government stock; and for Canada, average yield on government bonds with residual maturities of over ten years.

[4]August 1995 data refer to yield on ten-year government bonds.

## Table A19. Industrial Countries: Exchange Rates

| | 1987 | 1988 | 1989 | 1990 | 1991 | 1992 | 1993 | 1994 | August[1] 1995 |
|---|---|---|---|---|---|---|---|---|---|
| | *National currency units per U.S. dollar* | | | | | | | | |
| **U.S. dollar nominal exchange rates** | | | | | | | | | |
| Japanese yen | 144.6 | 128.2 | 138.0 | 144.8 | 134.7 | 126.7 | 111.2 | 102.2 | 93.5 |
| Deutsche mark | 1.80 | 1.76 | 1.88 | 1.62 | 1.66 | 1.56 | 1.65 | 1.62 | 1.43 |
| French franc | 6.01 | 5.96 | 6.38 | 5.45 | 5.64 | 5.29 | 5.66 | 5.55 | 4.93 |
| Pound sterling[2] | 1.63 | 1.78 | 1.64 | 1.78 | 1.76 | 1.76 | 1.50 | 1.53 | 1.58 |
| Italian lira | 1296 | 1302 | 1372 | 1198 | 1241 | 1232 | 1574 | 1612 | 1599 |
| Canadian dollar | 1.33 | 1.23 | 1.18 | 1.17 | 1.15 | 1.21 | 1.29 | 1.37 | 1.36 |
| Spanish peseta | 123.5 | 116.5 | 118.4 | 101.9 | 103.9 | 102.4 | 127.3 | 134.0 | 122.3 |
| Dutch guilder | 2.03 | 1.98 | 2.12 | 1.82 | 1.87 | 1.76 | 1.86 | 1.82 | 1.61 |
| Belgian franc | 37.3 | 36.8 | 39.4 | 33.4 | 34.1 | 32.1 | 34.6 | 33.5 | 29.5 |
| Swedish krona | 6.34 | 6.13 | 6.45 | 5.92 | 6.05 | 5.82 | 7.78 | 7.72 | 7.19 |
| Austrian schilling | 12.6 | 12.3 | 13.2 | 11.4 | 11.7 | 11.0 | 11.6 | 11.4 | 10.1 |
| Danish krone | 6.84 | 6.73 | 7.31 | 6.19 | 6.40 | 6.04 | 6.48 | 6.36 | 5.56 |
| Finnish markka | 4.40 | 4.18 | 4.29 | 3.82 | 4.04 | 4.48 | 5.71 | 5.22 | 4.27 |
| Greek drachma | 135.4 | 141.9 | 162.4 | 158.5 | 182.3 | 190.6 | 229.2 | 242.6 | 230.4 |
| Portuguese escudo | 140.9 | 144.0 | 157.5 | 142.6 | 144.5 | 135.0 | 160.8 | 166.0 | 148.6 |
| Irish pound | 0.67 | 0.66 | 0.71 | 0.60 | 0.62 | 0.59 | 0.68 | 0.67 | 0.62 |
| Swiss franc | 1.49 | 1.46 | 1.64 | 1.39 | 1.43 | 1.41 | 1.48 | 1.37 | 1.19 |
| Norwegian krone | 6.74 | 6.52 | 6.90 | 6.26 | 6.48 | 6.21 | 7.09 | 7.06 | 6.30 |
| Icelandic krona | 38.7 | 43.0 | 57.0 | 58.3 | 59.0 | 57.5 | 67.6 | 69.9 | 64.6 |
| Australian dollar | 1.43 | 1.28 | 1.26 | 1.28 | 1.28 | 1.36 | 1.47 | 1.37 | 1.35 |
| New Zealand dollar | 1.69 | 1.53 | 1.67 | 1.68 | 1.73 | 1.86 | 1.85 | 1.69 | 1.51 |
| | *Annual percent change* | | | | | | | | |
| **Real effective exchange rates[3]** | | | | | | | | | |
| United States | −13.2 | −6.2 | 3.4 | −4.7 | −1.7 | −2.1 | 3.8 | −0.4 | ... |
| Japan | 4.7 | 5.1 | −6.1 | −10.6 | 5.9 | 3.0 | 17.0 | 7.2 | ... |
| Germany | 6.8 | −0.1 | −1.6 | 5.7 | −0.5 | 2.8 | 8.1 | −0.1 | ... |
| France | −2.0 | −3.1 | −2.2 | 3.0 | −4.1 | 1.1 | 2.1 | 1.1 | ... |
| United Kingdom | 2.6 | 7.5 | 0.1 | −5.8 | 3.8 | −0.2 | −6.6 | 1.4 | ... |
| Italy | 0.9 | −0.9 | 4.3 | 3.8 | 1.1 | −1.9 | −16.8 | −4.3 | ... |
| Canada | 4.4 | 9.3 | 6.4 | 1.6 | 3.1 | −5.3 | −7.7 | −10.7 | ... |
| Spain | 1.8 | 4.6 | 8.2 | 6.2 | 1.7 | 0.6 | −8.5 | −7.6 | ... |
| Netherlands | 3.3 | −3.2 | −5.2 | 1.2 | −1.1 | 4.1 | 2.6 | 1.5 | ... |
| Belgium | 0.9 | −2.8 | −0.6 | 4.5 | 0.1 | 1.8 | 0.2 | 1.4 | ... |
| Sweden | 0.1 | 3.8 | 7.2 | 1.0 | 0.3 | 1.0 | −23.5 | −1.3 | ... |
| Austria | 0.9 | −3.5 | −3.0 | −1.1 | −3.0 | 0.6 | — | −1.6 | ... |
| Denmark | 9.7 | −0.3 | −1.3 | 6.6 | −3.5 | −0.1 | 1.9 | 0.1 | ... |
| Finland | −0.8 | 2.6 | 5.1 | 3.3 | −8.0 | −18.0 | −16.4 | 5.5 | ... |
| Ireland | −6.5 | −5.6 | −6.8 | 1.7 | −6.1 | −2.0 | −7.7 | −3.9 | ... |
| Switzerland | 1.2 | −2.8 | −7.9 | 2.0 | −2.5 | −4.0 | −1.8 | 4.7 | ... |
| Norway | 4.1 | 1.6 | −2.0 | −1.0 | −2.7 | −0.4 | −2.9 | 0.3 | ... |

[1]August data refer to the average for August 1–23, the reference period for the exchange rate assumptions. See "Assumptions" in the introduction to this Statistical Appendix.

[2]Expressed in U.S. dollars per pound.

[3]Defined as the ratio, in common currency, of the normalized unit labor costs in the manufacturing sector to the weighted average of those of its industrial country trading partners, using 1989–91 trade weights.

**Table A20. Developing Countries: Central Government Fiscal Balances**

*(In percent of GDP)*

|  | 1987 | 1988 | 1989 | 1990 | 1991 | 1992 | 1993 | 1994 | 1995 | 1996 |
|---|---|---|---|---|---|---|---|---|---|---|
| **Developing countries** | **−5.8** | **−5.3** | **−4.2** | **−3.1** | **−3.3** | **−2.7** | **−3.0** | **−2.5** | **−2.0** | **−1.2** |
| **By region** | | | | | | | | | | |
| Africa | −6.0 | −6.3 | −4.6 | −3.3 | −4.5 | −6.1 | −8.3 | −6.0 | −3.8 | −2.0 |
| Asia | −3.9 | −3.5 | −3.0 | −2.6 | −2.6 | −2.6 | −2.4 | −2.2 | −2.1 | −1.5 |
| Middle East and Europe | −11.7 | −12.2 | −9.1 | −9.5 | −11.4 | −5.5 | −7.0 | −6.0 | −4.6 | −3.5 |
| Western Hemisphere | −6.0 | −4.9 | −4.1 | −0.3 | −0.2 | −0.1 | −0.2 | −0.4 | 0.2 | 1.2 |
| Sub-Saharan Africa | −8.1 | −7.3 | −6.7 | −7.0 | −7.0 | −7.9 | −7.7 | −6.7 | −4.8 | −3.6 |
| Four newly industrializing | | | | | | | | | | |
| Asian economies | 0.8 | 2.0 | 1.5 | 1.0 | — | −0.1 | 0.6 | 0.9 | — | 0.4 |
| **By predominant export** | | | | | | | | | | |
| Fuel | −11.8 | −13.6 | −7.7 | −5.2 | −5.9 | −4.6 | −8.8 | −7.1 | −3.9 | −2.2 |
| Nonfuel exports | −5.0 | −4.3 | −3.8 | −2.8 | −3.0 | −2.5 | −2.4 | −2.1 | −1.8 | −1.1 |
| Manufactures | −1.6 | −1.4 | −1.6 | −1.4 | −1.8 | −1.8 | −1.3 | −1.3 | −1.4 | −0.6 |
| Primary products | −5.8 | −5.7 | −6.4 | −3.9 | −3.6 | −3.3 | −3.0 | −2.5 | −2.4 | −1.6 |
| Agricultural products | −6.3 | −7.4 | −8.8 | −4.5 | −4.3 | −4.2 | −3.7 | −3.8 | −3.0 | −2.3 |
| Minerals | −4.8 | −2.2 | −1.5 | −2.6 | −2.2 | −1.4 | −1.5 | 0.2 | −0.9 | −0.3 |
| Services, income, and | | | | | | | | | | |
| private transfers | −10.2 | −10.4 | −10.0 | −14.3 | −19.5 | −8.1 | −5.9 | −5.6 | −4.8 | −3.4 |
| Diversified export base | −6.1 | −5.1 | −4.2 | −2.5 | −2.3 | −2.3 | −2.7 | −2.3 | −1.8 | −1.3 |
| **By financial criteria** | | | | | | | | | | |
| Net creditor countries | −9.7 | −6.5 | −2.2 | −6.9 | −15.7 | −6.7 | −5.9 | −4.8 | −4.1 | −2.9 |
| Net debtor countries | −5.6 | −5.2 | −4.3 | −2.8 | −2.6 | −2.5 | −2.8 | −2.4 | −1.9 | −1.1 |
| Market borrowers | −4.0 | −3.4 | −2.6 | −0.6 | −0.8 | −0.8 | −1.0 | −1.0 | −0.6 | 0.2 |
| Diversified borrowers | −6.6 | −6.7 | −6.0 | −5.1 | −4.4 | −4.2 | −4.9 | −4.2 | −3.8 | −3.1 |
| Official borrowers | −9.5 | −9.7 | −8.4 | −7.8 | −7.0 | −6.4 | −6.8 | −5.6 | −4.4 | −3.2 |
| Countries with recent debt- | | | | | | | | | | |
| servicing difficulties | −7.8 | −7.3 | −6.1 | −3.2 | −2.5 | −2.2 | −2.5 | −2.2 | −1.3 | −0.1 |
| Countries without debt- | | | | | | | | | | |
| servicing difficulties | −4.1 | −3.9 | −3.3 | −2.7 | −2.7 | −2.6 | −3.0 | −2.5 | −2.2 | −1.6 |
| **Other groups** | | | | | | | | | | |
| Small low-income economies | −10.3 | −11.0 | −9.4 | −9.0 | −8.1 | −7.2 | −7.8 | −6.2 | −4.8 | −3.5 |
| Least developed countries | −9.1 | −9.5 | −8.2 | −8.3 | −7.5 | −7.8 | −7.3 | −7.8 | −7.0 | −6.3 |
| *Memorandum* | | | | | | | | | | |
| **Median** | | | | | | | | | | |
| Developing countries | −5.3 | −5.3 | −4.7 | −4.2 | −4.4 | −4.0 | −4.3 | −4.2 | −3.0 | −2.4 |
| By region | | | | | | | | | | |
| Africa | −6.4 | −6.8 | −5.9 | −5.2 | −5.4 | −6.5 | −6.8 | −6.1 | −4.3 | −3.4 |
| Asia | −5.1 | −2.6 | −3.5 | −6.3 | −4.7 | −3.7 | −3.4 | −3.4 | −3.0 | −2.9 |
| Middle East and Europe | −11.9 | −11.7 | −5.1 | −4.5 | −6.6 | −4.4 | −6.3 | −5.1 | −4.0 | −3.1 |
| Western Hemisphere | −3.2 | −4.4 | −3.9 | −1.7 | −2.1 | −1.9 | −1.9 | −2.1 | −1.2 | −0.8 |

## Table A21.  Developing Countries: Broad Money Aggregates

*(Annual percent change)*

|  | 1987 | 1988 | 1989 | 1990 | 1991 | 1992 | 1993 | 1994 | 1995 | 1996 |
|---|---|---|---|---|---|---|---|---|---|---|
| **Developing countries** | **44.2** | **74.2** | **84.5** | **79.2** | **57.9** | **66.2** | **73.4** | **55.6** | **25.7** | **20.3** |
| **By region** | | | | | | | | | | |
| Africa | 20.7 | 25.5 | 15.9 | 18.1 | 31.4 | 32.1 | 26.2 | 31.9 | 20.6 | 12.1 |
| Asia | 27.5 | 25.0 | 23.5 | 22.2 | 22.0 | 20.5 | 20.8 | 19.1 | 18.6 | 16.5 |
| Middle East and Europe | 16.4 | 18.5 | 19.9 | 19.6 | 24.3 | 24.6 | 28.4 | 32.0 | 26.2 | 22.8 |
| Western Hemisphere | 126.3 | 376.8 | 541.3 | 454.6 | 210.7 | 284.2 | 322.3 | 172.7 | 37.6 | 26.4 |
| Sub-Saharan Africa | 27.7 | 26.2 | 22.0 | 21.4 | 57.1 | 57.3 | 44.8 | 58.2 | 28.4 | 15.7 |
| Four newly industrializing | | | | | | | | | | |
|    Asian economies | 23.1 | 20.0 | 18.8 | 15.9 | 19.3 | 15.4 | 15.4 | 15.7 | 14.4 | 13.3 |
| **By predominant export** | | | | | | | | | | |
| Fuel | 14.0 | 17.2 | 15.9 | 18.8 | 20.9 | 20.2 | 25.6 | 23.0 | 27.2 | 19.4 |
| Nonfuel exports | 54.7 | 95.5 | 109.2 | 99.4 | 69.6 | 82.9 | 88.4 | 63.2 | 25.5 | 20.4 |
|   Manufactures | 24.2 | 20.8 | 18.9 | 21.2 | 22.8 | 23.0 | 22.5 | 24.3 | 20.9 | 17.8 |
|   Primary products | 101.7 | 237.3 | 451.0 | 332.6 | 101.1 | 57.6 | 45.2 | 31.2 | 14.0 | 15.2 |
|     Agricultural products | 112.8 | 262.4 | 518.0 | 299.3 | 85.4 | 47.0 | 38.1 | 22.2 | 9.4 | 13.6 |
|     Minerals | 66.4 | 164.4 | 276.9 | 443.8 | 151.8 | 93.8 | 71.6 | 69.6 | 33.2 | 21.5 |
|   Services, income, and | | | | | | | | | | |
|     private transfers | 12.2 | 12.8 | 14.3 | 17.8 | 15.9 | 14.0 | 12.9 | 11.9 | 11.7 | 14.2 |
|   Diversified export base | 66.3 | 130.2 | 136.6 | 133.8 | 103.4 | 147.2 | 171.3 | 112.8 | 33.3 | 24.2 |
| **By financial criteria** | | | | | | | | | | |
| Net creditor countries | 11.1 | 8.0 | 8.5 | 7.0 | 12.4 | 9.9 | 8.5 | 8.1 | 8.5 | 7.8 |
| Net debtor countries | 48.0 | 82.4 | 93.7 | 88.0 | 63.0 | 72.9 | 81.9 | 61.7 | 27.7 | 21.6 |
|   Market borrowers | 63.4 | 123.5 | 149.3 | 135.2 | 83.6 | 99.7 | 118.3 | 81.4 | 29.9 | 22.2 |
|   Diversified borrowers | 23.7 | 23.9 | 26.9 | 22.1 | 26.1 | 24.7 | 25.0 | 29.8 | 25.3 | 21.5 |
|   Official borrowers | 38.6 | 63.2 | 41.9 | 42.2 | 39.3 | 38.3 | 30.8 | 30.8 | 21.1 | 19.0 |
| Countries with recent debt- | | | | | | | | | | |
|   servicing difficulties | 84.2 | 203.8 | 260.4 | 237.3 | 136.6 | 177.4 | 193.9 | 116.6 | 34.4 | 24.4 |
| Countries without debt- | | | | | | | | | | |
|   servicing difficulties | 23.1 | 21.4 | 21.4 | 22.6 | 24.9 | 24.3 | 26.1 | 26.3 | 21.4 | 18.7 |
| **Other groups** | | | | | | | | | | |
| Small low-income economies | 40.7 | 67.8 | 45.4 | 45.2 | 42.2 | 43.8 | 35.8 | 35.4 | 23.4 | 20.3 |
| Least developed countries | 27.6 | 33.1 | 30.9 | 30.7 | 62.5 | 60.4 | 48.1 | 46.4 | 28.8 | 22.8 |
| *Memorandum* | | | | | | | | | | |
| **Median** | | | | | | | | | | |
| Developing countries | 16.1 | 18.4 | 16.5 | 17.2 | 18.1 | 15.6 | 14.5 | 15.7 | 12.4 | 11.1 |
| By region | | | | | | | | | | |
|   Africa | 13.9 | 14.6 | 12.8 | 11.5 | 16.1 | 13.5 | 11.7 | 18.5 | 11.9 | 10.4 |
|   Asia | 17.7 | 19.5 | 19.1 | 18.9 | 19.8 | 16.0 | 17.1 | 16.0 | 15.1 | 14.4 |
|   Middle East and Europe | 9.7 | 9.1 | 13.0 | 10.7 | 14.5 | 10.7 | 9.0 | 9.7 | 10.2 | 9.5 |
|   Western Hemisphere | 21.0 | 23.6 | 18.2 | 27.5 | 30.9 | 19.9 | 15.2 | 14.5 | 11.3 | 10.1 |

## Table A22. Summary of World Trade Volumes and Prices

*(Annual percent change)*

| | Average 1977–86 | 1987 | 1988 | 1989 | 1990 | 1991 | 1992 | 1993 | 1994 | 1995 | 1996 |
|---|---|---|---|---|---|---|---|---|---|---|---|
| **Trade in goods and services** | | | | | | | | | | | |
| **World trade[1]** | | | | | | | | | | | |
| Volume | 3.9 | 6.2 | 8.0 | 7.5 | 5.5 | 3.5 | 5.7 | 3.9 | 8.7 | 7.9 | 6.5 |
| Price deflator | | | | | | | | | | | |
| In U.S. dollars | 4.5 | 11.2 | 5.6 | 0.8 | 8.5 | −0.6 | 1.4 | −4.2 | 2.1 | 8.0 | 1.5 |
| In SDRs | 4.3 | 0.9 | 1.6 | 5.7 | 2.5 | −1.4 | −1.4 | −3.4 | −0.4 | 1.3 | 2.4 |
| **Volume of trade** | | | | | | | | | | | |
| Exports | | | | | | | | | | | |
| Industrial countries | 4.3 | 4.5 | 7.6 | 8.1 | 6.8 | 3.2 | 4.3 | 2.5 | 8.1 | 6.9 | 5.0 |
| Developing countries | 2.0 | 13.7 | 10.8 | 6.4 | 6.6 | 6.5 | 10.0 | 7.3 | 11.3 | 11.0 | 9.6 |
| Imports | | | | | | | | | | | |
| Industrial countries | 4.2 | 6.4 | 8.0 | 8.1 | 5.1 | 2.1 | 4.0 | 1.1 | 9.2 | 7.1 | 5.5 |
| Developing countries | 3.8 | 7.2 | 9.3 | 7.7 | 7.5 | 11.1 | 10.2 | 9.3 | 8.5 | 11.1 | 9.5 |
| **Terms of trade** | | | | | | | | | | | |
| Industrial countries | 0.3 | 0.7 | 0.6 | −1.0 | −1.6 | 0.7 | 0.5 | 1.1 | 0.4 | 0.3 | 0.6 |
| Developing countries | 1.0 | 0.7 | −3.2 | 1.4 | 1.2 | −2.5 | −1.7 | 0.8 | 0.2 | −0.6 | −0.6 |
| **Trade in goods** | | | | | | | | | | | |
| **World trade[1]** | | | | | | | | | | | |
| Volume | 4.0 | 6.7 | 10.2 | 7.4 | 4.8 | 3.6 | 5.1 | 3.9 | 9.3 | 8.3 | 6.4 |
| Price deflator | | | | | | | | | | | |
| In U.S. dollars | 4.2 | 11.0 | 5.0 | 0.9 | 7.9 | −1.5 | 1.4 | −4.7 | 2.6 | 8.2 | 1.7 |
| In SDRs | 4.0 | 0.7 | 1.0 | 5.8 | 2.0 | −2.4 | −1.5 | −3.8 | 0.1 | 1.5 | 2.5 |
| **World trade prices in U.S. dollars[2]** | | | | | | | | | | | |
| Manufactures | 5.0 | 12.3 | 6.3 | −0.2 | 9.3 | −0.3 | 3.6 | −5.8 | 2.8 | 4.0 | 2.0 |
| Oil | . . . | 28.7 | −20.4 | 21.5 | 28.2 | −17.0 | −0.5 | −11.5 | −4.1 | 7.8 | −6.9 |
| Nonfuel primary commodities | 0.8 | 9.3 | 24.2 | −1.6 | −6.4 | −5.7 | 0.1 | 1.8 | 13.6 | 8.6 | −1.1 |
| **World trade prices in SDRs[2]** | | | | | | | | | | | |
| Manufactures | 4.8 | 1.9 | 2.2 | 4.6 | 3.2 | −1.2 | 0.7 | −5.0 | 0.3 | −2.5 | 2.8 |
| Oil | . . . | 16.8 | −23.5 | 27.4 | 21.2 | −17.7 | −3.3 | −10.7 | −6.5 | 1.1 | −6.1 |
| Nonfuel primary commodities | 0.6 | −0.8 | 19.5 | 3.2 | −11.6 | −6.5 | −2.8 | 2.7 | 10.8 | 1.8 | −0.2 |

## Table A22 *(concluded)*

| | Average 1977–86 | 1987 | 1988 | 1989 | 1990 | 1991 | 1992 | 1993 | 1994 | 1995 | 1996 |
|---|---|---|---|---|---|---|---|---|---|---|---|
| **Trade in goods** | | | | | | | | | | | |
| **Volume of trade** | | | | | | | | | | | |
| Exports | | | | | | | | | | | |
| Industrial countries | 4.5 | 4.5 | 12.1 | 7.4 | 6.2 | 3.3 | 4.0 | 2.2 | 8.4 | 7.4 | 4.8 |
| Developing countries | 1.6 | 14.6 | 13.5 | 9.3 | 6.3 | 6.0 | 9.8 | 6.7 | 10.8 | 10.8 | 9.5 |
| Fuel exporters | −5.4 | 4.0 | 10.9 | 9.2 | 10.7 | −3.4 | 3.2 | −4.2 | −1.3 | 1.3 | 1.6 |
| Nonfuel exporters | 6.0 | 16.8 | 14.1 | 9.3 | 5.5 | 8.2 | 11.1 | 8.6 | 12.7 | 12.0 | 10.5 |
| Imports | | | | | | | | | | | |
| Industrial countries | 4.6 | 6.4 | 8.0 | 7.4 | 4.4 | 3.3 | 4.1 | 1.4 | 10.4 | 7.4 | 5.1 |
| Developing countries | 4.1 | 10.0 | 12.3 | 10.9 | 7.3 | 9.4 | 13.3 | 10.5 | 8.5 | 10.3 | 9.9 |
| Fuel exporters | 1.1 | −8.3 | 4.9 | 1.0 | — | −2.9 | 15.9 | −6.2 | −12.8 | −4.7 | 2.3 |
| Nonfuel exporters | 4.9 | 14.0 | 13.6 | 12.5 | 8.4 | 11.2 | 12.9 | 12.6 | 10.7 | 11.4 | 10.4 |
| **Price deflators in SDRs** | | | | | | | | | | | |
| Exports | | | | | | | | | | | |
| Industrial countries | 4.0 | 1.9 | 2.1 | 4.7 | 2.0 | −2.2 | −0.4 | −4.7 | 0.3 | 2.7 | 2.6 |
| Developing countries | 4.7 | — | −2.2 | 8.3 | 0.7 | −1.9 | −2.6 | 0.6 | 0.4 | −1.0 | 2.0 |
| Fuel exporters | 2.0 | 8.2 | −15.3 | 18.7 | 14.7 | −8.3 | −4.1 | −4.6 | −0.5 | 0.1 | −1.2 |
| Nonfuel exporters | 4.6 | −1.7 | 0.5 | 6.5 | −2.0 | −0.4 | −2.3 | 1.5 | 0.6 | −1.2 | 2.4 |
| Imports | | | | | | | | | | | |
| Industrial countries | 3.5 | 1.0 | 1.2 | 6.0 | 3.6 | −4.0 | −2.1 | −6.5 | −0.8 | 2.2 | 2.5 |
| Developing countries | 3.9 | −2.4 | 1.9 | 6.9 | −0.4 | 1.3 | −2.7 | — | −0.1 | −1.2 | 2.9 |
| Fuel exporters | 2.6 | −1.7 | −0.4 | 7.4 | 2.5 | 9.2 | −7.6 | −3.1 | −4.5 | 7.9 | 2.5 |
| Nonfuel exporters | 4.4 | −2.6 | 2.3 | 6.9 | −0.8 | 0.1 | −2.1 | 0.4 | 0.4 | −1.9 | 2.9 |
| **Terms of trade** | | | | | | | | | | | |
| Industrial countries | 0.5 | 0.9 | 0.9 | −1.3 | −1.5 | 1.8 | 1.8 | 2.0 | 1.1 | 0.5 | 0.1 |
| Developing countries | 0.8 | 2.5 | −4.0 | 1.3 | 1.1 | −3.1 | 0.1 | 0.6 | 0.5 | 0.2 | −0.9 |
| Fuel exporters | −0.6 | 10.1 | −14.9 | 10.6 | 12.0 | −16.0 | 3.8 | −1.5 | 4.3 | −7.2 | −3.6 |
| Nonfuel exporters | 0.3 | 0.9 | −1.7 | −0.3 | −1.2 | −0.5 | −0.3 | 1.1 | 0.1 | 0.7 | −0.5 |
| ***Memorandum*** | | | | | | | | | | | |
| **World exports in billions of U.S. dollars** | | | | | | | | | | | |
| Goods and services | 2,154 | 3,085 | 3,505 | 3,794 | 4,346 | 4,457 | 4,783 | 4,774 | 5,289 | 6,148 | 6,648 |
| Goods | 1,708 | 2,415 | 2,760 | 2,985 | 3,378 | 3,450 | 3,682 | 3,662 | 4,095 | 4,796 | 5,174 |

[1]Average of annual percent change for world exports and imports. The estimates of world trade comprise, in addition to trade of industrial and developing countries (which is summarized in the table), trade of countries in transition.

[2]As represented, respectively, by the export unit value index for the manufactures of the industrial countries the average of U.K. Brent, Dubai, and Alaska North Slope crude oil spot prices; and the average of world market prices for nonfuel primary commodities weighted by their 1987–89 shares in world commodity exports.

## Table A23. Industrial Countries: Export Volumes, Import Volumes, and Terms of Trade

*(Annual percent change)*

| | Average 1977–86 | 1987 | 1988 | 1989 | 1990 | 1991 | 1992 | 1993 | 1994 | 1995 | 1996 |
|---|---|---|---|---|---|---|---|---|---|---|---|
| **Trade in goods and services** | | | | | | | | | | | |
| **Export volume** | | | | | | | | | | | |
| **Industrial countries** | **4.3** | **4.5** | **7.6** | **8.1** | **6.8** | **3.2** | **4.3** | **2.5** | **8.1** | **6.9** | **5.0** |
| Major industrial countries | 4.1 | 4.2 | 8.1 | 9.0 | 7.5 | 2.9 | 4.4 | 2.3 | 8.2 | 7.0 | 4.8 |
| United States | 3.1 | 10.5 | 15.8 | 11.9 | 8.2 | 6.3 | 6.7 | 4.1 | 9.0 | 10.5 | 6.5 |
| Japan | 6.4 | 0.1 | 7.0 | 9.0 | 7.3 | 5.2 | 5.2 | 1.3 | 5.1 | 2.6 | 1.6 |
| Germany[1] | 4.1 | 0.4 | 5.5 | 10.2 | 10.4 | 0.1 | −0.3 | −4.7 | 7.5 | 3.6 | 4.2 |
| France | 3.6 | 3.1 | 7.9 | 10.3 | 5.4 | 4.1 | 4.9 | −0.4 | 5.9 | 6.9 | 4.3 |
| Italy | 3.9 | 4.7 | 5.4 | 8.8 | 7.0 | 0.5 | 5.0 | 9.4 | 10.9 | 9.5 | 5.8 |
| United Kingdom | 3.1 | 5.8 | 0.5 | 4.7 | 5.0 | −0.7 | 3.1 | 4.2 | 8.2 | 7.5 | 8.2 |
| Canada | 6.6 | 3.5 | 9.5 | 0.8 | 4.1 | 1.4 | 7.6 | 10.4 | 14.2 | 8.2 | 2.5 |
| Other industrial countries | 4.6 | 5.3 | 6.3 | 5.6 | 5.2 | 4.0 | 4.3 | 2.8 | 7.9 | 6.7 | 5.5 |
| *Memorandum* | | | | | | | | | | | |
| European Union | 4.1 | 3.9 | 5.6 | 7.7 | 6.7 | 2.0 | 3.2 | 1.5 | 8.1 | 6.6 | 5.4 |
| **Import volume** | | | | | | | | | | | |
| **Industrial countries** | **4.2** | **6.4** | **8.0** | **8.1** | **5.1** | **2.1** | **4.0** | **1.1** | **9.2** | **7.1** | **5.5** |
| Major industrial countries | 4.4 | 6.2 | 8.2 | 7.8 | 5.5 | 2.1 | 4.4 | 1.8 | 9.6 | 7.2 | 5.3 |
| United States | 6.9 | 4.6 | 3.7 | 3.8 | 3.6 | −0.5 | 8.7 | 10.7 | 13.4 | 10.0 | 4.1 |
| Japan | 2.1 | 7.8 | 18.7 | 17.6 | 8.6 | −4.1 | −0.4 | 2.7 | 8.4 | 9.2 | 7.4 |
| Germany[1] | 3.1 | 4.2 | 5.1 | 8.4 | 9.4 | 13.4 | 2.2 | −5.2 | 7.1 | 2.5 | 5.3 |
| France | 2.7 | 7.7 | 8.3 | 8.3 | 6.1 | 3.0 | 1.1 | −3.4 | 6.8 | 5.7 | 5.2 |
| Italy | 3.6 | 9.1 | 6.8 | 7.6 | 8.0 | 3.4 | 4.6 | −7.8 | 9.8 | 8.5 | 6.0 |
| United Kingdom | 3.9 | 7.8 | 12.6 | 7.4 | 0.5 | −5.3 | 6.2 | 3.1 | 6.1 | 4.5 | 7.0 |
| Canada | 5.8 | 7.0 | 13.8 | 6.3 | 2.0 | 3.3 | 5.6 | 8.8 | 10.5 | 7.2 | 1.7 |
| Other industrial countries | 3.6 | 6.8 | 7.6 | 8.7 | 4.1 | 2.2 | 2.9 | −0.5 | 8.2 | 6.9 | 6.0 |
| *Memorandum* | | | | | | | | | | | |
| European Union | 3.4 | 7.4 | 8.0 | 8.2 | 5.9 | 4.3 | 3.3 | −2.8 | 7.4 | 5.5 | 5.9 |
| **Terms of trade** | | | | | | | | | | | |
| **Industrial countries** | **0.3** | **0.7** | **0.6** | **−1.0** | **−1.6** | **0.7** | **0.5** | **1.1** | **0.4** | **0.3** | **0.6** |
| Major industrial countries | 0.3 | 0.8 | 0.4 | −1.5 | −2.6 | 1.2 | 1.0 | 1.3 | 0.4 | 0.3 | 0.7 |
| United States | 0.3 | −3.8 | 0.3 | −0.4 | −1.8 | 2.2 | 0.5 | 1.3 | 0.5 | −0.1 | 1.2 |
| Japan | −0.5 | 0.8 | −0.5 | −3.7 | −5.9 | 3.5 | 2.1 | 2.7 | 0.4 | −0.7 | 1.6 |
| Germany[1] | −0.1 | 3.9 | 0.1 | −2.3 | −6.5 | −0.8 | 2.5 | 1.7 | 0.1 | 1.3 | — |
| France | — | 0.1 | — | −1.6 | — | 0.7 | 0.9 | 1.2 | 0.4 | −0.6 | −0.1 |
| Italy | 0.7 | 0.3 | −0.7 | −3.0 | −0.2 | 1.7 | −1.2 | −2.4 | 0.2 | 0.4 | 1.1 |
| United Kingdom | 0.9 | 0.4 | 1.1 | 1.6 | 1.0 | 1.3 | 1.5 | 0.5 | −1.1 | −2.3 | −0.5 |
| Canada | −0.1 | 3.3 | 2.3 | 2.1 | −2.1 | −1.5 | −0.5 | 0.3 | 0.5 | 1.9 | 1.3 |
| Other industrial countries | 0.3 | 0.5 | 1.2 | 0.4 | 0.8 | −0.6 | −0.7 | 0.4 | 0.4 | 0.3 | 0.4 |
| *Memorandum* | | | | | | | | | | | |
| European Union | 0.4 | 1.2 | 0.3 | −0.7 | −1.5 | 0.1 | 0.8 | 0.5 | −0.1 | 0.2 | 0.2 |
| *Memorandum* | | | | | | | | | | | |
| **Trade in goods** | | | | | | | | | | | |
| Industrial countries | | | | | | | | | | | |
| Export volume | 4.5 | 4.5 | 12.1 | 7.4 | 6.2 | 3.3 | 4.0 | 2.2 | 8.4 | 7.4 | 4.8 |
| Import volume | 4.6 | 6.4 | 8.0 | 7.4 | 4.4 | 3.3 | 4.1 | 1.4 | 10.4 | 7.4 | 5.1 |
| Terms of trade | 0.5 | 0.9 | 0.9 | −1.3 | −1.5 | 1.8 | 1.8 | 2.0 | 1.1 | 0.5 | 0.1 |

[1]Data through June 1990 apply to west Germany only.

## Table A24. Developing Countries—by Region: Total Trade in Goods

*(Annual percent change)*

| | Average 1977–86 | 1987 | 1988 | 1989 | 1990 | 1991 | 1992 | 1993 | 1994 | 1995 | 1996 |
|---|---|---|---|---|---|---|---|---|---|---|---|
| **Developing countries** | | | | | | | | | | | |
| Value in U.S. dollars | | | | | | | | | | | |
| Exports | 5.5 | 25.2 | 14.7 | 12.5 | 13.6 | 4.9 | 9.7 | 6.1 | 13.6 | 16.6 | 10.6 |
| Imports | 7.6 | 17.4 | 18.5 | 10.5 | 12.9 | 11.6 | 13.0 | 9.5 | 10.8 | 15.7 | 12.1 |
| Volume | | | | | | | | | | | |
| Exports | 1.6 | 14.6 | 13.5 | 9.3 | 6.3 | 6.0 | 9.8 | 6.7 | 10.8 | 10.8 | 9.5 |
| Imports | 4.1 | 10.0 | 12.3 | 10.9 | 7.3 | 9.4 | 13.3 | 10.5 | 8.5 | 10.3 | 9.9 |
| Unit value in U.S. dollars | | | | | | | | | | | |
| Exports | 4.9 | 10.2 | 1.6 | 3.3 | 6.6 | −1.1 | 0.3 | −0.3 | 3.0 | 5.5 | 1.2 |
| Imports | 4.1 | 7.5 | 5.9 | 2.0 | 5.4 | 2.1 | 0.1 | −0.8 | 2.5 | 5.3 | 2.0 |
| Terms of trade | 0.8 | 2.5 | −4.0 | 1.3 | 1.1 | −3.1 | 0.1 | 0.6 | 0.5 | 0.2 | −0.9 |
| *Memorandum* | | | | | | | | | | | |
| Real GDP growth in developing country trading partners | 4.0 | 5.1 | 5.5 | 3.9 | 3.6 | 2.7 | 3.0 | 2.9 | 4.1 | 3.8 | 3.7 |
| Market prices of nonfuel commodities exported by developing countries | 0.6 | 4.1 | 17.8 | −2.7 | −5.4 | −3.4 | −2.4 | 2.5 | 18.0 | 8.4 | −2.9 |
| **By region** | | | | | | | | | | | |
| **Africa** | | | | | | | | | | | |
| Value in U.S. dollars | | | | | | | | | | | |
| Exports | 4.1 | 12.0 | 2.2 | 7.2 | 16.5 | −3.9 | −1.7 | −3.9 | 0.5 | 13.0 | 8.0 |
| Imports | 3.8 | 6.7 | 11.3 | 4.9 | 8.3 | −1.9 | 5.9 | −2.7 | 5.1 | 16.0 | 4.6 |
| Volume | | | | | | | | | | | |
| Exports | 0.9 | −2.4 | 5.2 | 4.0 | 4.9 | 2.2 | −1.4 | 3.0 | −0.4 | 4.2 | 5.3 |
| Imports | 0.1 | −4.8 | 7.2 | 3.7 | −1.8 | −3.6 | 1.7 | 0.4 | 2.7 | 7.6 | 1.9 |
| Unit value in U.S. dollars | | | | | | | | | | | |
| Exports | 5.0 | 15.4 | −2.3 | 3.1 | 11.3 | −5.5 | 0.3 | −6.3 | 6.4 | 8.8 | 2.9 |
| Imports | 4.8 | 12.8 | 5.0 | 2.0 | 11.0 | 2.6 | 4.8 | −2.2 | 5.2 | 8.0 | 2.8 |
| Terms of trade | 0.2 | 2.3 | −7.0 | 1.1 | 0.3 | −7.9 | −4.3 | −4.3 | 1.2 | 0.7 | 0.2 |
| **Asia** | | | | | | | | | | | |
| Value in U.S. dollars | | | | | | | | | | | |
| Exports | 12.6 | 31.6 | 23.2 | 11.6 | 11.0 | 13.9 | 13.4 | 10.5 | 17.3 | 18.8 | 13.5 |
| Imports | 12.2 | 24.5 | 27.1 | 13.4 | 13.4 | 14.6 | 13.0 | 13.3 | 15.1 | 19.6 | 15.0 |
| Volume | | | | | | | | | | | |
| Exports | 8.7 | 23.0 | 18.7 | 9.5 | 7.9 | 12.8 | 12.1 | 9.3 | 13.9 | 13.2 | 11.9 |
| Imports | 8.4 | 18.4 | 21.0 | 11.3 | 9.6 | 13.8 | 13.0 | 13.6 | 12.1 | 14.3 | 12.6 |
| Unit value in U.S. dollars | | | | | | | | | | | |
| Exports | 4.3 | 7.8 | 4.0 | 1.8 | 2.8 | 1.1 | 1.1 | 1.2 | 2.7 | 5.1 | 1.5 |
| Imports | 4.1 | 5.9 | 5.2 | 2.3 | 3.5 | 0.8 | 0.2 | −0.1 | 3.0 | 4.6 | 2.1 |
| Terms of trade | 0.2 | 1.8 | −1.1 | −0.5 | −0.8 | 0.4 | 0.9 | 1.4 | −0.3 | 0.4 | −0.7 |

## Table A24 (concluded)

| | Average 1977–86 | 1987 | 1988 | 1989 | 1990 | 1991 | 1992 | 1993 | 1994 | 1995 | 1996 |
|---|---|---|---|---|---|---|---|---|---|---|---|
| **Middle East and Europe** | | | | | | | | | | | |
| Value in U.S. dollars | | | | | | | | | | | |
| Exports | −2.4 | 26.3 | 2.2 | 21.0 | 22.9 | −9.6 | 8.0 | −3.4 | 4.4 | 6.8 | 1.5 |
| Imports | 5.6 | 9.5 | 5.9 | 7.4 | 13.9 | 5.8 | 10.3 | 3.0 | −7.3 | 8.8 | 6.1 |
| Volume | | | | | | | | | | | |
| Exports | −5.9 | 10.8 | 9.6 | 17.7 | 1.5 | −9.6 | 12.0 | −2.0 | 5.9 | 1.8 | 1.8 |
| Imports | 2.6 | 1.1 | −0.8 | 20.7 | 4.2 | −2.2 | 17.1 | 5.3 | −7.5 | 0.9 | 4.6 |
| Unit value in U.S. dollars | | | | | | | | | | | |
| Exports | 4.1 | 15.2 | −5.7 | 6.0 | 19.6 | −1.7 | −1.2 | −1.7 | −0.4 | 5.1 | −0.5 |
| Imports | 3.2 | 8.1 | 6.8 | −1.2 | 9.6 | 7.3 | −5.5 | −3.5 | −1.8 | 9.6 | 1.3 |
| Terms of trade | 0.8 | 6.6 | −11.7 | 7.2 | 9.1 | −8.4 | 4.5 | 1.8 | 1.4 | −4.1 | −1.8 |
| **Western Hemisphere** | | | | | | | | | | | |
| Value in U.S. dollars | | | | | | | | | | | |
| Exports | 6.5 | 16.3 | 12.6 | 10.1 | 9.9 | −1.5 | 4.5 | 5.1 | 14.6 | 18.3 | 7.2 |
| Imports | 3.8 | 15.3 | 11.6 | 7.2 | 12.7 | 16.2 | 21.0 | 8.5 | 15.3 | 5.9 | 7.3 |
| Volume | | | | | | | | | | | |
| Exports | 4.1 | 8.0 | 7.8 | 4.1 | 7.0 | 3.7 | 6.0 | 6.6 | 8.3 | 11.1 | 7.1 |
| Imports | 0.1 | 7.1 | 3.4 | 2.2 | 8.6 | 15.1 | 17.4 | 8.7 | 11.7 | 2.1 | 5.1 |
| Unit value in U.S. dollars | | | | | | | | | | | |
| Exports | 3.5 | 8.4 | 4.7 | 5.7 | 2.9 | −4.9 | −1.4 | −1.3 | 5.7 | 6.3 | 0.4 |
| Imports | 4.6 | 7.9 | 7.9 | 4.7 | 3.9 | 0.8 | 3.5 | −0.1 | 3.3 | 3.9 | 1.9 |
| Terms of trade | −1.0 | 0.4 | −2.9 | 1.0 | −1.0 | −5.7 | −4.7 | −1.3 | 2.4 | 2.3 | −1.5 |
| **Sub-Saharan Africa** | | | | | | | | | | | |
| Value in U.S. dollars | | | | | | | | | | | |
| Exports | 4.9 | 5.0 | 2.5 | 4.0 | 5.6 | −3.9 | −3.9 | −2.8 | 7.4 | 14.3 | 8.4 |
| Imports | 5.4 | 12.4 | 6.8 | 1.6 | 7.3 | −0.9 | 0.8 | −2.0 | −0.4 | 11.8 | 7.2 |
| Volume | | | | | | | | | | | |
| Exports | 0.9 | −1.2 | 0.6 | 2.8 | 2.6 | −1.9 | −2.8 | 2.5 | 5.8 | 7.5 | 3.6 |
| Imports | −0.5 | 1.6 | 0.8 | −0.4 | −3.0 | −3.5 | −1.4 | −3.2 | −5.2 | 5.6 | 2.8 |
| Unit value in U.S. dollars | | | | | | | | | | | |
| Exports | 8.5 | 7.4 | 3.5 | 2.2 | 4.5 | −1.3 | 0.7 | −3.6 | 20.3 | 7.3 | 5.2 |
| Imports | 8.5 | 12.5 | 8.0 | 4.1 | 12.7 | 5.0 | 3.9 | 3.3 | 11.9 | 6.7 | 4.8 |
| Terms of trade | — | −4.6 | −4.2 | −1.8 | −7.3 | −5.9 | −3.1 | −6.6 | 7.5 | 0.6 | 0.4 |
| **Four newly industrializing Asian economies** | | | | | | | | | | | |
| Value in U.S. dollars | | | | | | | | | | | |
| Exports | 15.7 | 34.7 | 26.0 | 10.3 | 8.0 | 14.3 | 12.3 | 10.4 | 12.5 | 16.8 | 12.5 |
| Imports | 12.9 | 35.0 | 32.6 | 12.7 | 13.7 | 16.6 | 12.5 | 9.8 | 13.9 | 18.3 | 13.0 |
| Volume | | | | | | | | | | | |
| Exports | 12.0 | 29.3 | 20.3 | 8.1 | 6.1 | 12.8 | 12.8 | 9.8 | 10.0 | 11.2 | 11.1 |
| Imports | 8.6 | 30.0 | 26.1 | 10.2 | 12.0 | 16.4 | 14.5 | 9.3 | 11.4 | 12.7 | 10.4 |
| Unit value in U.S. dollars | | | | | | | | | | | |
| Exports | 3.8 | 4.6 | 4.8 | 1.9 | 1.6 | 1.4 | −0.6 | 0.7 | 1.8 | 5.2 | 1.3 |
| Imports | 4.3 | 4.9 | 5.4 | 2.4 | 1.5 | 0.1 | −1.5 | 0.5 | 2.9 | 4.8 | 2.3 |
| Terms of trade | −0.5 | −0.2 | −0.5 | −0.5 | 0.1 | 1.2 | 0.8 | 0.2 | −1.0 | 0.4 | −0.9 |

## Table A25. Developing Countries—by Predominant Export: Total Trade in Goods

*(Annual percent change)*

| | Average 1977–86 | 1987 | 1988 | 1989 | 1990 | 1991 | 1992 | 1993 | 1994 | 1995 | 1996 |
|---|---|---|---|---|---|---|---|---|---|---|---|
| **Fuel** | | | | | | | | | | | |
| Value in U.S. dollars | | | | | | | | | | | |
| Exports | −3.3 | 23.6 | −2.5 | 23.8 | 34.0 | −8.6 | 1.5 | −8.8 | −1.4 | 7.8 | — |
| Imports | 3.8 | — | 9.0 | 4.5 | 8.9 | 8.4 | 10.0 | −6.4 | −12.0 | 7.6 | 4.4 |
| Volume | | | | | | | | | | | |
| Exports | −5.4 | 4.0 | 10.9 | 9.2 | 10.7 | −3.4 | 3.2 | −4.2 | −1.3 | 1.3 | 1.6 |
| Imports | 1.1 | −8.3 | 4.9 | 1.0 | — | −2.9 | 15.9 | −6.2 | −12.8 | −4.7 | 2.3 |
| Unit value in U.S. dollars | | | | | | | | | | | |
| Exports | 2.1 | 19.2 | −11.9 | 13.3 | 21.5 | −7.5 | −1.3 | −5.4 | 2.0 | 6.7 | −2.0 |
| Imports | 2.7 | 8.3 | 3.5 | 2.4 | 8.4 | 10.1 | −4.9 | −4.0 | −2.1 | 15.1 | 1.7 |
| Terms of trade | −0.6 | 10.1 | −14.9 | 10.6 | 12.0 | −16.0 | 3.8 | −1.5 | 4.3 | −7.2 | −3.6 |
| **Nonfuel exports** | | | | | | | | | | | |
| Value in U.S. dollars | | | | | | | | | | | |
| Exports | 9.9 | 25.6 | 18.8 | 10.3 | 9.2 | 8.4 | 11.5 | 9.2 | 16.1 | 17.9 | 12.0 |
| Imports | 8.8 | 21.6 | 20.3 | 11.5 | 13.5 | 12.0 | 13.5 | 11.9 | 13.6 | 16.5 | 12.7 |
| Volume | | | | | | | | | | | |
| Exports | 6.0 | 16.8 | 14.1 | 9.3 | 5.5 | 8.2 | 11.1 | 8.6 | 12.7 | 12.0 | 10.5 |
| Imports | 4.9 | 14.0 | 13.6 | 12.5 | 8.4 | 11.2 | 12.9 | 12.6 | 10.7 | 11.4 | 10.4 |
| Unit value in U.S. dollars | | | | | | | | | | | |
| Exports | 4.8 | 8.3 | 4.5 | 1.6 | 3.7 | 0.4 | 0.6 | 0.6 | 3.1 | 5.4 | 1.5 |
| Imports | 4.5 | 7.4 | 6.3 | 1.9 | 5.0 | 1.0 | 0.8 | −0.4 | 2.9 | 4.6 | 2.1 |
| Terms of trade | 0.3 | 0.9 | −1.7 | −0.3 | −1.2 | −0.5 | −0.3 | 1.1 | 0.1 | 0.7 | −0.5 |
| **Manufactures** | | | | | | | | | | | |
| Value in U.S. dollars | | | | | | | | | | | |
| Exports | 15.1 | 33.8 | 24.1 | 9.4 | 9.7 | 13.7 | 13.1 | 9.6 | 16.8 | 18.4 | 13.3 |
| Imports | 13.4 | 27.8 | 29.4 | 10.6 | 9.3 | 16.6 | 14.5 | 13.6 | 13.1 | 18.7 | 15.2 |
| Volume | | | | | | | | | | | |
| Exports | 11.2 | 27.5 | 17.6 | 7.3 | 7.1 | 12.0 | 13.1 | 9.2 | 13.8 | 12.9 | 11.9 |
| Imports | 8.9 | 21.7 | 22.7 | 7.9 | 6.9 | 16.4 | 15.6 | 13.3 | 10.6 | 13.5 | 12.8 |
| Unit value in U.S. dollars | | | | | | | | | | | |
| Exports | 4.1 | 5.3 | 5.7 | 1.9 | 2.2 | 1.5 | −0.1 | 0.5 | 2.2 | 5.0 | 1.2 |
| Imports | 4.6 | 5.9 | 5.7 | 2.6 | 2.4 | 0.1 | −0.8 | 0.3 | 2.7 | 4.5 | 2.1 |
| Terms of trade | −0.5 | −0.5 | — | −0.7 | −0.2 | 1.4 | 0.7 | 0.1 | −0.5 | 0.5 | −0.8 |
| **Primary products** | | | | | | | | | | | |
| Value in U.S. dollars | | | | | | | | | | | |
| Exports | 4.6 | 7.3 | 9.4 | 9.2 | 8.5 | −1.1 | 2.6 | 3.2 | 15.5 | 21.4 | 7.7 |
| Imports | 5.1 | 16.2 | −3.8 | 2.3 | 7.4 | 14.0 | 21.9 | 6.3 | 11.1 | 8.0 | 8.8 |
| Volume | | | | | | | | | | | |
| Exports | 3.1 | 2.0 | 1.1 | 5.2 | 12.7 | 2.6 | 4.4 | 6.2 | 7.5 | 13.6 | 6.1 |
| Imports | 0.5 | 5.9 | −8.7 | 4.8 | −1.5 | 11.3 | 19.9 | 5.9 | 7.3 | 3.1 | 5.5 |
| Unit value in U.S. dollars | | | | | | | | | | | |
| Exports | 3.6 | 5.8 | 10.5 | 4.2 | −2.4 | −3.0 | −0.9 | −2.2 | 9.7 | 7.3 | 1.8 |
| Imports | 5.9 | 10.9 | 6.8 | 2.4 | 10.4 | 4.5 | 2.8 | 1.5 | 5.2 | 5.0 | 3.3 |
| Terms of trade | −2.2 | −4.6 | 3.5 | 1.8 | −11.6 | −7.2 | −3.6 | −3.6 | 4.2 | 2.2 | −1.4 |

**Table A25** *(concluded)*

| | Average 1977–86 | 1987 | 1988 | 1989 | 1990 | 1991 | 1992 | 1993 | 1994 | 1995 | 1996 |
|---|---|---|---|---|---|---|---|---|---|---|---|
| **Agricultural products** | | | | | | | | | | | |
| Value in U.S. dollars | | | | | | | | | | | |
|   Exports | 4.3 | 2.6 | 4.6 | 5.1 | 15.7 | –0.6 | 2.2 | 9.4 | 15.2 | 21.2 | 9.2 |
|   Imports | 6.1 | 15.5 | –10.0 | –2.9 | 5.3 | 22.7 | 27.1 | 9.0 | 14.1 | 4.4 | 7.8 |
| Volume | | | | | | | | | | | |
|   Exports | 3.0 | 2.6 | –0.1 | 2.2 | 22.3 | 2.6 | 5.6 | 9.2 | 9.2 | 15.3 | 7.1 |
|   Imports | 1.0 | 5.9 | –14.6 | 1.7 | –3.6 | 17.9 | 23.0 | 7.3 | 10.3 | –0.3 | 4.0 |
| Unit value in U.S. dollars | | | | | | | | | | | |
|   Exports | 4.0 | 0.9 | 8.3 | 3.5 | –3.7 | –2.0 | –2.3 | 1.1 | 6.4 | 5.7 | 2.2 |
|   Imports | 6.6 | 9.9 | 7.1 | 3.1 | 10.5 | 7.3 | 5.6 | 3.2 | 4.7 | 5.1 | 3.8 |
| Terms of trade | –2.4 | –8.2 | 1.2 | 0.4 | –12.9 | –8.7 | –7.5 | –2.1 | 1.7 | 0.6 | –1.5 |
| **Minerals** | | | | | | | | | | | |
| Value in U.S. dollars | | | | | | | | | | | |
|   Exports | 5.1 | 15.5 | 16.8 | 14.9 | –0.5 | –1.9 | 3.2 | –5.8 | 15.9 | 21.8 | 5.2 |
|   Imports | 3.4 | 17.6 | 9.0 | 11.2 | 10.6 | 1.7 | 13.0 | 1.0 | 4.9 | 16.2 | 10.9 |
| Volume | | | | | | | | | | | |
|   Exports | 3.1 | 1.1 | 2.9 | 9.4 | 0.6 | 2.6 | 2.8 | 1.7 | 4.5 | 10.6 | 4.5 |
|   Imports | –0.4 | 5.9 | 3.3 | 10.1 | 1.6 | 1.9 | 14.6 | 3.1 | 1.1 | 10.8 | 8.4 |
| Unit value in U.S. dollars | | | | | | | | | | | |
|   Exports | 2.8 | 14.3 | 14.0 | 5.1 | –0.6 | –4.5 | 1.2 | –7.0 | 15.3 | 10.1 | 1.2 |
|   Imports | 4.4 | 12.9 | 6.3 | 1.1 | 10.4 | 0.5 | –1.8 | –1.9 | 6.4 | 4.8 | 2.4 |
| Terms of trade | –1.5 | 1.2 | 7.2 | 3.9 | –10.0 | –5.0 | 3.0 | –5.3 | 8.3 | 5.0 | –1.2 |
| **Services, income, and**<br>  **private transfers** | | | | | | | | | | | |
| Value in U.S. dollars | | | | | | | | | | | |
|   Exports | 0.5 | 13.1 | 4.2 | 23.9 | –10.5 | –30.6 | 37.8 | 18.4 | 14.7 | 8.8 | 5.2 |
|   Imports | 6.8 | 11.4 | 10.4 | 2.0 | 5.1 | 2.9 | 12.2 | 2.8 | 5.1 | 6.5 | 5.2 |
| Volume | | | | | | | | | | | |
|   Exports | –3.6 | 2.6 | –2.1 | 56.7 | –20.5 | –28.1 | 50.5 | 11.4 | 22.9 | 4.0 | 3.8 |
|   Imports | 3.0 | 3.8 | –0.9 | 56.3 | –5.4 | –2.2 | 12.6 | 3.2 | 3.7 | 4.3 | 3.6 |
| Unit value in U.S. dollars | | | | | | | | | | | |
|   Exports | 5.3 | 14.0 | 6.9 | –12.1 | 13.0 | 4.8 | –2.9 | 5.0 | –4.8 | 5.1 | 1.5 |
|   Imports | 4.3 | 7.5 | 12.5 | –13.9 | 11.0 | 5.7 | 1.9 | –0.2 | 1.4 | 2.1 | 1.6 |
| Terms of trade | 1.0 | 6.1 | –4.9 | 2.1 | 1.7 | –0.8 | –4.7 | 5.2 | –6.1 | 3.0 | –0.1 |
| **Diversified export base** | | | | | | | | | | | |
| Value in U.S. dollars | | | | | | | | | | | |
|   Exports | 8.8 | 21.9 | 15.6 | 10.6 | 10.8 | 6.7 | 9.3 | 8.8 | 15.4 | 17.2 | 11.3 |
|   Imports | 6.3 | 17.6 | 16.8 | 16.6 | 21.8 | 7.4 | 10.8 | 11.8 | 15.8 | 16.2 | 10.8 |
| Volume | | | | | | | | | | | |
|   Exports | 4.6 | 9.7 | 14.1 | 8.4 | 4.6 | 7.5 | 7.2 | 7.8 | 11.0 | 10.9 | 9.4 |
|   Imports | 3.2 | 9.0 | 10.7 | 12.3 | 14.6 | 6.5 | 8.2 | 14.3 | 12.3 | 10.9 | 8.7 |
| Unit value in U.S. dollars | | | | | | | | | | | |
|   Exports | 5.1 | 11.8 | 1.4 | 1.9 | 6.0 | –0.7 | 2.0 | 1.1 | 4.0 | 5.6 | 1.9 |
|   Imports | 4.1 | 8.1 | 5.8 | 3.9 | 6.4 | 0.8 | 2.5 | –1.9 | 3.1 | 4.9 | 1.9 |
| Terms of trade | 0.9 | 3.3 | –4.2 | –1.9 | –0.4 | –1.4 | –0.5 | 3.0 | 0.9 | 0.6 | — |

## Table A26. Nonfuel Commodity Prices[1]
*(Annual percent change; U.S. dollar terms)*

| | Average 1977–86 | 1987 | 1988 | 1989 | 1990 | 1991 | 1992 | 1993 | 1994 | 1995 | 1996 |
|---|---|---|---|---|---|---|---|---|---|---|---|
| **Nonfuel primary commodities** | **0.8** | **9.3** | **24.2** | **−1.6** | **−6.4** | **−5.7** | **0.1** | **1.8** | **13.6** | **8.6** | **−1.1** |
| **By commodity group** | | | | | | | | | | | |
| Food | −1.0 | 4.7 | 28.8 | 1.8 | −9.6 | −0.9 | 2.3 | −1.3 | 5.1 | 4.3 | — |
| Beverages | 2.0 | −30.1 | 2.8 | −17.2 | −12.7 | −6.5 | −13.9 | 6.3 | 74.9 | 2.0 | −7.6 |
| Agricultural raw materials | 2.8 | 28.1 | 7.9 | 3.3 | 2.8 | −3.6 | 2.7 | 16.2 | 10.1 | 5.7 | 1.4 |
| Metals | 1.0 | 22.9 | 49.5 | −5.7 | −10.7 | −14.3 | −2.3 | −14.2 | 16.6 | 23.6 | −4.0 |
| Fertilizers | −0.1 | 1.2 | 15.4 | 2.1 | −4.5 | 3.2 | −5.0 | −15.4 | 8.0 | 6.7 | 2.0 |
| **Developing countries** | **0.6** | **4.1** | **17.8** | **−2.7** | **−5.4** | **−3.4** | **−2.4** | **2.5** | **18.0** | **8.4** | **−2.9** |
| **By region** | | | | | | | | | | | |
| Africa | 0.9 | −2.1 | 10.3 | −3.9 | −3.4 | −5.3 | −6.5 | 2.7 | 21.9 | 6.5 | −4.1 |
| Asia | 0.2 | 17.3 | 15.4 | −0.7 | −5.1 | −0.9 | 2.7 | 8.3 | 14.2 | 10.2 | −2.2 |
| Middle East and Europe | −0.1 | 18.1 | 14.6 | 4.5 | −3.2 | −6.1 | −5.3 | −9.2 | 16.6 | 9.7 | −5.2 |
| Western Hemisphere | 1.0 | −5.4 | 24.8 | −4.8 | −6.9 | −4.9 | −5.8 | −3.5 | 21.4 | 7.1 | −3.1 |
| Sub-Saharan Africa | 1.0 | −4.2 | 8.0 | −5.4 | −3.5 | −5.3 | −7.2 | 6.8 | 24.6 | 5.5 | −5.0 |
| Four newly industrializing Asian economies | 0.9 | 16.4 | 16.9 | −3.9 | −6.2 | −4.5 | 4.3 | 1.9 | 21.2 | 17.5 | −1.1 |
| **By predominant export** | | | | | | | | | | | |
| Fuel | 1.6 | 22.2 | 29.1 | −12.3 | −10.0 | −10.5 | 0.1 | 11.6 | 10.4 | 10.0 | −2.2 |
| Nonfuel exports | 0.6 | 3.6 | 17.5 | −2.3 | −5.3 | −3.2 | −2.4 | 2.2 | 18.3 | 8.4 | −2.9 |
| Manufactures | −0.1 | 14.8 | 15.8 | 0.2 | −5.0 | −4.9 | −1.0 | 0.6 | 14.8 | 11.9 | −1.9 |
| Primary products | 0.4 | 3.2 | 20.2 | −2.5 | −5.4 | −6.0 | −4.6 | −2.5 | 20.0 | 10.1 | −4.8 |
| Agricultural products | 0.5 | −2.6 | 11.0 | −4.6 | −6.0 | −4.2 | −6.3 | 4.7 | 21.7 | 4.1 | −3.5 |
| Minerals | 0.3 | 15.0 | 36.0 | 0.3 | −4.7 | −8.4 | −2.1 | −12.0 | 17.4 | 20.0 | −6.7 |
| Services, income, and private transfers | 0.1 | 11.9 | 20.1 | −1.3 | −2.5 | −7.7 | −7.0 | −2.4 | 18.8 | 8.5 | −5.2 |
| Diversified export base | 0.8 | 1.8 | 16.3 | −2.7 | −5.3 | −1.3 | −1.5 | 4.8 | 18.1 | 7.1 | −2.2 |
| **By financial criteria** | | | | | | | | | | | |
| Net creditor countries | 0.3 | 14.6 | 39.5 | −2.7 | −14.7 | −11.2 | 6.1 | −6.8 | 14.0 | 15.1 | −3.0 |
| Net debtor countries | 0.6 | 4.0 | 17.7 | −2.7 | −5.3 | −3.4 | −2.4 | 2.5 | 18.1 | 8.4 | −2.9 |
| Market borrowers | 0.2 | 9.1 | 21.5 | −3.4 | −6.5 | −3.1 | −0.6 | 3.0 | 14.0 | 10.4 | −2.5 |
| Diversified borrowers | 1.3 | −3.1 | 13.5 | −1.5 | −3.9 | −2.4 | −2.6 | 2.3 | 22.4 | 4.8 | −2.0 |
| Official borrowers | 0.6 | 2.6 | 13.0 | −2.5 | −4.0 | −6.2 | −8.5 | 1.3 | 24.6 | 8.5 | −6.1 |
| Countries with recent debt-servicing difficulties | 0.7 | 0.7 | 19.8 | −3.5 | −5.5 | −4.7 | −4.8 | −2.0 | 18.2 | 7.6 | −3.2 |
| Countries without debt-servicing difficulties | 0.6 | 8.1 | 15.3 | −1.7 | −5.2 | −1.8 | 0.2 | 7.4 | 17.9 | 9.2 | −2.7 |
| **Other groups** | | | | | | | | | | | |
| Small low-income economies | 0.6 | 1.6 | 17.5 | −0.7 | −6.5 | −8.0 | −5.1 | −6.4 | 29.8 | 11.5 | −5.2 |
| Least developed countries | 1.1 | −3.5 | 16.8 | −1.7 | −4.1 | −6.3 | −9.1 | −1.6 | 29.4 | 10.9 | −7.5 |
| *Memorandum* | | | | | | | | | | | |
| Average oil spot price[2] | ... | 28.7 | −20.4 | 21.5 | 28.2 | −17.0 | −0.5 | −11.5 | −4.1 | 7.8 | −6.9 |
| In U.S. dollars a barrel | ... | 17.79 | 14.15 | 17.19 | 22.05 | 18.30 | 18.22 | 16.13 | 15.47 | 16.67 | 15.51 |
| Export unit value of manufactures[3] | 5.1 | 13.2 | 6.6 | −0.6 | 9.7 | −0.3 | 3.9 | −6.3 | 3.3 | 6.9 | 2.0 |

[1]Averages of world market prices weighted by 1987–89 exports as a share of world or group commodity estimates.
[2]Average of U.K. Brent, Dubai, and Alaska North Slope crude oil spot prices.
[3]For the manufactures exported by the industrial countries.

## Table A27.  Summary of Payments Balances on Current Account
*(In billions of U.S. dollars)*

| | 1987 | 1988 | 1989 | 1990 | 1991 | 1992 | 1993 | 1994 | 1995 | 1996 |
|---|---|---|---|---|---|---|---|---|---|---|
| **Industrial countries** | **−70.6** | **−63.8** | **−92.0** | **−112.4** | **−31.3** | **−34.2** | **28.8** | **−6.3** | **−19.1** | **−20.1** |
| United States | −166.3 | −127.1 | −103.8 | −92.7 | −7.4 | −61.5 | −99.9 | −151.2 | −175.9 | −173.1 |
| European Union | 26.3 | 6.2 | −10.8 | −30.4 | −78.0 | −75.3 | 10.0 | 26.9 | 51.7 | 50.6 |
| Japan | 87.0 | 79.6 | 57.2 | 35.8 | 72.9 | 117.6 | 131.4 | 129.1 | 116.1 | 104.3 |
| Other industrial countries | −19.6 | −26.2 | −43.4 | −37.3 | −28.6 | −27.8 | −18.3 | −11.1 | −6.8 | 4.2 |
| **Developing countries** | **−1.3** | **−16.2** | **−9.8** | **−2.2** | **−82.5** | **−68.8** | **−98.5** | **−68.4** | **−63.7** | **−76.6** |
| **By region** | | | | | | | | | | |
| Africa | −4.1 | −8.7 | −7.4 | −2.6 | −4.2 | −8.5 | −8.6 | −11.2 | −14.5 | −11.6 |
| Asia | 23.3 | 12.7 | 4.9 | 2.3 | 3.1 | 3.4 | −11.2 | 4.0 | −4.0 | −13.1 |
| Middle East and Europe | −11.3 | −12.0 | −1.8 | 0.2 | −63.4 | −28.2 | −33.5 | −14.4 | −15.4 | −21.4 |
| Western Hemisphere | −9.3 | −8.2 | −5.6 | −2.2 | −18.0 | −35.5 | −45.2 | −46.8 | −29.7 | −30.5 |
| **By analytical criteria** | | | | | | | | | | |
| Fuel exporters | −14.6 | −23.8 | −10.5 | 10.7 | −33.1 | −29.0 | −29.8 | −10.9 | −8.9 | −13.7 |
| Nonfuel exporters | 13.3 | 7.6 | 0.7 | −12.9 | −49.4 | −39.8 | −68.6 | −57.5 | −54.8 | −62.9 |
| Net creditor countries | 16.0 | 8.1 | 14.6 | 19.8 | −39.4 | −8.8 | −9.3 | −5.9 | −2.9 | −5.6 |
| Net debtor countries | −17.3 | −24.3 | −24.4 | −22.0 | −43.1 | −60.0 | −89.2 | −62.5 | −60.8 | −71.0 |
| Countries with recent debt-servicing difficulties | −20.8 | −24.1 | −18.7 | −13.5 | −25.1 | −44.8 | −56.1 | −57.9 | −41.3 | −40.6 |
| Countries without debt-servicing difficulties | 3.5 | −0.2 | −5.7 | −8.5 | −18.0 | −15.2 | −33.0 | −4.6 | −19.4 | −30.4 |
| **Countries in transition** | **8.0** | **2.2** | **−5.9** | **−19.4** | **−7.4** | **−2.8** | **−3.3** | **−1.8** | **−7.6** | **−17.8** |
| Central and eastern Europe | ... | ... | ... | ... | −11.0 | — | −7.8 | −4.1 | −6.4 | −9.0 |
| Excluding Belarus and Ukraine | ... | ... | ... | ... | −2.8 | 0.4 | −6.6 | −2.2 | −4.7 | −7.1 |
| Russia | ... | ... | ... | ... | 4.1 | −1.2 | 5.4 | 3.4 | −0.9 | −6.0 |
| Transcaucasus and central Asia | ... | ... | ... | ... | −0.5 | −1.6 | −0.9 | −1.1 | −0.4 | −2.8 |
| **Total[1]** | **−64.0** | **−77.8** | **−107.7** | **−133.9** | **−121.2** | **−105.8** | **−73.0** | **−76.5** | **−90.4** | **−114.6** |
| In percent of sum of world exports and imports of goods and services | −1.0 | −1.1 | −1.4 | −1.5 | −1.4 | −1.1 | −0.8 | −0.7 | −0.7 | −0.9 |

[1]Reflects errors, omissions, and asymmetries in balance of payments statistics on current account, as well as the exclusion of data for international organizations and a limited number of countries. See "Classification of Countries" in the introduction to this Statistical Appendix.

## Table A28. Industrial Countries: Balance of Payments on Current Account

| | 1987 | 1988 | 1989 | 1990 | 1991 | 1992 | 1993 | 1994 | 1995 | 1996 |
|---|---|---|---|---|---|---|---|---|---|---|
| | | | | | *In billions of U.S. dollars* | | | | | |
| **Balance on current account** | | | | | | | | | | |
| **Industrial countries** | **−70.6** | **−63.8** | **−92.0** | **−112.4** | **−31.3** | **−34.2** | **28.8** | **−6.3** | **−19.1** | **−20.1** |
| Major industrial countries | −63.6 | −54.7 | −65.6 | −90.3 | −21.4 | −28.3 | −1.2 | −36.4 | −58.5 | −66.8 |
| United States | −166.3 | −127.1 | −103.8 | −92.7 | −7.4 | −61.5 | −99.9 | −151.2 | −175.9 | −173.1 |
| Japan | 87.0 | 79.6 | 57.2 | 35.8 | 72.9 | 117.6 | 131.4 | 129.1 | 116.1 | 104.3 |
| Germany[1] | 45.9 | 50.6 | 57.2 | 48.9 | −19.2 | −21.6 | −15.6 | −20.6 | −16.5 | −27.1 |
| France | −8.0 | −4.8 | −4.6 | −9.7 | −5.9 | 3.9 | 10.5 | 9.7 | 16.0 | 15.8 |
| Italy | −2.2 | −6.3 | −11.8 | −17.0 | −23.6 | −27.8 | 11.3 | 15.5 | 22.4 | 26.5 |
| United Kingdom | −8.2 | −29.6 | −36.9 | −34.0 | −14.5 | −17.4 | −16.6 | −2.6 | −7.4 | −4.2 |
| Canada | −11.8 | −17.2 | −22.8 | −21.6 | −23.6 | −21.4 | −22.3 | −16.3 | −13.3 | −9.1 |
| Other industrial countries | −7.0 | −9.0 | −26.3 | −22.1 | −9.9 | −5.9 | 30.0 | 30.0 | 39.4 | 46.7 |
| Spain | — | −3.7 | −11.5 | −16.9 | −16.7 | −18.4 | −4.0 | −3.7 | −2.4 | −1.2 |
| Netherlands | 3.2 | 5.3 | 8.3 | 10.5 | 7.9 | 7.6 | 10.2 | 10.3 | 12.9 | 11.3 |
| Belgium-Luxembourg | 2.8 | 3.7 | 3.6 | 3.6 | 4.9 | 6.6 | 11.3 | 12.6 | 16.5 | 17.6 |
| Sweden | −0.1 | −0.7 | −3.4 | −6.5 | −3.4 | −7.9 | −4.0 | 0.9 | 4.9 | 7.4 |
| Austria | −0.2 | −0.2 | 0.2 | 1.2 | 0.1 | −0.1 | −0.7 | −2.0 | −3.3 | −2.6 |
| Denmark | −3.0 | −1.3 | −1.1 | 1.4 | 2.0 | 4.2 | 4.7 | 3.4 | 3.8 | 3.7 |
| Finland | −1.7 | −2.7 | −5.7 | −6.9 | −6.6 | −4.9 | −0.8 | 1.1 | 2.7 | 1.4 |
| Greece | −2.5 | −3.0 | −4.6 | −4.9 | −3.7 | −2.0 | −0.7 | −0.1 | −1.5 | −1.9 |
| Portugal | 0.4 | −1.1 | 0.1 | −0.2 | −0.7 | — | 0.8 | −1.0 | −0.7 | −0.4 |
| Ireland | −0.1 | 0.1 | −0.5 | 0.1 | 1.5 | 2.4 | 3.6 | 3.2 | 4.2 | 4.4 |
| Switzerland | 7.6 | 9.0 | 7.0 | 8.6 | 10.6 | 15.1 | 18.3 | 18.5 | 18.1 | 17.1 |
| Norway | −4.1 | −3.9 | 0.1 | 3.9 | 5.1 | 2.9 | 2.4 | 3.2 | 5.2 | 9.9 |
| Iceland | −0.2 | −0.2 | −0.1 | −0.1 | −0.3 | −0.2 | — | 0.1 | 0.2 | 0.2 |
| Australia | −7.3 | −9.9 | −17.2 | −14.6 | −9.5 | −10.1 | −10.4 | −15.5 | −19.8 | −19.6 |
| New Zealand | −1.8 | −0.5 | −1.6 | −1.2 | −1.0 | −1.2 | −0.8 | −1.1 | −1.4 | −0.6 |
| *Memorandum* | | | | | | | | | | |
| European Union | 26.3 | 6.2 | −10.8 | −30.4 | −78.0 | −75.3 | 10.0 | 26.9 | 51.7 | 50.6 |
| | | | | | *In percent of GDP* | | | | | |
| **Balance on current account** | | | | | | | | | | |
| United States | −3.7 | −2.6 | −2.0 | −1.7 | −0.1 | −1.0 | −1.6 | −2.2 | −2.5 | −2.3 |
| Japan | 3.6 | 2.7 | 2.0 | 1.2 | 2.2 | 3.2 | 3.1 | 2.8 | 2.3 | 2.0 |
| Germany[1] | 4.1 | 4.2 | 4.8 | 3.0 | −1.1 | −1.1 | −0.8 | −1.0 | −0.7 | −1.1 |
| France | −0.9 | −0.5 | −0.5 | −0.8 | −0.5 | 0.3 | 0.8 | 0.7 | 1.0 | 1.0 |
| Italy | −0.3 | −0.8 | −1.4 | −1.6 | −2.1 | −2.3 | 1.1 | 1.5 | 2.1 | 2.3 |
| United Kingdom | −1.2 | −3.5 | −4.4 | −3.5 | −1.4 | −1.6 | −1.8 | −0.3 | −0.7 | −0.4 |
| Canada | −2.8 | −3.5 | −4.1 | −3.8 | −4.0 | −3.8 | −4.0 | −3.0 | −2.3 | −1.5 |
| Spain | — | −1.1 | −3.0 | −3.4 | −3.2 | −3.2 | −0.8 | −0.8 | −0.4 | −0.2 |
| Netherlands | 1.5 | 2.3 | 3.6 | 3.7 | 2.7 | 2.4 | 3.3 | 3.1 | 3.3 | 2.8 |
| Belgium-Luxembourg | 2.0 | 2.4 | 2.3 | 1.9 | 2.5 | 3.0 | 5.4 | 5.6 | 6.1 | 6.1 |
| Sweden | −0.1 | −0.4 | −1.8 | −2.8 | −1.4 | −3.2 | −2.2 | 0.4 | 2.2 | 3.2 |
| Austria | −0.2 | −0.2 | 0.2 | 0.8 | — | −0.1 | −0.4 | −1.0 | −1.4 | −1.1 |
| Denmark | −2.9 | −1.2 | −1.1 | 1.1 | 1.6 | 3.0 | 3.5 | 2.4 | 2.1 | 2.0 |
| Finland | −1.9 | −2.6 | −5.1 | −5.1 | −5.4 | −4.6 | −1.0 | 1.1 | 2.1 | 1.0 |
| Greece | −4.4 | −4.7 | −7.0 | −5.9 | −4.3 | −2.1 | −0.7 | −0.1 | −1.4 | −1.6 |
| Portugal | 1.2 | −2.2 | 0.3 | −0.3 | −0.9 | — | 0.9 | −1.1 | −0.7 | −0.3 |
| Ireland | −0.3 | 0.3 | −1.4 | 0.1 | 3.3 | 4.8 | 7.6 | 6.1 | 7.2 | 7.0 |
| Switzerland | 4.4 | 4.9 | 4.0 | 3.8 | 4.6 | 6.3 | 7.9 | 7.2 | 5.9 | 5.4 |
| Norway | −4.9 | −4.3 | 0.1 | 3.7 | 4.8 | 2.6 | 2.3 | 2.9 | 4.4 | 8.1 |
| Iceland | −3.4 | −3.5 | −1.4 | −2.1 | −4.6 | −3.1 | — | 2.1 | 2.2 | 2.6 |
| Australia | −3.7 | −4.0 | −6.1 | −4.9 | −3.2 | −3.5 | −3.7 | −4.8 | −5.7 | −5.3 |
| New Zealand | −5.0 | −1.1 | −3.7 | −2.8 | −2.3 | −2.9 | −1.7 | −2.3 | −2.4 | −1.0 |

[1]Data through June 1990 apply to west Germany only.

**Table A29. Industrial Countries: Current Account Transactions**

*(In billions of U.S. dollars)*

| | 1987 | 1988 | 1989 | 1990 | 1991 | 1992 | 1993 | 1994 | 1995 | 1996 |
|---|---|---|---|---|---|---|---|---|---|---|
| Exports | 1,687.9 | 1,944.6 | 2,098.4 | 2,410.9 | 2,453.3 | 2,614.2 | 2,520.7 | 2,800.6 | 3,285.3 | 3,505.0 |
| Imports | 1,719.9 | 1,956.5 | 2,139.1 | 2,456.9 | 2,455.8 | 2,578.1 | 2,429.8 | 2,716.8 | 3,173.9 | 3,388.1 |
| Trade balance | −32.0 | −11.9 | −40.7 | −46.0 | −2.5 | 36.1 | 90.9 | 83.9 | 111.5 | 116.9 |
| Services, credits | 515.1 | 572.7 | 616.6 | 750.6 | 788.9 | 864.3 | 850.2 | 899.0 | 1,020.9 | 1,110.0 |
| Services, debits | 495.6 | 567.1 | 611.6 | 742.7 | 766.1 | 848.7 | 827.4 | 876.1 | 1,003.8 | 1,072.5 |
| Balance on services | 19.4 | 5.6 | 5.0 | 7.9 | 22.8 | 15.6 | 22.7 | 22.9 | 17.1 | 37.6 |
| Balance on goods and services | −16.0 | −7.7 | −31.1 | −37.9 | 17.9 | 50.2 | 112.6 | 89.3 | 86.5 | 93.4 |
| Factor income, net | −3.4 | −1.4 | 4.7 | 0.1 | −2.3 | −1.5 | −1.1 | −17.5 | −42.1 | −61.1 |
| Current transfers, net | −54.6 | −56.1 | −60.9 | −74.4 | −49.2 | −84.4 | −83.8 | −95.6 | −105.7 | −113.5 |
| **Current account balance** | **−70.6** | **−63.8** | **−92.0** | **−112.4** | **−31.3** | **−34.2** | **28.8** | **−6.3** | **−19.1** | **−20.1** |
| **Balance on goods and services** | | | | | | | | | | |
| **Industrial countries** | **−12.6** | **−6.3** | **−35.8** | **−38.1** | **20.2** | **51.7** | **113.6** | **106.8** | **128.6** | **154.5** |
| Major industrial countries | −24.9 | −19.4 | −34.6 | −47.8 | 0.1 | 24.5 | 57.6 | 44.1 | 53.2 | 69.3 |
| United States | −152.7 | −115.3 | −91.4 | −80.0 | −29.4 | −39.5 | −74.8 | −106.2 | −116.0 | −91.4 |
| Japan | 74.0 | 62.7 | 37.9 | 18.0 | 58.7 | 86.0 | 96.2 | 95.6 | 81.2 | 65.0 |
| Germany[1] | 58.1 | 63.5 | 61.3 | 56.1 | 0.6 | −0.7 | 8.1 | 12.2 | 27.2 | 23.7 |
| France | 2.0 | 3.4 | 3.5 | 1.7 | 6.5 | 21.8 | 25.5 | 27.6 | 33.3 | 33.9 |
| Italy | −1.3 | −4.9 | −9.2 | −14.7 | −17.7 | −22.2 | 16.7 | 21.2 | 28.0 | 32.6 |
| United Kingdom | −8.8 | −31.2 | −35.0 | −27.0 | −11.6 | −15.9 | −11.6 | −10.4 | −10.8 | −9.7 |
| Canada | 3.7 | 2.4 | −1.8 | −2.0 | −6.9 | −5.0 | −2.5 | 4.1 | 10.3 | 15.2 |
| Other industrial countries | 12.3 | 13.0 | −1.1 | 9.7 | 20.2 | 27.2 | 56.0 | 62.7 | 75.4 | 85.1 |
| *Memorandum* | | | | | | | | | | |
| European Union | 56.6 | 34.4 | 13.6 | 9.1 | −27.5 | −16.6 | 66.3 | 86.2 | 127.7 | 135.1 |
| **Factor income, net** | | | | | | | | | | |
| **Industrial countries** | **−3.4** | **−1.4** | **4.7** | **0.1** | **−2.3** | **−1.5** | **−1.1** | **−17.5** | **−42.1** | **−61.1** |
| Major industrial countries | 20.4 | 27.9 | 38.0 | 41.0 | 38.8 | 43.9 | 35.8 | 24.3 | 2.7 | −14.5 |
| United States | 9.5 | 13.3 | 13.7 | 20.7 | 15.1 | 10.1 | 9.0 | −9.3 | −24.3 | −42.9 |
| Japan | 16.7 | 21.0 | 23.4 | 23.2 | 26.7 | 36.2 | 41.4 | 41.0 | 43.2 | 47.9 |
| Germany[1] | 3.9 | 5.2 | 15.5 | 16.8 | 17.9 | 14.4 | 11.0 | 4.9 | 0.9 | −4.4 |
| France | −1.6 | −1.5 | −0.6 | −3.2 | −5.1 | −9.1 | −8.9 | −9.5 | −7.5 | −7.8 |
| Italy | 1.2 | 1.7 | 1.7 | 1.4 | 1.3 | 1.2 | 0.7 | 2.2 | 2.2 | 2.3 |
| United Kingdom | 6.2 | 7.9 | 5.6 | 1.8 | −0.4 | 7.6 | 2.8 | 16.1 | 12.3 | 15.3 |
| Canada | −15.4 | −19.8 | −21.2 | −19.6 | −16.7 | −16.5 | −20.2 | −21.2 | −24.1 | −24.9 |
| Other industrial countries | −23.8 | −29.2 | −33.4 | −40.9 | −41.1 | −45.3 | −36.9 | −41.8 | −44.8 | −46.6 |
| *Memorandum* | | | | | | | | | | |
| European Union | −3.9 | −2.3 | 5.9 | −5.6 | −8.8 | −14.2 | −15.6 | −9.6 | −16.9 | −21.0 |

[1]Data through June 1990 apply to west Germany only.

## Table A30. Developing Countries: Payments Balances on Current Account

| | 1987 | 1988 | 1989 | 1990 | 1991 | 1992 | 1993 | 1994 | 1995 | 1996 |
|---|---|---|---|---|---|---|---|---|---|---|
| | | | | | *In billions of U.S. dollars* | | | | | |
| **Developing countries** | **−1.3** | **−16.2** | **−9.8** | **−2.2** | **−82.5** | **−68.8** | **−98.5** | **−68.4** | **−63.7** | **−76.6** |
| **By region** | | | | | | | | | | |
| Africa | −4.1 | −8.7 | −7.4 | −2.6 | −4.2 | −8.5 | −8.6 | −11.2 | −14.5 | −11.6 |
| Asia | 23.3 | 12.7 | 4.9 | 2.3 | 3.1 | 3.4 | −11.2 | 4.0 | −4.0 | −13.1 |
| Middle East and Europe | −11.3 | −12.0 | −1.8 | 0.2 | −63.4 | −28.2 | −33.5 | −14.4 | −15.4 | −21.4 |
| Western Hemisphere | −9.3 | −8.2 | −5.6 | −2.2 | −18.0 | −35.5 | −45.2 | −46.8 | −29.7 | −30.5 |
| Sub-Saharan Africa | −6.0 | −6.8 | −6.8 | −8.2 | −8.3 | −9.1 | −8.6 | −6.0 | −6.5 | −5.7 |
| Four newly industrializing Asian economies | 32.8 | 30.7 | 27.4 | 18.4 | 14.0 | 16.0 | 21.8 | 21.4 | 18.2 | 21.4 |
| **By predominant export** | | | | | | | | | | |
| Fuel | −14.6 | −23.8 | −10.5 | 10.7 | −33.1 | −29.0 | −29.8 | −10.9 | −8.9 | −13.7 |
| Nonfuel exports | 13.3 | 7.6 | 0.7 | −12.9 | −49.4 | −39.8 | −68.6 | −57.5 | −54.8 | −62.9 |
| Manufactures | 33.4 | 26.6 | 23.9 | 30.1 | 24.6 | 19.8 | 5.2 | 22.2 | 20.2 | 13.3 |
| Primary products | −15.7 | −10.6 | −6.6 | −5.1 | −11.4 | −19.6 | −21.3 | −21.5 | −14.1 | −16.7 |
| Agricultural products | −12.0 | −7.5 | −4.7 | −1.9 | −7.6 | −14.5 | −15.1 | −16.5 | −10.1 | −11.1 |
| Minerals | −3.6 | −3.1 | −1.9 | −3.2 | −3.8 | −5.1 | −6.2 | −5.0 | −4.1 | −5.6 |
| Services, income, and private transfers | 1.1 | 1.0 | 5.9 | 1.6 | −26.5 | −1.1 | 3.6 | 1.9 | 2.2 | 2.5 |
| Diversified export base | −5.6 | −9.4 | −22.4 | −39.4 | −36.1 | −38.9 | −56.2 | −60.1 | −63.0 | −62.0 |
| **By financial criteria** | | | | | | | | | | |
| Net creditor countries | 16.0 | 8.1 | 14.6 | 19.8 | −39.4 | −8.8 | −9.3 | −5.9 | −2.9 | −5.6 |
| Net debtor countries | −17.3 | −24.3 | −24.4 | −22.0 | −43.1 | −60.0 | −89.2 | −62.5 | −60.8 | −71.0 |
| Market borrowers | 10.3 | 7.4 | 6.9 | 12.9 | −21.8 | −31.8 | −49.5 | −29.4 | −19.3 | −29.4 |
| Diversified borrowers | −14.5 | −16.7 | −18.1 | −25.8 | −12.5 | −16.3 | −24.0 | −18.6 | −27.1 | −28.3 |
| Official borrowers | −13.1 | −15.0 | −13.2 | −9.0 | −8.9 | −11.9 | −15.7 | −14.5 | −14.4 | −13.3 |
| Countries with recent debt-servicing difficulties | −20.8 | −24.1 | −18.7 | −13.5 | −25.1 | −44.8 | −56.1 | −57.9 | −41.3 | −40.6 |
| Countries without debt-servicing difficulties | 3.5 | −0.2 | −5.7 | −8.5 | −18.0 | −15.2 | −33.0 | −4.6 | −19.4 | −30.4 |
| **Other groups** | | | | | | | | | | |
| Small low-income economies | −13.1 | −16.0 | −12.2 | −9.0 | −9.7 | −11.3 | −13.8 | −13.1 | −12.8 | −12.6 |
| Least developed countries | −5.5 | −6.4 | −5.9 | −7.3 | −7.7 | −8.0 | −7.8 | −6.9 | −7.3 | −7.8 |

## Table A30 (concluded)

| | Average 1977–86 | 1987 | 1988 | 1989 | 1990 | 1991 | 1992 | 1993 | 1994 | 1995 | 1996 |
|---|---|---|---|---|---|---|---|---|---|---|---|
| | | | | | *In percent of exports of goods and services* | | | | | | |
| **Developing countries** | **–3.9** | **–0.2** | **–2.1** | **–1.1** | **–0.2** | **–7.9** | **–6.0** | **–8.1** | **–4.9** | **–4.0** | **–4.3** |
| **By region** | | | | | | | | | | | |
| Africa | –14.7 | –5.3 | –11.0 | –8.8 | –2.6 | –4.5 | –9.0 | –9.4 | –12.1 | –13.9 | –10.3 |
| Asia | –5.0 | 6.9 | 3.1 | 1.1 | 0.4 | 0.5 | 0.5 | –1.5 | 0.5 | –0.4 | –1.1 |
| Middle East and Europe | 6.2 | –7.8 | –8.1 | –1.0 | 0.1 | –33.2 | –13.7 | –16.7 | –6.9 | –6.9 | –9.3 |
| Western Hemisphere | –18.7 | –7.9 | –6.2 | –3.8 | –1.3 | –11.1 | –20.8 | –24.7 | –22.6 | –12.4 | –11.9 |
| Sub-Saharan Africa | –27.0 | –20.7 | –22.8 | –21.8 | –24.7 | –26.1 | –29.4 | –27.9 | –18.4 | –17.5 | –14.2 |
| Four newly industrializing Asian economies | 0.9 | 15.8 | 11.8 | 9.5 | 5.8 | 3.9 | 4.0 | 4.9 | 4.2 | 3.1 | 3.2 |
| **By predominant export** | | | | | | | | | | | |
| Fuel | 1.3 | –11.7 | –19.7 | –7.2 | 5.7 | –19.2 | –16.7 | –18.6 | –7.0 | –5.3 | –8.1 |
| Nonfuel exports | –8.7 | 2.4 | 1.2 | 0.1 | –1.6 | –5.7 | –4.1 | –6.5 | –4.7 | –3.8 | –3.9 |
| Manufactures | 2.5 | 12.6 | 8.2 | 6.7 | 7.6 | 5.5 | 3.9 | 0.9 | 3.4 | 2.6 | 1.5 |
| Primary products | –26.0 | –33.8 | –21.4 | –12.2 | –8.6 | –19.1 | –31.8 | –33.2 | –29.3 | –16.1 | –17.6 |
| Agricultural products | –26.1 | –42.2 | –25.9 | –15.1 | –5.3 | –21.2 | –39.0 | –37.4 | –35.7 | –18.1 | –18.4 |
| Minerals | –26.8 | –20.4 | –15.0 | –8.3 | –13.4 | –16.1 | –20.7 | –26.1 | –18.4 | –12.5 | –16.3 |
| Services, income, and private transfers | 13.1 | 3.3 | 2.7 | 14.4 | 3.8 | –73.6 | –2.5 | 7.5 | 3.5 | 3.7 | 3.9 |
| Diversified export base | –19.5 | –2.7 | –3.9 | –8.4 | –13.0 | –11.2 | –11.0 | –14.5 | –13.5 | –12.2 | –10.9 |
| **By financial criteria** | | | | | | | | | | | |
| Net creditor countries | 15.5 | 12.6 | 6.0 | 9.3 | 10.9 | –21.2 | –4.4 | –4.6 | –2.8 | –1.3 | –2.3 |
| Net debtor countries | 0.9 | –3.2 | –3.8 | –3.4 | –2.7 | –5.0 | –6.3 | –8.7 | –5.3 | –4.4 | –4.6 |
| Market borrowers | –7.7 | 2.9 | 1.7 | 1.4 | 2.3 | –3.6 | –4.6 | –6.6 | –3.4 | –1.9 | –2.5 |
| Diversified borrowers | –13.7 | –11.1 | –11.7 | –11.4 | –15.1 | –7.6 | –9.3 | –12.6 | –8.7 | –11.2 | –10.7 |
| Official borrowers | –25.6 | –22.1 | –23.2 | –18.8 | –11.0 | –10.7 | –13.8 | –18.3 | –16.0 | –13.9 | –11.9 |
| Countries with recent debt-servicing difficulties | –18.3 | –10.5 | –11.1 | –7.7 | –5.1 | –10.1 | –17.2 | –20.7 | –19.3 | –11.9 | –10.9 |
| Countries without debt-servicing difficulties | –26.1 | 1.0 | — | –1.2 | –1.6 | –3.0 | –2.2 | –4.4 | –0.5 | –1.9 | –2.6 |
| **Other groups** | | | | | | | | | | | |
| Small low-income economies | –26.9 | –28.3 | –33.1 | –22.9 | –14.2 | –15.3 | –17.3 | –21.0 | –18.8 | –15.9 | –14.4 |
| Least developed countries | –40.0 | –33.5 | –35.6 | –31.4 | –37.0 | –40.6 | –42.6 | –39.9 | –31.6 | –29.2 | –28.7 |
| ***Memorandum*** | | | | | | | | | | | |
| **Median** | | | | | | | | | | | |
| Developing countries | –17.5 | –13.1 | –13.0 | –11.1 | –14.5 | –12.7 | –14.2 | –15.7 | –11.4 | –12.3 | –10.8 |

## Table A31. Developing Countries—by Region: Current Account Transactions

*(In billions of U.S. dollars)*

| | 1987 | 1988 | 1989 | 1990 | 1991 | 1992 | 1993 | 1994 | 1995 | 1996 |
|---|---|---|---|---|---|---|---|---|---|---|
| **Developing countries** | | | | | | | | | | |
| Exports | 552.8 | 634.3 | 713.6 | 810.7 | 850.2 | 932.3 | 989.3 | 1,123.7 | 1,310.0 | 1,449.1 |
| Imports | 509.8 | 603.9 | 667.1 | 753.0 | 840.0 | 949.2 | 1,039.4 | 1,151.2 | 1,332.3 | 1,493.1 |
| Trade balance | 43.0 | 30.3 | 46.4 | 57.7 | 10.1 | −16.9 | −50.0 | −27.7 | −23.5 | −44.3 |
| Services, net | −13.4 | −13.5 | −23.1 | −23.8 | −40.9 | −34.1 | −22.2 | −11.5 | −11.4 | −6.3 |
| Balance on goods and services | 29.6 | 16.8 | 23.3 | 33.9 | −30.8 | −51.0 | −72.2 | −39.2 | −34.9 | −50.6 |
| Factor income, net | −52.1 | −54.7 | −58.9 | −57.7 | −54.9 | −53.3 | −57.5 | −63.5 | −67.4 | −64.5 |
| Current transfers, net | 21.2 | 21.7 | 25.7 | 21.7 | 3.1 | 35.5 | 31.4 | 34.2 | 37.2 | 38.1 |
| **Current account balance** | **−1.3** | **−16.2** | **−9.8** | **−2.2** | **−82.5** | **−68.8** | **−98.5** | **−68.4** | **−63.7** | **−76.6** |
| *Memorandum* | | | | | | | | | | |
| Exports of goods and services | 676.0 | 772.3 | 868.8 | 989.7 | 1,040.9 | 1,147.3 | 1,221.8 | 1,386.4 | 1,606.2 | 1,776.2 |
| Interest payments | 74.3 | 79.6 | 88.2 | 91.7 | 87.4 | 87.2 | 88.7 | 96.5 | 110.2 | 114.0 |
| Oil trade balance | 83.3 | 77.5 | 103.1 | 134.5 | 112.4 | 115.3 | 98.4 | 93.4 | 98.1 | 108.6 |
| **By region** | | | | | | | | | | |
| **Africa** | | | | | | | | | | |
| Exports | 65.7 | 67.2 | 72.0 | 83.9 | 80.6 | 79.3 | 76.1 | 76.5 | 86.4 | 93.3 |
| Imports | 58.4 | 64.9 | 68.1 | 73.7 | 72.4 | 76.6 | 74.5 | 78.3 | 90.9 | 95.0 |
| Trade balance | 7.4 | 2.3 | 3.9 | 10.2 | 8.3 | 2.7 | 1.6 | −1.9 | −4.5 | −1.7 |
| Services, net | −8.5 | −8.7 | −9.6 | −11.6 | −10.7 | −10.3 | −10.1 | −9.0 | −9.6 | −8.9 |
| Balance on goods and services | −1.2 | −6.4 | −5.7 | −1.4 | −2.4 | −7.6 | −8.5 | −11.0 | −14.1 | −10.7 |
| Factor income, net | −12.0 | −12.6 | −13.2 | −13.8 | −14.5 | −13.8 | −12.4 | −12.2 | −13.0 | −13.6 |
| Current transfers, net | 9.1 | 10.3 | 11.5 | 12.7 | 12.7 | 12.9 | 12.3 | 12.0 | 12.4 | 12.6 |
| **Current account balance** | **−4.1** | **−8.7** | **−7.4** | **−2.6** | **−4.2** | **−8.5** | **−8.6** | **−11.2** | **−14.5** | **−11.6** |
| *Memorandum* | | | | | | | | | | |
| Exports of goods and services | 76.6 | 79.3 | 84.4 | 96.9 | 94.3 | 94.4 | 91.6 | 92.6 | 104.7 | 112.8 |
| Interest payments | 13.3 | 14.2 | 14.7 | 15.5 | 15.4 | 15.0 | 14.0 | 13.9 | 15.3 | 15.5 |
| Oil trade balance | 10.5 | 10.1 | 15.2 | 23.7 | 21.5 | 20.8 | 18.4 | 14.7 | 16.6 | 17.8 |
| **Asia** | | | | | | | | | | |
| Exports | 284.1 | 349.9 | 390.4 | 433.3 | 493.7 | 559.6 | 618.5 | 725.5 | 861.7 | 977.8 |
| Imports | 267.1 | 339.5 | 385.0 | 436.6 | 500.3 | 565.1 | 640.3 | 737.1 | 881.3 | 1,013.8 |
| Trade balance | 17.1 | 10.4 | 5.4 | −3.3 | −6.6 | −5.5 | −21.9 | −11.6 | −19.6 | −36.0 |
| Services, net | 5.0 | 4.3 | 3.7 | 7.0 | 6.5 | 3.5 | 4.6 | 8.0 | 4.3 | 7.2 |
| Balance on goods and services | 22.0 | 14.7 | 9.1 | 3.7 | −0.1 | −2.0 | −17.3 | −3.6 | −15.2 | −28.8 |
| Factor income, net | −6.0 | −8.5 | −8.5 | −6.7 | −7.6 | −6.2 | −5.5 | −5.9 | −3.1 | 1.0 |
| Current transfers, net | 7.3 | 6.5 | 4.3 | 5.3 | 10.8 | 11.6 | 11.6 | 13.6 | 14.3 | 14.8 |
| **Current account balance** | **23.3** | **12.7** | **4.9** | **2.3** | **3.1** | **3.4** | **−11.2** | **4.0** | **−4.0** | **−13.1** |
| *Memorandum* | | | | | | | | | | |
| Exports of goods and services | 338.0 | 413.6 | 464.0 | 521.6 | 593.3 | 675.8 | 746.7 | 878.8 | 1,038.9 | 1,177.5 |
| Interest payments | 18.7 | 19.2 | 20.5 | 21.2 | 23.6 | 25.8 | 26.2 | 30.9 | 35.2 | 37.0 |
| Oil trade balance | −5.8 | −6.7 | −9.2 | −13.1 | −14.8 | −18.7 | −19.0 | −19.8 | −23.8 | −26.1 |

**Table A31** *(concluded)*

| | 1987 | 1988 | 1989 | 1990 | 1991 | 1992 | 1993 | 1994 | 1995 | 1996 |
|---|---|---|---|---|---|---|---|---|---|---|
| **Middle East and Europe** | | | | | | | | | | |
| Exports | 109.0 | 111.4 | 134.8 | 165.6 | 149.8 | 161.8 | 156.3 | 163.1 | 174.3 | 176.9 |
| Imports | 109.1 | 115.5 | 124.1 | 141.3 | 149.6 | 164.9 | 169.8 | 157.4 | 171.3 | 181.7 |
| Trade balance | −0.1 | −4.1 | 10.7 | 24.3 | 0.2 | −3.1 | −13.5 | 5.8 | 3.0 | −4.8 |
| Services, net | −13.2 | −12.4 | −20.5 | −21.7 | −37.3 | −28.6 | −20.0 | −15.9 | −14.6 | −13.5 |
| Balance on goods and services | −13.3 | −16.6 | −9.8 | 2.6 | −37.0 | −31.7 | −33.6 | −10.1 | −11.6 | −18.3 |
| Factor income, net | 1.4 | 4.0 | 5.2 | 4.0 | 5.0 | 4.4 | 3.2 | −0.8 | −1.0 | −0.5 |
| Current transfers, net | 0.6 | 0.6 | 2.8 | −6.4 | −31.3 | −0.8 | −3.2 | −3.5 | −2.8 | −2.6 |
| **Current account balance** | **−11.3** | **−12.0** | **−1.8** | **0.2** | **−63.4** | **−28.2** | **−33.5** | **−14.4** | **−15.4** | **−21.4** |
| *Memorandum* | | | | | | | | | | |
| Exports of goods and services | 143.9 | 148.3 | 173.5 | 207.7 | 191.2 | 206.1 | 200.7 | 208.2 | 223.4 | 229.4 |
| Interest payments | 7.6 | 10.8 | 11.8 | 12.7 | 10.0 | 9.5 | 9.7 | 11.6 | 13.4 | 12.9 |
| Oil trade balance | 65.1 | 63.0 | 82.6 | 103.6 | 89.1 | 97.7 | 85.4 | 83.1 | 87.6 | 100.3 |
| **Western Hemisphere** | | | | | | | | | | |
| Exports | 93.9 | 105.8 | 116.4 | 127.9 | 126.1 | 131.7 | 138.4 | 158.6 | 187.6 | 201.1 |
| Imports | 75.3 | 84.0 | 90.0 | 101.4 | 117.8 | 142.6 | 154.7 | 178.4 | 188.9 | 202.6 |
| Trade balance | 18.7 | 21.8 | 26.4 | 26.5 | 8.2 | −10.9 | −16.2 | −19.9 | −2.4 | −1.8 |
| Services, net | 3.4 | 3.3 | 3.3 | 2.5 | 0.6 | 1.2 | 3.3 | 5.4 | 8.4 | 9.0 |
| Balance on goods and services | 22.0 | 25.1 | 29.6 | 29.0 | 8.8 | −9.7 | −12.8 | −14.5 | 6.0 | 7.2 |
| Factor income, net | −35.5 | −37.6 | −42.4 | −41.1 | −37.7 | −37.6 | −42.9 | −44.6 | −50.4 | −51.4 |
| Current transfers, net | 4.3 | 4.3 | 7.2 | 10.0 | 10.9 | 11.8 | 10.7 | 12.2 | 13.2 | 13.3 |
| **Current account balance** | **−9.3** | **−8.2** | **−5.6** | **−2.2** | **−18.0** | **−35.5** | **−45.2** | **−46.8** | **−29.7** | **−30.5** |
| *Memorandum* | | | | | | | | | | |
| Exports of goods and services | 117.5 | 131.1 | 147.0 | 163.5 | 162.1 | 171.1 | 182.9 | 206.9 | 239.2 | 256.5 |
| Interest payments | 34.7 | 35.4 | 41.3 | 42.3 | 38.3 | 36.9 | 38.8 | 40.1 | 46.3 | 48.5 |
| Oil trade balance | 13.5 | 11.1 | 14.5 | 20.3 | 16.6 | 15.5 | 13.5 | 15.3 | 17.7 | 16.7 |
| **Four newly industrializing Asian economies** | | | | | | | | | | |
| Exports | 175.5 | 221.1 | 243.8 | 263.3 | 301.0 | 338.1 | 373.4 | 420.1 | 490.6 | 552.1 |
| Imports | 150.0 | 198.9 | 224.2 | 254.8 | 297.0 | 334.1 | 366.9 | 417.8 | 494.2 | 558.6 |
| Trade balance | 25.5 | 22.2 | 19.6 | 8.5 | 4.0 | 4.0 | 6.5 | 2.4 | −3.6 | −6.6 |
| Services, net | 7.7 | 7.8 | 6.9 | 6.6 | 6.1 | 7.8 | 13.6 | 17.6 | 16.4 | 20.2 |
| Balance on goods and services | 33.2 | 30.0 | 26.5 | 15.1 | 10.1 | 11.7 | 20.1 | 20.0 | 12.8 | 13.6 |
| Factor income, net | −0.6 | 1.5 | 3.1 | 4.2 | 4.8 | 4.7 | 2.8 | 2.6 | 5.9 | 8.1 |
| Current transfers, net | 0.3 | −0.8 | −2.2 | −0.8 | −0.9 | −0.5 | −1.1 | −1.2 | −0.5 | −0.3 |
| **Current account balance** | **32.8** | **30.7** | **27.4** | **18.4** | **14.0** | **16.0** | **21.8** | **21.4** | **18.2** | **21.4** |
| *Memorandum* | | | | | | | | | | |
| Exports of goods and services | 208.3 | 260.8 | 290.1 | 316.2 | 359.9 | 405.3 | 448.4 | 506.3 | 591.6 | 666.6 |
| Interest payments | 4.9 | 4.5 | 4.9 | 4.8 | 4.7 | 4.6 | 4.3 | 4.8 | 5.5 | 5.6 |
| Oil trade balance | −7.6 | −7.2 | −9.0 | −11.7 | −12.0 | −14.5 | −13.5 | −13.9 | −15.4 | −15.6 |

## Table A32. Developing Countries—by Analytical Criteria: Current Account Transactions

*(In billions of U.S. dollars)*

| | 1987 | 1988 | 1989 | 1990 | 1991 | 1992 | 1993 | 1994 | 1995 | 1996 |
|---|---|---|---|---|---|---|---|---|---|---|
| **By predominant export** | | | | | | | | | | |
| **Fuel** | | | | | | | | | | |
| Exports | 105.2 | 102.5 | 126.9 | 170.0 | 155.4 | 157.7 | 143.8 | 141.8 | 152.8 | 152.8 |
| Imports | 82.7 | 90.2 | 94.2 | 102.6 | 111.2 | 122.3 | 114.4 | 100.7 | 108.4 | 113.1 |
| Trade balance | 22.5 | 12.4 | 32.7 | 67.5 | 44.2 | 35.4 | 29.3 | 41.0 | 44.4 | 39.7 |
| Services, net | −20.4 | −19.2 | −25.8 | −32.9 | −45.5 | −40.8 | −32.8 | −27.6 | −28.0 | −27.9 |
| Balance on goods and services | 2.1 | −6.9 | 6.9 | 34.6 | −1.3 | −5.5 | −3.5 | 13.4 | 16.4 | 11.8 |
| Factor income, net | −5.6 | −6.3 | −7.8 | −5.0 | −4.8 | −6.0 | −6.9 | −6.6 | −7.6 | −7.7 |
| Current transfers, net | −11.0 | −10.6 | −9.7 | −18.9 | −27.0 | −17.6 | −19.5 | −17.7 | −17.7 | −17.8 |
| **Current account balance** | **−14.6** | **−23.8** | **−10.5** | **10.7** | **−33.1** | **−29.0** | **−29.8** | **−10.9** | **−8.9** | **−13.7** |
| *Memorandum* | | | | | | | | | | |
| Exports of goods and services | 124.1 | 121.0 | 146.3 | 187.7 | 172.5 | 173.9 | 160.4 | 156.0 | 168.1 | 169.6 |
| Interest payments | 10.1 | 11.2 | 11.7 | 11.9 | 9.1 | 9.1 | 8.3 | 8.8 | 10.4 | 10.5 |
| Oil trade balance | 86.4 | 81.1 | 103.2 | 143.5 | 129.3 | 131.3 | 114.0 | 106.6 | 113.9 | 127.3 |
| **Nonfuel exports** | | | | | | | | | | |
| Exports | 447.6 | 531.7 | 586.7 | 640.7 | 694.8 | 774.6 | 845.5 | 981.9 | 1,157.2 | 1,296.3 |
| Imports | 427.0 | 513.8 | 573.0 | 650.5 | 728.8 | 826.9 | 924.9 | 1,050.5 | 1,223.9 | 1,380.0 |
| Trade balance | 20.6 | 18.0 | 13.8 | −9.8 | −34.0 | −52.3 | −79.3 | −68.7 | −67.9 | −84.0 |
| Services, net | 6.9 | 5.7 | 2.7 | 9.1 | 4.5 | 6.7 | 10.6 | 16.1 | 16.6 | 21.6 |
| Balance on goods and services | 27.5 | 23.7 | 16.5 | −0.7 | −29.5 | −45.6 | −68.7 | −52.6 | −51.3 | −62.4 |
| Factor income, net | −46.5 | −48.4 | −51.1 | −52.7 | −50.1 | −47.4 | −50.6 | −56.9 | −59.8 | −56.8 |
| Current transfers, net | 32.3 | 32.3 | 35.4 | 40.6 | 30.2 | 53.1 | 50.8 | 51.8 | 54.9 | 55.9 |
| **Current account balance** | **13.3** | **7.6** | **0.7** | **−12.9** | **−49.4** | **−39.8** | **−68.6** | **−57.5** | **−54.8** | **−62.9** |
| *Memorandum* | | | | | | | | | | |
| Exports of goods and services | 551.9 | 651.3 | 722.5 | 802.0 | 868.4 | 973.4 | 1,061.4 | 1,230.4 | 1,438.0 | 1,606.6 |
| Interest payments | 64.2 | 68.4 | 76.5 | 79.8 | 78.3 | 78.1 | 80.3 | 87.7 | 99.9 | 103.5 |
| Oil trade balance | −3.1 | −3.6 | −0.1 | −8.9 | −16.9 | −16.0 | −15.6 | −13.1 | −15.9 | −18.7 |
| **Manufactures** | | | | | | | | | | |
| Exports | 220.3 | 273.4 | 299.0 | 328.0 | 372.9 | 421.8 | 462.4 | 540.1 | 639.3 | 724.2 |
| Imports | 201.4 | 260.5 | 288.2 | 315.0 | 367.4 | 420.4 | 477.6 | 540.2 | 641.1 | 738.6 |
| Trade balance | 18.9 | 12.9 | 10.9 | 13.0 | 5.5 | 1.4 | −15.2 | −0.1 | −1.9 | −14.5 |
| Services, net | 11.3 | 7.6 | 6.7 | 7.6 | 8.2 | 6.5 | 9.1 | 13.4 | 9.5 | 12.2 |
| Balance on goods and services | 30.3 | 20.5 | 17.5 | 20.6 | 13.7 | 7.9 | −6.0 | 13.3 | 7.6 | −2.2 |
| Factor income, net | −2.2 | 1.7 | 3.0 | 4.1 | 4.3 | 4.3 | 4.5 | 1.8 | 4.6 | 6.8 |
| Current transfers, net | 5.3 | 4.5 | 3.3 | 5.4 | 6.6 | 7.5 | 6.8 | 7.0 | 8.0 | 8.8 |
| **Current account balance** | **33.4** | **26.6** | **23.9** | **30.1** | **24.6** | **19.8** | **5.2** | **22.2** | **20.2** | **13.3** |
| *Memorandum* | | | | | | | | | | |
| Exports of goods and services | 264.5 | 325.6 | 358.6 | 397.1 | 450.2 | 512.6 | 561.4 | 657.5 | 774.7 | 877.7 |
| Interest payments | 6.5 | 8.7 | 9.2 | 9.6 | 10.6 | 12.9 | 12.7 | 16.0 | 18.7 | 19.0 |
| Oil trade balance | −5.5 | −5.7 | −7.4 | −9.9 | −10.5 | −13.5 | −12.9 | −13.3 | −14.5 | −13.8 |

## Table A32 *(continued)*

| | 1987 | 1988 | 1989 | 1990 | 1991 | 1992 | 1993 | 1994 | 1995 | 1996 |
|---|---|---|---|---|---|---|---|---|---|---|
| **Primary products** | | | | | | | | | | |
| Exports | 38.0 | 41.6 | 45.4 | 49.3 | 48.7 | 50.0 | 51.6 | 59.6 | 72.4 | 78.0 |
| Imports | 40.4 | 38.9 | 39.8 | 42.7 | 48.7 | 59.3 | 63.1 | 70.1 | 75.7 | 82.4 |
| Trade balance | –2.4 | 2.7 | 5.6 | 6.6 | — | –9.4 | –11.5 | –10.6 | –3.4 | –4.4 |
| Services, net | –6.3 | –6.7 | –6.6 | –6.9 | –7.0 | –7.4 | –7.7 | –6.6 | –6.2 | –5.8 |
| Balance on goods and services | –8.7 | –4.0 | –1.0 | –0.3 | –6.9 | –16.7 | –19.2 | –17.2 | –9.5 | –10.3 |
| Factor income, net | –12.2 | –12.2 | –12.2 | –11.6 | –12.1 | –11.4 | –9.8 | –11.9 | –12.4 | –14.0 |
| Current transfers, net | 5.2 | 5.6 | 6.5 | 6.8 | 7.7 | 8.5 | 7.7 | 7.5 | 7.7 | 7.6 |
| **Current account balance** | **–15.7** | **–10.6** | **–6.6** | **–5.1** | **–11.4** | **–19.6** | **–21.3** | **–21.5** | **–14.1** | **–16.7** |
| *Memorandum* | | | | | | | | | | |
| Exports of goods and services | 46.4 | 49.5 | 54.6 | 59.6 | 59.6 | 61.7 | 64.0 | 73.2 | 87.9 | 94.8 |
| Interest payments | 13.2 | 13.1 | 15.4 | 14.5 | 13.8 | 12.7 | 11.8 | 12.8 | 14.0 | 15.1 |
| Oil trade balance | –3.2 | –3.3 | –3.2 | –3.1 | –3.2 | –2.4 | –1.7 | –1.8 | –1.8 | –1.8 |
| **Services, income, and private transfers** | | | | | | | | | | |
| Exports | 18.4 | 19.2 | 23.8 | 21.3 | 14.7 | 20.3 | 24.1 | 27.6 | 30.0 | 31.6 |
| Imports | 30.9 | 34.1 | 34.8 | 36.6 | 37.7 | 42.3 | 43.4 | 45.6 | 48.6 | 51.1 |
| Trade balance | –12.5 | –15.0 | –11.1 | –15.4 | –22.9 | –21.9 | –19.4 | –18.1 | –18.6 | –19.5 |
| Services, net | 3.8 | 4.4 | 3.5 | 7.1 | 4.2 | 7.4 | 10.1 | 10.4 | 11.5 | 12.4 |
| Balance on goods and services | –8.7 | –10.6 | –7.5 | –8.3 | –18.8 | –14.5 | –9.4 | –7.7 | –7.1 | –7.1 |
| Factor income, net | 2.5 | 3.4 | 4.9 | 3.0 | 3.6 | 3.2 | 2.2 | 0.2 | 0.2 | 0.4 |
| Current transfers, net | 7.4 | 8.1 | 8.5 | 6.8 | –11.3 | 10.3 | 10.7 | 9.3 | 9.1 | 9.1 |
| **Current account balance** | **1.1** | **1.0** | **5.9** | **1.6** | **–26.5** | **–1.1** | **3.6** | **1.9** | **2.2** | **2.5** |
| *Memorandum* | | | | | | | | | | |
| Exports of goods and services | 34.8 | 36.4 | 41.0 | 41.6 | 36.0 | 44.2 | 48.8 | 54.0 | 58.8 | 62.6 |
| Interest payments | 5.6 | 5.5 | 6.2 | 7.1 | 6.1 | 4.9 | 5.0 | 5.3 | 5.3 | 5.1 |
| Oil trade balance | 5.4 | 5.1 | 9.2 | 5.0 | –0.3 | 4.8 | 7.1 | 9.7 | 10.2 | 10.0 |
| **Diversified export base** | | | | | | | | | | |
| Exports | 170.9 | 197.6 | 218.6 | 242.1 | 258.4 | 282.4 | 307.4 | 354.6 | 415.5 | 462.6 |
| Imports | 154.3 | 180.3 | 210.2 | 256.1 | 275.1 | 304.8 | 340.8 | 394.6 | 458.5 | 507.9 |
| Trade balance | 16.6 | 17.3 | 8.4 | –14.0 | –16.7 | –22.4 | –33.3 | –40.0 | –44.0 | –45.5 |
| Services, net | –1.9 | 0.4 | –0.9 | 1.2 | –0.8 | 0.1 | –0.8 | –1.1 | 1.8 | 2.7 |
| Balance on goods and services | 14.6 | 17.7 | 7.4 | –12.7 | –17.5 | –22.3 | –34.1 | –41.1 | –42.2 | –42.8 |
| Factor income, net | –34.5 | –41.3 | –46.9 | –48.2 | –45.8 | –43.4 | –47.5 | –47.1 | –52.2 | –49.9 |
| Current transfers, net | 14.3 | 14.2 | 17.0 | 21.6 | 27.2 | 26.8 | 25.6 | 28.1 | 30.1 | 30.3 |
| **Current account balance** | **–5.6** | **–9.4** | **–22.4** | **–39.4** | **–36.1** | **–38.9** | **–56.2** | **–60.1** | **–63.0** | **–62.0** |
| *Memorandum* | | | | | | | | | | |
| Exports of goods and services | 206.3 | 239.8 | 268.4 | 303.7 | 322.6 | 354.9 | 387.2 | 445.8 | 516.6 | 571.6 |
| Interest payments | 38.8 | 41.1 | 45.8 | 48.7 | 47.8 | 47.7 | 50.8 | 53.6 | 61.8 | 64.3 |
| Oil trade balance | 0.2 | 0.3 | 1.3 | –0.9 | –3.0 | –4.8 | –8.2 | –7.8 | –9.8 | –13.0 |

## Table A32 (continued)

| | 1987 | 1988 | 1989 | 1990 | 1991 | 1992 | 1993 | 1994 | 1995 | 1996 |
|---|---|---|---|---|---|---|---|---|---|---|
| **By financial criteria** | | | | | | | | | | |
| **Net debtor countries** | | | | | | | | | | |
| Exports | 444.2 | 518.8 | 579.2 | 650.1 | 685.7 | 753.9 | 813.2 | 939.4 | 1,104.0 | 1,234.5 |
| Imports | 438.1 | 514.6 | 572.6 | 652.7 | 723.2 | 812.8 | 899.3 | 1,005.8 | 1,169.9 | 1,319.0 |
| Trade balance | 6.1 | 4.2 | 6.6 | –2.6 | –37.5 | –58.9 | –86.0 | –66.5 | –67.0 | –84.8 |
| Services, net | 3.0 | 1.0 | –2.4 | 2.3 | 4.3 | 5.4 | 8.2 | 16.9 | 22.2 | 28.6 |
| Balance on goods and services | 9.1 | 5.2 | 4.3 | –0.3 | –33.1 | –53.4 | –77.8 | –49.7 | –44.8 | –56.2 |
| Factor income, net | –61.4 | –66.6 | –72.1 | –71.3 | –67.0 | –64.4 | –67.1 | –70.4 | –77.2 | –76.1 |
| Current transfers, net | 34.9 | 37.1 | 43.4 | 49.6 | 57.0 | 57.8 | 55.9 | 57.4 | 59.7 | 60.9 |
| **Current account balance** | **–17.3** | **–24.3** | **–24.4** | **–22.0** | **–43.1** | **–60.0** | **–89.2** | **–62.5** | **–60.8** | **–71.0** |
| *Memorandum* | | | | | | | | | | |
| Exports of goods and services | 548.7 | 636.8 | 712.6 | 807.9 | 854.9 | 946.0 | 1,021.2 | 1,179.5 | 1,376.4 | 1,535.5 |
| Interest payments | 72.5 | 77.6 | 85.4 | 89.1 | 85.0 | 84.7 | 86.3 | 93.3 | 107.5 | 111.6 |
| Oil trade balance | 39.6 | 35.7 | 49.2 | 58.9 | 41.0 | 36.0 | 27.8 | 25.3 | 26.3 | 38.4 |
| **Market borrowers** | | | | | | | | | | |
| Exports | 296.9 | 358.8 | 399.8 | 453.7 | 497.6 | 557.9 | 608.8 | 713.8 | 847.5 | 954.7 |
| Imports | 267.8 | 329.4 | 372.8 | 427.3 | 504.5 | 574.7 | 640.8 | 731.1 | 853.7 | 976.2 |
| Trade balance | 29.1 | 29.4 | 27.0 | 26.4 | –7.0 | –16.8 | –31.8 | –17.3 | –7.3 | –21.8 |
| Services, net | 11.3 | 7.0 | 7.0 | 7.9 | 5.4 | 3.8 | 6.1 | 12.1 | 16.3 | 19.7 |
| Balance on goods and services | 40.4 | 36.4 | 34.1 | 34.3 | –1.5 | –13.0 | –25.6 | –5.2 | 9.0 | –2.1 |
| Factor income, net | –38.6 | –38.3 | –41.5 | –36.9 | –36.2 | –36.7 | –41.4 | –44.3 | –50.3 | –49.3 |
| Current transfers, net | 8.6 | 9.3 | 14.3 | 15.5 | 16.0 | 18.0 | 17.8 | 20.1 | 20.6 | 21.7 |
| **Current account balance** | **10.3** | **7.4** | **6.9** | **12.9** | **–21.8** | **–31.8** | **–49.5** | **–29.4** | **–19.3** | **–29.4** |
| *Memorandum* | | | | | | | | | | |
| Exports of goods and services | 359.0 | 429.7 | 483.2 | 554.2 | 607.3 | 684.0 | 745.4 | 874.0 | 1,030.9 | 1,160.3 |
| Interest payments | 40.5 | 43.5 | 49.1 | 50.7 | 48.1 | 49.4 | 51.2 | 55.9 | 66.4 | 69.4 |
| Oil trade balance | 27.3 | 22.2 | 27.5 | 42.8 | 36.2 | 32.2 | 27.9 | 27.8 | 28.3 | 26.3 |
| **Official borrowers** | | | | | | | | | | |
| Exports | 43.0 | 45.7 | 51.7 | 60.6 | 59.5 | 59.6 | 58.5 | 61.8 | 70.9 | 76.6 |
| Imports | 63.3 | 68.3 | 70.9 | 79.4 | 81.4 | 86.6 | 87.9 | 90.1 | 99.9 | 105.9 |
| Trade balance | –20.3 | –22.6 | –19.1 | –18.8 | –21.9 | –26.9 | –29.5 | –28.4 | –29.2 | –29.3 |
| Services, net | –1.3 | –0.5 | –3.2 | –1.4 | –2.3 | — | –0.1 | 1.2 | 2.0 | 3.8 |
| Balance on goods and services | –21.7 | –23.1 | –22.3 | –20.2 | –24.2 | –27.0 | –29.6 | –27.2 | –27.1 | –25.5 |
| Factor income, net | –8.4 | –9.3 | –9.0 | –11.0 | –11.3 | –10.6 | –10.5 | –10.7 | –11.2 | –12.0 |
| Current transfers, net | 17.0 | 17.4 | 18.1 | 22.2 | 26.6 | 25.7 | 24.4 | 23.3 | 23.9 | 24.1 |
| **Current account balance** | **–13.1** | **–15.0** | **–13.2** | **–9.0** | **–8.9** | **–11.9** | **–15.7** | **–14.5** | **–14.4** | **–13.3** |
| *Memorandum* | | | | | | | | | | |
| Exports of goods and services | 59.4 | 64.6 | 70.3 | 82.5 | 83.2 | 85.9 | 85.8 | 90.9 | 103.4 | 111.7 |
| Interest payments | 11.8 | 12.8 | 13.5 | 14.7 | 14.6 | 13.5 | 13.3 | 13.5 | 14.0 | 13.8 |
| Oil trade balance | 1.3 | 2.3 | 6.2 | 9.1 | 7.3 | 7.4 | 6.2 | 4.4 | 5.3 | 4.6 |

**Table A32** *(concluded)*

| | 1987 | 1988 | 1989 | 1990 | 1991 | 1992 | 1993 | 1994 | 1995 | 1996 |
|---|---|---|---|---|---|---|---|---|---|---|
| **Countries with recent debt-servicing difficulties** | | | | | | | | | | |
| Exports | 162.2 | 178.0 | 198.2 | 212.7 | 197.6 | 203.9 | 211.0 | 233.9 | 273.2 | 293.5 |
| Imports | 145.8 | 161.4 | 170.3 | 185.1 | 194.6 | 224.7 | 237.2 | 265.5 | 287.9 | 309.1 |
| Trade balance | 16.5 | 16.6 | 27.9 | 27.6 | 3.1 | −20.7 | −26.0 | −31.7 | −15.9 | −15.9 |
| Services, net | −9.2 | −10.9 | −14.8 | −14.3 | −10.7 | −8.7 | −9.6 | −7.5 | −3.8 | −2.1 |
| Balance on goods and services | 7.2 | 5.7 | 13.2 | 13.3 | −7.6 | −29.4 | −35.6 | −39.2 | −19.7 | −18.0 |
| Factor income, net | −45.1 | −48.0 | −53.8 | −54.4 | −46.3 | −44.5 | −47.9 | −46.9 | −51.7 | −52.1 |
| Current transfers, net | 17.1 | 18.3 | 21.9 | 27.7 | 28.8 | 29.2 | 27.6 | 28.0 | 28.6 | 29.2 |
| **Current account balance** | **−20.8** | **−24.1** | **−18.7** | **−13.5** | **−25.1** | **−44.8** | **−56.1** | **−57.9** | **−41.3** | **−40.6** |
| *Memorandum* | | | | | | | | | | |
| Exports of goods and services | 198.7 | 216.3 | 242.3 | 263.5 | 248.8 | 260.5 | 271.7 | 299.6 | 346.2 | 372.8 |
| Interest payments | 50.3 | 52.1 | 59.4 | 61.1 | 54.3 | 51.3 | 52.8 | 53.6 | 60.6 | 62.9 |
| Oil trade balance | 27.7 | 27.5 | 39.2 | 42.3 | 27.4 | 26.5 | 23.4 | 23.3 | 26.3 | 40.6 |
| **Countries without debt-servicing difficulties** | | | | | | | | | | |
| Exports | 281.9 | 340.9 | 381.0 | 437.5 | 488.1 | 550.0 | 602.2 | 705.5 | 830.8 | 941.1 |
| Imports | 292.3 | 353.3 | 402.3 | 467.6 | 528.6 | 588.1 | 662.1 | 740.3 | 881.9 | 1,010.0 |
| Trade balance | −10.4 | −12.4 | −21.3 | −30.1 | −40.5 | −38.1 | −59.9 | −34.8 | −51.1 | −68.9 |
| Services, net | 12.3 | 12.0 | 12.4 | 16.6 | 15.0 | 14.2 | 17.8 | 24.3 | 26.0 | 30.7 |
| Balance on goods and services | 1.9 | −0.4 | −8.9 | −13.6 | −25.5 | −24.0 | −42.2 | −10.5 | −25.1 | −38.2 |
| Factor income, net | −16.3 | −18.6 | −18.3 | −16.9 | −20.8 | −19.9 | −19.2 | −23.5 | −25.4 | −24.0 |
| Current transfers, net | 17.9 | 18.8 | 21.6 | 22.0 | 28.3 | 28.7 | 28.3 | 29.4 | 31.1 | 31.7 |
| **Current account balance** | **3.5** | **−0.2** | **−5.7** | **−8.5** | **−18.0** | **−15.2** | **−33.0** | **−4.6** | **−19.4** | **−30.4** |
| *Memorandum* | | | | | | | | | | |
| Exports of goods and services | 350.0 | 420.5 | 470.2 | 544.4 | 606.0 | 685.5 | 749.5 | 879.9 | 1,030.2 | 1,162.7 |
| Interest payments | 22.2 | 25.5 | 26.0 | 28.0 | 30.7 | 33.4 | 33.5 | 39.7 | 46.8 | 48.6 |
| Oil trade balance | 11.9 | 8.2 | 10.0 | 16.6 | 13.7 | 9.4 | 4.4 | 2.0 | — | −2.2 |
| **Other groups** | | | | | | | | | | |
| **Least developed countries** | | | | | | | | | | |
| Exports | 12.6 | 14.1 | 15.1 | 15.5 | 14.9 | 14.3 | 14.9 | 16.9 | 19.5 | 21.2 |
| Imports | 21.6 | 23.1 | 23.3 | 25.1 | 24.7 | 25.4 | 25.9 | 27.1 | 30.3 | 32.9 |
| Trade balance | −9.0 | −9.0 | −8.3 | −9.6 | −9.9 | −11.1 | −11.0 | −10.2 | −10.9 | −11.7 |
| Services, net | −2.9 | −3.3 | −4.3 | −3.7 | −3.8 | −3.5 | −3.6 | −3.6 | −3.8 | −3.0 |
| Balance on goods and services | −11.9 | −12.3 | −12.6 | −13.3 | −13.7 | −14.6 | −14.7 | −13.8 | −14.6 | −14.8 |
| Factor income, net | −2.4 | −2.5 | −2.0 | −2.4 | −2.5 | −2.4 | −2.2 | −2.4 | −2.5 | −2.5 |
| Current transfers, net | 8.7 | 8.4 | 8.7 | 8.4 | 8.4 | 9.0 | 9.0 | 9.2 | 9.8 | 9.5 |
| **Current account balance** | **−5.5** | **−6.4** | **−5.9** | **−7.3** | **−7.7** | **−8.0** | **−7.8** | **−6.9** | **−7.3** | **−7.8** |
| *Memorandum* | | | | | | | | | | |
| Exports of goods and services | 16.4 | 18.0 | 18.7 | 19.8 | 19.0 | 18.7 | 19.6 | 21.9 | 25.0 | 27.2 |
| Interest payments | 3.3 | 3.4 | 4.1 | 3.5 | 3.4 | 3.6 | 3.6 | 3.8 | 4.1 | 3.5 |
| Oil trade balance | −5.3 | −3.6 | −2.7 | −3.8 | −4.2 | −4.2 | −4.3 | −4.1 | −3.9 | −4.4 |

## Table A33. Summary of Balance of Payments and External Financing

*(In billions of U.S. dollars)*

| | 1987 | 1988 | 1989 | 1990 | 1991 | 1992 | 1993 | 1994 | 1995 | 1996 |
|---|---|---|---|---|---|---|---|---|---|---|
| **Developing countries** | | | | | | | | | | |
| **Balance of payments** | | | | | | | | | | |
| Balance on current account | −1.3 | −16.2 | −9.8 | −2.2 | −82.5 | −68.8 | −98.5 | −68.4 | −63.7 | −76.6 |
| Balance on capital and financial account | 1.3 | 16.2 | 9.8 | 2.2 | 82.5 | 68.8 | 98.5 | 68.4 | 63.7 | 76.6 |
| *By balance of payments component* | | | | | | | | | | |
| Capital transfers[1] | 0.8 | 1.4 | 1.4 | 14.9 | 2.5 | 2.1 | 3.1 | 1.9 | 1.3 | 2.5 |
| Net capital flows | 40.3 | 21.3 | 33.6 | 44.3 | 150.9 | 140.2 | 170.4 | 137.4 | 116.2 | 118.2 |
| Errors and omissions, net | 5.5 | −1.1 | 7.5 | −1.9 | 6.0 | −13.5 | −7.6 | −6.9 | 5.2 | −3.4 |
| Change in reserves (− = increase) | −45.4 | −5.4 | −32.7 | −55.2 | −76.8 | −60.0 | −67.3 | −64.1 | −59.0 | −40.7 |
| *By type of financing flow* | | | | | | | | | | |
| Nonexceptional financing flows | −0.6 | −5.2 | 3.9 | 5.9 | 125.0 | 96.8 | 132.0 | 110.0 | 105.3 | 88.3 |
| Exceptional financing flows | 47.3 | 26.8 | 38.7 | 51.4 | 34.4 | 32.0 | 33.8 | 22.4 | 17.4 | 28.9 |
| Arrears on debt service | 9.2 | 12.9 | 16.8 | 25.0 | 0.7 | 12.0 | 14.3 | −5.8 | ... | ... |
| Debt forgiveness | — | 0.3 | 0.2 | 13.6 | 1.6 | 0.8 | 1.7 | 1.8 | ... | ... |
| Rescheduling of debt service | 37.4 | 21.6 | 16.9 | 16.4 | 14.1 | 13.3 | 17.3 | 13.0 | ... | ... |
| Change in reserves (− = increase) | −45.4 | −5.4 | −32.7 | −55.2 | −76.8 | −60.0 | −67.3 | −64.1 | −59.0 | −40.7 |
| **External financing** | | | | | | | | | | |
| Balance on current account | −1.3 | −16.2 | −9.8 | −2.2 | −82.5 | −68.8 | −98.5 | −68.4 | −63.7 | −76.6 |
| Change in reserves (− = increase)[2] | −45.4 | −5.4 | −32.7 | −55.2 | −76.8 | −60.0 | −67.3 | −64.1 | −59.0 | −40.7 |
| Asset transactions, including net errors and omissions[3] | −1.6 | −22.1 | −17.6 | −37.4 | 46.8 | −23.6 | −34.8 | −24.1 | −25.4 | −37.7 |
| **Total, net external financing[4]** | **48.3** | **43.7** | **60.1** | **94.7** | **112.6** | **152.5** | **200.5** | **156.6** | **148.0** | **155.0** |
| Non-debt-creating flows, net | 12.8 | 15.2 | 16.0 | 29.6 | 30.6 | 40.9 | 74.8 | 80.1 | 71.6 | 74.7 |
| Capital transfers[1] | 0.8 | 1.4 | 1.4 | 14.9 | 2.5 | 2.1 | 3.1 | 1.9 | 1.3 | 2.5 |
| Direct investment and related flows | 11.9 | 13.8 | 14.6 | 14.7 | 28.1 | 38.8 | 71.8 | 78.2 | 70.3 | 72.2 |
| Net credit and loans from IMF[5] | −4.7 | −4.1 | −1.5 | −1.9 | 1.1 | −0.2 | −0.2 | −0.8 | ... | ... |
| Net external borrowing[6] | 40.2 | 32.6 | 45.7 | 67.1 | 80.9 | 111.7 | 125.9 | 77.3 | 63.1 | 81.9 |
| Borrowing from official creditors[7] | 23.5 | 19.2 | 20.9 | 11.3 | 21.5 | 6.0 | 20.5 | 13.9 | 36.6 | 4.6 |
| Borrowing from banks[8] | 20.0 | 0.2 | 3.9 | 36.6 | 35.6 | 23.2 | 25.9 | −11.4 | 5.1 | 12.3 |
| Other borrowing[9] | −3.3 | 13.2 | 20.9 | 19.2 | 23.8 | 82.6 | 79.5 | 74.8 | 21.4 | 65.0 |
| *Memorandum* | | | | | | | | | | |
| Balance on goods and services in percent of GDP[10] | 1.0 | 0.5 | 0.7 | 0.9 | −0.8 | −1.2 | −1.5 | −0.8 | −0.6 | −0.8 |
| Scheduled amortization of external debt | 99.7 | 95.9 | 88.0 | 95.2 | 98.4 | 114.0 | 120.1 | 130.3 | 123.5 | 122.9 |
| Gross external financing[11] | 148.0 | 139.6 | 148.1 | 190.0 | 211.0 | 266.4 | 320.6 | 286.9 | 271.5 | 277.9 |
| Gross external borrowing[11] | 139.9 | 128.5 | 133.6 | 162.3 | 179.3 | 225.7 | 246.0 | 207.6 | 186.6 | 204.7 |
| **Countries in transition** | | | | | | | | | | |
| **Balance of payments** | | | | | | | | | | |
| Balance on current account | 8.0 | 2.2 | −5.9 | −19.4 | −7.4 | −2.8 | −3.3 | −1.8 | −7.6 | −17.8 |
| Balance on capital and financial account | −8.0 | −2.2 | 5.9 | 19.4 | 7.4 | 2.8 | 3.3 | 1.8 | 7.6 | 17.8 |
| *By balance of payments component* | | | | | | | | | | |
| Capital transfers[1] | — | — | 0.4 | 0.1 | 1.3 | 3.9 | 7.7 | 6.2 | 7.8 | 7.0 |
| Net capital flows | −6.4 | −0.9 | 6.8 | 12.7 | 3.4 | 4.8 | 13.2 | 7.1 | 24.5 | 24.1 |
| Errors and omissions, net | 0.3 | 3.9 | 5.3 | 2.9 | −4.1 | −3.6 | −4.0 | −5.1 | −1.5 | −1.4 |
| Change in reserves (− = increase) | −1.8 | −5.2 | −6.7 | 3.8 | 6.7 | −2.4 | −13.6 | −6.4 | −23.2 | −11.8 |

## Table A33 (concluded)

| | 1987 | 1988 | 1989 | 1990 | 1991 | 1992 | 1993 | 1994 | 1995 | 1996 |
|---|---|---|---|---|---|---|---|---|---|---|
| *By type of financing flow* | | | | | | | | | | |
| Nonexceptional financing flows | −12.3 | −3.7 | 9.9 | −1.7 | −13.8 | −16.0 | −6.5 | −11.0 | 14.5 | 22.0 |
| Exceptional financing flows | 6.1 | 6.7 | 2.7 | 17.3 | 14.5 | 21.2 | 23.4 | 19.2 | 16.3 | 7.7 |
| Arrears on debt service | 0.3 | 0.1 | 0.8 | 9.0 | 6.1 | 7.2 | 4.3 | 3.2 | ... | ... |
| Debt forgiveness | — | — | 0.4 | — | 0.9 | 2.4 | 2.1 | — | ... | ... |
| Rescheduling of debt service | 5.8 | 6.5 | 1.5 | 8.3 | 7.2 | 9.5 | 17.1 | 14.7 | ... | ... |
| Change in reserves (− = increase) | −1.8 | −5.2 | −6.7 | 3.8 | 6.7 | −2.4 | −13.6 | −6.4 | −23.2 | −11.8 |
| **External financing** | | | | | | | | | | |
| Balance on current account | 8.0 | 2.2 | −5.9 | −19.4 | −7.4 | −2.8 | −3.3 | −1.8 | −7.6 | −17.8 |
| Change in reserves (− = increase)[2] | −1.8 | −5.2 | −6.7 | 3.8 | 6.7 | −2.4 | −13.6 | −6.4 | −23.2 | −11.8 |
| Asset transactions, including net errors and omissions[3] | −2.4 | — | 2.9 | −2.3 | −2.7 | −3.0 | 2.9 | 2.2 | 5.4 | 3.1 |
| **Total, net external financing[4]** | **−3.8** | **3.0** | **9.6** | **17.9** | **3.4** | **8.2** | **14.0** | **6.0** | **25.4** | **26.5** |
| Non-debt-creating flows, net | −0.2 | 0.5 | 0.6 | 0.1 | 3.7 | 8.0 | 13.6 | 9.4 | 14.9 | 17.5 |
| Capital transfers[1] | — | — | 0.4 | 0.1 | 1.3 | 3.9 | 7.7 | 6.2 | 7.8 | 7.0 |
| Direct investment and related flows | −0.2 | 0.5 | 0.2 | — | 2.3 | 4.0 | 5.9 | 3.2 | 7.1 | 10.6 |
| Net credit and loans from IMF[5] | −1.1 | −0.9 | −0.9 | 0.1 | 3.1 | 1.6 | 2.0 | 2.4 | ... | ... |
| Net external borrowing[6] | −2.5 | 3.4 | 9.9 | 17.8 | −3.4 | −1.5 | −1.6 | −5.7 | 2.8 | 9.0 |
| Borrowing from official creditors[7] | — | −2.2 | — | 10.8 | 20.7 | 13.4 | 2.1 | 3.2 | −0.9 | 7.2 |
| Borrowing from banks[8] | 1.7 | 5.6 | 11.1 | −3.1 | −5.8 | −1.1 | 4.2 | 4.6 | 0.5 | 0.6 |
| Other borrowing[9] | −4.2 | — | −1.3 | 10.0 | −18.2 | −13.8 | −7.9 | −13.5 | 3.2 | 1.1 |
| *Memorandum* | | | | | | | | | | |
| Balance on goods and services in percent of GDP[10] | 0.7 | 0.3 | −0.2 | −1.0 | −0.3 | −0.1 | −0.4 | 0.1 | −0.5 | −0.8 |
| Scheduled amortization of external debt | 19.9 | 22.9 | 17.1 | 29.1 | 28.0 | 30.4 | 27.3 | 30.3 | 27.6 | 26.3 |
| Gross external financing[11] | 16.1 | 25.9 | 26.8 | 47.0 | 31.4 | 38.6 | 41.3 | 36.3 | 53.0 | 52.8 |
| Gross external borrowing[11] | 17.5 | 26.3 | 27.0 | 46.8 | 24.6 | 28.9 | 25.7 | 24.6 | 30.4 | 35.2 |

[1]Comprise debt forgiveness as well as all other identified transactions on capital account as defined in the 5th edition of the IMF's *Balance of Payments Manual*.

[2]Positioned here to reflect the discretionary nature of many countries' transactions in reserves.

[3]Include changes in recorded private external assets (mainly portfolio investment), export credit, the collateral for debt-reduction operations, and the net change in unrecorded balance of payments flows (net errors and omissions).

[4]Equals, with opposite sign, the sum of transactions listed above. It is the amount required to finance the deficit on goods and services, factor income, and current transfers; the increase in the official reserve level; the net asset transactions; and the transactions underlying net errors and omissions.

[5]Comprise use of IMF resources under the General Resources Account, Trust Fund, structural adjustment facility (SAF), and enhanced structural adjustment facility (ESAF). For further detail, see Table A37.

[6]Net disbursement of long- and short-term credits (including exceptional financing) by both official and private creditors.

[7]Net disbursements by official creditors (other than monetary authorities) based on directly reported flows, and flows derived from statistics on debt stocks. The estimates include the increase in official claims caused by the transfer of officially guaranteed claims to the guarantor agency in the creditor country, usually in the context of debt rescheduling.

[8]Net disbursements by commercial banks based on directly reported flows and on cross-border claims and liabilities reported in the International Banking section of the IMF's *International Financial Statistics*.

[9]Includes primary bond issues and loans on the international capital markets. Since the estimates are residually derived, they also reflect any underrecording or misclassification of official and commercial bank credits above.

[10]This is often referred to as the "resource balance" and, with opposite sign, the "net resource transfer."

[11]Net external financing/borrowing (see footnotes 4 and 6, respectively) plus amortization due on external debt.

## Table A34. Developing Countries—by Region: Balance of Payments and External Financing[1]

*(In billions of U.S. dollars)*

| | 1987 | 1988 | 1989 | 1990 | 1991 | 1992 | 1993 | 1994 | 1995 | 1996 |
|---|---|---|---|---|---|---|---|---|---|---|
| **Africa** | | | | | | | | | | |
| Balance on current account | −4.1 | −8.7 | −7.4 | −2.6 | −4.2 | −8.5 | −8.6 | −11.2 | −14.5 | −11.6 |
| Change in reserves (− = increase) | −1.0 | 0.4 | −2.3 | −4.1 | −5.6 | 5.6 | −1.2 | −4.9 | −1.8 | −3.8 |
| Asset transactions, including net errors and omissions | 1.9 | 2.9 | 1.0 | −0.5 | 3.8 | −2.5 | −0.9 | −0.4 | 1.0 | 0.1 |
| **Total, net external financing** | **3.2** | **5.4** | **8.7** | **7.2** | **6.0** | **5.4** | **10.8** | **16.4** | **15.3** | **15.2** |
| Non-debt-creating flows, net | 1.1 | 0.7 | 4.3 | 4.3 | 2.3 | 3.3 | 1.8 | 3.4 | 2.7 | 3.6 |
| Net credit and loans from IMF | −1.1 | −0.3 | 0.1 | −0.6 | 0.2 | −0.2 | 0.2 | 0.9 | . . . | . . . |
| Net external borrowing | 3.2 | 4.9 | 4.4 | 3.4 | 3.6 | 2.4 | 8.8 | 12.0 | 10.7 | 10.7 |
| From official creditors | 5.5 | 5.2 | 3.1 | 4.3 | 6.2 | 1.2 | 4.8 | 10.8 | 8.5 | 5.7 |
| From banks | −0.9 | −1.6 | −3.4 | 3.9 | 2.9 | 1.1 | 4.8 | 2.0 | 5.1 | 3.4 |
| Other | −1.4 | 1.3 | 4.7 | −4.7 | −5.5 | 0.1 | −0.8 | −0.8 | −2.9 | 1.5 |
| *Memorandum* | | | | | | | | | | |
| Net capital flows | 2.4 | 4.8 | 7.5 | 3.7 | 4.4 | 4.0 | 9.1 | 15.4 | 14.4 | 14.5 |
| Exceptional financing | 14.2 | 7.0 | 15.8 | 13.1 | 10.6 | 10.1 | 7.8 | 14.3 | 13.4 | 25.0 |
| **Asia** | | | | | | | | | | |
| Balance on current account | 23.3 | 12.7 | 4.9 | 2.3 | 3.1 | 3.4 | −11.2 | 4.0 | −4.0 | −13.1 |
| Change in reserves (− = increase) | −41.8 | −16.2 | −18.3 | −27.1 | −46.5 | −34.4 | −50.6 | −68.7 | −52.3 | −47.5 |
| Asset transactions, including net errors and omissions | −2.2 | −16.8 | −14.5 | −16.8 | −19.5 | −25.5 | −30.3 | −26.8 | −30.7 | −27.7 |
| **Total, net external financing** | **20.6** | **20.3** | **27.9** | **41.5** | **62.9** | **56.5** | **92.0** | **91.5** | **87.0** | **88.3** |
| Non-debt-creating flows, net | 7.7 | 9.4 | 6.4 | 10.7 | 14.6 | 18.7 | 34.7 | 42.2 | 37.5 | 34.2 |
| Net credit and loans from IMF | −2.4 | −2.4 | −1.1 | −2.4 | 1.9 | 1.3 | 0.6 | −0.8 | . . . | . . . |
| Net external borrowing | 15.3 | 13.3 | 22.6 | 33.3 | 46.4 | 36.5 | 56.8 | 50.1 | 51.2 | 55.4 |
| From official creditors | −0.7 | 6.7 | 6.2 | 4.6 | 9.9 | 8.1 | 8.8 | 6.3 | 8.5 | 8.0 |
| From banks | 13.9 | 9.5 | 8.0 | 13.3 | 19.1 | 13.6 | 15.0 | 16.9 | 11.3 | 10.3 |
| Other | 2.2 | −2.8 | 8.4 | 15.4 | 17.4 | 14.8 | 33.0 | 26.9 | 31.5 | 37.2 |
| *Memorandum* | | | | | | | | | | |
| Net capital flows | 18.1 | 9.3 | 11.1 | 25.0 | 50.5 | 38.3 | 73.5 | 72.7 | 54.7 | 60.1 |
| Exceptional financing | 2.1 | 1.9 | 1.8 | 2.2 | 2.4 | 2.1 | 1.6 | 1.1 | — | — |
| **Middle East and Europe** | | | | | | | | | | |
| Balance on current account | −11.3 | −12.0 | −1.8 | 0.2 | −63.4 | −28.2 | −33.5 | −14.4 | −15.4 | −21.4 |
| Change in reserves (− = increase) | 0.8 | 9.4 | −10.3 | −6.2 | −8.3 | −10.2 | 5.7 | 2.4 | 2.9 | 11.2 |
| Asset transactions, including net errors and omissions | −0.8 | −4.5 | 0.9 | −5.9 | 62.2 | 11.9 | 5.5 | 18.6 | 8.6 | 3.0 |
| **Total, net external financing** | **11.3** | **7.1** | **11.1** | **11.9** | **9.5** | **26.5** | **22.3** | **−6.6** | **3.9** | **7.2** |
| Non-debt-creating flows, net | 1.0 | 1.3 | 1.2 | 11.9 | 1.3 | 1.7 | 1.7 | 0.6 | −0.6 | 2.1 |
| Net credit and loans from IMF | −0.4 | −0.5 | −0.2 | −0.1 | — | 0.4 | — | 0.4 | . . . | . . . |
| Net external borrowing | 10.7 | 6.4 | 10.1 | 0.1 | 8.2 | 24.4 | 20.7 | −7.5 | 4.3 | 5.3 |
| From official creditors | 11.3 | 2.6 | 3.5 | −5.8 | 2.0 | −2.0 | 6.5 | −0.8 | −3.7 | −6.4 |
| From banks | 3.8 | 7.5 | −1.1 | 2.0 | 8.9 | 10.2 | −0.5 | −1.1 | −5.0 | −1.3 |
| Other | −4.4 | −3.7 | 7.8 | 3.9 | −2.8 | 16.3 | 14.6 | −5.6 | 13.0 | 13.1 |
| *Memorandum* | | | | | | | | | | |
| Net capital flows | 10.3 | 0.1 | 8.2 | −3.4 | 72.9 | 44.5 | 27.5 | 8.0 | 17.8 | 12.6 |
| Exceptional financing | 0.3 | — | 1.1 | 14.3 | 7.0 | 6.7 | 16.1 | 5.4 | 1.7 | 1.5 |

## Table A34 *(concluded)*

| | 1987 | 1988 | 1989 | 1990 | 1991 | 1992 | 1993 | 1994 | 1995 | 1996 |
|---|---|---|---|---|---|---|---|---|---|---|
| **Western Hemisphere** | | | | | | | | | | |
| Balance on current account | −9.3 | −8.2 | −5.6 | −2.2 | −18.0 | −35.5 | −45.2 | −46.8 | −29.7 | −30.5 |
| Change in reserves (− = increase) | −3.4 | 1.0 | −1.9 | −17.7 | −16.4 | −21.1 | −21.2 | 7.2 | −7.7 | −0.5 |
| Asset transactions, including | | | | | | | | | | |
| net errors and omissions | −0.4 | −3.7 | −4.9 | −14.2 | 0.3 | −7.5 | −9.0 | −15.5 | −4.4 | −13.2 |
| **Total, net external financing** | **13.1** | **10.9** | **12.4** | **34.1** | **34.1** | **64.1** | **75.5** | **55.2** | **41.0** | **44.0** |
| Non-debt-creating flows, net | 6.3 | 9.0 | 7.1 | 7.1 | 11.6 | 13.0 | 14.1 | 14.9 | 17.9 | 17.4 |
| Net credit and loans from IMF | −0.8 | −0.9 | −0.2 | 1.2 | −1.0 | −1.6 | −0.9 | −1.3 | ... | ... |
| Net external borrowing | 7.5 | 2.8 | 5.5 | 25.8 | 23.5 | 52.7 | 62.3 | 41.6 | 10.2 | 27.6 |
| From official creditors | 7.4 | 4.7 | 8.2 | 8.2 | 3.3 | −1.3 | 0.3 | −2.4 | 23.3 | −2.7 |
| From banks | 3.3 | −15.1 | 0.4 | 17.4 | 4.7 | −1.7 | 6.6 | −29.2 | −6.3 | −0.1 |
| Other | −3.2 | 13.2 | −3.0 | 0.2 | 15.6 | 55.7 | 55.3 | 73.1 | −6.9 | 30.4 |
| *Memorandum* | | | | | | | | | | |
| Net capital flows | 9.5 | 7.1 | 6.8 | 19.0 | 23.0 | 53.4 | 60.3 | 41.3 | 29.2 | 30.9 |
| Exceptional financing | 30.7 | 17.9 | 20.0 | 21.8 | 14.3 | 13.1 | 8.2 | 1.5 | 2.3 | 2.5 |
| **Sub-Saharan Africa** | | | | | | | | | | |
| Balance on current account | −6.0 | −6.8 | −6.8 | −8.2 | −8.3 | −9.1 | −8.6 | −6.0 | −6.5 | −5.7 |
| Change in reserves (− = increase) | −0.8 | −0.2 | −1.1 | −0.3 | −4.2 | 2.7 | −0.9 | −3.3 | −1.7 | −1.3 |
| Asset transactions, including | | | | | | | | | | |
| net errors and omissions | 1.1 | 0.9 | 1.1 | 1.7 | 5.4 | −0.8 | 1.7 | 0.7 | 0.8 | 0.5 |
| **Total, net external financing** | **5.7** | **6.1** | **6.8** | **6.9** | **7.2** | **7.3** | **7.8** | **8.6** | **7.4** | **6.5** |
| Non-debt-creating flows, net | 0.5 | 0.5 | 1.4 | 1.0 | 1.3 | 1.5 | 1.1 | 1.7 | 0.5 | 1.3 |
| Net credit and loans from IMF | −0.5 | −0.2 | −0.4 | −0.3 | — | — | −0.2 | 0.5 | ... | ... |
| Net external borrowing | 5.7 | 5.8 | 5.8 | 6.1 | 5.9 | 5.8 | 6.9 | 6.4 | 5.7 | 5.1 |
| From official creditors | 4.9 | 4.2 | 3.3 | 5.6 | 6.5 | 0.8 | 4.2 | 5.1 | 3.7 | 2.4 |
| From banks | 0.3 | 0.3 | 0.1 | 0.9 | 0.1 | 0.3 | 0.6 | −0.5 | 0.3 | 0.3 |
| Other | 0.5 | 1.3 | 2.4 | −0.4 | −0.6 | 4.7 | 2.2 | 1.8 | 1.7 | 2.5 |
| *Memorandum* | | | | | | | | | | |
| Net capital flows | 5.0 | 5.4 | 5.6 | 6.4 | 6.0 | 6.2 | 6.2 | 7.6 | 6.5 | 5.7 |
| Exceptional financing | 5.1 | 6.0 | 6.8 | 7.3 | 7.2 | 8.1 | 7.8 | 8.6 | 7.1 | 5.2 |
| **Four newly industrializing Asian economies** | | | | | | | | | | |
| Balance on current account | 32.8 | 30.7 | 27.4 | 18.4 | 14.0 | 16.0 | 21.8 | 21.4 | 18.2 | 21.4 |
| Change in reserves (− = increase) | −36.0 | −14.5 | −13.3 | −7.7 | −19.5 | −19.1 | −23.4 | −26.4 | −25.5 | −26.1 |
| Asset transactions, including | | | | | | | | | | |
| net errors and omissions | −0.7 | −11.7 | −14.5 | −17.3 | −12.5 | −16.1 | −23.1 | −20.4 | −15.5 | −13.1 |
| **Total, net external financing** | **3.9** | **−4.4** | **0.5** | **6.6** | **18.0** | **19.1** | **24.6** | **25.4** | **22.9** | **17.9** |
| Non-debt-creating flows, net | 3.1 | 1.1 | −3.0 | −0.1 | 2.4 | 2.8 | 1.9 | 0.6 | −0.7 | −2.1 |
| Net credit and loans from IMF | −1.2 | −0.5 | — | — | — | — | — | — | ... | ... |
| Net external borrowing | 2.0 | −5.0 | 3.5 | 6.7 | 15.5 | 16.3 | 22.7 | 24.8 | 23.6 | 19.9 |
| From official creditors | −5.9 | −2.0 | −1.7 | −0.8 | 0.2 | −0.6 | −1.9 | −0.3 | −0.6 | −0.5 |
| From banks | 7.5 | −1.8 | −0.3 | −0.6 | 4.3 | 0.5 | 0.4 | 2.5 | −0.7 | −0.7 |
| Other | 0.4 | −1.2 | 5.5 | 8.1 | 11.0 | 16.3 | 24.2 | 22.6 | 24.9 | 21.1 |
| *Memorandum* | | | | | | | | | | |
| Net capital flows | 1.9 | −14.7 | −14.7 | −7.5 | 6.9 | 3.1 | 5.8 | 7.4 | 7.8 | 5.3 |
| Exceptional financing | — | — | — | — | — | — | — | — | — | — |

[1]For definitions, see footnotes to Table A33.

**Table A35. Developing Countries—by Analytical Criteria: Balance of Payments and External Financing**[1]

*(In billions of U.S. dollars)*

| | 1987 | 1988 | 1989 | 1990 | 1991 | 1992 | 1993 | 1994 | 1995 | 1996 |
|---|---|---|---|---|---|---|---|---|---|---|
| **By predominant export** | | | | | | | | | | |
| **Fuel** | | | | | | | | | | |
| Balance on current account | −14.6 | −23.8 | −10.5 | 10.7 | −33.1 | −29.0 | −29.8 | −10.9 | −8.9 | −13.7 |
| Change in reserves (− = increase) | 2.9 | 12.6 | −5.6 | −9.4 | −3.3 | 5.0 | 9.5 | 1.3 | 6.5 | 6.8 |
| Asset transactions, including | | | | | | | | | | |
| net errors and omissions | 3.3 | 4.0 | 9.8 | −6.2 | 28.9 | 18.4 | 15.5 | 14.5 | 3.1 | 2.6 |
| **Total, net external financing** | **8.4** | **7.3** | **6.3** | **4.9** | **7.5** | **5.6** | **4.8** | **−5.0** | **−0.8** | **4.4** |
| Non-debt-creating flows, net | 0.6 | 0.7 | 3.0 | 0.8 | 2.4 | 1.6 | 1.1 | 1.4 | 1.5 | 2.4 |
| Net credit and loans from IMF | — | 0.2 | 1.7 | 1.9 | 0.5 | −0.5 | −0.8 | 0.4 | . . . | . . . |
| Net external borrowing | 7.8 | 6.4 | 1.7 | 2.1 | 4.5 | 4.5 | 4.5 | −6.8 | −2.9 | 1.1 |
| From official creditors | 2.2 | 3.2 | 0.2 | 2.1 | 0.5 | −1.1 | 0.6 | 4.8 | 1.0 | −1.6 |
| From banks | −1.9 | −0.6 | — | 4.2 | 12.3 | 6.6 | 6.1 | — | 3.2 | 4.4 |
| Other | 7.4 | 3.8 | 1.5 | −4.1 | −8.2 | −1.0 | −2.2 | −11.6 | −7.1 | −1.7 |
| *Memorandum* | | | | | | | | | | |
| Net capital flows | 11.7 | 7.3 | 13.6 | −0.5 | 30.3 | 22.5 | 14.6 | 6.5 | 5.1 | 7.4 |
| Exceptional financing | 8.1 | 0.7 | 10.7 | 4.4 | 3.9 | 5.1 | 12.7 | 10.3 | 6.2 | 20.3 |
| **Nonfuel exports** | | | | | | | | | | |
| Balance on current account | 13.3 | 7.6 | 0.7 | −12.9 | −49.4 | −39.8 | −68.6 | −57.5 | −54.8 | −62.9 |
| Change in reserves (− = increase) | −48.3 | −18.0 | −27.2 | −45.7 | −73.5 | −65.0 | −76.8 | −65.4 | −65.5 | −47.4 |
| Asset transactions, including | | | | | | | | | | |
| net errors and omissions | −4.8 | −26.1 | −27.4 | −31.3 | 17.9 | −42.0 | −50.3 | −38.7 | −28.5 | −40.3 |
| **Total, net external financing** | **39.9** | **36.4** | **53.8** | **89.9** | **105.1** | **146.8** | **195.8** | **161.5** | **148.0** | **150.4** |
| Non-debt-creating flows, net | 15.6 | 19.7 | 16.1 | 33.1 | 27.3 | 35.0 | 51.2 | 59.7 | 56.0 | 55.0 |
| Net credit and loans from IMF | −4.7 | −4.2 | −3.2 | −3.8 | 0.6 | 0.3 | 0.6 | −1.3 | . . . | . . . |
| Net external borrowing | 29.0 | 21.0 | 40.9 | 60.6 | 77.2 | 111.5 | 144.1 | 103.0 | 79.3 | 97.9 |
| From official creditors | 21.2 | 16.0 | 20.7 | 9.2 | 21.0 | 7.0 | 19.9 | 9.1 | 35.5 | 6.2 |
| From banks | 22.0 | 0.8 | 3.9 | 32.5 | 23.4 | 16.6 | 19.8 | −11.4 | 1.9 | 7.9 |
| Other | −14.2 | 4.2 | 16.4 | 19.0 | 32.9 | 87.8 | 104.3 | 105.3 | 41.8 | 83.8 |
| *Memorandum* | | | | | | | | | | |
| Net capital flows | 28.6 | 14.0 | 20.0 | 44.8 | 120.6 | 117.8 | 155.8 | 131.0 | 111.1 | 110.8 |
| Exceptional financing | 39.2 | 26.1 | 28.0 | 47.0 | 30.5 | 26.9 | 21.1 | 12.1 | 11.1 | 8.6 |
| **By financial criteria** | | | | | | | | | | |
| **Net creditor countries** | | | | | | | | | | |
| Balance on current account | 16.0 | 8.1 | 14.6 | 19.8 | −39.4 | −8.8 | −9.3 | −5.9 | −2.9 | −5.6 |
| Change in reserves (− = increase) | −23.1 | 10.3 | 0.8 | 4.6 | −13.2 | −3.8 | 9.3 | −1.1 | 4.2 | 6.8 |
| Asset transactions, including | | | | | | | | | | |
| net errors and omissions | −1.8 | −11.9 | −8.8 | −21.5 | 49.1 | 4.9 | −6.9 | −1.6 | 0.5 | −4.8 |
| **Total, net external financing** | **8.8** | **−6.5** | **−6.6** | **−2.9** | **3.6** | **7.7** | **6.9** | **8.5** | **−1.8** | **3.6** |
| Non-debt-creating flows, net | −0.5 | −3.5 | −6.1 | −4.0 | −0.7 | −2.0 | −2.2 | −1.4 | −5.1 | −1.9 |
| Net credit and loans from IMF | — | — | — | — | — | — | — | — | . . . | . . . |
| Net external borrowing | 9.3 | −2.9 | −0.6 | 1.1 | 4.3 | 9.7 | 9.1 | 9.9 | 3.2 | 5.5 |
| From official creditors | −1.2 | −0.2 | — | — | — | — | — | — | — | — |
| From banks | 6.7 | −2.3 | −0.9 | −1.3 | 9.6 | 4.9 | 3.3 | 2.3 | −4.8 | −2.5 |
| Other | 3.8 | −0.4 | 0.3 | 2.4 | −5.3 | 4.8 | 5.8 | 7.6 | 8.0 | 8.1 |
| *Memorandum* | | | | | | | | | | |
| Net capital flows | 7.8 | −18.3 | −14.5 | −19.4 | 64.5 | 22.3 | 5.4 | 10.1 | 2.5 | −0.3 |
| Exceptional financing | — | — | — | — | — | — | — | — | — | — |

## Table A35 *(continued)*

| | 1987 | 1988 | 1989 | 1990 | 1991 | 1992 | 1993 | 1994 | 1995 | 1996 |
|---|---|---|---|---|---|---|---|---|---|---|
| **Net debtor countries** | | | | | | | | | | |
| Balance on current account | −17.3 | −24.3 | −24.4 | −22.0 | −43.1 | −60.0 | −89.2 | −62.5 | −60.8 | −71.0 |
| Change in reserves (− = increase) | −22.3 | −15.7 | −33.6 | −59.8 | −63.6 | −56.2 | −76.6 | −63.0 | −63.2 | −47.5 |
| Asset transactions, including net errors and omissions | 0.2 | −10.2 | −8.8 | −15.9 | −2.3 | −28.5 | −27.8 | −22.5 | −25.9 | −33.0 |
| **Total, net external financing** | **39.5** | **50.2** | **66.8** | **97.7** | **109.0** | **144.7** | **193.7** | **147.9** | **149.0** | **151.2** |
| Non-debt-creating flows, net | 16.7 | 23.9 | 25.1 | 37.9 | 30.4 | 38.6 | 54.4 | 62.5 | 62.6 | 59.3 |
| Net credit and loans from IMF | −4.7 | −4.1 | −1.5 | −1.9 | 1.1 | −0.2 | −0.2 | −0.8 | ... | ... |
| Net external borrowing | 27.5 | 30.3 | 43.2 | 61.7 | 77.5 | 106.3 | 139.5 | 86.3 | 73.1 | 93.5 |
| From official creditors | 24.7 | 19.3 | 20.9 | 11.3 | 21.5 | 6.0 | 20.5 | 13.9 | 36.6 | 4.6 |
| From banks | 13.3 | 2.5 | 4.8 | 38.0 | 26.0 | 18.3 | 22.6 | −13.7 | 9.9 | 14.9 |
| Other | −10.5 | 8.4 | 17.5 | 12.4 | 29.9 | 82.0 | 96.3 | 86.1 | 26.7 | 74.0 |
| *Memorandum* | | | | | | | | | | |
| Net capital flows | 32.5 | 39.6 | 48.2 | 63.7 | 86.4 | 117.9 | 165.0 | 127.4 | 113.7 | 118.5 |
| Exceptional financing | 47.3 | 26.8 | 38.7 | 51.4 | 34.4 | 32.0 | 33.8 | 22.4 | 17.4 | 28.9 |
| **Market borrowers** | | | | | | | | | | |
| Balance on current account | 10.3 | 7.4 | 6.9 | 12.9 | −21.8 | −31.8 | −49.5 | −29.4 | −19.3 | −29.4 |
| Change in reserves (− = increase) | −19.6 | −15.3 | −25.2 | −46.1 | −40.1 | −43.4 | −59.8 | −49.9 | −56.6 | −42.5 |
| Asset transactions, including net errors and omissions | −4.2 | −13.6 | −14.4 | −24.0 | −11.9 | −30.9 | −28.7 | −29.3 | −27.1 | −34.0 |
| **Total, net external financing** | **13.5** | **21.5** | **32.8** | **57.1** | **73.7** | **106.1** | **138.1** | **108.6** | **102.2** | **105.6** |
| Non-debt-creating flows, net | 11.5 | 17.8 | 14.7 | 16.4 | 20.9 | 26.3 | 42.7 | 49.1 | 43.5 | 39.9 |
| Net credit and loans from IMF | −1.8 | −1.4 | 0.2 | 0.7 | −1.2 | −1.6 | −1.2 | −0.7 | ... | ... |
| Net external borrowing | 3.8 | 5.1 | 17.9 | 39.9 | 54.1 | 81.4 | 96.6 | 60.3 | 45.6 | 66.3 |
| From official creditors | −2.2 | 1.8 | 5.0 | 5.9 | 7.5 | 2.1 | 5.6 | 6.5 | 29.8 | 1.1 |
| From banks | 7.6 | −7.2 | 3.5 | 27.8 | 21.4 | 17.6 | 18.8 | −17.1 | 9.4 | 15.4 |
| Other | −1.5 | 10.5 | 9.5 | 6.2 | 25.1 | 61.7 | 72.2 | 70.9 | 6.4 | 49.8 |
| *Memorandum* | | | | | | | | | | |
| Net capital flows | 8.7 | 12.4 | 16.4 | 39.0 | 57.0 | 82.9 | 113.1 | 88.3 | 70.0 | 72.8 |
| Exceptional financing | 27.1 | 14.4 | 15.9 | 18.6 | 11.1 | 12.8 | 16.8 | 8.1 | 8.0 | 6.6 |
| **Diversified borrowers** | | | | | | | | | | |
| Balance on current account | −14.5 | −16.7 | −18.1 | −25.8 | −12.5 | −16.3 | −24.0 | −18.6 | −27.1 | −28.3 |
| Change in reserves (− = increase) | −1.0 | 0.1 | −6.5 | −6.9 | −14.3 | −10.8 | −11.7 | −7.0 | −4.5 | −4.4 |
| Asset transactions, including net errors and omissions | 1.7 | 1.5 | 5.6 | 5.9 | 4.3 | 0.7 | −2.5 | 6.8 | 2.8 | 0.9 |
| **Total, net external financing** | **13.8** | **15.1** | **19.0** | **26.8** | **22.5** | **26.5** | **38.2** | **18.8** | **28.8** | **31.8** |
| Non-debt-creating flows, net | 2.5 | 3.2 | 4.2 | 3.8 | 4.3 | 5.6 | 4.7 | 6.8 | 11.7 | 12.8 |
| Net credit and loans from IMF | −2.2 | −1.9 | −1.5 | −1.5 | 2.0 | 1.1 | 1.4 | −0.5 | ... | ... |
| Net external borrowing | 13.5 | 13.8 | 16.2 | 24.5 | 16.2 | 19.8 | 32.1 | 12.5 | 17.5 | 19.5 |
| From official creditors | 15.1 | 5.3 | 6.6 | 7.8 | 8.5 | 4.0 | 8.0 | 0.9 | 2.7 | 0.2 |
| From banks | 6.5 | 10.8 | 3.0 | 11.0 | 4.6 | 3.5 | 6.1 | 4.2 | −0.5 | −0.3 |
| Other | −8.1 | −2.4 | 6.6 | 5.7 | 3.1 | 12.2 | 18.0 | 7.4 | 15.4 | 19.6 |
| *Memorandum* | | | | | | | | | | |
| Net capital flows | 13.9 | 14.6 | 20.2 | 27.9 | 21.4 | 23.4 | 37.3 | 20.5 | 29.2 | 33.7 |
| Exceptional financing | 4.7 | 5.5 | 6.5 | 6.7 | 6.3 | 5.2 | 4.4 | 5.6 | 2.2 | 2.5 |

## Table A35  (continued)

| | 1987 | 1988 | 1989 | 1990 | 1991 | 1992 | 1993 | 1994 | 1995 | 1996 |
|---|---|---|---|---|---|---|---|---|---|---|
| **Official borrowers** | | | | | | | | | | |
| Balance on current account | −13.1 | −15.0 | −13.2 | −9.0 | −8.9 | −11.9 | −15.7 | −14.5 | −14.4 | −13.3 |
| Change in reserves (− = increase) | −1.7 | −0.5 | −1.9 | −6.8 | −9.1 | −2.0 | −5.1 | −6.1 | −2.1 | −0.6 |
| Asset transactions, including | | | | | | | | | | |
| net errors and omissions | 2.7 | 1.9 | — | 2.1 | 5.3 | 1.6 | 3.3 | — | −1.5 | 0.1 |
| **Total, net external financing** | **12.2** | **13.6** | **15.1** | **13.7** | **12.7** | **12.2** | **17.4** | **20.5** | **18.0** | **13.8** |
| Non-debt-creating flows, net | 2.7 | 3.0 | 6.2 | 17.6 | 5.2 | 6.7 | 7.0 | 6.6 | 7.3 | 6.6 |
| Net credit and loans from IMF | −0.7 | −0.8 | −0.2 | −1.1 | 0.3 | 0.3 | −0.3 | 0.4 | ... | ... |
| Net external borrowing | 10.2 | 11.4 | 9.1 | −2.8 | 7.2 | 5.2 | 10.7 | 13.5 | 10.0 | 7.7 |
| From official creditors | 11.8 | 12.2 | 9.3 | −2.4 | 5.4 | −0.1 | 6.9 | 6.5 | 4.1 | 3.2 |
| From banks | −0.7 | −1.1 | −1.7 | −0.9 | — | −2.8 | −2.3 | −0.8 | 1.0 | −0.2 |
| Other | −0.9 | 0.3 | 1.4 | 0.6 | 1.7 | 8.1 | 6.1 | 7.8 | 4.9 | 4.7 |
| *Memorandum* | | | | | | | | | | |
| Net capital flows | 9.9 | 12.6 | 11.5 | −3.3 | 8.0 | 11.6 | 14.6 | 18.5 | 14.5 | 12.0 |
| Exceptional financing | 15.5 | 6.9 | 16.3 | 26.2 | 17.0 | 14.0 | 12.6 | 8.7 | 7.1 | 19.8 |
| **Countries with recent debt-servicing difficulties** | | | | | | | | | | |
| Balance on current account | −20.8 | −24.1 | −18.7 | −13.5 | −25.1 | −44.8 | −56.1 | −57.9 | −41.3 | −40.6 |
| Change in reserves (− = increase) | −7.8 | 0.8 | −8.9 | −26.3 | −24.4 | −24.7 | −24.8 | 2.4 | −8.3 | −1.2 |
| Asset transactions, including | | | | | | | | | | |
| net errors and omissions | 3.1 | 0.5 | −1.7 | −10.6 | 1.1 | −5.2 | −10.4 | −14.9 | −5.1 | −13.3 |
| **Total, net external financing** | **25.6** | **22.8** | **29.3** | **50.3** | **48.4** | **74.6** | **91.4** | **70.4** | **54.0** | **54.8** |
| Non-debt-creating flows, net | 8.6 | 11.2 | 12.3 | 22.4 | 14.7 | 17.4 | 17.3 | 17.3 | 20.6 | 19.2 |
| Net credit and loans from IMF | −1.8 | −1.3 | −0.5 | 0.4 | −1.0 | −1.8 | −0.3 | −1.1 | ... | ... |
| Net external borrowing | 18.7 | 12.9 | 17.5 | 27.5 | 34.7 | 59.0 | 74.5 | 54.1 | 19.2 | 35.8 |
| From official creditors | 21.5 | 13.4 | 15.6 | 3.8 | 6.1 | −0.2 | 6.9 | 3.3 | 26.3 | −0.8 |
| From banks | 2.9 | −12.7 | −5.5 | 16.6 | 3.0 | −6.6 | 3.4 | −29.6 | −4.8 | 1.6 |
| Other | −5.7 | 12.2 | 7.3 | 7.1 | 25.7 | 65.8 | 64.1 | 80.4 | −2.3 | 35.0 |
| *Memorandum* | | | | | | | | | | |
| Net capital flows | 21.5 | 20.2 | 23.1 | 20.9 | 34.3 | 64.5 | 74.0 | 56.4 | 39.2 | 40.4 |
| Exceptional financing | 47.2 | 26.7 | 38.6 | 51.3 | 33.8 | 29.3 | 21.8 | 13.2 | 10.5 | 23.8 |
| **Countries without debt-servicing difficulties** | | | | | | | | | | |
| Balance on current account | 3.5 | −0.2 | −5.7 | −8.5 | −18.0 | −15.2 | −33.0 | −4.6 | −19.4 | −30.4 |
| Change in reserves (− = increase) | −14.5 | −16.5 | −24.7 | −33.5 | −39.2 | −31.5 | −51.8 | −65.4 | −54.9 | −46.3 |
| Asset transactions, including | | | | | | | | | | |
| net errors and omissions | −2.9 | −10.6 | −7.1 | −5.4 | −3.4 | −23.4 | −17.4 | −7.6 | −20.7 | −19.7 |
| **Total, net external financing** | **13.9** | **27.3** | **37.5** | **47.4** | **60.6** | **70.2** | **102.3** | **77.6** | **95.0** | **96.4** |
| Non-debt-creating flows, net | 8.0 | 12.7 | 12.8 | 15.5 | 15.7 | 21.2 | 37.1 | 45.1 | 42.0 | 40.1 |
| Net credit and loans from IMF | −2.9 | −2.8 | −1.0 | −2.3 | 2.1 | 1.6 | 0.2 | 0.3 | ... | ... |
| Net external borrowing | 8.7 | 17.4 | 25.7 | 34.2 | 42.7 | 47.3 | 65.0 | 32.2 | 53.9 | 57.7 |
| From official creditors | 3.2 | 5.9 | 5.2 | 7.5 | 15.4 | 6.2 | 13.6 | 10.6 | 10.2 | 5.3 |
| From banks | 10.4 | 15.2 | 10.3 | 21.3 | 23.1 | 24.9 | 19.2 | 16.0 | 14.7 | 13.3 |
| Other | −4.9 | −3.8 | 10.2 | 5.3 | 4.3 | 16.3 | 32.2 | 5.6 | 29.0 | 39.0 |
| *Memorandum* | | | | | | | | | | |
| Net capital flows | 11.0 | 19.4 | 25.1 | 42.7 | 52.1 | 53.4 | 91.0 | 71.0 | 74.5 | 78.1 |
| Exceptional financing | — | — | 0.1 | 0.1 | 0.5 | 2.8 | 12.1 | 9.3 | 6.9 | 5.1 |

**Table A35** *(concluded)*

| | 1987 | 1988 | 1989 | 1990 | 1991 | 1992 | 1993 | 1994 | 1995 | 1996 |
|---|---|---|---|---|---|---|---|---|---|---|
| **Other groups** | | | | | | | | | | |
| **Small low-income countries** | | | | | | | | | | |
| Balance on current account | −13.1 | −16.0 | −12.2 | −9.0 | −9.7 | −11.3 | −13.8 | −13.1 | −12.8 | −12.6 |
| Change in reserves (− = increase) | −0.5 | 1.1 | −1.5 | −4.1 | −7.8 | −0.5 | −5.7 | −7.2 | −2.5 | −0.5 |
| Asset transactions, including | | | | | | | | | | |
| net errors and omissions | 2.1 | 1.3 | 0.8 | 1.6 | 5.5 | 2.2 | 3.0 | 0.5 | −1.6 | 0.2 |
| **Total, net external financing** | **11.5** | **13.6** | **12.8** | **11.6** | **12.0** | **9.6** | **16.4** | **19.8** | **16.9** | **12.8** |
| Non-debt-creating flows, net | 2.3 | 2.3 | 5.0 | 13.7 | 4.1 | 4.9 | 5.1 | 4.3 | 5.3 | 4.7 |
| Net credit and loans from IMF | −0.9 | −0.6 | −0.2 | −0.6 | 0.4 | 0.5 | — | 0.9 | . . . | . . . |
| Net external borrowing | 10.1 | 11.9 | 8.0 | −1.5 | 7.6 | 4.2 | 11.4 | 14.6 | 10.4 | 8.5 |
| From official creditors | 9.3 | 9.9 | 7.6 | −1.5 | 5.0 | −0.8 | 6.2 | 5.3 | 4.8 | 3.1 |
| From banks | −0.3 | −0.6 | −1.4 | −0.2 | −0.4 | −2.9 | −2.2 | 0.3 | 0.7 | 0.3 |
| Other | 1.0 | 2.5 | 1.7 | 0.2 | 3.0 | 7.9 | 7.4 | 9.0 | 5.0 | 5.0 |
| *Memorandum* | | | | | | | | | | |
| Net capital flows | 9.4 | 12.9 | 9.8 | −2.4 | 7.2 | 8.9 | 14.2 | 18.6 | 13.4 | 11.2 |
| Exceptional financing | 13.6 | 6.1 | 14.8 | 21.4 | 15.7 | 13.3 | 11.5 | 10.4 | 7.4 | 21.0 |
| **Least developed countries** | | | | | | | | | | |
| Balance on current account | −5.5 | −6.4 | −5.9 | −7.3 | −7.7 | −8.0 | −7.8 | −6.9 | −7.3 | −7.8 |
| Change in reserves (− = increase) | −1.5 | −0.1 | −0.9 | — | −4.3 | 2.1 | −1.4 | −2.4 | −1.7 | −1.1 |
| Asset transactions, including | | | | | | | | | | |
| net errors and omissions | 0.6 | −0.1 | 0.2 | 0.4 | 4.8 | −2.0 | 1.2 | 1.0 | 1.1 | 1.1 |
| **Total, net external financing** | **6.4** | **6.6** | **6.6** | **7.0** | **7.2** | **7.9** | **8.0** | **8.2** | **7.9** | **7.7** |
| Non-debt-creating flows, net | 0.4 | 0.6 | 1.2 | 1.3 | 2.2 | 2.6 | 2.7 | 1.9 | 1.2 | 2.2 |
| Net credit and loans from IMF | — | −0.1 | −0.3 | −0.4 | 0.1 | 0.2 | −0.1 | 0.2 | . . . | . . . |
| Net external borrowing | 6.0 | 6.2 | 5.8 | 6.0 | 4.9 | 5.1 | 5.4 | 6.1 | 5.8 | 5.7 |
| From official creditors | 4.5 | 5.0 | 4.5 | 5.5 | 6.7 | 1.1 | 4.3 | 4.9 | 4.5 | 3.3 |
| From banks | 0.3 | −0.4 | 0.7 | 0.6 | 0.1 | — | −0.1 | −0.8 | — | — |
| Other | 1.1 | 1.7 | 0.6 | −0.1 | −1.8 | 4.0 | 1.2 | 2.0 | 1.3 | 2.4 |
| *Memorandum* | | | | | | | | | | |
| Net capital flows | 2.2 | 2.3 | 1.4 | 2.0 | 1.2 | 1.1 | 1.1 | 1.9 | 2.9 | 3.5 |
| Exceptional financing | 3.9 | 4.2 | 4.7 | 5.1 | 5.7 | 6.5 | 6.6 | 6.4 | 5.0 | 4.3 |

[1]For definitions, see footnotes to Table A33.

## Table A36. Developing Countries: Reserves[1]

| | 1987 | 1988 | 1989 | 1990 | 1991 | 1992 | 1993 | 1994 | 1995 | 1996 |
|---|---|---|---|---|---|---|---|---|---|---|
| | *In billions of U.S. dollars* | | | | | | | | | |
| **Developing countries** | **258.9** | **252.5** | **275.5** | **325.0** | **396.7** | **419.8** | **480.9** | **556.0** | **603.2** | **632.0** |
| **By region** | | | | | | | | | | |
| Africa | 11.0 | 10.4 | 12.0 | 16.7 | 19.7 | 16.2 | 16.7 | 21.4 | 21.8 | 24.8 |
| Asia | 148.5 | 158.6 | 168.6 | 194.4 | 238.9 | 239.8 | 275.4 | 347.9 | 390.6 | 426.2 |
| Middle East and Europe | 61.0 | 52.4 | 61.6 | 65.6 | 72.1 | 75.1 | 79.6 | 81.5 | 78.7 | 68.6 |
| Western Hemisphere | 38.3 | 31.1 | 33.3 | 48.3 | 66.0 | 88.7 | 109.2 | 105.2 | 112.1 | 112.4 |
| Sub-Saharan Africa | 6.0 | 6.2 | 6.5 | 7.7 | 8.4 | 7.6 | 7.7 | 9.3 | 9.5 | 10.1 |
| Four newly industrializing Asian economies | 102.8 | 111.4 | 117.7 | 126.3 | 143.6 | 152.7 | 165.5 | 189.7 | 205.6 | 219.7 |
| **By predominant export** | | | | | | | | | | |
| Fuel | 52.7 | 43.6 | 46.9 | 54.0 | 57.0 | 47.1 | 47.0 | 47.4 | 41.0 | 35.3 |
| Nonfuel exports | 206.3 | 208.9 | 228.6 | 271.0 | 339.7 | 372.8 | 433.9 | 508.6 | 562.2 | 596.7 |
| Manufactures | 126.5 | 136.0 | 142.9 | 163.9 | 196.0 | 181.0 | 197.6 | 254.4 | 291.0 | 315.7 |
| Primary products | 11.8 | 13.9 | 14.0 | 20.9 | 26.6 | 33.5 | 38.7 | 48.9 | 61.6 | 65.4 |
| Agricultural products | 5.2 | 6.8 | 5.3 | 8.8 | 11.7 | 15.7 | 19.4 | 21.4 | 22.8 | 25.9 |
| Minerals | 6.6 | 7.2 | 8.7 | 12.1 | 14.9 | 17.8 | 19.3 | 27.5 | 38.9 | 39.5 |
| Services, income, and private transfers | 11.6 | 8.8 | 10.7 | 12.3 | 17.2 | 24.3 | 27.1 | 28.1 | 28.1 | 25.4 |
| Diversified export base | 56.4 | 50.2 | 60.9 | 73.8 | 99.9 | 134.0 | 170.5 | 177.2 | 181.5 | 190.3 |
| **By financial criteria** | | | | | | | | | | |
| Net creditor countries | 117.1 | 107.9 | 105.0 | 100.1 | 112.2 | 109.2 | 109.5 | 116.4 | 112.2 | 105.4 |
| Net debtor countries | 141.8 | 144.6 | 170.5 | 224.9 | 284.5 | 310.6 | 371.4 | 439.6 | 491.1 | 526.7 |
| Market borrowers | 96.9 | 100.5 | 116.7 | 160.0 | 199.7 | 214.5 | 262.4 | 308.7 | 355.0 | 386.4 |
| Diversified borrowers | 30.0 | 29.3 | 37.5 | 42.4 | 55.8 | 63.8 | 73.6 | 88.9 | 93.4 | 97.8 |
| Official borrowers | 14.9 | 14.8 | 16.3 | 22.5 | 29.0 | 32.2 | 35.5 | 42.0 | 42.6 | 42.5 |
| Countries with recent debt-servicing difficulties | 47.7 | 39.5 | 48.6 | 70.9 | 97.7 | 123.0 | 145.8 | 144.3 | 150.4 | 150.5 |
| Countries without debt-servicing difficulties | 94.1 | 105.1 | 121.9 | 154.0 | 186.8 | 187.7 | 225.7 | 295.3 | 340.7 | 376.1 |
| **Other groups** | | | | | | | | | | |
| Small low-income economies | 9.3 | 8.1 | 9.0 | 12.8 | 18.0 | 20.7 | 24.5 | 29.0 | 30.0 | 29.7 |
| Least developed countries | 7.2 | 7.1 | 6.9 | 8.3 | 9.5 | 9.2 | 9.6 | 11.1 | 11.4 | 11.7 |

## Table A36  *(concluded)*

| | 1987 | 1988 | 1989 | 1990 | 1991 | 1992 | 1993 | 1994 | 1995 | 1996 |
|---|---|---|---|---|---|---|---|---|---|---|
| | *Ratio of reserves to imports of goods and services*[2] | | | | | | | | | |
| **Developing countries** | **40.1** | **33.4** | **32.6** | **34.0** | **37.0** | **35.0** | **37.2** | **39.0** | **36.8** | **34.6** |
| **By region** | | | | | | | | | | |
| Africa | 14.2 | 12.2 | 13.3 | 17.0 | 20.4 | 15.8 | 16.7 | 20.7 | 18.3 | 20.1 |
| Asia | 47.0 | 39.8 | 37.1 | 37.5 | 40.3 | 35.4 | 36.1 | 39.4 | 37.1 | 35.3 |
| Middle East and Europe | 38.8 | 31.8 | 33.6 | 32.0 | 31.6 | 31.6 | 34.0 | 37.3 | 33.5 | 27.7 |
| Western Hemisphere | 40.1 | 29.4 | 28.4 | 35.9 | 43.0 | 49.1 | 55.8 | 47.5 | 48.1 | 45.1 |
| Sub-Saharan Africa | 16.3 | 15.7 | 16.0 | 17.7 | 19.5 | 17.6 | 18.0 | 22.1 | 20.4 | 20.6 |
| Four newly industrializing | | | | | | | | | | |
| Asian economies | 58.7 | 48.2 | 44.6 | 41.9 | 41.1 | 38.8 | 38.7 | 39.0 | 35.5 | 33.7 |
| **By predominant export** | | | | | | | | | | |
| Fuel | 43.2 | 34.1 | 33.7 | 35.3 | 32.8 | 26.2 | 28.7 | 33.2 | 27.0 | 22.4 |
| Nonfuel exports | 39.3 | 33.3 | 32.4 | 33.8 | 37.8 | 36.6 | 38.4 | 39.6 | 37.8 | 35.8 |
| Manufactures | 54.0 | 44.6 | 41.9 | 43.5 | 44.9 | 35.9 | 34.8 | 39.5 | 37.9 | 35.9 |
| Primary products | 21.3 | 26.0 | 25.2 | 34.9 | 40.0 | 42.7 | 46.5 | 54.1 | 63.2 | 62.2 |
| Agricultural products | 14.2 | 20.3 | 16.0 | 24.7 | 28.2 | 30.8 | 35.1 | 35.1 | 35.9 | 38.0 |
| Minerals | 35.2 | 35.4 | 39.0 | 49.7 | 59.5 | 64.7 | 69.0 | 93.2 | 114.3 | 107.0 |
| Services, income, and | | | | | | | | | | |
| private transfers | 26.6 | 18.8 | 22.0 | 24.7 | 31.4 | 41.3 | 46.6 | 45.6 | 42.7 | 36.4 |
| Diversified export base | 29.4 | 22.6 | 23.4 | 23.3 | 29.4 | 35.5 | 40.5 | 36.4 | 32.5 | 31.0 |
| **By financial criteria** | | | | | | | | | | |
| Net creditor countries | 109.7 | 87.0 | 76.5 | 67.8 | 61.1 | 54.9 | 56.1 | 59.2 | 51.0 | 44.8 |
| Net debtor countries | 26.3 | 22.9 | 24.1 | 27.8 | 32.0 | 31.1 | 33.8 | 35.8 | 34.6 | 33.1 |
| Market borrowers | 30.4 | 25.6 | 26.0 | 30.8 | 32.8 | 30.8 | 34.0 | 35.1 | 34.7 | 33.2 |
| Diversified borrowers | 21.5 | 19.4 | 22.5 | 22.9 | 32.5 | 33.7 | 34.6 | 38.4 | 34.8 | 33.5 |
| Official borrowers | 18.4 | 16.9 | 17.6 | 21.9 | 27.0 | 28.6 | 30.7 | 35.6 | 32.6 | 31.0 |
| Countries with recent debt- | | | | | | | | | | |
| servicing difficulties | 24.9 | 18.8 | 21.2 | 28.4 | 38.1 | 42.4 | 47.4 | 42.6 | 41.1 | 38.5 |
| Countries without debt- | | | | | | | | | | |
| servicing difficulties | 27.0 | 25.0 | 25.4 | 27.6 | 29.6 | 26.4 | 28.5 | 33.2 | 32.3 | 31.3 |
| **Other groups** | | | | | | | | | | |
| Small low-income economies | 13.8 | 11.3 | 12.1 | 15.7 | 20.9 | 23.2 | 26.8 | 31.0 | 29.0 | 27.1 |
| Least developed countries | 25.5 | 23.3 | 22.1 | 25.1 | 28.9 | 27.7 | 28.2 | 31.2 | 28.7 | 27.8 |

[1]In this table, official holdings of gold are valued at SDR 35 an ounce. This convention results in a marked underestimate of reserves for countries that have substantial gold holdings.

[2]Reserves at year-end in percent of imports of goods and services for the year indicated.

## Table A37. Net Credit and Loans from IMF[1]

*(In billions of U.S. dollars)*

| | 1987 | 1988 | 1989 | 1990 | 1991 | 1992 | 1993 | 1994 |
|---|---|---|---|---|---|---|---|---|
| **Developing countries** | **−4.7** | **−4.1** | **−1.5** | **−1.9** | **1.1** | **−0.2** | **−0.2** | **−0.8** |
| **By region** | | | | | | | | |
| Africa | −1.1 | −0.3 | 0.1 | −0.6 | 0.2 | −0.2 | 0.2 | 0.9 |
| Asia | −2.4 | −2.4 | −1.1 | −2.4 | 1.9 | 1.3 | 0.6 | −0.8 |
| Middle East and Europe | −0.4 | −0.5 | −0.2 | −0.1 | — | 0.4 | — | 0.4 |
| Western Hemisphere | −0.8 | −0.9 | −0.2 | 1.2 | −1.0 | −1.6 | −0.9 | −1.3 |
| Sub-Saharan Africa | −0.5 | −0.2 | −0.4 | −0.3 | — | — | −0.2 | 0.5 |
| **By predominant export** | | | | | | | | |
| Fuel | — | 0.2 | 1.7 | 1.9 | 0.5 | −0.5 | −0.8 | 0.4 |
| Nonfuel exports | −4.7 | −4.2 | −3.2 | −3.8 | 0.6 | 0.3 | 0.6 | −1.3 |
| Manufactures | −1.2 | −0.6 | −0.1 | −0.5 | −0.5 | 0.3 | — | — |
| Primary products | — | −0.4 | −0.9 | −0.8 | −0.9 | −0.1 | 1.1 | 0.6 |
| Services, income, and private transfers | −0.2 | −0.3 | −0.2 | −0.3 | — | 0.1 | 0.1 | — |
| Diversified export base | −3.2 | −2.9 | −2.0 | −2.3 | 1.9 | 0.1 | −0.6 | −1.9 |
| **By financial criteria** | | | | | | | | |
| Net creditor countries | — | — | — | — | — | — | — | — |
| Net debtor countries | −4.7 | −4.1 | −1.5 | −1.9 | 1.1 | −0.2 | −0.2 | −0.8 |
| Market borrowers | −1.8 | −1.4 | 0.2 | 0.7 | −1.2 | −1.6 | −1.2 | −0.7 |
| Official borrowers | −0.7 | −0.8 | −0.2 | −1.1 | 0.3 | 0.3 | −0.3 | 0.4 |
| Countries with recent debt-servicing difficulties | −1.8 | −1.3 | −0.5 | 0.4 | −1.0 | −1.8 | −0.3 | −1.1 |
| Countries without debt-servicing difficulties | −2.9 | −2.8 | −1.0 | −2.3 | 2.1 | 1.6 | 0.2 | 0.3 |
| **Other groups** | | | | | | | | |
| Small low-income economies | −0.9 | −0.6 | −0.2 | −0.6 | 0.4 | 0.5 | — | 0.9 |
| Least developed countries | — | −0.1 | −0.3 | −0.4 | 0.1 | 0.2 | −0.1 | 0.2 |
| **Countries in transition** | **−1.1** | **−0.9** | **−0.9** | **0.1** | **3.5** | **1.7** | **2.1** | **2.4** |
| Central and eastern Europe | ... | ... | ... | ... | 3.5 | 0.7 | 0.4 | 0.5 |
| Excluding Belarus and Ukraine | ... | ... | ... | ... | 3.5 | 0.7 | 0.3 | 0.2 |
| Russia | ... | ... | ... | ... | — | 1.0 | 1.5 | 1.5 |
| Transcaucasus and central Asia | ... | ... | ... | ... | — | — | 0.2 | 0.3 |
| *Memorandum* | | | | | | | | |
| **Total, nonindustrial countries** | | | | | | | | |
| Net credit provided under: | | | | | | | | |
| General Resources Account | −5.642 | −4.875 | −3.121 | −2.148 | 3.606 | 0.842 | 1.711 | 0.594 |
| Trust Fund | −0.711 | −0.669 | −0.509 | −0.365 | −0.069 | — | −0.060 | −0.014 |
| SAF | 0.522 | 0.413 | 0.902 | 0.131 | 0.242 | 0.024 | −0.064 | −0.185 |
| ESAF | — | 0.138 | 0.330 | 0.557 | 0.804 | 0.706 | 0.317 | 1.139 |
| Disbursements at year-end under:[2] | | | | | | | | |
| General Resources Account | 40.267 | 33.314 | 29.334 | 29.503 | 33.434 | 32.961 | 34.609 | 37.389 |
| Trust Fund | 1.946 | 1.177 | 0.627 | 0.296 | 0.226 | 0.217 | 0.157 | 0.153 |
| SAF | 0.688 | 1.067 | 1.967 | 2.403 | 2.670 | 2.590 | 2.524 | 2.494 |
| ESAF | — | 0.138 | 0.473 | 0.959 | 1.805 | 2.424 | 2.734 | 4.068 |

[1]Excludes industrial countries' net credit from IMF. Includes net disbursements from programs under the General Resources Account, Trust Fund, SAF, and ESAF. The data are on a transactions basis, with conversions to U.S. dollar values at annual average exchange rates.

[2]Converted to U.S. dollar values at end-of-period exchange rates.

## Table A38. Summary of External Debt and Debt Service

| | 1987 | 1988 | 1989 | 1990 | 1991 | 1992 | 1993 | 1994 | 1995 | 1996 |
|---|---|---|---|---|---|---|---|---|---|---|
| | | | | | *In billions of U.S. dollars* | | | | | |
| **External debt** | | | | | | | | | | |
| **Developing countries** | **1,156.5** | **1,166.3** | **1,195.5** | **1,273.7** | **1,359.2** | **1,439.8** | **1,571.2** | **1,704.7** | **1,852.1** | **1,934.2** |
| **By region** | | | | | | | | | | |
| Africa | 203.0 | 204.9 | 212.7 | 223.9 | 234.7 | 235.4 | 246.7 | 256.0 | 277.9 | 288.1 |
| Asia | 317.6 | 327.8 | 335.4 | 368.9 | 414.9 | 455.6 | 518.6 | 582.0 | 659.8 | 703.6 |
| Middle East and Europe | 209.3 | 218.1 | 230.6 | 243.2 | 257.6 | 276.8 | 303.9 | 317.1 | 333.9 | 337.7 |
| Western Hemisphere | 426.7 | 415.5 | 416.7 | 437.8 | 452.0 | 472.0 | 502.0 | 549.6 | 580.5 | 604.8 |
| **By financial criteria** | | | | | | | | | | |
| Net creditor countries | 30.3 | 28.2 | 27.2 | 25.7 | 30.6 | 38.5 | 42.0 | 46.1 | 48.9 | 51.4 |
| Net debtor countries | 1,126.3 | 1,138.1 | 1,168.3 | 1,248.1 | 1,328.6 | 1,401.3 | 1,529.2 | 1,658.6 | 1,803.2 | 1,882.9 |
| Market borrowers | 543.6 | 530.8 | 534.5 | 570.0 | 618.7 | 669.0 | 752.9 | 834.8 | 916.0 | 972.3 |
| Diversified borrowers | 347.4 | 363.4 | 381.7 | 414.9 | 433.7 | 454.5 | 486.6 | 513.2 | 555.7 | 572.8 |
| Official borrowers | 235.2 | 243.8 | 252.1 | 263.2 | 276.2 | 277.9 | 289.7 | 310.6 | 331.4 | 337.8 |
| Countries with recent debt-servicing difficulties | 716.0 | 717.2 | 732.6 | 770.0 | 796.3 | 818.6 | 857.9 | 924.2 | 981.6 | 1,013.1 |
| Countries without debt-servicing difficulties | 410.2 | 420.9 | 435.7 | 478.0 | 532.3 | 582.7 | 671.3 | 734.4 | 821.6 | 869.8 |
| **Countries in transition** | **145.7** | **144.1** | **152.3** | **196.1** | **202.8** | **215.5** | **230.9** | **240.8** | **260.4** | **274.4** |
| Central and eastern Europe | ... | ... | ... | ... | 107.4 | 109.7 | 116.6 | 115.2 | 125.6 | 131.7 |
| Excluding Belarus and Ukraine | ... | ... | ... | ... | 107.4 | 105.6 | 112.0 | 109.6 | 116.9 | 120.5 |
| Russia | ... | ... | ... | ... | 95.3 | 105.4 | 110.4 | 119.8 | 130.4 | 136.4 |
| Transcaucasus and central Asia | ... | ... | ... | ... | 0.1 | 0.4 | 3.9 | 5.9 | 4.4 | 6.3 |
| **Debt-service payments[1]** | | | | | | | | | | |
| **Developing countries** | **131.1** | **137.7** | **134.4** | **146.2** | **171.3** | **175.5** | **186.1** | **207.4** | **232.0** | **219.1** |
| **By region** | | | | | | | | | | |
| Africa | 23.8 | 21.4 | 24.3 | 26.9 | 27.7 | 32.2 | 27.6 | 26.8 | 32.5 | 33.2 |
| Asia | 46.8 | 44.4 | 48.3 | 48.4 | 49.1 | 54.9 | 62.9 | 65.6 | 77.1 | 84.2 |
| Middle East and Europe | 14.0 | 16.6 | 17.4 | 23.5 | 24.2 | 19.4 | 20.0 | 33.5 | 31.7 | 27.2 |
| Western Hemisphere | 46.4 | 55.3 | 44.4 | 47.4 | 70.3 | 69.0 | 75.6 | 81.5 | 90.6 | 74.5 |
| **By financial criteria** | | | | | | | | | | |
| Net creditor countries | 4.9 | 4.5 | 4.4 | 4.2 | 3.2 | 3.3 | 3.1 | 6.5 | 5.5 | 4.5 |
| Net debtor countries | 126.2 | 133.2 | 130.0 | 142.0 | 168.1 | 172.2 | 183.0 | 200.9 | 226.6 | 214.7 |
| Market borrowers | 76.0 | 84.1 | 76.3 | 79.1 | 104.6 | 105.5 | 119.1 | 124.9 | 131.0 | 128.4 |
| Diversified borrowers | 29.3 | 35.0 | 36.2 | 38.8 | 39.7 | 42.8 | 44.9 | 53.7 | 75.8 | 64.6 |
| Official borrowers | 20.9 | 14.1 | 17.4 | 24.0 | 23.8 | 23.9 | 19.0 | 22.3 | 19.7 | 21.7 |
| Countries with recent debt-servicing difficulties | 68.8 | 71.9 | 64.3 | 73.6 | 95.2 | 94.7 | 97.8 | 106.3 | 119.9 | 104.7 |
| Countries without debt-servicing difficulties | 57.4 | 61.3 | 65.6 | 68.4 | 72.9 | 77.5 | 85.2 | 94.7 | 106.7 | 110.0 |
| **Countries in transition** | **24.0** | **27.1** | **25.1** | **30.7** | **...** | **26.3** | **18.2** | **25.2** | **26.0** | **37.7** |
| Central and eastern Europe | ... | ... | ... | ... | 11.5 | 13.6 | 13.0 | 17.7 | 16.3 | 20.7 |
| Excluding Belarus and Ukraine | ... | ... | ... | ... | 11.5 | 13.6 | 12.9 | 15.8 | 18.2 | 19.8 |
| Russia | ... | ... | ... | ... | ... | 12.6 | 5.0 | 6.9 | 8.2 | 15.8 |
| Transcaucasus and central Asia | ... | ... | ... | ... | — | 0.1 | 0.1 | 0.6 | 1.5 | 1.2 |

149

## Table A38 (concluded)

| | 1987 | 1988 | 1989 | 1990 | 1991 | 1992 | 1993 | 1994 | 1995 | 1996 |
|---|---|---|---|---|---|---|---|---|---|---|
| | | | | | *In percent of exports of goods and services* | | | | | |
| **External debt**[2] | | | | | | | | | | |
| **Developing countries** | **171.1** | **151.0** | **137.6** | **128.7** | **130.6** | **125.5** | **128.6** | **123.0** | **115.3** | **108.9** |
| **By region** | | | | | | | | | | |
| Africa | 265.0 | 258.4 | 252.2 | 231.1 | 248.8 | 249.4 | 269.5 | 276.5 | 265.5 | 255.5 |
| Asia | 94.0 | 79.3 | 72.3 | 70.7 | 69.9 | 67.4 | 69.5 | 66.2 | 63.5 | 59.8 |
| Middle East and Europe | 145.5 | 147.0 | 133.0 | 117.1 | 134.8 | 134.3 | 151.4 | 152.3 | 149.4 | 147.2 |
| Western Hemisphere | 363.1 | 316.9 | 283.5 | 267.7 | 278.8 | 276.0 | 274.5 | 265.6 | 242.7 | 235.8 |
| **By financial criteria** | | | | | | | | | | |
| Net creditor countries | 23.8 | 20.8 | 17.4 | 14.1 | 16.4 | 19.1 | 20.9 | 22.3 | 21.3 | 21.3 |
| Net debtor countries | 205.3 | 178.7 | 164.0 | 154.5 | 155.4 | 148.1 | 149.7 | 140.6 | 131.0 | 122.6 |
| Market borrowers | 151.4 | 123.6 | 110.6 | 102.8 | 101.9 | 97.8 | 101.0 | 95.5 | 88.9 | 83.8 |
| Diversified borrowers | 266.8 | 255.0 | 240.0 | 242.3 | 264.0 | 258.0 | 256.2 | 239.0 | 229.6 | 217.4 |
| Official borrowers | 396.0 | 377.3 | 358.7 | 319.1 | 331.9 | 323.4 | 337.5 | 341.9 | 320.5 | 302.4 |
| Countries with recent debt-servicing difficulties | 360.4 | 331.6 | 302.3 | 292.2 | 320.0 | 314.2 | 315.8 | 308.4 | 283.6 | 271.7 |
| Countries without debt-servicing difficulties | 117.2 | 100.1 | 92.6 | 87.8 | 87.8 | 85.0 | 89.6 | 83.5 | 79.8 | 74.8 |
| **Countries in transition** | **70.7** | **66.9** | **72.5** | **100.6** | **116.7** | **137.4** | **127.5** | **118.5** | **110.4** | **106.7** |
| Central and eastern Europe | ... | ... | ... | ... | 138.0 | 124.6 | 115.0 | 101.9 | 93.0 | 89.6 |
| Excluding Belarus and Ukraine | ... | ... | ... | ... | 153.5 | 135.0 | 135.9 | 114.9 | 99.9 | 94.5 |
| Russia | ... | ... | ... | ... | 154.8 | 183.4 | 169.4 | 154.4 | 152.0 | 149.6 |
| Transcaucasus and central Asia | ... | ... | ... | ... | 0.2 | 3.9 | 27.0 | 46.1 | 29.7 | 33.4 |
| **Debt-service payments** | | | | | | | | | | |
| **Developing countries** | **19.4** | **17.8** | **15.5** | **14.8** | **16.5** | **15.3** | **15.2** | **15.0** | **14.4** | **12.3** |
| **By region** | | | | | | | | | | |
| Africa | 31.1 | 27.0 | 28.8 | 27.8 | 29.3 | 34.1 | 30.2 | 28.9 | 31.0 | 29.5 |
| Asia | 13.9 | 10.7 | 10.4 | 9.3 | 8.3 | 8.1 | 8.4 | 7.5 | 7.4 | 7.2 |
| Middle East and Europe | 9.7 | 11.2 | 10.0 | 11.3 | 12.7 | 9.4 | 9.9 | 16.1 | 14.2 | 11.8 |
| Western Hemisphere | 39.5 | 42.2 | 30.2 | 29.0 | 43.4 | 40.3 | 41.4 | 39.4 | 37.9 | 29.0 |
| **By financial criteria** | | | | | | | | | | |
| Net creditor countries | 3.8 | 3.3 | 2.8 | 2.3 | 1.7 | 1.6 | 1.5 | 3.1 | 2.4 | 1.9 |
| Net debtor countries | 23.0 | 20.9 | 18.2 | 17.6 | 19.7 | 18.2 | 17.9 | 17.0 | 16.5 | 14.0 |
| Market borrowers | 21.2 | 19.6 | 15.8 | 14.3 | 17.2 | 15.4 | 16.0 | 14.3 | 12.7 | 11.1 |
| Diversified borrowers | 22.5 | 24.6 | 22.8 | 22.7 | 24.1 | 24.3 | 23.6 | 25.0 | 31.3 | 24.5 |
| Official borrowers | 35.2 | 21.8 | 24.8 | 29.1 | 28.6 | 27.8 | 22.2 | 24.6 | 19.1 | 19.4 |
| Countries with recent debt-servicing difficulties | 34.6 | 33.3 | 26.5 | 27.9 | 38.3 | 36.4 | 36.0 | 35.5 | 34.6 | 28.1 |
| Countries without debt-servicing difficulties | 16.4 | 14.6 | 14.0 | 12.6 | 12.0 | 11.3 | 11.4 | 10.8 | 10.4 | 9.5 |
| **Countries in transition** | **11.6** | **12.6** | **11.9** | **15.7** | **...** | **16.7** | **10.0** | **12.4** | **11.0** | **14.7** |
| Central and eastern Europe | ... | ... | ... | ... | 14.7 | 15.4 | 12.9 | 15.6 | 12.1 | 14.1 |
| Excluding Belarus and Ukraine | ... | ... | ... | ... | 16.4 | 17.4 | 15.6 | 16.6 | 15.5 | 15.5 |
| Russia | ... | ... | ... | ... | ... | 21.9 | 7.7 | 8.9 | 9.6 | 17.3 |
| Transcaucasus and central Asia | ... | ... | ... | ... | — | 0.7 | 0.9 | 4.6 | 10.1 | 6.5 |

[1]Debt-service payments refer to actual payments of interest on total debt plus actual amortization payments on long-term debt. The projections incorporate the impact of exceptional financing items.

[2]Total debt at year-end in percent of exports of goods and services in year indicated.

## Table A39. Developing Countries—by Region: External Debt, by Maturity and Type of Creditor

*(In billions of U.S. dollars)*

| | 1987 | 1988 | 1989 | 1990 | 1991 | 1992 | 1993 | 1994 | 1995 | 1996 |
|---|---|---|---|---|---|---|---|---|---|---|
| **Developing countries** | | | | | | | | | | |
| **Total debt** | **1,156.5** | **1,166.3** | **1,195.5** | **1,273.7** | **1,359.2** | **1,439.8** | **1,571.2** | **1,704.7** | **1,852.1** | **1,934.2** |
| By maturity | | | | | | | | | | |
| Short-term | 185.4 | 189.3 | 200.2 | 228.6 | 252.7 | 274.6 | 306.4 | 326.0 | 367.6 | 396.3 |
| Long-term | 971.1 | 977.0 | 995.3 | 1,045.1 | 1,106.5 | 1,165.2 | 1,264.8 | 1,378.7 | 1,484.6 | 1,538.1 |
| By type of creditor | | | | | | | | | | |
| Official | 527.1 | 539.0 | 560.4 | 607.2 | 645.8 | 659.9 | 691.2 | 747.7 | 828.4 | 825.2 |
| Banks | 482.3 | 462.7 | 449.3 | 457.3 | 490.2 | 500.8 | 532.4 | 509.8 | 518.8 | 532.2 |
| Other private | 147.1 | 164.6 | 185.8 | 209.3 | 223.2 | 279.1 | 347.6 | 447.2 | 504.9 | 576.8 |
| **By region** | | | | | | | | | | |
| **Africa** | | | | | | | | | | |
| **Total debt** | **203.0** | **204.9** | **212.7** | **223.9** | **234.7** | **235.4** | **246.7** | **256.0** | **277.9** | **288.1** |
| By maturity | | | | | | | | | | |
| Short-term | 29.5 | 27.9 | 29.7 | 29.9 | 29.1 | 26.8 | 26.6 | 27.7 | 28.6 | 32.6 |
| Long-term | 173.5 | 177.0 | 183.1 | 194.1 | 205.6 | 208.6 | 220.2 | 228.3 | 249.3 | 255.5 |
| By type of creditor | | | | | | | | | | |
| Official | 126.5 | 127.9 | 135.0 | 147.1 | 153.5 | 156.6 | 164.3 | 175.8 | 188.8 | 190.3 |
| Banks | 57.2 | 55.3 | 53.5 | 56.9 | 56.2 | 50.7 | 51.8 | 46.2 | 49.8 | 51.1 |
| Other private | 19.4 | 21.6 | 24.3 | 19.9 | 25.1 | 28.0 | 30.6 | 34.0 | 39.3 | 46.8 |
| **Asia** | | | | | | | | | | |
| **Total debt** | **317.6** | **327.8** | **335.4** | **368.9** | **414.9** | **455.6** | **518.6** | **582.0** | **659.8** | **703.6** |
| By maturity | | | | | | | | | | |
| Short-term | 55.7 | 61.3 | 63.9 | 73.4 | 90.7 | 100.4 | 118.7 | 139.8 | 174.9 | 192.6 |
| Long-term | 261.8 | 266.5 | 271.5 | 295.5 | 324.2 | 355.2 | 399.9 | 442.2 | 484.9 | 511.0 |
| By type of creditor | | | | | | | | | | |
| Official | 181.1 | 183.1 | 186.5 | 200.4 | 210.7 | 225.3 | 243.5 | 267.1 | 288.3 | 294.5 |
| Banks | 107.0 | 112.9 | 115.7 | 127.5 | 150.9 | 168.5 | 182.2 | 206.8 | 225.3 | 240.0 |
| Other private | 29.5 | 31.8 | 33.2 | 41.0 | 53.2 | 61.7 | 92.9 | 108.1 | 146.1 | 169.1 |
| **Middle East and Europe** | | | | | | | | | | |
| **Total debt** | **209.3** | **218.1** | **230.6** | **243.2** | **257.6** | **276.8** | **303.9** | **317.1** | **333.9** | **337.7** |
| By maturity | | | | | | | | | | |
| Short-term | 42.2 | 39.9 | 43.7 | 47.4 | 49.7 | 59.0 | 72.4 | 57.7 | 60.4 | 65.9 |
| Long-term | 167.1 | 178.2 | 186.9 | 195.7 | 207.9 | 217.7 | 231.6 | 259.4 | 273.5 | 271.8 |
| By type of creditor | | | | | | | | | | |
| Official | 111.8 | 114.0 | 116.9 | 116.5 | 124.2 | 120.4 | 123.8 | 137.9 | 141.1 | 134.9 |
| Banks | 47.0 | 47.7 | 52.5 | 51.9 | 60.8 | 62.7 | 75.6 | 68.8 | 61.3 | 59.6 |
| Other private | 50.5 | 56.4 | 61.2 | 74.7 | 72.7 | 93.8 | 104.5 | 110.4 | 131.5 | 143.1 |
| **Western Hemisphere** | | | | | | | | | | |
| **Total debt** | **426.7** | **415.5** | **416.7** | **437.8** | **452.0** | **472.0** | **502.0** | **549.6** | **580.5** | **604.8** |
| By maturity | | | | | | | | | | |
| Short-term | 58.0 | 60.1 | 62.8 | 77.9 | 83.2 | 88.3 | 88.8 | 100.9 | 103.7 | 105.2 |
| Long-term | 368.7 | 355.4 | 353.8 | 359.9 | 368.8 | 383.7 | 413.2 | 448.8 | 476.9 | 499.8 |
| By type of creditor | | | | | | | | | | |
| Official | 107.8 | 114.0 | 122.0 | 143.2 | 157.4 | 157.6 | 159.6 | 166.9 | 210.2 | 205.5 |
| Banks | 271.2 | 246.7 | 227.6 | 221.0 | 222.3 | 218.9 | 222.8 | 188.1 | 182.4 | 181.5 |
| Other private | 47.7 | 54.8 | 67.1 | 73.6 | 72.3 | 95.6 | 119.6 | 194.7 | 187.9 | 217.8 |
| **Sub-Saharan Africa** | | | | | | | | | | |
| **Total debt** | **101.9** | **103.2** | **107.7** | **119.2** | **129.7** | **135.0** | **140.1** | **146.7** | **158.8** | **163.5** |
| By maturity | | | | | | | | | | |
| Short-term | 8.3 | 8.3 | 9.4 | 9.9 | 10.6 | 11.2 | 13.9 | 14.1 | 13.2 | 14.4 |
| Long-term | 93.6 | 94.9 | 98.3 | 109.3 | 119.2 | 123.8 | 126.2 | 132.5 | 145.6 | 149.0 |
| By type of creditor | | | | | | | | | | |
| Official | 77.8 | 80.0 | 82.9 | 92.8 | 101.5 | 103.5 | 107.7 | 116.2 | 126.3 | 128.5 |
| Banks | 11.2 | 11.1 | 11.3 | 14.1 | 13.9 | 14.5 | 15.4 | 11.0 | 11.5 | 11.6 |
| Other private | 12.9 | 12.2 | 13.5 | 12.3 | 14.3 | 17.0 | 16.9 | 19.5 | 21.0 | 23.3 |

## Table A40. Developing Countries—by Analytical Criteria: External Debt, by Maturity and Type of Creditor
*(In billions of U.S. dollars)*

| | 1987 | 1988 | 1989 | 1990 | 1991 | 1992 | 1993 | 1994 | 1995 | 1996 |
|---|---|---|---|---|---|---|---|---|---|---|
| **By predominant export** | | | | | | | | | | |
| **Fuel** | | | | | | | | | | |
| **Total debt** | **151.2** | **159.7** | **170.3** | **180.4** | **194.2** | **200.4** | **217.1** | **217.5** | **222.5** | **223.6** |
| By maturity | | | | | | | | | | |
| Short-term | 26.2 | 27.3 | 29.2 | 24.6 | 28.2 | 32.7 | 37.1 | 29.8 | 26.4 | 27.4 |
| Long-term | 125.0 | 132.4 | 141.1 | 155.8 | 166.0 | 167.7 | 180.0 | 187.7 | 196.2 | 196.3 |
| By type of creditor | | | | | | | | | | |
| Official | 42.3 | 44.3 | 52.0 | 58.3 | 66.0 | 70.5 | 77.1 | 88.5 | 88.3 | 82.8 |
| Banks | 69.5 | 66.3 | 70.8 | 66.1 | 75.2 | 71.8 | 88.6 | 76.7 | 73.8 | 76.1 |
| Other private | 39.4 | 49.2 | 47.5 | 56.0 | 53.0 | 58.1 | 51.4 | 52.3 | 60.4 | 64.8 |
| **Nonfuel exports** | | | | | | | | | | |
| **Total debt** | **1,005.3** | **1,006.5** | **1,025.2** | **1,093.3** | **1,165.0** | **1,239.5** | **1,354.1** | **1,487.3** | **1,629.6** | **1,710.6** |
| By maturity | | | | | | | | | | |
| Short-term | 159.2 | 161.9 | 171.0 | 204.0 | 224.5 | 241.9 | 269.3 | 296.2 | 341.2 | 368.8 |
| Long-term | 846.1 | 844.6 | 854.2 | 889.4 | 940.5 | 997.6 | 1,084.8 | 1,191.0 | 1,288.4 | 1,341.8 |
| By type of creditor | | | | | | | | | | |
| Official | 484.8 | 494.7 | 508.5 | 549.0 | 579.8 | 589.5 | 614.1 | 659.2 | 740.1 | 742.5 |
| Banks | 412.7 | 396.4 | 378.4 | 391.1 | 415.0 | 429.0 | 443.8 | 433.2 | 445.0 | 456.1 |
| Other private | 107.7 | 115.4 | 138.3 | 153.2 | 170.2 | 221.0 | 296.2 | 394.9 | 444.5 | 512.0 |
| **Manufactures** | | | | | | | | | | |
| **Total debt** | **124.2** | **125.8** | **125.0** | **133.3** | **155.8** | **171.2** | **206.0** | **240.8** | **272.3** | **293.2** |
| By maturity | | | | | | | | | | |
| Short-term | 38.9 | 40.3 | 42.4 | 45.4 | 57.1 | 60.4 | 73.7 | 88.8 | 107.3 | 114.8 |
| Long-term | 85.3 | 85.6 | 82.5 | 87.9 | 98.7 | 110.8 | 132.3 | 152.0 | 165.0 | 178.4 |
| By type of creditor | | | | | | | | | | |
| Official | 33.0 | 32.8 | 32.3 | 34.3 | 36.3 | 34.2 | 36.8 | 40.4 | 43.6 | 44.9 |
| Banks | 60.8 | 61.1 | 56.8 | 57.7 | 70.7 | 73.4 | 80.8 | 91.8 | 97.2 | 101.6 |
| Other private | 30.4 | 31.9 | 35.9 | 41.2 | 48.7 | 63.6 | 88.4 | 108.5 | 131.6 | 146.7 |
| **Primary products** | | | | | | | | | | |
| **Total debt** | **195.8** | **196.9** | **205.7** | **219.0** | **232.0** | **239.6** | **248.6** | **278.7** | **295.5** | **313.0** |
| By maturity | | | | | | | | | | |
| Short-term | 25.6 | 28.8 | 31.8 | 36.5 | 41.2 | 44.5 | 38.2 | 40.8 | 40.6 | 42.6 |
| Long-term | 170.2 | 168.1 | 173.8 | 182.5 | 190.8 | 195.1 | 210.4 | 237.9 | 254.9 | 270.3 |
| By type of creditor | | | | | | | | | | |
| Official | 99.3 | 103.2 | 108.9 | 123.8 | 134.0 | 134.0 | 141.3 | 152.6 | 166.2 | 168.9 |
| Banks | 65.8 | 61.5 | 60.0 | 58.2 | 57.4 | 57.3 | 56.7 | 53.7 | 53.9 | 53.9 |
| Other private | 30.7 | 32.2 | 36.8 | 37.0 | 40.6 | 48.3 | 50.6 | 72.4 | 75.4 | 90.1 |
| **Agricultural products** | | | | | | | | | | |
| **Total debt** | **129.4** | **130.1** | **138.9** | **144.4** | **155.8** | **158.9** | **163.0** | **182.7** | **195.0** | **208.2** |
| By maturity | | | | | | | | | | |
| Short-term | 16.4 | 17.6 | 19.0 | 21.6 | 26.7 | 27.3 | 19.8 | 21.4 | 20.2 | 22.0 |
| Long-term | 113.0 | 112.4 | 119.9 | 122.9 | 129.1 | 131.6 | 143.1 | 161.3 | 174.7 | 186.2 |
| By type of creditor | | | | | | | | | | |
| Official | 64.5 | 66.7 | 70.1 | 76.8 | 84.8 | 84.6 | 88.5 | 95.3 | 106.1 | 108.6 |
| Banks | 45.1 | 43.5 | 44.4 | 42.0 | 41.2 | 40.6 | 39.2 | 36.1 | 37.8 | 37.0 |
| Other private | 19.8 | 19.9 | 24.4 | 25.6 | 29.7 | 33.7 | 35.3 | 51.3 | 51.1 | 62.6 |
| **Minerals** | | | | | | | | | | |
| **Total debt** | **66.3** | **66.9** | **66.8** | **74.5** | **76.2** | **80.7** | **85.6** | **96.0** | **100.5** | **104.8** |
| By maturity | | | | | | | | | | |
| Short-term | 9.2 | 11.2 | 12.8 | 14.9 | 14.6 | 17.2 | 18.3 | 19.4 | 20.4 | 20.6 |
| Long-term | 57.2 | 55.6 | 54.0 | 59.6 | 61.7 | 63.5 | 67.3 | 76.6 | 80.2 | 84.2 |
| By type of creditor | | | | | | | | | | |
| Official | 34.7 | 36.5 | 38.8 | 47.0 | 49.1 | 49.4 | 52.8 | 57.3 | 60.1 | 60.3 |
| Banks | 20.7 | 18.1 | 15.7 | 16.2 | 16.2 | 16.7 | 17.4 | 17.6 | 16.2 | 17.0 |
| Other private | 10.9 | 12.3 | 12.4 | 11.4 | 10.9 | 14.7 | 15.4 | 21.1 | 24.3 | 27.5 |

## Table A40 *(continued)*

| | 1987 | 1988 | 1989 | 1990 | 1991 | 1992 | 1993 | 1994 | 1995 | 1996 |
|---|---|---|---|---|---|---|---|---|---|---|
| **Services, income, and private transfers** | | | | | | | | | | |
| **Total debt** | **88.0** | **90.6** | **92.2** | **90.5** | **88.0** | **95.4** | **98.2** | **103.6** | **105.4** | **101.8** |
| By maturity | | | | | | | | | | |
| Short-term | 18.9 | 18.3 | 17.3 | 15.4 | 7.8 | 7.4 | 8.4 | 10.2 | 9.9 | 7.1 |
| Long-term | 69.1 | 72.3 | 75.0 | 75.1 | 80.1 | 88.0 | 89.8 | 93.4 | 95.5 | 94.8 |
| By type of creditor | | | | | | | | | | |
| Official | 60.4 | 62.7 | 64.0 | 60.8 | 60.0 | 57.6 | 58.9 | 63.1 | 66.8 | 67.9 |
| Banks | 19.4 | 18.9 | 18.7 | 19.6 | 21.0 | 25.8 | 23.7 | 23.6 | 22.5 | 19.0 |
| Other private | 8.2 | 9.0 | 9.5 | 10.0 | 7.0 | 12.0 | 15.6 | 16.9 | 16.2 | 14.9 |
| **Diversified export base** | | | | | | | | | | |
| **Total debt** | **597.3** | **593.2** | **602.3** | **650.6** | **689.3** | **733.2** | **801.4** | **864.2** | **956.3** | **1,002.6** |
| By maturity | | | | | | | | | | |
| Short-term | 75.9 | 74.5 | 79.5 | 106.7 | 118.4 | 129.6 | 149.1 | 156.4 | 183.3 | 204.3 |
| Long-term | 521.5 | 518.7 | 522.9 | 543.9 | 570.9 | 603.6 | 652.3 | 707.8 | 773.0 | 798.3 |
| By type of creditor | | | | | | | | | | |
| Official | 292.1 | 296.0 | 303.3 | 330.0 | 349.5 | 363.7 | 377.1 | 403.1 | 463.5 | 460.8 |
| Banks | 266.8 | 254.9 | 242.9 | 255.5 | 265.9 | 272.6 | 282.7 | 264.1 | 271.5 | 281.6 |
| Other private | 38.4 | 42.3 | 56.1 | 65.1 | 73.9 | 97.0 | 141.5 | 197.0 | 221.3 | 260.3 |
| **By financial criteria** | | | | | | | | | | |
| **Net creditor countries** | | | | | | | | | | |
| **Total debt** | **30.3** | **28.2** | **27.2** | **25.7** | **30.6** | **38.5** | **42.0** | **46.1** | **48.9** | **51.4** |
| By maturity | | | | | | | | | | |
| Short-term | 24.9 | 22.8 | 21.6 | 20.2 | 23.7 | 24.3 | 27.5 | 30.2 | 33.5 | 38.4 |
| Long-term | 5.3 | 5.3 | 5.6 | 5.5 | 6.9 | 14.2 | 14.5 | 15.9 | 15.4 | 13.0 |
| By type of creditor | | | | | | | | | | |
| Official | 2.3 | 2.1 | 1.1 | 1.1 | 1.1 | 1.0 | 1.0 | 1.0 | 1.1 | 1.1 |
| Banks | 26.3 | 24.0 | 23.8 | 22.5 | 32.1 | 37.0 | 40.2 | 42.8 | 38.6 | 36.0 |
| Other private | 1.7 | 2.1 | 2.3 | 2.1 | −2.5 | 0.5 | 0.8 | 2.3 | 9.3 | 14.3 |
| **Net debtor countries** | | | | | | | | | | |
| **Total debt** | **1,126.3** | **1,138.1** | **1,168.3** | **1,248.1** | **1,328.6** | **1,401.3** | **1,529.2** | **1,658.6** | **1,803.2** | **1,882.9** |
| By maturity | | | | | | | | | | |
| Short-term | 160.5 | 166.4 | 178.6 | 208.5 | 229.0 | 250.3 | 278.9 | 295.8 | 334.1 | 357.9 |
| Long-term | 965.8 | 971.7 | 989.7 | 1,039.6 | 1,099.6 | 1,151.0 | 1,250.3 | 1,362.8 | 1,469.2 | 1,525.1 |
| By type of creditor | | | | | | | | | | |
| Official | 524.8 | 536.9 | 559.4 | 606.2 | 644.8 | 658.9 | 690.2 | 746.7 | 827.3 | 824.2 |
| Banks | 456.0 | 438.7 | 425.5 | 434.8 | 458.1 | 463.8 | 492.2 | 467.0 | 480.3 | 496.2 |
| Other private | 145.4 | 162.5 | 183.4 | 207.1 | 225.7 | 278.5 | 346.8 | 444.9 | 495.6 | 562.5 |
| **Market borrowers** | | | | | | | | | | |
| **Total debt** | **543.6** | **530.8** | **534.5** | **570.0** | **618.7** | **669.0** | **752.9** | **834.8** | **916.0** | **972.3** |
| By maturity | | | | | | | | | | |
| Short-term | 87.2 | 92.6 | 100.5 | 124.3 | 146.4 | 163.9 | 181.3 | 196.2 | 226.8 | 244.5 |
| Long-term | 456.4 | 438.3 | 434.0 | 445.7 | 472.4 | 505.0 | 571.5 | 638.5 | 689.3 | 728.0 |
| By type of creditor | | | | | | | | | | |
| Official | 133.8 | 134.1 | 141.5 | 161.5 | 183.4 | 185.6 | 197.6 | 217.7 | 263.0 | 258.3 |
| Banks | 331.3 | 307.2 | 285.6 | 282.9 | 302.8 | 307.1 | 334.7 | 306.3 | 314.6 | 331.6 |
| Other private | 78.6 | 89.6 | 107.4 | 125.6 | 132.5 | 176.3 | 220.6 | 310.8 | 338.4 | 382.5 |
| **Diversified borrowers** | | | | | | | | | | |
| **Total debt** | **347.4** | **363.4** | **381.7** | **414.9** | **433.7** | **454.5** | **486.6** | **513.2** | **555.7** | **572.8** |
| By maturity | | | | | | | | | | |
| Short-term | 52.7 | 53.9 | 56.0 | 63.8 | 64.7 | 69.8 | 78.1 | 77.4 | 86.8 | 94.3 |
| Long-term | 294.7 | 309.5 | 325.8 | 351.1 | 369.0 | 384.6 | 408.6 | 435.8 | 469.0 | 478.5 |
| By type of creditor | | | | | | | | | | |
| Official | 200.1 | 203.8 | 210.1 | 226.3 | 238.0 | 247.4 | 261.3 | 277.2 | 296.4 | 295.6 |
| Banks | 96.2 | 103.0 | 111.8 | 122.6 | 126.5 | 132.5 | 136.1 | 139.7 | 143.0 | 142.4 |
| Other private | 51.1 | 56.7 | 59.9 | 66.0 | 69.2 | 74.5 | 89.3 | 96.3 | 116.4 | 134.7 |

**Table A40** *(concluded)*

| | 1987 | 1988 | 1989 | 1990 | 1991 | 1992 | 1993 | 1994 | 1995 | 1996 |
|---|---|---|---|---|---|---|---|---|---|---|
| **Official borrowers** | | | | | | | | | | |
| **Total debt** | **235.2** | **243.8** | **252.1** | **263.2** | **276.2** | **277.9** | **289.7** | **310.6** | **331.4** | **337.8** |
| By maturity | | | | | | | | | | |
| Short-term | 20.6 | 19.9 | 22.2 | 20.4 | 17.9 | 16.5 | 19.5 | 22.2 | 20.6 | 19.1 |
| Long-term | 214.7 | 223.9 | 229.9 | 242.8 | 258.3 | 261.4 | 270.2 | 288.4 | 310.9 | 318.7 |
| By type of creditor | | | | | | | | | | |
| Official | 190.9 | 199.1 | 207.8 | 218.3 | 223.4 | 225.9 | 231.3 | 251.7 | 268.0 | 270.3 |
| Banks | 28.6 | 28.5 | 28.1 | 29.3 | 28.8 | 24.2 | 21.5 | 21.1 | 22.7 | 22.2 |
| Other private | 15.7 | 16.2 | 16.2 | 15.6 | 24.0 | 27.8 | 36.8 | 37.8 | 40.8 | 45.3 |
| **Countries with recent debt-servicing difficulties** | | | | | | | | | | |
| **Total debt** | **716.0** | **717.2** | **732.6** | **770.0** | **796.3** | **818.6** | **857.9** | **924.2** | **981.6** | **1,013.1** |
| By maturity | | | | | | | | | | |
| Short-term | 101.0 | 100.6 | 104.7 | 118.0 | 121.2 | 123.9 | 122.9 | 139.2 | 144.0 | 147.6 |
| Long-term | 615.0 | 616.6 | 627.9 | 652.1 | 675.1 | 694.7 | 735.0 | 785.0 | 837.6 | 865.6 |
| By type of creditor | | | | | | | | | | |
| Official | 297.3 | 308.4 | 327.3 | 360.5 | 378.0 | 382.8 | 394.5 | 420.0 | 481.0 | 478.6 |
| Banks | 329.9 | 303.6 | 284.3 | 278.2 | 278.2 | 268.0 | 262.8 | 224.9 | 222.3 | 222.8 |
| Other private | 88.8 | 105.2 | 121.1 | 131.4 | 140.1 | 167.8 | 200.6 | 279.3 | 278.2 | 311.8 |
| **Countries without debt-servicing difficulties** | | | | | | | | | | |
| **Total debt** | **410.2** | **420.9** | **435.7** | **478.0** | **532.3** | **582.7** | **671.3** | **734.4** | **821.6** | **869.8** |
| By maturity | | | | | | | | | | |
| Short-term | 59.5 | 65.8 | 73.9 | 90.5 | 107.8 | 126.4 | 156.0 | 156.6 | 190.1 | 210.3 |
| Long-term | 350.8 | 355.1 | 361.8 | 387.5 | 424.5 | 456.3 | 515.3 | 577.8 | 631.6 | 659.5 |
| By type of creditor | | | | | | | | | | |
| Official | 227.5 | 228.5 | 232.1 | 245.7 | 266.8 | 276.2 | 295.7 | 326.6 | 346.3 | 345.6 |
| Banks | 126.2 | 135.0 | 141.2 | 156.6 | 179.9 | 195.8 | 229.4 | 242.1 | 258.0 | 273.4 |
| Other private | 56.6 | 57.3 | 62.4 | 75.7 | 85.6 | 110.7 | 146.2 | 165.6 | 217.4 | 250.7 |
| **Other groups** | | | | | | | | | | |
| **Small low-income economies** | | | | | | | | | | |
| **Total debt** | **216.3** | **222.8** | **232.0** | **242.1** | **255.4** | **254.7** | **268.6** | **287.7** | **308.3** | **315.7** |
| By maturity | | | | | | | | | | |
| Short-term | 17.4 | 18.1 | 20.5 | 18.1 | 16.1 | 14.3 | 16.2 | 18.2 | 16.5 | 15.2 |
| Long-term | 198.9 | 204.7 | 211.6 | 224.1 | 239.3 | 240.4 | 252.5 | 269.5 | 291.8 | 300.5 |
| By type of creditor | | | | | | | | | | |
| Official | 169.3 | 176.7 | 186.0 | 194.6 | 203.1 | 203.8 | 211.7 | 230.0 | 246.0 | 248.1 |
| Banks | 25.3 | 25.7 | 26.1 | 28.8 | 28.5 | 24.8 | 22.8 | 19.6 | 21.1 | 21.4 |
| Other private | 21.6 | 20.4 | 19.9 | 18.7 | 23.9 | 26.1 | 34.1 | 38.1 | 41.3 | 46.2 |
| **Least developed countries** | | | | | | | | | | |
| **Total debt** | **88.0** | **91.9** | **96.3** | **107.2** | **116.7** | **117.9** | **125.8** | **136.6** | **145.8** | **151.1** |
| By maturity | | | | | | | | | | |
| Short-term | 6.5 | 5.5 | 6.6 | 6.8 | 7.5 | 8.1 | 8.9 | 9.6 | 8.9 | 10.7 |
| Long-term | 81.5 | 86.3 | 89.7 | 100.4 | 109.2 | 109.9 | 116.9 | 127.1 | 136.8 | 140.4 |
| By type of creditor | | | | | | | | | | |
| Official | 75.8 | 78.5 | 82.3 | 93.2 | 100.0 | 99.2 | 104.8 | 115.5 | 124.3 | 127.1 |
| Banks | 6.8 | 6.7 | 7.0 | 7.5 | 7.3 | 7.2 | 7.3 | 6.8 | 7.2 | 7.2 |
| Other private | 5.4 | 6.6 | 7.0 | 6.5 | 9.4 | 11.6 | 13.8 | 14.3 | 14.3 | 16.8 |

## Table A41. Developing Countries: Ratio of External Debt to GDP[1]

| | 1987 | 1988 | 1989 | 1990 | 1991 | 1992 | 1993 | 1994 | 1995 | 1996 |
|---|---|---|---|---|---|---|---|---|---|---|
| **Developing countries** | **40.6** | **37.2** | **35.2** | **34.3** | **34.7** | **33.4** | **33.1** | **33.0** | **31.2** | **29.6** |
| **By region** | | | | | | | | | | |
| Africa | 62.9 | 60.0 | 62.8 | 59.4 | 63.5 | 60.8 | 63.6 | 66.9 | 62.9 | 65.7 |
| Asia | 26.9 | 23.9 | 21.8 | 22.6 | 23.8 | 23.5 | 23.7 | 25.0 | 23.8 | 22.0 |
| Middle East and Europe | 37.1 | 38.7 | 41.4 | 37.6 | 38.2 | 36.4 | 37.6 | 36.3 | 32.7 | 29.7 |
| Western Hemisphere | 54.7 | 48.6 | 43.4 | 41.2 | 40.1 | 38.4 | 36.8 | 34.9 | 34.3 | 34.3 |
| Sub-Saharan Africa | 86.4 | 79.5 | 84.2 | 86.6 | 94.1 | 94.0 | 94.5 | 111.7 | 101.1 | 95.2 |
| Four newly industrializing | | | | | | | | | | |
| Asian economies | 18.2 | 12.8 | 10.1 | 9.2 | 10.1 | 9.8 | 11.3 | 11.9 | 12.9 | 13.2 |
| **By predominant export** | | | | | | | | | | |
| Fuel | 33.6 | 35.8 | 37.4 | 35.7 | 38.0 | 35.2 | 36.9 | 32.6 | 27.8 | 26.2 |
| Nonfuel exports | 41.9 | 37.4 | 34.9 | 34.1 | 34.2 | 33.1 | 32.6 | 33.1 | 31.8 | 30.1 |
| Manufactures | 19.1 | 15.5 | 13.3 | 13.8 | 14.5 | 14.1 | 14.9 | 17.0 | 15.7 | 14.6 |
| Primary products | 56.8 | 59.6 | 71.3 | 59.4 | 51.6 | 45.1 | 41.3 | 42.0 | 39.3 | 37.3 |
| Agricultural products | 48.4 | 52.1 | 70.4 | 53.3 | 46.1 | 38.7 | 34.6 | 34.8 | 33.2 | 31.6 |
| Minerals | 86.2 | 82.9 | 73.3 | 76.2 | 68.2 | 66.6 | 65.4 | 68.9 | 61.3 | 57.8 |
| Services, income, and | | | | | | | | | | |
| private transfers | 59.1 | 54.3 | 82.3 | 78.8 | 77.8 | 73.9 | 68.7 | 64.9 | 59.9 | 52.2 |
| Diversified export base | 47.5 | 43.1 | 37.7 | 37.0 | 38.9 | 39.2 | 39.5 | 38.3 | 38.7 | 38.0 |
| **By financial criteria** | | | | | | | | | | |
| Net creditor countries | 11.8 | 10.1 | 8.4 | 7.0 | 7.8 | 8.7 | 9.3 | 9.6 | 9.5 | 9.5 |
| Net debtor countries | 43.4 | 39.9 | 38.0 | 37.3 | 37.7 | 36.2 | 35.6 | 35.4 | 33.3 | 31.4 |
| Market borrowers | 37.3 | 31.3 | 27.9 | 27.8 | 28.1 | 27.4 | 27.8 | 28.5 | 27.3 | 26.3 |
| Diversified borrowers | 46.6 | 47.4 | 46.0 | 44.4 | 47.0 | 46.1 | 44.4 | 42.3 | 39.2 | 35.8 |
| Official borrowers | 60.6 | 62.4 | 76.8 | 72.2 | 69.8 | 63.2 | 59.5 | 57.7 | 51.9 | 48.9 |
| Countries with recent debt- | | | | | | | | | | |
| servicing difficulties | 58.4 | 55.4 | 54.0 | 51.1 | 50.0 | 46.4 | 42.8 | 39.6 | 37.4 | 35.9 |
| Countries without debt- | | | | | | | | | | |
| servicing difficulties | 30.0 | 27.0 | 25.4 | 26.0 | 27.6 | 27.7 | 29.3 | 31.3 | 29.4 | 27.4 |
| **Other groups** | | | | | | | | | | |
| Small low-income economies | 62.0 | 64.7 | 82.7 | 78.4 | 76.6 | 68.3 | 64.5 | 62.1 | 55.0 | 52.3 |
| Least developed countries | 79.4 | 73.0 | 69.9 | 68.1 | 66.8 | 56.7 | 50.8 | 49.3 | 42.8 | 36.8 |

[1]Debt at year-end in percent of GDP in year indicated.

## Table A42. Developing Countries: Debt-Service Ratios[1]

*(In percent of exports of goods and services)*

| | 1987 | 1988 | 1989 | 1990 | 1991 | 1992 | 1993 | 1994 | 1995 | 1996 |
|---|---|---|---|---|---|---|---|---|---|---|
| **Interest payments[2]** | | | | | | | | | | |
| **Developing countries** | **9.1** | **8.7** | **7.3** | **6.5** | **7.3** | **6.1** | **5.9** | **5.6** | **6.2** | **5.8** |
| **By region** | | | | | | | | | | |
| Africa | 16.6 | 12.3 | 13.2 | 12.0 | 13.0 | 11.9 | 11.8 | 11.3 | 10.3 | 13.8 |
| Asia | 5.4 | 4.8 | 4.5 | 4.2 | 3.8 | 3.7 | 3.4 | 3.2 | 3.1 | 2.9 |
| Middle East and Europe | 3.7 | 4.4 | 4.1 | 4.5 | 5.8 | 4.6 | 4.9 | 5.3 | 5.8 | 5.3 |
| Western Hemisphere | 21.3 | 23.7 | 16.2 | 13.5 | 18.7 | 14.3 | 14.5 | 13.7 | 18.2 | 16.2 |
| Sub-Saharan Africa | 10.8 | 11.6 | 11.3 | 9.9 | 11.0 | 10.6 | 11.8 | 11.1 | 11.1 | 11.8 |
| Four newly industrializing Asian economies | 2.4 | 1.7 | 1.7 | 1.5 | 1.3 | 1.1 | 1.0 | 1.0 | 0.9 | 0.8 |
| **By predominant export** | | | | | | | | | | |
| Fuel | 7.2 | 4.8 | 4.8 | 3.7 | 4.6 | 4.5 | 4.4 | 4.3 | 4.8 | 6.8 |
| Nonfuel exports | 9.5 | 9.4 | 7.7 | 7.2 | 7.9 | 6.4 | 6.2 | 5.8 | 6.4 | 5.7 |
| Manufactures | 2.4 | 2.7 | 2.5 | 2.3 | 2.4 | 2.5 | 2.4 | 2.4 | 2.4 | 2.2 |
| Primary products | 18.9 | 16.0 | 12.4 | 12.8 | 22.5 | 11.6 | 9.4 | 10.1 | 8.0 | 7.9 |
| Agricultural products | 20.9 | 17.0 | 12.1 | 13.3 | 12.8 | 10.3 | 7.9 | 9.2 | 6.2 | 6.0 |
| Minerals | 15.7 | 14.5 | 12.8 | 12.0 | 37.1 | 13.5 | 12.0 | 11.6 | 11.0 | 11.2 |
| Services, income, and private transfers | 12.0 | 6.8 | 7.9 | 13.5 | 16.2 | 9.0 | 8.6 | 8.5 | 7.8 | 6.6 |
| Diversified export base | 16.0 | 17.6 | 13.7 | 11.6 | 11.9 | 10.8 | 10.9 | 9.6 | 11.9 | 10.6 |
| **By financial criteria** | | | | | | | | | | |
| Net creditor countries | 2.0 | 1.9 | 2.1 | 1.7 | 1.3 | 1.2 | 1.2 | 1.5 | 1.2 | 1.0 |
| Net debtor countries | 10.7 | 10.1 | 8.4 | 7.6 | 8.6 | 7.1 | 6.9 | 6.3 | 7.0 | 6.5 |
| Market borrowers | 9.8 | 10.2 | 7.6 | 6.3 | 7.3 | 6.1 | 6.0 | 5.2 | 6.0 | 5.6 |
| Diversified borrowers | 9.4 | 9.8 | 9.2 | 9.1 | 11.7 | 10.4 | 9.8 | 9.6 | 12.1 | 10.6 |
| Official borrowers | 19.2 | 10.4 | 12.3 | 13.5 | 12.8 | 9.0 | 8.3 | 8.8 | 5.5 | 6.9 |
| Countries with recent debt-servicing difficulties | 19.6 | 18.6 | 14.4 | 13.4 | 18.3 | 14.2 | 14.2 | 13.7 | 15.4 | 14.8 |
| Countries without debt-servicing difficulties | 5.7 | 5.8 | 5.3 | 4.8 | 4.7 | 4.5 | 4.2 | 3.8 | 4.2 | 3.9 |
| **Other groups** | | | | | | | | | | |
| Small low-income economies | 21.9 | 11.0 | 13.8 | 15.5 | 14.3 | 9.5 | 8.5 | 9.5 | 4.3 | 6.1 |
| Least developed countries | 9.9 | 9.9 | 9.8 | 8.0 | 9.2 | 8.6 | 10.2 | 9.3 | 10.3 | 9.2 |

**Table A42** *(concluded)*

|  | 1987 | 1988 | 1989 | 1990 | 1991 | 1992 | 1993 | 1994 | 1995 | 1996 |
|---|---|---|---|---|---|---|---|---|---|---|
| **Amortization[2]** | | | | | | | | | | |
| **Developing countries** | **10.3** | **9.1** | **8.2** | **8.2** | **9.1** | **9.2** | **9.3** | **9.4** | **8.2** | **6.5** |
| **By region** | | | | | | | | | | |
| Africa | 14.5 | 14.7 | 15.7 | 15.8 | 16.4 | 22.2 | 18.4 | 17.6 | 20.7 | 15.7 |
| Asia | 8.4 | 6.0 | 5.9 | 5.1 | 4.5 | 4.5 | 5.0 | 4.3 | 4.3 | 4.3 |
| Middle East and Europe | 6.0 | 6.8 | 5.9 | 6.8 | 6.8 | 4.8 | 5.0 | 10.8 | 8.4 | 6.5 |
| Western Hemisphere | 18.3 | 18.4 | 13.9 | 15.4 | 24.7 | 26.0 | 26.9 | 25.7 | 19.7 | 12.9 |
| Sub-Saharan Africa | 15.2 | 15.3 | 14.8 | 11.7 | 12.1 | 13.2 | 13.5 | 15.5 | 30.3 | 11.8 |
| Four newly industrializing Asian economies | 6.3 | 3.2 | 2.7 | 2.4 | 2.1 | 2.2 | 2.4 | 1.5 | 1.5 | 1.6 |
| **By predominant export** | | | | | | | | | | |
| Fuel | 8.3 | 8.9 | 7.9 | 8.1 | 8.7 | 10.7 | 10.0 | 13.8 | 10.1 | 8.2 |
| Nonfuel exports | 10.8 | 9.2 | 8.3 | 8.3 | 9.2 | 8.9 | 9.2 | 8.8 | 8.0 | 6.4 |
| Manufactures | 6.3 | 3.5 | 3.8 | 3.0 | 2.5 | 2.6 | 3.0 | 2.4 | 2.4 | 2.4 |
| Primary products | 11.8 | 17.8 | 17.4 | 17.6 | 26.6 | 17.3 | 18.4 | 18.0 | 21.6 | 13.4 |
| Agricultural products | 14.8 | 25.4 | 24.9 | 23.9 | 19.6 | 21.2 | 20.4 | 21.4 | 28.3 | 15.6 |
| Minerals | 7.0 | 7.0 | 7.5 | 8.1 | 37.0 | 11.2 | 14.9 | 12.1 | 10.2 | 9.5 |
| Services, income, and private transfers | 11.0 | 9.0 | 6.1 | 14.4 | 17.2 | 7.9 | 6.1 | 5.0 | 3.8 | 3.4 |
| Diversified export base | 16.3 | 15.2 | 12.7 | 12.4 | 14.5 | 16.7 | 17.0 | 17.3 | 14.7 | 11.7 |
| **By financial criteria** | | | | | | | | | | |
| Net creditor countries | 1.9 | 1.4 | 0.8 | 0.7 | 0.4 | 0.4 | 0.4 | 1.6 | 1.2 | 0.8 |
| Net debtor countries | 12.3 | 10.8 | 9.8 | 9.9 | 11.0 | 11.1 | 11.0 | 10.7 | 9.4 | 7.4 |
| Market borrowers | 11.3 | 9.4 | 8.2 | 8.0 | 10.0 | 9.4 | 10.0 | 9.0 | 6.7 | 5.5 |
| Diversified borrowers | 13.1 | 14.8 | 13.6 | 13.5 | 12.5 | 13.9 | 13.8 | 15.4 | 19.2 | 13.9 |
| Official borrowers | 16.0 | 11.5 | 12.4 | 15.6 | 15.8 | 18.8 | 14.0 | 15.8 | 13.6 | 12.6 |
| Countries with recent debt-servicing difficulties | 15.1 | 14.7 | 12.1 | 14.5 | 20.0 | 22.2 | 21.9 | 21.8 | 19.2 | 13.3 |
| Countries without debt-servicing difficulties | 10.7 | 8.8 | 8.7 | 7.7 | 7.3 | 6.8 | 7.1 | 7.0 | 6.1 | 5.6 |
| **Other groups** | | | | | | | | | | |
| Small low-income economies | 17.6 | 13.0 | 14.8 | 17.9 | 17.7 | 21.6 | 14.4 | 17.5 | 21.0 | 12.9 |
| Least developed countries | 12.9 | 11.5 | 14.3 | 12.7 | 14.1 | 14.9 | 14.6 | 14.7 | 18.4 | 10.9 |

[1]Excludes service payments to the IMF.

[2]Interest payments on total debt and amortization on long-term debt. Estimates through 1994 reflect debt-service payments actually made. The estimates for 1995 and 1996 take into account projected exceptional financing items, including accumulation of arrears and rescheduling agreements. In some cases, amortization on account of debt-reduction operations is included.

## Table A43. IMF Charges and Repurchases to the IMF[1]

*(In percent of exports of goods and services)*

| | 1987 | 1988 | 1989 | 1990 | 1991 | 1992 | 1993 | 1994 |
|---|---|---|---|---|---|---|---|---|
| **Developing countries** | **1.7** | **1.2** | **1.0** | **1.0** | **0.8** | **0.6** | **0.6** | **0.4** |
| **By region** | | | | | | | | |
| Africa | 3.0 | 2.1 | 2.2 | 1.7 | 1.3 | 1.2 | 1.2 | 0.9 |
| Asia | 1.2 | 0.8 | 0.5 | 0.5 | 0.4 | 0.2 | 0.1 | 0.2 |
| Middle East and Europe | 0.4 | 0.4 | 0.2 | 0.1 | 0.1 | — | — | — |
| Western Hemisphere | 3.7 | 3.1 | 2.9 | 3.2 | 3.0 | 2.7 | 2.6 | 1.5 |
| Sub-Saharan Africa | 4.6 | 4.5 | 4.8 | 3.4 | 2.6 | 2.2 | 1.7 | 1.2 |
| **By predominant export** | | | | | | | | |
| Fuel | — | — | 0.1 | 0.1 | 0.3 | 0.5 | 0.6 | 0.4 |
| Nonfuel exports | 2.0 | 1.4 | 1.2 | 1.2 | 0.9 | 0.7 | 0.6 | 0.4 |
| **By financial criteria** | | | | | | | | |
| Net creditor countries | — | — | — | — | — | — | — | — |
| Net debtor countries | 2.0 | 1.5 | 1.2 | 1.2 | 1.0 | 0.8 | 0.7 | 0.5 |
| Market borrowers | 1.4 | 1.0 | 0.9 | 1.0 | 0.8 | 0.7 | 0.7 | 0.4 |
| Official borrowers | 4.1 | 3.2 | 3.0 | 2.6 | 1.9 | 1.4 | 1.2 | 0.7 |
| Countries with recent debt-servicing difficulties | 3.4 | 2.6 | 2.5 | 2.6 | 2.5 | 2.2 | 2.1 | 1.4 |
| Countries without debt-servicing difficulties | 1.3 | 0.9 | 0.6 | 0.5 | 0.4 | 0.2 | 0.2 | 0.2 |
| **Other groups** | | | | | | | | |
| Small low-income economies | 4.5 | 3.8 | 3.5 | 2.7 | 1.9 | 1.5 | 1.2 | 0.8 |
| Least developed countries | 4.9 | 3.5 | 4.9 | 4.0 | 2.9 | 1.8 | 1.4 | 1.0 |
| **Countries in transition** | **0.7** | **0.7** | **0.5** | **0.4** | **0.3** | **0.6** | **0.4** | **1.1** |
| Central and eastern Europe | ... | ... | ... | ... | 0.6 | 1.1 | 0.7 | 2.0 |
| Excluding Belarus and Ukraine | ... | ... | ... | ... | 0.7 | 1.3 | 0.8 | 2.3 |
| Russia | ... | ... | ... | ... | — | — | — | — |
| Transcaucasus and central Asia | ... | ... | ... | ... | — | — | — | 0.1 |
| *Memorandum* | | | | | | | | |
| **Total, in billions of U.S. dollars** | | | | | | | | |
| General Resources Account | 12.580 | 10.890 | 10.000 | 10.538 | 9.010 | 8.348 | 7.593 | 8.173 |
| Charges | 2.673 | 2.428 | 2.422 | 2.596 | 2.525 | 2.427 | 2.341 | 1.804 |
| Repurchases | 9.907 | 8.462 | 7.578 | 7.941 | 6.485 | 5.921 | 5.330 | 6.544 |
| Trust Fund | 0.708 | 0.673 | 0.513 | 0.367 | 0.070 | — | 0.063 | 0.015 |
| Interest | 0.005 | 0.004 | 0.004 | 0.002 | 0.001 | — | 0.003 | — |
| Repayments | 0.703 | 0.669 | 0.509 | 0.365 | 0.069 | — | 0.060 | 0.014 |
| SAF | 0.001 | 0.003 | 0.006 | 0.010 | 0.014 | 0.045 | 0.138 | 0.314 |
| Interest | 0.001 | 0.003 | 0.006 | 0.010 | 0.014 | 0.012 | 0.012 | 0.010 |
| Repayments | — | — | — | — | — | 0.033 | 0.126 | 0.304 |
| ESAF | — | — | 0.001 | 0.003 | 0.007 | 0.010 | 0.013 | 0.016 |
| Interest | — | — | 0.001 | 0.003 | 0.007 | 0.010 | 0.013 | 0.014 |
| Repayments | — | — | — | — | — | — | — | 0.002 |

[1]Excludes industrial countries. Charges on, and repurchases (or repayments of principal) for, use of IMF credit.

## Table A44. Summary of Sources and Uses of World Saving

*(In percent of GDP)*

| | Averages 1973–80 | Averages 1981–87 | 1988 | 1989 | 1990 | 1991 | 1992 | 1993 | 1994 | 1995 | 1996 |
|---|---|---|---|---|---|---|---|---|---|---|---|
| **World** | | | | | | | | | | | |
| Saving | 24.9 | 22.4 | 23.5 | 23.8 | 23.5 | 22.6 | 21.9 | 21.9 | 23.1 | 23.6 | 23.7 |
| Investment | 24.8 | 23.3 | 24.1 | 24.5 | 23.8 | 23.5 | 23.1 | 23.0 | 23.7 | 24.4 | 24.8 |
| **Industrial countries** | | | | | | | | | | | |
| Saving | 23.5 | 20.9 | 21.4 | 21.6 | 20.9 | 20.6 | 19.6 | 19.3 | 19.9 | 20.0 | 20.3 |
| Private | 21.6 | 20.7 | 19.9 | 19.4 | 19.3 | 19.9 | 20.1 | 20.1 | 20.1 | 19.8 | 19.8 |
| Public | 1.8 | 0.2 | 1.5 | 2.2 | 1.6 | 0.7 | −0.4 | −0.8 | −0.1 | 0.2 | 0.5 |
| Investment | 23.3 | 21.2 | 21.7 | 22.2 | 21.6 | 20.7 | 20.0 | 19.4 | 20.0 | 20.4 | 20.6 |
| Private | 18.8 | 17.5 | 18.2 | 18.6 | 17.9 | 17.2 | 16.4 | 15.6 | 16.4 | 16.8 | 17.0 |
| Public | 4.5 | 3.8 | 3.4 | 3.6 | 3.6 | 3.5 | 3.6 | 3.7 | 3.6 | 3.6 | 3.6 |
| Net lending | 0.2 | −0.4 | −0.3 | −0.5 | −0.7 | −0.1 | −0.4 | — | — | −0.4 | −0.3 |
| Private | 2.8 | 3.3 | 1.7 | 0.8 | 1.4 | 2.7 | 3.7 | 4.5 | 3.7 | 3.0 | 2.8 |
| Public | −2.6 | −3.6 | −1.9 | −1.3 | −2.0 | −2.8 | −4.1 | −4.5 | −3.7 | −3.4 | −3.1 |
| Current transfers | −0.4 | −0.4 | −0.4 | −0.4 | −0.4 | −0.2 | −0.4 | −0.4 | −0.4 | −0.4 | −0.4 |
| Factor income | 0.7 | 0.2 | 0.5 | 0.3 | 0.2 | 0.1 | — | — | 0.2 | −0.2 | −0.3 |
| Resource balance | −0.1 | −0.2 | −0.4 | −0.4 | −0.4 | −0.1 | 0.1 | 0.3 | 0.2 | 0.3 | 0.4 |
| **United States** | | | | | | | | | | | |
| Saving | 20.3 | 17.6 | 16.5 | 16.4 | 15.3 | 15.4 | 14.2 | 14.6 | 15.7 | 15.6 | 15.9 |
| Private | 18.6 | 18.4 | 16.4 | 15.6 | 15.5 | 16.4 | 16.3 | 15.8 | 15.6 | 15.4 | 15.9 |
| Public | 1.6 | −0.7 | 0.1 | 0.8 | −0.3 | −1.0 | −2.1 | −1.2 | 0.1 | 0.2 | 0.1 |
| Investment | 20.0 | 19.4 | 18.3 | 18.1 | 16.8 | 15.3 | 15.3 | 16.1 | 17.4 | 18.0 | 18.1 |
| Private | 17.4 | 17.2 | 16.2 | 15.8 | 14.6 | 13.0 | 13.1 | 13.9 | 15.3 | 16.0 | 16.1 |
| Public | 2.6 | 2.2 | 2.1 | 2.2 | 2.2 | 2.3 | 2.2 | 2.2 | 2.0 | 2.0 | 2.0 |
| Net lending | 0.3 | −1.8 | −1.8 | −1.7 | −1.6 | 0.1 | −1.1 | −1.5 | −1.7 | −2.4 | −2.1 |
| Private | 1.2 | 1.2 | 0.2 | −0.2 | 0.9 | 3.4 | 3.2 | 1.9 | 0.3 | −0.5 | −0.2 |
| Public | −1.0 | −2.9 | −2.0 | −1.5 | −2.5 | −3.2 | −4.3 | −3.4 | −2.0 | −1.9 | −2.0 |
| Current transfers | −0.3 | −0.5 | −0.5 | −0.5 | −0.6 | 0.1 | −0.5 | −0.5 | −0.5 | −0.5 | −0.5 |
| Factor income | 1.1 | 1.0 | 1.0 | 0.5 | 0.5 | 0.5 | 0.1 | 0.2 | 0.4 | −0.3 | −0.4 |
| Resource balance | −0.6 | −2.2 | −2.4 | −1.7 | −1.4 | −0.5 | −0.7 | −1.2 | −1.6 | −1.6 | −1.2 |
| **European Union** | | | | | | | | | | | |
| Saving | 23.4 | 20.2 | 21.5 | 22.0 | 21.5 | 20.1 | 19.1 | 18.6 | 19.5 | 20.1 | 20.6 |
| Private | 22.2 | 20.8 | 21.1 | 21.0 | 21.4 | 21.1 | 21.1 | 21.2 | 21.4 | 22.0 | 21.7 | 21.4 |
| Public | 1.2 | −0.6 | 0.4 | 1.0 | 0.1 | −1.0 | −2.1 | −2.9 | −2.5 | −1.6 | −0.7 |
| Investment | 23.2 | 20.0 | 21.2 | 22.0 | 21.8 | 21.2 | 20.2 | 18.4 | 19.0 | 19.4 | 19.8 |
| Private | 18.2 | 16.2 | 17.7 | 18.3 | 18.0 | 18.0 | 16.8 | 15.1 | 15.9 | 16.3 | 16.8 |
| Public | 5.0 | 3.8 | 3.5 | 3.7 | 3.7 | 3.2 | 3.3 | 3.3 | 3.0 | 3.1 | 3.1 |
| Net lending | 0.2 | 0.2 | 0.3 | — | −0.3 | −1.1 | −1.1 | 0.2 | 0.6 | 0.7 | 0.8 |
| Private | 4.1 | 4.6 | 3.3 | 2.7 | 3.3 | 3.1 | 4.4 | 6.4 | 6.0 | 5.4 | 4.6 |
| Public | −3.8 | −4.4 | −3.1 | −2.7 | −3.7 | −4.3 | −5.4 | −6.2 | −5.5 | −4.7 | −3.8 |
| Current transfers | −0.8 | −0.3 | −0.4 | −0.5 | −0.4 | −0.5 | −0.5 | −0.4 | −0.5 | −0.5 | −0.6 |
| Factor income | 0.6 | — | 0.2 | 0.4 | 0.2 | −0.1 | −0.2 | −0.2 | — | −0.1 | — |
| Resource balance | 0.4 | 0.5 | 0.4 | 0.1 | −0.1 | −0.5 | −0.4 | 0.8 | 1.0 | 1.3 | 1.4 |
| **Japan** | | | | | | | | | | | |
| Saving | 33.2 | 31.2 | 33.3 | 33.7 | 33.9 | 34.6 | 34.3 | 33.1 | 31.7 | 31.0 | 30.8 |
| Private | 29.1 | 26.7 | 25.5 | 24.1 | 23.5 | 24.9 | 25.6 | 26.9 | 26.0 | 25.8 | 26.1 |
| Public | 4.1 | 4.5 | 7.9 | 9.6 | 10.4 | 9.7 | 8.6 | 6.2 | 5.7 | 5.2 | 4.7 |
| Investment | 33.3 | 28.8 | 30.6 | 31.8 | 32.8 | 32.5 | 31.1 | 29.9 | 28.8 | 28.8 | 28.8 |
| Private | 23.9 | 21.0 | 24.0 | 25.3 | 26.1 | 25.8 | 23.5 | 21.3 | 19.8 | 19.9 | 19.7 |
| Public | 9.4 | 7.8 | 6.6 | 6.5 | 6.6 | 6.7 | 7.6 | 8.6 | 9.0 | 8.9 | 9.2 |
| Net lending | −0.1 | 2.4 | 2.7 | 1.9 | 1.1 | 2.1 | 3.2 | 3.1 | 2.8 | 2.2 | 2.0 |
| Private | 5.2 | 5.7 | 1.5 | −1.2 | −2.6 | −0.9 | 2.2 | 5.6 | 6.2 | 6.0 | 6.4 |
| Public | −5.3 | −3.3 | 1.2 | 3.1 | 3.8 | 3.1 | 1.0 | −2.5 | −3.3 | −3.8 | −4.4 |
| Current transfers | −0.1 | −0.1 | −0.1 | −0.1 | −0.2 | −0.4 | −0.1 | −0.1 | −0.2 | −0.2 | −0.2 |
| Factor income | −0.2 | 0.3 | 0.7 | 0.7 | 0.7 | 0.7 | 1.0 | 1.0 | 0.9 | 0.8 | 0.9 |
| Resource balance | 0.1 | 2.2 | 2.2 | 1.3 | 0.6 | 1.8 | 2.4 | 2.3 | 2.1 | 1.6 | 1.3 |

159

## Table A44  (continued)

| | Averages | | 1988 | 1989 | 1990 | 1991 | 1992 | 1993 | 1994 | 1995 | 1996 |
|---|---|---|---|---|---|---|---|---|---|---|---|
| | 1973–80 | 1981–87 | | | | | | | | | |
| **Developing countries** | | | | | | | | | | | |
| Saving | 25.7 | 22.6 | 25.0 | 25.7 | 26.3 | 24.2 | 24.6 | 25.2 | 27.6 | 28.6 | 28.3 |
| Investment | 25.6 | 24.6 | 26.3 | 26.8 | 26.1 | 26.1 | 26.6 | 27.9 | 28.9 | 29.8 | 30.1 |
| Net lending | 0.1 | −2.0 | −1.4 | −1.1 | 0.2 | −1.9 | −2.0 | −2.7 | −1.3 | −1.1 | −1.7 |
| Current transfers | 0.9 | 1.0 | 1.0 | 1.3 | 1.3 | 0.9 | 1.5 | 1.3 | 1.2 | 1.2 | 1.1 |
| Factor income | −1.5 | −1.8 | −2.1 | −1.9 | −1.1 | −1.7 | −1.9 | −1.6 | −1.4 | −1.4 | −1.6 |
| Resource balance | 0.7 | −1.2 | −0.2 | −0.5 | 0.1 | −1.2 | −1.6 | −2.5 | −1.1 | −0.9 | −1.3 |
| *Memorandum* | | | | | | | | | | | |
| Acquisition of foreign assets | 3.6 | 0.5 | 0.6 | 0.9 | 2.5 | 1.2 | 1.5 | 1.7 | 2.5 | 2.0 | 1.3 |
| Change in reserves | 2.0 | 0.1 | 0.1 | 0.7 | 1.8 | 2.3 | 1.3 | 1.4 | 2.1 | 1.3 | 0.6 |
| **By region** | | | | | | | | | | | |
| **Africa** | | | | | | | | | | | |
| Saving | 26.5 | 20.1 | 17.3 | 17.9 | 18.1 | 18.4 | 16.1 | 15.3 | 17.3 | 18.7 | 19.2 |
| Investment | 31.8 | 24.4 | 21.0 | 21.5 | 19.5 | 21.3 | 20.9 | 19.6 | 21.7 | 23.5 | 24.5 |
| Net lending | −5.2 | −4.3 | −3.7 | −3.6 | −1.4 | −3.0 | −4.8 | −4.3 | −4.4 | −4.8 | −5.4 |
| Current transfers | 2.0 | 2.6 | 4.1 | 4.7 | 4.9 | 4.8 | 4.8 | 4.9 | 4.9 | 4.6 | 4.6 |
| Factor income | −4.5 | −3.5 | −4.4 | −4.8 | −4.3 | −5.5 | −5.9 | −4.9 | −3.9 | −3.6 | −5.9 |
| Resource balance | −2.7 | −3.4 | −3.4 | −3.4 | −2.0 | −2.2 | −3.8 | −4.4 | −5.4 | −5.8 | −4.0 |
| *Memorandum* | | | | | | | | | | | |
| Acquisition of foreign assets | 1.9 | −0.3 | −0.7 | 0.6 | 1.5 | 0.5 | −1.6 | 0.4 | 1.5 | 0.2 | 0.9 |
| Change in reserves | 1.0 | −0.4 | — | 0.8 | 1.5 | 1.8 | −1.7 | 0.4 | 1.6 | 0.5 | 1.0 |
| **Asia** | | | | | | | | | | | |
| Saving | 24.9 | 26.6 | 30.4 | 30.5 | 30.1 | 30.0 | 29.9 | 31.2 | 34.0 | 35.2 | 34.0 |
| Investment | 25.9 | 27.6 | 30.8 | 31.5 | 30.6 | 30.3 | 30.5 | 32.9 | 34.5 | 35.6 | 35.1 |
| Net lending | −0.9 | −1.1 | −0.4 | −1.0 | −0.5 | −0.2 | −0.6 | −1.7 | −0.4 | −0.4 | −1.1 |
| Current transfers | 1.1 | 0.8 | 0.6 | 0.5 | 0.5 | 0.9 | 0.9 | 0.8 | 0.9 | 0.8 | 0.7 |
| Factor income | −0.7 | −0.4 | −0.6 | −0.7 | −0.8 | −0.9 | −0.8 | −0.5 | −0.6 | −0.3 | −0.4 |
| Resource balance | −1.3 | −1.5 | −0.4 | −0.8 | −0.2 | −0.2 | −0.7 | −2.0 | −0.7 | −0.8 | −1.4 |
| *Memorandum* | | | | | | | | | | | |
| Acquisition of foreign assets | 1.4 | 1.3 | 1.5 | 1.1 | 2.4 | 3.5 | 2.2 | 2.8 | 4.5 | 3.0 | 2.0 |
| Change in reserves | 1.3 | 1.1 | 0.7 | 0.7 | 1.8 | 2.6 | 1.2 | 1.9 | 3.5 | 1.8 | 1.1 |
| **Middle East and Europe** | | | | | | | | | | | |
| Saving | 35.9 | 19.2 | 18.5 | 20.8 | 23.0 | 15.0 | 20.2 | 19.3 | 21.1 | 20.6 | 21.0 |
| Investment | 24.7 | 23.4 | 21.5 | 21.5 | 23.1 | 24.4 | 24.9 | 24.5 | 20.8 | 21.2 | 21.8 |
| Net lending | 11.2 | −4.2 | −3.0 | −0.7 | −0.1 | −9.4 | −4.6 | −5.2 | 0.4 | −0.6 | −0.8 |
| Current transfers | 1.0 | 1.5 | 0.6 | 3.0 | 2.3 | −2.4 | 2.4 | 1.6 | 1.2 | 1.1 | 1.3 |
| Factor income | −0.1 | −0.4 | −0.7 | 0.3 | — | 1.5 | −1.3 | −0.5 | 0.3 | −0.4 | 0.1 |
| Resource balance | 10.3 | −5.2 | −2.9 | −4.1 | −2.4 | −8.5 | −5.8 | −6.3 | −1.1 | −1.3 | −2.2 |
| *Memorandum* | | | | | | | | | | | |
| Acquisition of foreign assets | 12.8 | −0.5 | −0.8 | 1.0 | 1.9 | −8.5 | 0.5 | −1.5 | −2.4 | −0.2 | −1.5 |
| Change in reserves | 6.8 | −1.5 | −1.3 | 1.6 | 1.6 | 2.0 | 2.9 | 0.1 | 0.4 | −0.1 | −1.5 |
| **Western Hemisphere** | | | | | | | | | | | |
| Saving | 20.6 | 19.0 | 20.5 | 21.2 | 23.0 | 18.2 | 17.9 | 17.3 | 18.2 | 18.7 | 19.9 |
| Investment | 23.6 | 20.2 | 21.9 | 21.7 | 20.2 | 19.6 | 20.6 | 20.8 | 21.4 | 20.8 | 22.4 |
| Net lending | −3.0 | −1.2 | −1.5 | −0.5 | 2.8 | −1.4 | −2.7 | −3.4 | −3.2 | −2.1 | −2.5 |
| Current transfers | 0.2 | 0.4 | 0.6 | 1.0 | 1.2 | 1.2 | 1.2 | 1.0 | 1.0 | 1.1 | 1.0 |
| Factor income | −2.1 | −4.1 | −4.9 | −4.5 | −1.2 | −3.6 | −3.3 | −3.6 | −3.5 | −4.1 | −4.2 |
| Resource balance | −1.1 | 2.5 | 2.8 | 3.0 | 2.9 | 1.0 | −0.6 | −0.8 | −0.6 | 1.0 | 0.7 |
| *Memorandum* | | | | | | | | | | | |
| Acquisition of foreign assets | 1.4 | 0.2 | — | 0.5 | 3.4 | 1.2 | 1.7 | 1.5 | 0.4 | 1.3 | 0.9 |
| Change in reserves | 0.5 | −0.2 | −0.4 | 0.2 | 1.9 | 1.8 | 1.7 | 1.5 | −0.6 | 1.0 | 0.1 |

## Table A44 *(continued)*

| | Averages | | 1988 | 1989 | 1990 | 1991 | 1992 | 1993 | 1994 | 1995 | 1996 |
|---|---|---|---|---|---|---|---|---|---|---|---|
| | 1973–80 | 1981–87 | | | | | | | | | |
| **By predominant export** | | | | | | | | | | | |
| **Fuel** | | | | | | | | | | | |
| Saving | 42.0 | 20.2 | 16.5 | 19.1 | 23.3 | 20.6 | 20.1 | 17.0 | 21.1 | 21.3 | 20.5 |
| Investment | 30.6 | 24.5 | 22.3 | 21.3 | 20.4 | 25.0 | 26.5 | 22.9 | 20.2 | 21.3 | 22.3 |
| Net lending | 11.4 | −4.3 | −5.8 | −2.2 | 2.9 | −4.4 | −6.4 | −5.9 | 0.9 | — | −1.8 |
| Current transfers | −2.2 | −1.9 | −1.7 | −1.0 | −1.8 | −2.8 | −1.7 | −2.0 | −1.7 | −1.6 | −1.4 |
| Factor income | −2.1 | −1.5 | −2.2 | −3.1 | −2.1 | −1.0 | −3.4 | −2.8 | −1.0 | −1.3 | −2.9 |
| Resource balance | 15.7 | −0.9 | −1.8 | 1.9 | 6.9 | −0.5 | −1.3 | −1.1 | 3.7 | 2.9 | 2.6 |
| *Memorandum* | | | | | | | | | | | |
| Acquisition of foreign assets | 13.2 | −1.8 | −3.8 | −0.8 | 3.9 | −4.0 | −4.3 | −4.4 | −2.0 | −0.5 | −0.5 |
| Change in reserves | 7.7 | −2.6 | −2.8 | 1.5 | 2.4 | 0.5 | −1.7 | −1.2 | 0.2 | −0.8 | −0.7 |
| **Nonfuel exports** | | | | | | | | | | | |
| Saving | 22.4 | 22.9 | 26.0 | 26.5 | 26.7 | 24.6 | 25.2 | 26.1 | 28.3 | 29.3 | 29.1 |
| Investment | 24.6 | 24.6 | 26.8 | 27.4 | 26.8 | 26.3 | 26.6 | 28.5 | 29.8 | 30.6 | 30.8 |
| Net lending | −2.2 | −1.6 | −0.8 | −0.9 | −0.1 | −1.7 | −1.5 | −2.4 | −1.5 | −1.3 | −1.7 |
| Current transfers | 1.5 | 1.5 | 1.3 | 1.6 | 1.7 | 1.4 | 1.9 | 1.7 | 1.6 | 1.5 | 1.4 |
| Factor income | −1.5 | −1.8 | −2.1 | −1.7 | −1.0 | −1.8 | −1.7 | −1.5 | −1.5 | −1.4 | −1.5 |
| Resource balance | −2.2 | −1.3 | — | −0.8 | −0.7 | −1.3 | −1.6 | −2.6 | −1.6 | −1.3 | −1.6 |
| *Memorandum* | | | | | | | | | | | |
| Acquisition of foreign assets | 1.7 | 0.9 | 1.1 | 1.1 | 2.3 | 1.8 | 2.2 | 2.4 | 3.0 | 2.3 | 1.5 |
| Change in reserves | 0.8 | 0.6 | 0.4 | 0.6 | 1.7 | 2.5 | 1.6 | 1.7 | 2.3 | 1.5 | 0.7 |
| **By financial criteria** | | | | | | | | | | | |
| **Net creditor countries** | | | | | | | | | | | |
| Saving | 47.4 | 29.4 | 26.1 | 24.8 | 26.3 | 5.9 | 19.7 | 20.8 | 20.8 | 23.1 | 22.9 |
| Investment | 25.0 | 23.5 | 21.8 | 21.1 | 20.8 | 22.5 | 22.6 | 23.8 | 22.2 | 22.4 | 22.0 |
| Net lending | 22.5 | 5.9 | 4.2 | 3.7 | 5.5 | −16.6 | −2.9 | −3.0 | −1.5 | 0.7 | 0.8 |
| Current transfers | −7.3 | −5.4 | −5.8 | −6.0 | −8.2 | −19.4 | −5.4 | −6.1 | −5.6 | −5.2 | −5.0 |
| Factor income | 0.3 | 2.8 | 6.0 | 4.0 | 4.9 | 4.3 | 2.0 | 1.8 | 1.2 | 2.8 | 3.6 |
| Resource balance | 29.5 | 8.5 | 4.0 | 5.6 | 8.9 | −1.5 | 0.6 | 1.3 | 2.9 | 3.1 | 2.3 |
| *Memorandum* | | | | | | | | | | | |
| Acquisition of foreign assets | 21.6 | 7.1 | 0.3 | 1.4 | 4.9 | −16.5 | −1.6 | −1.2 | 0.3 | −1.0 | −0.1 |
| Change in reserves | 6.9 | 3.4 | −3.8 | −0.4 | −1.7 | 3.6 | 0.8 | −2.3 | 0.3 | −0.8 | −1.2 |
| **Net debtor countries** | | | | | | | | | | | |
| Saving | 24.4 | 22.2 | 24.9 | 25.7 | 26.3 | 25.2 | 24.9 | 25.4 | 28.0 | 28.9 | 28.6 |
| Investment | 25.7 | 24.7 | 26.6 | 27.1 | 26.4 | 26.3 | 26.8 | 28.2 | 29.2 | 30.1 | 30.5 |
| Net lending | −1.3 | −2.5 | −1.7 | −1.3 | — | −1.1 | −1.9 | −2.7 | −1.3 | −1.2 | −1.9 |
| Current transfers | 1.4 | 1.4 | 1.3 | 1.7 | 1.8 | 2.0 | 1.9 | 1.7 | 1.6 | 1.5 | 1.5 |
| Factor income | −1.7 | −2.1 | −2.5 | −2.2 | −1.4 | −2.0 | −2.1 | −1.8 | −1.6 | −1.6 | −1.9 |
| Resource balance | −1.0 | −1.8 | −0.5 | −0.9 | −0.4 | −1.2 | −1.7 | −2.7 | −1.3 | −1.1 | −1.5 |
| *Memorandum* | | | | | | | | | | | |
| Acquisition of foreign assets | 2.5 | 0.1 | 0.6 | 0.9 | 2.4 | 2.1 | 1.7 | 1.9 | 2.6 | 2.2 | 1.4 |
| Change in reserves | 1.7 | −0.1 | 0.3 | 0.8 | 2.0 | 2.2 | 1.3 | 1.6 | 2.2 | 1.4 | 0.7 |
| **Market borrowers** | | | | | | | | | | | |
| Saving | 26.4 | 25.9 | 29.2 | 29.7 | 30.6 | 28.5 | 28.5 | 29.7 | 33.3 | 34.5 | 33.6 |
| Investment | 27.9 | 26.5 | 29.6 | 30.0 | 28.4 | 28.8 | 29.7 | 32.1 | 33.8 | 34.7 | 34.7 |
| Net lending | −1.5 | −0.6 | −0.3 | −0.3 | 2.2 | −0.2 | −1.2 | −2.4 | −0.4 | −0.2 | −1.1 |
| Current transfers | 0.4 | 0.4 | 0.4 | 0.6 | 0.6 | 0.6 | 0.6 | 0.6 | 0.6 | 0.6 | 0.6 |
| Factor income | −1.6 | −2.2 | −2.3 | −2.0 | −0.2 | −1.2 | −1.5 | −1.4 | −1.3 | −1.4 | −1.6 |
| Resource balance | −0.3 | 1.2 | 1.5 | 1.1 | 1.8 | 0.4 | −0.3 | −1.7 | 0.2 | 0.7 | −0.1 |
| *Memorandum* | | | | | | | | | | | |
| Acquisition of foreign assets | 2.3 | 0.9 | 1.2 | 1.4 | 3.7 | 2.7 | 2.3 | 2.4 | 3.9 | 3.4 | 2.2 |
| Change in reserves | 1.0 | 0.4 | 0.5 | 1.0 | 2.5 | 2.2 | 1.2 | 1.6 | 2.8 | 2.1 | 1.0 |

## Table A44 *(concluded)*

| | Averages | | 1988 | 1989 | 1990 | 1991 | 1992 | 1993 | 1994 | 1995 | 1996 |
|---|---|---|---|---|---|---|---|---|---|---|---|
| | 1973–80 | 1981–87 | | | | | | | | | |
| **Official borrowers** | | | | | | | | | | | |
| Saving | 18.3 | 14.4 | 12.9 | 14.9 | 15.1 | 15.5 | 14.1 | 13.2 | 13.8 | 14.8 | 16.2 |
| Investment | 25.3 | 21.1 | 18.8 | 19.2 | 18.6 | 19.1 | 19.3 | 18.6 | 18.9 | 19.9 | 21.5 |
| Net lending | −7.0 | −6.7 | −5.8 | −4.3 | −3.5 | −3.7 | −5.2 | −5.4 | −5.1 | −5.1 | −5.2 |
| Current transfers | 4.7 | 5.0 | 5.0 | 6.9 | 7.9 | 9.0 | 8.1 | 7.5 | 6.6 | 6.2 | 6.2 |
| Factor income | −5.1 | −2.7 | −3.5 | −2.3 | −4.0 | −4.7 | −5.2 | −4.3 | −3.9 | −3.9 | −5.2 |
| Resource balance | −6.6 | −9.0 | −7.3 | −9.0 | −7.4 | −8.0 | −8.1 | −8.6 | −7.9 | −7.4 | −6.3 |
| *Memorandum* | | | | | | | | | | | |
| Acquisition of foreign assets | 2.0 | −0.6 | −0.5 | 0.3 | 1.6 | 1.8 | 0.4 | 0.9 | 1.5 | 0.8 | — |
| Change in reserves | 1.1 | −0.2 | 0.1 | 0.3 | 2.3 | 2.9 | 1.7 | 1.8 | 1.7 | 0.4 | −0.1 |
| **Countries with recent debt-servicing difficulties** | | | | | | | | | | | |
| Saving | 23.2 | 17.8 | 18.4 | 19.8 | 21.1 | 17.5 | 17.1 | 16.4 | 17.3 | 18.0 | 19.4 |
| Investment | 25.5 | 21.1 | 21.1 | 21.1 | 20.0 | 19.7 | 20.4 | 20.1 | 20.8 | 20.5 | 22.4 |
| Net lending | −2.3 | −3.4 | −2.7 | −1.3 | 1.1 | −2.2 | −3.3 | −3.7 | −3.5 | −2.6 | −3.0 |
| Current transfers | 1.2 | 1.6 | 1.8 | 2.7 | 3.2 | 3.2 | 2.9 | 2.6 | 2.4 | 2.3 | 2.3 |
| Factor income | −2.4 | −3.7 | −4.7 | −3.8 | −2.1 | −3.7 | −3.5 | −3.3 | −3.0 | −3.4 | −3.9 |
| Resource balance | −1.1 | −1.3 | 0.2 | −0.2 | −0.1 | −1.7 | −2.7 | −3.0 | −2.9 | −1.5 | −1.4 |
| *Memorandum* | | | | | | | | | | | |
| Acquisition of foreign assets | 2.7 | −0.5 | −0.3 | 0.7 | 3.0 | 1.6 | 1.4 | 1.5 | 0.7 | 1.2 | 0.6 |
| Change in reserves | 2.0 | −0.6 | −0.3 | 0.6 | 2.3 | 2.1 | 1.8 | 1.5 | 0.1 | 0.8 | 0.1 |
| **Countries without debt-servicing difficulties** | | | | | | | | | | | |
| Saving | 25.5 | 25.5 | 29.0 | 29.3 | 29.3 | 29.4 | 29.1 | 30.0 | 33.1 | 34.0 | 32.8 |
| Investment | 25.8 | 27.2 | 30.0 | 30.7 | 30.0 | 30.0 | 30.2 | 32.2 | 33.3 | 34.6 | 34.1 |
| Net lending | −0.3 | −1.7 | −1.0 | −1.4 | −0.7 | −0.5 | −1.2 | −2.2 | −0.2 | −0.6 | −1.3 |
| Current transfers | 1.6 | 1.2 | 1.0 | 1.1 | 1.0 | 1.4 | 1.3 | 1.3 | 1.3 | 1.1 | 1.1 |
| Factor income | −0.9 | −0.7 | −1.2 | −1.2 | −1.0 | −1.1 | −1.4 | −1.0 | −0.9 | −0.8 | −0.9 |
| Resource balance | −1.0 | −2.1 | −0.9 | −1.2 | −0.6 | −0.9 | −1.1 | −2.5 | −0.6 | −0.9 | −1.5 |
| *Memorandum* | | | | | | | | | | | |
| Acquisition of foreign assets | 2.2 | 0.6 | 1.2 | 1.0 | 2.0 | 2.4 | 1.8 | 2.1 | 3.6 | 2.7 | 1.7 |
| Change in reserves | 1.5 | 0.4 | 0.6 | 0.9 | 1.8 | 2.3 | 1.0 | 1.7 | 3.2 | 1.7 | 1.0 |
| **Countries in transition** | | | | | | | | | | | |
| **Central and eastern Europe excluding Belarus and Ukraine** | | | | | | | | | | | |
| Saving | 34.6 | 32.2 | 33.6 | 30.8 | 30.5 | 22.6 | 22.0 | 16.9 | 19.0 | 18.2 | 18.2 |
| Investment | 32.3 | 31.8 | 31.8 | 30.3 | 30.0 | 25.3 | 21.4 | 19.8 | 20.0 | 20.3 | 21.5 |
| Net lending | 2.3 | 0.4 | 1.8 | 0.5 | 0.5 | −2.7 | 0.7 | −2.9 | −1.1 | −2.1 | −3.3 |
| Current transfers | 1.6 | 1.8 | 2.1 | 1.8 | 2.0 | 0.5 | 1.7 | 1.2 | 1.2 | 0.8 | 0.7 |
| Factor income | 3.6 | −0.6 | — | −1.4 | −0.9 | −3.5 | −0.1 | −0.8 | −1.5 | −1.8 | −2.3 |
| Resource balance | −3.0 | −0.9 | −0.3 | 0.1 | −0.6 | 0.3 | −0.9 | −3.3 | −0.7 | −1.1 | −1.6 |
| *Memorandum* | | | | | | | | | | | |
| Acquisition of foreign assets | 0.6 | 1.1 | 1.3 | 1.3 | 4.3 | 1.9 | 2.5 | 2.5 | 3.4 | 2.6 | 1.2 |
| Change in reserves | 0.2 | 0.2 | 0.8 | 1.5 | 1.9 | 1.0 | 1.5 | 3.1 | 3.3 | 3.4 | 1.5 |

Note: The estimates in this table are based on individual countries' national accounts and balance of payments statistics. For many countries, the estimates of national saving are built up from national accounts data on gross domestic investment and from balance-of-payments-based data on net foreign investment. The latter, which is equivalent to the current account balance, comprises three components: current transfers, net factor income, and the resource balance. The mixing of data sources, which is dictated by availability, implies that the estimates for national saving that are derived incorporate the statistical discrepancies. Furthermore, errors, omissions, and asymmetries in balance of payments statistics affect the estimates for net lending; at the global level, net lending, which in theory would be zero, equals the world current account discrepancy. Notwithstanding these statistical shortcomings, flow of funds estimates, such as those presented in this table, provide a useful framework for analyzing development in saving and investment, both over time and across regions and countries. Country group composites are weighted by GDP valued at purchasing power parities (PPPs) as a share of total world GDP.

## Table A45. Summary of Medium-Term Baseline Scenario

| | Eight-Year Averages | | Four-Year Average 1993–96 | 1993 | 1994 | 1995 | 1996 | Four-Year Average 1997–2000 |
|---|---|---|---|---|---|---|---|---|
| | 1977–84 | 1985–92 | | | | | | |
| | | | | *Annual percent change unless otherwise noted* | | | | |
| **Industrial countries** | | | | | | | | |
| Real GDP | 2.6 | 2.7 | 2.3 | 1.1 | 3.1 | 2.5 | 2.4 | 2.7 |
| Real total domestic demand | 2.4 | 2.8 | 2.3 | 0.9 | 3.3 | 2.6 | 2.5 | 2.7 |
| GDP deflator | 7.9 | 3.9 | 2.2 | 2.5 | 1.9 | 2.0 | 2.5 | 2.4 |
| Real six-month LIBOR (in percent)[1] | 4.4 | 3.7 | 3.0 | 1.2 | 3.0 | 4.3 | 3.5 | 3.5 |
| **World prices in U.S. dollars** | | | | | | | | |
| Manufactures | 4.0 | 6.0 | 0.7 | −5.8 | 2.8 | 4.0 | 2.0 | 1.6 |
| Oil | . . . | . . . | −3.9 | −11.5 | −4.1 | 7.8 | −6.9 | 1.4 |
| Nonfuel primary commodities | 2.9 | 0.1 | 5.6 | 1.8 | 13.6 | 8.6 | −1.1 | 0.7 |
| **Developing countries** | | | | | | | | |
| Real GDP | 4.4 | 5.0 | 6.2 | 6.1 | 6.2 | 6.1 | 6.3 | 6.5 |
| Export volume[2] | 1.4 | 8.1 | 9.4 | 6.7 | 10.8 | 10.8 | 9.5 | 9.6 |
| Terms of trade[2] | 2.9 | −2.2 | 0.1 | 0.6 | 0.5 | 0.2 | −0.9 | −0.1 |
| Import volume[2] | 5.4 | 7.5 | 9.8 | 10.5 | 8.5 | 10.3 | 9.9 | 9.3 |
| **World trade, volume[2]** | **4.0** | **5.3** | **6.7** | **3.9** | **8.7** | **7.9** | **6.5** | **6.2** |
| **World real GDP** | **3.2** | **3.2** | **3.5** | **2.5** | **3.6** | **3.7** | **4.1** | **4.5** |

| | Four-Year Average 1985–88 | 1988 | 1992 | 1993 | 1994 | 1995 | 1996 | 2000 |
|---|---|---|---|---|---|---|---|---|
| | | | | *In percent of exports of goods and services* | | | | |
| **Developing countries** | | | | | | | | |
| Current account balance | −3.7 | −2.1 | −6.0 | −8.1 | −4.9 | −4.0 | −4.3 | −2.0 |
| Total external debt | 162.9 | 151.0 | 125.5 | 128.6 | 123.0 | 115.3 | 108.9 | 89.4 |
| Debt-service payments[3] | 20.2 | 17.8 | 15.3 | 15.2 | 15.0 | 14.4 | 12.3 | 9.5 |
| Interest | 10.9 | 8.7 | 6.1 | 5.9 | 5.6 | 6.2 | 5.8 | 3.9 |
| Amortization | 9.3 | 9.1 | 9.2 | 9.3 | 9.4 | 8.2 | 6.5 | 5.5 |
| *Memorandum* | | | | | | | | |
| **Net debtor countries** | | | | | | | | |
| Current account balance | −6.6 | −3.8 | −6.3 | −8.7 | −5.3 | −4.4 | −4.6 | −2.4 |
| Total external debt | 198.1 | 178.7 | 148.1 | 149.7 | 140.6 | 131.0 | 122.6 | 98.0 |
| Debt-service payments[3] | 24.3 | 20.9 | 18.2 | 17.9 | 17.0 | 16.5 | 14.0 | 10.6 |
| Interest | 13.1 | 10.1 | 7.1 | 6.9 | 6.3 | 7.0 | 6.5 | 4.4 |
| Amortization | 11.2 | 10.8 | 11.1 | 11.0 | 10.7 | 9.4 | 7.4 | 6.2 |

[1]London interbank offered rate on U.S. dollar deposits less percent change in U.S. GDP deflator.

[2]Data refer to trade in goods only.

[3]Interest payments on total debt, plus amortization payments on long-term debt only. Projections incorporate the impact of exceptional financing items. Excludes service payments to the IMF.

## Table A46. Developing Countries—Medium-Term Baseline Scenario: Selected Economic Indicators

| | Averages | | | 1993 | 1994 | 1995 | 1996 | Average 1997–2000 |
|---|---|---|---|---|---|---|---|---|
| | 1977–84 | 1985–92 | 1993–96 | | | | | |
| | *Annual percent change* | | | | | | | |
| **Developing countries** | | | | | | | | |
| Real GDP | 4.4 | 5.0 | 6.2 | 6.1 | 6.2 | 6.1 | 6.3 | 6.5 |
| Export volume[1] | 1.4 | 8.1 | 9.4 | 6.7 | 10.8 | 10.8 | 9.5 | 9.6 |
| Terms of trade[1] | 2.9 | −2.2 | 0.1 | 0.6 | 0.5 | 0.2 | −0.9 | −0.1 |
| Import volume[1] | 5.4 | 7.5 | 9.8 | 10.5 | 8.5 | 10.3 | 9.9 | 9.3 |
| **By region** | | | | | | | | |
| **Africa** | | | | | | | | |
| Real GDP | 1.7 | 2.5 | 2.9 | 0.8 | 2.6 | 3.0 | 5.2 | 4.8 |
| Export volume[1] | −0.2 | 2.8 | 3.0 | 3.0 | −0.4 | 4.2 | 5.3 | 4.2 |
| Terms of trade[1] | 3.1 | −4.7 | −0.6 | −4.3 | 1.2 | 0.7 | 0.2 | 0.3 |
| Import volume[1] | 1.9 | −1.4 | 3.1 | 0.4 | 2.7 | 7.6 | 1.9 | 3.6 |
| **Asia** | | | | | | | | |
| Real GDP | 6.6 | 7.2 | 8.4 | 8.7 | 8.5 | 8.7 | 7.9 | 7.5 |
| Export volume[1] | 9.1 | 12.2 | 12.1 | 9.3 | 13.9 | 13.2 | 11.9 | 11.1 |
| Terms of trade[1] | 0.8 | −0.5 | 0.2 | 1.4 | −0.3 | 0.4 | −0.7 | −0.4 |
| Import volume[1] | 9.5 | 11.9 | 13.2 | 13.6 | 12.1 | 14.3 | 12.6 | 10.6 |
| **Middle East and Europe** | | | | | | | | |
| Real GDP | 2.7 | 3.1 | 2.4 | 3.6 | 0.3 | 2.4 | 3.2 | 4.0 |
| Export volume[1] | −6.6 | 4.1 | 1.8 | −2.0 | 5.9 | 1.8 | 1.8 | 6.6 |
| Terms of trade[1] | 5.2 | −3.3 | −0.7 | 1.8 | 1.4 | −4.1 | −1.8 | 1.2 |
| Import volume[1] | 6.0 | 2.0 | 0.7 | 5.3 | −7.5 | 0.9 | 4.6 | 7.2 |
| **Western Hemisphere** | | | | | | | | |
| Real GDP | 3.1 | 2.5 | 3.5 | 3.3 | 4.6 | 2.1 | 4.0 | 5.3 |
| Export volume[1] | 5.5 | 4.2 | 8.3 | 6.6 | 8.3 | 11.1 | 7.1 | 6.5 |
| Terms of trade[1] | 0.7 | −3.6 | 0.5 | −1.3 | 2.4 | 2.3 | −1.5 | −0.1 |
| Import volume[1] | −0.6 | 7.3 | 6.8 | 8.7 | 11.7 | 2.1 | 5.1 | 6.5 |
| **By financial criteria** | | | | | | | | |
| **Countries with recent debt-servicing difficulties** | | | | | | | | |
| Real GDP | 2.9 | 2.5 | 3.4 | 2.7 | 4.1 | 2.4 | 4.2 | 5.3 |
| Export volume[1] | 2.1 | 4.0 | 7.1 | 6.1 | 6.8 | 9.7 | 6.0 | 7.7 |
| Terms of trade[1] | 2.3 | −4.2 | 0.4 | −2.4 | 2.6 | 1.9 | −0.4 | 0.2 |
| Import volume[1] | 1.4 | 3.4 | 6.1 | 5.8 | 9.3 | 4.0 | 5.2 | 7.6 |
| **Countries without debt-servicing difficulties** | | | | | | | | |
| Real GDP | 5.7 | 6.6 | 7.7 | 8.0 | 7.4 | 8.0 | 7.5 | 7.2 |
| Export volume[1] | 4.1 | 9.9 | 12.1 | 9.8 | 14.0 | 13.3 | 11.6 | 10.7 |
| Terms of trade[1] | 2.5 | −1.0 | 0.3 | 1.8 | 0.9 | −1.1 | −0.4 | — |
| Import volume[1] | 7.3 | 8.9 | 12.7 | 14.8 | 10.1 | 13.7 | 12.2 | 10.4 |

## Table A46 (concluded)

| | 1984 | 1988 | 1992 | 1993 | 1994 | 1995 | 1996 | 2000 |
|---|---|---|---|---|---|---|---|---|
| | *In percent of exports of goods and services* | | | | | | | |
| **Developing countries** | | | | | | | | |
| Current account balance | −5.0 | −2.1 | −6.0 | −8.1 | −4.9 | −4.0 | −4.3 | −2.0 |
| Total external debt | 142.6 | 151.0 | 125.5 | 128.6 | 123.0 | 115.3 | 108.9 | 89.4 |
| Debt-service payments[2] | 19.8 | 17.8 | 15.3 | 15.2 | 15.0 | 14.4 | 12.3 | 9.5 |
| Interest payments | 11.6 | 8.7 | 6.1 | 5.9 | 5.6 | 6.2 | 5.8 | 3.9 |
| Amortization | 8.2 | 9.1 | 9.2 | 9.3 | 9.4 | 8.2 | 6.5 | 5.5 |
| **By region** | | | | | | | | |
| **Africa** | | | | | | | | |
| Current account balance | −11.4 | −11.0 | −9.0 | −9.4 | −12.1 | −13.9 | −10.3 | −4.5 |
| Total external debt | 186.6 | 258.4 | 249.4 | 269.5 | 276.5 | 265.5 | 255.5 | 220.6 |
| Debt-service payments[2] | 26.3 | 27.0 | 34.1 | 30.2 | 28.9 | 31.0 | 29.5 | 24.0 |
| Interest payments | 10.8 | 12.3 | 11.9 | 11.8 | 11.3 | 10.3 | 13.8 | 10.4 |
| Amortization | 15.5 | 14.7 | 22.2 | 18.4 | 17.6 | 20.7 | 15.7 | 13.6 |
| **Asia** | | | | | | | | |
| Current account balance | −1.5 | 3.1 | 0.5 | −1.5 | 0.5 | −0.4 | −1.1 | −0.4 |
| Total external debt | 95.9 | 79.3 | 67.4 | 69.5 | 66.2 | 63.5 | 59.8 | 51.8 |
| Debt-service payments[2] | 12.2 | 10.7 | 8.1 | 8.4 | 7.5 | 7.4 | 7.2 | 5.6 |
| Interest payments | 6.7 | 4.8 | 3.7 | 3.4 | 3.2 | 3.1 | 2.9 | 2.0 |
| Amortization | 5.5 | 6.0 | 4.5 | 5.0 | 4.3 | 4.3 | 4.3 | 3.6 |
| **Middle East and Europe** | | | | | | | | |
| Current account balance | −9.7 | −8.1 | −13.7 | −16.7 | −6.9 | −6.9 | −9.3 | −2.0 |
| Total external debt | 79.4 | 147.0 | 134.3 | 151.4 | 152.3 | 149.4 | 147.2 | 116.4 |
| Debt-service payments[2] | 9.2 | 11.2 | 9.4 | 9.9 | 16.1 | 14.2 | 11.8 | 7.8 |
| Interest payments | 4.9 | 4.4 | 4.6 | 4.9 | 5.3 | 5.8 | 5.3 | 4.1 |
| Amortization | 4.2 | 6.8 | 4.8 | 5.0 | 10.8 | 8.4 | 6.5 | 3.6 |
| **Western Hemisphere** | | | | | | | | |
| Current account balance | −1.0 | −6.2 | −20.8 | −24.7 | −22.6 | −12.4 | −11.9 | −9.5 |
| Total external debt | 300.2 | 316.9 | 276.0 | 274.5 | 265.6 | 242.7 | 235.8 | 210.7 |
| Debt-service payments[2] | 46.3 | 42.2 | 40.3 | 41.4 | 39.4 | 37.9 | 29.0 | 25.5 |
| Interest payments | 31.5 | 23.7 | 14.3 | 14.5 | 13.7 | 18.2 | 16.2 | 11.2 |
| Amortization | 14.8 | 18.4 | 26.0 | 26.9 | 25.7 | 19.7 | 12.9 | 14.3 |
| **By financial criteria** | | | | | | | | |
| **Countries with recent debt-servicing difficulties** | | | | | | | | |
| Current account balance | −10.6 | −11.1 | −17.2 | −20.7 | −19.3 | −11.9 | −10.9 | −6.5 |
| Total external debt | 276.7 | 331.6 | 314.2 | 315.8 | 308.4 | 283.6 | 271.7 | 218.7 |
| Debt-service payments[2] | 37.6 | 33.3 | 36.4 | 36.0 | 35.5 | 34.6 | 28.1 | 21.5 |
| Interest payments | 23.6 | 18.6 | 14.2 | 14.2 | 13.7 | 15.4 | 14.8 | 9.9 |
| Amortization | 14.1 | 14.7 | 22.2 | 21.9 | 21.8 | 19.2 | 13.3 | 11.7 |
| **Countries without debt-servicing difficulties** | | | | | | | | |
| Current account balance | −4.6 | — | −2.2 | −4.4 | −0.5 | −1.9 | −2.6 | −1.2 |
| Total external debt | 108.3 | 100.1 | 85.0 | 89.6 | 83.5 | 79.8 | 74.8 | 62.4 |
| Debt-service payments[2] | 15.3 | 14.6 | 11.3 | 11.4 | 10.8 | 10.4 | 9.5 | 7.3 |
| Interest payments | 7.9 | 5.8 | 4.5 | 4.2 | 3.8 | 4.2 | 3.9 | 2.7 |
| Amortization | 7.4 | 8.8 | 6.8 | 7.1 | 7.0 | 6.1 | 5.6 | 4.6 |

[1]Data refer to trade in goods only.

[2]Interest payments on total debt plus amortization payments on long-term debt only. Projections incorporate the impact of exceptional financing items. Excludes service payments to the IMF.

# World Economic and Financial Surveys

This series (ISSN 0258-7440) contains biannual, annual, and periodic studies covering monetary and financial issues of importance to the global economy. The core elements of the series are the *World Economic Outlook* report, usually published in May and October, and the annual report on *International Capital Markets*. Other studies assess international trade policy, private market and official financing for developing countries, exchange and payments systems, export credit policies, and issues raised in the *World Economic Outlook*.

## World Economic Outlook: A Survey by the Staff of the International Monetary Fund

The *World Economic Outlook,* published twice a year in English, French, Spanish, and Arabic, presents IMF staff economists' analyses of global economic developments during the near and medium term. Chapters give an overview of the world economy; consider issues affecting industrial countries, developing countries, and economies in transition to the market; and address topics of pressing current interest.

ISSN 0256-6877.
$34.00 (academic rate: $23.00; paper).
1995 (Oct). ISBN 1-55775-467-5. **Stock #WEO-295.**
1995 (May). ISBN 1-55775-468-3. **Stock #WEO-195.**
1994 (May). ISBN 1-55775-381-4. **Stock #WEO-194.**
1994 (Oct.). ISBN 1-55775-385-7. **Stock #WEO-294.**

## International Capital Markets: Developments, Prospects, and Policy Issues

This annual report reviews developments in international capital markets, including recent bond market turbulence and the role of hedge funds, supervision of banks and nonbanks and the regulation of derivatives, structural changes in government securities markets, and recent developments in private market financing for developing countries

$20.00 (academic rate: $12.00; paper).
1995 ISBN 1-55775-516-7. **Stock #WEO-695.**
1994. ISBN 1-55775-426-8. **Stock #WEO-694.**

## Staff Studies for the World Economic Outlook
*by the IMF's Research Department*

These studies, supporting analyses and scenarios of the *World Economic Outlook,* provide a detailed examination of theory and evidence on major issues currently affecting the global economy.

$20.00 (academic rate: $12.00; paper).
1995. ISBN 1-55775-499-3. **Stock #WEO-395.**
1993. ISBN 1-55775-337-7. **Stock #WEO-393.**

## Issues in International Exchange and Payments Systems
*by a Staff Team from the IMF's Monetary and Exchange Affairs Department*

The global trend toward liberalization in countries' international exchange and payments systems has been widespread in both industrial and developing countries and most dramatic in Central and Eastern Europe. Countries in general have brought their exchange systems more in line with market principles and moved toward more flexible exchange rate arrangements in recent years.

$20.00 (academic rate: $12.00; paper).
1995. ISBN 1-55775-480-2. **Stock #WEO-895.**

## Private Market Financing for Developing Countries
*by a Staff Team from the IMF's Policy Development and Review Department*

This study surveys recent trends in private market financing for developing countries, including flows to developing countries through banking and securities markets; the restoration of access to voluntary market financing for some developing countries; and the status of commercial bank debt in low-income countries.

$20.00 (academic rate: $12.00; paper).
1995 (November). ISBN 1-55775-526-4. **Stock #WEO-1595.**
1995 (March). ISBN 1-55775-456-X. **Stock #WEO-994.**

## International Trade Policies
*by a Staff Team led by Naheed Kirmani*

The study reviews major issues and developments in trade and their implications for the work of the IMF. Volume I, *The Uruguay Round and Beyond: Principal Issues*, gives an overview of the principal issues and developments in the world trading system. Volume II, *The Uruguay Round and Beyond: Background Papers*, presents detailed background papers on selected trade and trade-related issues. The study updates previous studies published under the title *Issues and Developments in International Trade Policy*.

$20.00 (academic rate: $12.00; paper).
1994. *Volume I. The Uruguay Round and Beyond: Principal Issues*
ISBN 1-55775-469-1. **Stock #WEO-1094.**
1994. *Volume II. The Uruguay Round and Beyond: Background Papers*
ISBN 1-55775-457-8. **Stock #WEO-1494.**
1992. ISBN 1-55775-311-1. **Stock #WEO-1092.**

## Official Financing for Developing Countries
*by a Staff Team from the IMF's Policy Development and Review Department*

This study provides information on official financing for developing countries, with the focus on low- and lower-middle-income countries. It updates and replaces *Multilateral Official Debt Rescheduling: Recent Experience* and reviews developments in direct financing by official and multilateral sources.

$20.00 (academic rate: $12.00; paper)
1995. ISBN 1-55775-527-2. **Stock #WEO-1395.**
1994. ISBN 1-55775-378-4. **Stock #WEO-1394.**

## Officially Supported Export Credits: Recent Developments and Prospects
*by Michael G. Kuhn, Balazs Horvath, Christopher J. Jarvis*

This study examines export credit and cover policies in major industrial countries.

$20.00 (academic rate: $12.00; paper).
1995. ISBN 1-55775-448-9. **Stock #WEO-595.**

---

*Available by series subscription or single title (including back issues); academic rate available only to full-time university faculty and students.*

Please send orders and inquiries to:
International Monetary Fund, Publication Services, 700 19th Street, N.W.
Washington, D.C. 20431, U.S.A.
Tel.: (202) 623-7430   Telefax: (202) 623-7201
Internet: publications@imf.org

# Staff Studies for the *World Economic Outlook*

*By the Research Department of the International Monetary Fund*

The analyses and recommendations contained in the Fund's *World Economic Outlook* draw on a broad range of supporting studies. Some of these are summarized in boxes or annexes to the *World Economic Outlook*. Other, more substantial studies have been published since 1986 in *Staff Studies for the World Economic Outlook*.

The current issue of *Staff Studies for the World Economic Outlook*, September 1995, includes the following studies:

Price: US$20.00 (US$12.00 to full-time faculty members and students at universities and colleges)

Please send orders to:
International Monetary Fund, Publication Services, 700 19th Street, N. W.
Washington, D.C. 20431, U.S.A.
Tel: (202) 623-7430    Telefax: (202) 623-7201
Internet: publications@imf.org